Virginia Woolf and Motherhood

Virginia Woolf and Motherhood

Charlotte Taylor Suppé

EDINBURGH
University Press

Edinburgh University Press is one of the leading university presses in the UK. We publish academic books and journals in our selected subject areas across the humanities and social sciences, combining cutting-edge scholarship with high editorial and production values to produce academic works of lasting importance. For more information visit our website: edinburghuniversitypress.com

© Charlotte Taylor Suppé 2025

Published with the support of the University of Edinburgh Scholarly Publishing Initiatives Fund.

Edinburgh University Press Ltd
13 Infirmary Street
Edinburgh EH1 1LT

Typeset in 11/13 Adobe Sabon by
IDSUK (DataConnection) Ltd, and
printed and bound in Great Britain.

A CIP record for this book is available from the British Library

ISBN 978 1 3995 2091 1 (hardback)
ISBN 978 1 3995 2093 5 (webready PDF)
ISBN 978 1 3995 2094 2 (epub)

The right of © Charlotte Taylor Suppé to be identified as the author of this work has been asserted in accordance with the Copyright, Designs and Patents Act 1988, and the Copyright and Related Rights Regulations 2003 (SI No. 2498).

Contents

List of Figures	vi
Acknowledgements	vii
Abbreviations	ix
Introduction	1
1. Motherhood and the Great War	24
2. Motherhood and Eugenics	86
3. Motherhood and Food	150
4. Motherhood and Psychoanalysis	227
Conclusion	260
Bibliography	263
Index	286

Figures

Figure 1 Wright's coal tar soap advertisement	27
Figure 2 'Women of Britain Say "Go"'	28
Figure 3 'A Native Woman and Child'	160
Figure 4 Glaxo 'Builds Bonnie Babies'	164
Figure 5 Glaxo 'Remembrance'	165

Acknowledgements

My initial acknowledgments go to Clara Jones and Anna Snaith, whose methodology, generosity, expert guidance, insight and energising discussion immeasurably enriched not only the doctoral thesis that became this book, but my own academic life. I am also indebted to my examiners Derek Ryan and Bryony Randall whose excellent advice and constructive criticism led to the creation of a new final chapter. Jackie Jones, Elizabeth Fraser and Susannah Butler at Edinburgh University Press have supported me through the publication process, for which I am incredibly grateful. My gratitude also extends to the EUP readers for their thoughtful comments. Thanks are also due to Lara Feigel and Max Saunders who oversaw the inception of the project.

The images in this book were sourced and licensed with the invaluable help of Genevieve Coyle and Casey Thomas in the Manuscripts and Archive department at Yale University Library, Jill Moretto at GlaxoSmithKline, the archive department of Lornamead and Christine Black of the Waiuku Museum Society. With additional thanks to Professor Mark Wollaeger. Two sections of Chapter 3 have been published in different forms. A version of the infant feeding sections appeared in *Women: A Cultural Review* while the section on 'Memories of a Working Women's Guild' is adapted for a chapter in *Virginia Woolf and Capitalism* (EUP).

My love and appreciation goes to my family (both here and in America). To my father, Peter Taylor, for his unwavering support and enthusiasm and my mother, Nina Taylor, who provides the many types of maternal sustenance that so often goes unrecognised. My children, who make the maternal personal: Elia, for a completely new understanding of how to ask questions, how to make friends and how to love reading and Alix, for showing me what pure determination and generosity of spirit looks like. The final, and greatest, of credits goes to the person who has read every iteration, who has

viii   *Acknowledgements*

provided support, love, grammatical advice, technical maintenance, encouragement, and perhaps the most difficult and essential thing, time: my husband, Steve Suppé, without whom this book would not exist. I dedicate this book to them all, and to the memory of my remarkable grandmother, Fay Weyman.

Abbreviations: Works by Virginia Woolf

AROO	*A Room of One's Own*
BA	*Between the Acts*
CSF	*The Complete Shorter Fiction of Virginia Woolf*
D1–5	*The Diary of Virginia Woolf* (5 vols)
E1–6	*The Essays of Virginia Woolf* (6 vols)
F	*Flush: A Biography*
H	*Virginia Woolf The Hours: The British Museum Manuscript of* Mrs Dalloway
JR	*Jacob's Room*
JRHD	*Virginia Woolf's* Jacob's Room: *The Holograph Draft*
L1–6	*The Letters of Virginia Woolf* (6 vols)
M	*Melymbrosia*
MB	*Moments of Being*
MD	*Mrs Dalloway*
ND	*Night and Day*
O	*Orlando: A Biography*
P	*The Pargiters: The Novel-Essay Portion of* The Years
PA	*A Passionate Apprentice: The Early Journals, 1897–1909*
PH	*Pointz Hall: The Earlier and Later Typescripts of* Between the Acts
RF	*Roger Fry: A Biography*
RN	*Virginia Woolf's Reading Notebooks*
TG	*Three Guineas*
TL	*To the Lighthouse*
VO	*The Voyage Out*
W	*The Waves*
WH	The Waves: *The Two Holograph Drafts*
Y	*The Years*

Introduction

Motherhood in the Writing of Virginia Woolf

Motherhood is one of the most important recurrent themes in Virginia Woolf's writing. The sheer number of texts that engage with maternal discourses, across a range of forms and genres, attest to the significance of the topic. References to motherhood can be found in every one of Woolf's novels, from *Melymbrosia*, where characters discuss the changing 'conditions' of maternity (*M* 137), to *Between the Acts*, where an empty cot in an empty nursery – 'The cradle of our race' (*BA* 45) – takes on a shadowy symbolism.[1] Maternal themes and characters can frequently be seen in Woolf's shorter fiction and her essays, and maternal discourses are prominent in the message of *A Room of One's Own* and *Three Guineas*, and the lectures and manuscripts connected with these works. Mentions of motherhood also regularly occur in Woolf's letters and diary, and her unpublished memoirs contain valuable studies of her mother, Julia Stephen, and mothering. This book explores Woolf's literary interest in motherhood, adding a fresh perspective to current scholarship on Woolf's feminist politics, and offering a deeper understanding of how personal and public events worked together to inform her creative processes.

For a number of reasons Woolf's engagement with the ideologies and discourses of motherhood has received relatively little scholarly attention. Jane Marcus notes that in the 1970s and 1980s critics 'fetishized' Woolf, framing her as 'the sign of feminist literary and political culture [. . .] as well as the icon of Women's Studies and Feminist Theory'.[2] Marcus and her contemporaries took inspiration from Woolf's figurative use of maternal metaphors, creating a female canon that concentrated on 'mother-muses' and 'aesthetic

2   Virginia Woolf and Motherhood

foremothers', and mythologising Woolf as 'Saint Virginia', the foremost of 'our sainted literary mothers'.[3] Given Woolf's status as a non-mother, and the lack of critical interest in her engagement with the prominent social issue of motherhood, it is perhaps ironic that she was appointed this matron saint of feminist studies.[4] While scholars paid little attention to the way Woolf used her mother characters as a form of socio-political critique, psychoanalytic research did dwell on the characters' subjective and biographical connotations.[5] For many decades, the image of the mother was seen to loom so large in Woolf's life as 'the Angel' or a traumatic loss that it was difficult to look beyond this to other ways in which she engaged with maternal discourses. In addition, scholarship on motherhood (which, since the late 1990s has widely been called 'motherhood studies' or 'maternal studies') habitually uses a personal approach, a methodology at odds with the language and perspective favoured by modernist and Woolf studies.

Woolf's attention to maternity can be approached from a number of different angles. The four chapters of this book are loosely based on four distinct ways motherhood appears in her writing: characters who are mothers, maternal metaphors, the material and functional aspects of motherhood and the psychological repercussions of mother–child relationships. Together, these chapters show the variety and depth of Woolf's engagement with the maternal discourses of her historical moment. They investigate how she used motherhood to further her radical discussion about women's place in society. They also prompt an examination of the diverse personal and public stimuli that inspired her to write so broadly on this topic.

Woolf began using motherhood as a form of characterisation early on in her writing. She depicted both mothers and non-mothers, sometimes with satirical exaggeration and sometimes with subtle restraint. In keeping with the diversity of their portrayals, these figures respond to maternity with an assortment of emotions including ambivalence, enthusiasm, compulsion and antipathy. The first chapter of this book surveys Woolf's writing in the years after the First World War (WW1) when she explored and condemned war-making with the aid of a series of mother characters such as *Jacob's Room*'s Betty Flanders and *Mrs Dalloway*'s Clarissa Dalloway. The second chapter investigates how Woolf used maternal metaphors to engage with eugenics, a popular scientific movement that engendered many public discourses concerning motherhood. Over time, Woolf created increasingly extended maternal metaphors fashioning this literary trope to suit her purposes by incorporating feminist eugenic concepts. By showing these maternal metaphors as subversive social commentary this chapter not only reconfirms Woolf's feminism but also portrays eugenics in a way rarely explored by Woolf scholars.

The third chapter considers the material aspects of motherhood by exploring Woolf's writing on the production, preparation and consumption of food. Woolf included these maternal tasks in her writing in order to comment on the performative aspect of women's lives. In doing so she highlighted systemic political and social strictures that restricted female autonomy and creativity. However this writing is complicated by the class collaboration intrinsic to such tasks. By using domestic acts to explore the curtailed creativity and autonomy of only her own class, without challenging the subordination of working-class women, Woolf inadvertently calls attention to the limitations of her social commentary. Since domestic interactions with the working class were also difficult for Woolf in real life (she felt uncomfortable taking on the role of a Victorian matriarch and longed to live without servants) personal anxiety emerges alongside professional unease in these alimentary episodes.

The final chapter of the book returns to both characterisation and war, this time considering not mothers themselves but the long-term effect that mothering has on an individual's disposition and motivations. In the late 1930s, after years of antipathy towards psychoanalysis, Woolf finally turned to it for a new perspective on human nature. Although her initial aim was to understand the psychology of fascism and war-making, she was quickly influenced by the way that psychoanalytic development theories foregrounded the formative effects of mother–child relationships. By examining how Woolf used these theories to hone both her fictional and non-fictional character outlines – defining her adult subjects through their relationships with their mothers – this chapter offers a fresh perspective on current psychoanalytic Woolf scholarship.

Woolf's fascination with the socio-politics of motherhood is clear from her earliest writing. In *Melymbrosia* the following conversation occurs when Mrs Thornbury and Mrs Elliot begin to discuss the unmarried writer Miss Allan:

> 'Oh, it *is* a hard life,' said Mrs Thornbury. 'Unmarried women – earning their livings – it's the hardest life of all.' [. . .]
> 'Yet she seems pretty cheerful,' said Mrs Elliot.
> 'I'm afraid it's all a great many can hope to have,' sighed Mrs Thornbury. 'I believe that there are more of us than ever now.

4   *Virginia Woolf and Motherhood*

> Sir Harley Lethbridge was telling me only the other day how difficult it is to find boys for the navy – partly because of their teeth, it is true. And I have heard young women talk quite openly of –.'
>
> 'Dreadful, dreadful!' exclaimed Mrs Elliot. 'The crown, as one may call it, of a woman's life. I, who know what it is to be childless – ' [. . .]
>
> 'Women without children can do so much for the children of others,' observed Mrs Thornbury gently.
>
> 'I sketch a great deal,' said Mrs Elliot, 'but that isn't really an occupation. It's so disconcerting to find girls just beginning doing better than one does oneself!'
>
> 'Are there not institutions – clubs – that you could help?' asked Mrs Thornbury.
>
> 'They are so exhausting,' said Mrs Elliot. 'I look strong, because of my colour; but I'm not; the youngest of eleven never is.'
>
> 'If the mother is careful before,' said Mrs Thornbury judicially, 'there is no reason why the size of the family should make any difference [. . .]
>
> But Mrs Elliot was inattentive to the elder lady's experience, and her eyes wandered about the hall.
>
> 'My mother had two miscarriages, I know,' she said suddenly. 'The first because she met one of those great dancing bears – they shouldn't be allowed; the other – it was a horrid story – our cook had a child and there was a dinner party. So I put my dyspepsia down to that.' (*M* 137–38)

This passage, which is reproduced exactly in *The Voyage Out*, is a good indication of the variety of maternal discourses that were playing out in the public domain. Sir Harley Lethbridge's concerns about 'the navy' and 'teeth' relate to the falling birth rate, eugenic unease, and the place of motherhood in imperial expansion and war-making. Contraception and female sexuality are hinted at by the unmentionable subject that Mrs Thornbury has, ironically, 'heard young women talk quite openly of'. The discussion about family size also speaks to arguments about birth control, as well as the public and philanthropic activism that women engaged in through maternal and infant health. Mrs Elliot's observation that sketching 'isn't really an occupation' – a direct response to thinking about a child-free woman's purpose – hints at Woolf's ongoing preoccupation with the contrast between artistic creation and procreation. The influence of class thinking on maternal discourses is shown in the divergent values placed on the pregnancies of Mrs Elliot's mother and the cook. And maternal bodies are shown to be a site of class difference not only through the miscarriage that occurs as a result of an upper-class woman performing a working-class woman's job, but also due to the analogy drawn between the post-partum cook and 'great dancing bears'.

The diversity of this commentary reinforces the now commonly accepted view of Woolf as engaged with the social and political events of her time. But while motherhood is at the heart of many public discourses, it is also a deeply personal and private concern. The influence that both public and personal issues of motherhood had on Woolf can be demonstrated by looking at her use of maternal metaphors – a trope which has, according to Susan Stanford Friedman's influential article on the subject, 'yoked artistic creativity and human procreativity for centuries in writers as disparate as Philip Sidney and Erica Jong, William Shakespeare and Mary Shelley'.[6] In her 'personal' writing – her letters and diaries – Woolf frequently used maternal metaphors to describe her own, and others', literary productions. A sequel to *A Room of One's Own* was 'conceived' 'while having my bath' (*D4* 6), *The Years* was 'like a long childbirth' (*D5* 31) and contrasted with *Three Guineas*, which was 'the mildest childbirth I have ever had [. . .] No book ever slid from me so secretly & smoothly' (*D5* 148, 149), a letter to Ottoline Morrell notes that: 'Everyone seems on the verge of having a book out – Desmond [MacCarthy] has them three at a birth' (*L2* 18), and Mary Hutchinson's book for the Hogarth Press, *Fugitive Pieces*, was 'half in and half out of the womb these 9 months' (*L3* 364). Woolf's fiction and polemical writing are also populated by maternal metaphors. Though live children are curiously absent from *Orlando*, its protagonist carries the manuscript of her poem 'fluttering above her heart' (*O* 192), and in *A Room of One's Own*, 'masterpieces are not single and solitary births; they are the outcome of many years of thinking in common' (*AROO* 59).

Friedman observes that literary childbirth metaphors are part of a linguistically encoded binary system, within which words such as *conceive, confinement, delivery* and *labour* establish universally acknowledged gender roles. She notes that 'the binary system [. . .] conceives woman and writer, motherhood and authorhood, babies and books, as mutually exclusive'. Thus, while male authors use such metaphors to elevate their art and, ultimately, reconfirm gender stereotypes, female authors employ them to 'confront the patriarchally imposed, essential dilemma of their artistic identity'. Friedman's examples of texts that demonstrate 'a fear of combining creation and procreation', include Mary Shelley's *Frankenstein*, and Sylvia Plath and Erica Jong's pregnancy and childbirth poetry.[7] While Friedman's binary delineations can be prescriptive (child-free female authors

6   *Virginia Woolf and Motherhood*

being one of the anomalies that unsettle such a reading), it is useful to think of these categories while examining the socio-political impact of Woolf's maternal metaphors. As Christine Froula points out, maternal figures in *A Room of One's Own* are 'subject not simply to the natural laws of human reproduction but to the fatality of maternity in a political economy of gender that sets nature (the female reproductive body) at war with nature (genius)'.[8] Portraying motherhood as lethal not only to artistry but to life in general, Woolf's maternal metaphors foreground artistic production over biological reproduction. Her overt ambivalence about maternity – an uncertainty which can be seen well before marriage – stems from a belief that becoming a mother stays artistic creation. As Rachel Bowlby notes, in 'Woolf's time [. . .] parenthood, and motherhood in particular, could be perceived as an obstacle to superior forms of achievement'.[9] Accordingly, Woolf observes that Britain's four most famous women novelists – 'Jane Austen and the Brontës and George Eliot' – had little in common: 'Save for the possibly relevant fact that not one of them had a child' (*AROO* 60).

One of the aims of this book is to uncover the creative ramifications of Woolf's relationship with motherhood. Maternal metaphors are excellent material for this because they also reveal some of the more personal motivations behind her art. The comparison of Woolf's most valued activity – writing – to childbirth establishes how personally significant motherhood was. Indeed, she acknowledged how her status as a non-mother stimulated her creativity, explaining to Gwen Raverat in a letter: 'I was going to have written to Jacques about his children, and about my having none – I mean, these efforts of mine to communicate with people are partly childlessness, and the horror that sometimes overcomes me' (*L3* 172). Woolf repeatedly contrasted her literary success with her sister Vanessa Bell's maternity. She praised Bell's art with: 'I am amazed, a little alarmed (for as you have the children, the fame by rights belongs to me)' (*L3* 271), and on comparing the disparity in their earnings she noted: 'I put my life blood into writing, & she had children' (*D5* 120). Often these thoughts occurred during moments of depression, such as this diary entry written while finishing *To the Lighthouse*:

> its coming – the horror – physically like a painful wave swelling about the heart – tossing me up. I'm unhappy unhappy! [. . .] But why am I feeling this? Let me watch the wave rise. I watch. Vanessa. Children. Failure. (*D3* 110)

These feelings were directly related to what Woolf saw as her 'failure' to fight off mental illness. She describes this culpability in another diary entry; 'my own fault too – a little more self control on my part, & we might have had a boy of 12, a girl of 10'. In response to these difficult emotions she determined to explore the benefits of being child-free, endeavouring 'to exploit my own possessions to the full' and to 'increase the pleasure of life enormously by living it carefully'. However she understood that such a premeditated outlook was difficult, if not impossible, when it came to something as emotive as maternity: 'No doubt', she concluded, 'this is a rationalisation of a state which is not really of that nature' (*D3* 107).[10]

As with her diary and letters, Woolf's forays into memoir cast light upon her personal relationship with motherhood, offering yet more biographical context for her foregrounding of books over babies, and indeed her writing about motherhood in general. Inspired by Vanessa's first pregnancy, 'Reminiscences' (1907) explores the Stephens' childhood through the biographies of Julia Stephen, Stella Duckworth and Vanessa.[11] The curious effect of this auto/biography is that although it depicts three women, it describes only one role in the family – that of matriarch. Alex Zwerdling describes the work as 'a tightly structured tale of an unwilled matrilineal succession, in which the family office of housekeeper and mother must be occupied by someone no matter at what cost'.[12] Woolf, who had a reputation for being virginal, appears to have been omitted from this legacy even before her marriage with Leonard and the decision not to have children. Read closely, the account shows that Woolf's emotional distance from motherhood was already present while she was in her twenties. Because it was intended for the pregnant Vanessa, 'Reminiscences' may venerate the maternal role, nonetheless, it explores Woolf's feelings about her mother's death from the 'labours' and 'toil' (*MB* 8–11) of domesticity, Stella's death in pregnancy and asserts Vanessa's place as the maternal heir (for example, Woolf repeats the family legend that even as a small child Vanessa 'was able to care for the three little creatures who were younger than she was' (*MB* 1)).

Written much later, 'A Sketch of the Past' (1939) is a more self-conscious attempt at memoir writing (in the first paragraph Woolf refers to herself as 'a great memoir reader' and notes 'the number of different ways in which memoirs can be written (*MB* 78)). Woolf's choice then, to begin the memoir with an image of her mother, reiterates how significant the maternal figure was to her life and work.

8   *Virginia Woolf and Motherhood*

'A Sketch' also negotiates how Julia Stephen inspired *To the Light-house*, while, perhaps paradoxically, offering the tantalising and subjective image of Stephen as:

> a person who died forty-four years ago at the age of forty-nine, without leaving a book, or a picture, or any piece of work – apart from the three children who now survive and the memory of her that remains in their minds. (*MB* 96)

This image contrasts with Stephen's dedication to philanthropic work and her actual – albeit small – body of published writing which included *Notes from Sick Rooms* and the entry 'Julia Margaret Cameron' in the *Dictionary of National Biography* (*DNB*). This disparity, plus Woolf's creative decision to take the 'measure' (*MB* 97) of her mother's character through an examination of her two marriages, offers a chance to explore the rupture not only between Woolf's modernism and the patriarchal culture of her childhood, but from the traditional structures of matriarchy too.

Motherhood and Maternalism: Historical and Critical Contexts

While Woolf's references to motherhood are often explicit there are also moments where such allusions are more subtle. In her earlier works (for example, 'The Journal of Mistress Joan Martyn', *The Voyage Out* and *Night and Day*), female protagonists grapple with the question of marriage, and motherhood is implied rather than stated. In the Victorian era – before birth control campaigns began in earnest – marriage was likely to end in motherhood and thus the terms could be used synonymously. However the reduction in family size that occurred between Woolf's parents' generation and her own was a signifier of the enormous social change these years had seen. Woolf used maternal discourses as an agent of modernity. To present motherhood as ambivalent, as a question, is consistent with her writing of gendered, avant-garde literature. Often this ambivalence is represented through formal experimentation. For example, in Mrs Thornbury and Mrs Elliot's conversation the actions of the young women who are mysteriously avoiding motherhood are represented with textual dashes ('Mrs Thornbury has 'heard young women talk quite openly of – ' (*M* 137)). Similarly, in the 1921 story 'A Society', discussions about chastity and pregnancy are full of ambivalent silences. Though no critics have specifically documented these moments of silence with regard to motherhood, Valentine Cunningham has noted that 'after 1914 [. . .] obscuration [. . .] would come to be accepted as the great grace of a whole modern literature of silence, exiled meanings, refusal', and Anne Toner is one of several critics that have shown how 'Woolf advanced a feminist argument' through her use of silence.[13]

Woolf's interest in maternal discourses is part of her general engagement with the place of women in society. As Elaine Showalter noted in her landmark book *A Literature of Their Own*: 'Woolf inherited a female tradition a century old; no woman writer has ever been more in touch with – even obsessed by – this tradition than she'.[14] In order to negotiate Woolf's writing about motherhood it is important to understand something of the history of this 'female tradition' and, more specifically, the history of maternal rhetoric. Early twentieth-century narratives about the domestic and social place of women can be traced back to the middle of the previous century, with the 1851 census acting a pivotal moment in the history of women's social inequality. The census showed some 512,361 more women than men living in Great Britain – meaning that for every 20 men there were 21 women.[15] For the first time the census also collected the marital status of the population, with figures showing that 25 per cent of women did not marry (compared to only 19 per cent of men).[16] Unmarried, middle-class women faced a difficult situation; they were labelled 'unproductive' by a society that morally objected to 'redundancy' among its citizens and were thought of as an economic 'burden', yet they were confined to the domestic sphere and supporting themselves was deemed socially unacceptable. The census report was released in 1854, the same year that Coventry Patmore published the first version of his poem *The Angel in the House*. Though their substance differed significantly, both publications would prove important in the subsequent movement for women's rights and employment, and in Woolf's feminist imagination.

Although middle-class women's employment underwent a transformation in the twentieth century, traces of *The Angel* and the 'surplus women' problem continued to be found in debates about female professional and domestic roles. *Melymbrosia*'s Mrs Thornbury articulates the continuing national concern about 'surplus women' when she observes that there are more 'Unmarried women – earning their livings [. . .] than ever now' (*M* 137), and Woolf famously discusses Patmore's 'Angel' in 'Professions for Women', where she recalls herself as a young unmarried woman beginning her professional life. In 'Professions', Woolf gives the title of 'Angel in the House' to 'the phantom [. . .] who used to come between me and my paper when I was writing reviews' (*E6* 480). However, by taking up her argument against the 'Angel', Woolf is also bringing herself into conflict with the image of the 'surplus woman'. Like *Melymbrosia*'s Miss Allan, the unmarried Virginia Stephen is freed from being a 'burden' by her professional life as a writer. Money is a fundamental part of this argument. Writing requires little funding, so young women writers make: 'No demand [. . .] upon the family purse' (*E6* 479). More importantly, Woolf specifically recalls receiving 'a cheque for one pound ten shillings and sixpence' (*E6* 480) for her first review, a payment that legitimises her younger self's professional life (though she also complicates and satirises this statement by acknowledging her privilege and class, explaining that 'instead of spending that sum upon bread and butter, rent, shoes and stockings, or butcher's bills, I went out and bought a cat – a beautiful cat, a Persian cat' (*E6* 480)). This pecuniary validation prevents Virginia Stephen from being 'surplus' and allows her to contribute to the intellectual and social endeavours of civilisation. As an author, Woolf explains, she strives to elucidate womanhood by writing the 'truth about my own experiences as a body' (*E6* 483). She goes on to make this undertaking collaborative, proposing that her audience – 'women practising for the first time in history I know not how many different professions' (*E6* 483) – expand on this 'extremely important piece of information' through 'experiments', 'failures and successes' 'in all the arts and professions open to human skill' (*E6* 481).

Woolf's focus on women as paid professionals is important because it distances them from the philanthropic 'work' of Victorian women – voluntary employment that is interwoven with the maternalist ideas of Mrs Thornbury. While scholars such as Clara Jones and Milena Radeva have explored Woolf's feelings about female philanthropy, little has been written about the links Woolf draws between motherhood and philanthropy, or how she criticises philanthropic maternalism in her fiction.[17] 'Maternalism', as defined by Seth Koven and Sonya Michel in their formative article on the subject, is a term applied to 'ideologies that exalted women's capacity to mother and extended to society as a whole the values of care, nurturance, and morality'.[18] While critics have primarily focused on maternalism during Woolf's lifetime, its rhetoric can also be traced back to the seismic shift of the 1851 census.[19] In 1855 Anna Jameson published two lectures on women's employment that firmly established maternalist ideals, calling for women to be allowed 'the power to carry into a wider sphere the duties of home – the wifely, motherly, sisterly instincts, which bind them to the other half of the human race'.[20] For Woolf and other women of her time, this maternalist idealism was outdated.[21] Woolf comments on late-Victorian maternalist philanthropy through figures such as Mrs Thornbury, or *To the Lighthouse*'s Mrs Ramsay. It is important to note that maternalist rhetoric did not exclude those without children, indeed many maternalist campaigners did not have children of their own (as Mrs Thornbury remarks: 'Women without children can do so much for the children of others' (*M* 138)).

Employing maternalist attitudes as an aid to characterisation was one of the earliest ways Woolf used maternal themes in her social criticism, and her critical practice continued to evolve alongside public maternal discourses. While sweeping changes in women's social position altered the nature of feminist rhetoric, motherhood continued to be an important political and social concern. In the wake of the suffrage campaign and WW1 there was some division among post-war activists about what feminism should fight for – equality with men, or rights for women on their own merits. Nonetheless, emerging groups of both 'old' (or 'equalitarian') and 'new' (or 'welfare') feminists continued to use motherhood in their campaigns, shifting the focus of their demands from enfranchisement and the philanthropic guardianship of the poor, to education, welfare, and family and employment legislation. This argument played out among women Woolf knew, feminists such as Independent MP Eleanor Rathbone, Margaret Llewelyn Davies, Ray Strachey and the Six Point Group – a society whose members included Winifred Holtby and Vera Brittain. While these disagreements occurred, Woolf continued to engage with this politicising of motherhood, reflecting Rathbone's campaign for state-funded maternal 'endowments' by appealing in *Three Guineas* for 'a wage to be paid by the State to those whose profession is marriage and motherhood' (*TG* 236). This demand directly challenged traditional maternalist ideals, which insisted that motherhood transcended payment. Indeed, Anna Jameson argued that maternalist philanthropists were an 'order of women, quite beyond the reach of any remuneration'.[22] Woolf was one of many public voices that reacted to essentialist theories about motherhood, and in doing so she engaged in an activity which is yet have a title, but which scholars Rebecca Jo Plant and Julie Stephens have respectively called 'antimaternalism' and 'postmaternalism'.[23] Incorporating a maternalist-adverse perspective in her writing helped Woolf express her ambivalence about the determinist aspects of gender. It also allowed her to articulate her anger at the way patriarchal society categorised women. As the above

12   *Virginia Woolf and Motherhood*

passage from *Melymbrosia* demonstrates, writing about motherhood with insight (and often irony) was an excellent way of challenging and disrupting gender expectations.

In this book I contend that Woolf engaged with maternal discourses as a part of her political and feminist response to society and to women's place in it.[24] This work aims not only to broaden academic understanding of how Woolf engaged with contemporary social issues, but also to explore how her personal feelings about motherhood affected her creative process and politics. The key critical context for this research is work produced within the broad spectrum of Woolf studies. More specifically, this book is a historicist, biographical, textual study concerned with Woolf's feminist social commentary across a range of genres.

The history of feminist criticism about Woolf – from the ideological and recuperative analyses of critics such as Marcus, Showalter, Sandra Gilbert and Susan Gubar, to the more contextualised readings of the early 2000s, such as Naomi Black's *Virginia Woolf as Feminist* and Julia Briggs's *Virginia Woolf: An Inner Life* – has already been recounted in many excellent ways.[25] Michael Whitworth traces the historicist branch of Woolf studies back to the 1950s, though he, like many scholars, registers Alex Zwerdling's *Virginia Woolf and the Real World* as a 'pioneering' text in the field.[26] Historicist Woolf criticism has since expressed varying degrees of interest in the events relevant to this book: war (seen, for example, in the work of Mark Hussey, Karen Levenback and Masami Usui), eugenics (Linden Peach and David Bradshaw), the changing domestic and class relations of women (Heather Levy, Natasha Periyan and Alison Light) and psychoanalysis (Elizabeth Abel and Nicky Platt).[27] In the past, critics have perceived a divide between feminist studies and historicism. Zwerdling, for example, branded feminist criticism 'ahistorical', and observed how it seemed 'to disregard the particular contribution of Woolf's work to the various social and political movements it engages'.[28] However, more recent scholarship has striven to change this view, with Linden Peach observing 'feminist literary critics, such as Jane Marcus [. . .], argued for the political significance of Woolf that studies of her art and aesthetics earlier in the century had overlooked'.[29] Ruptures between historicism and feminism have been blamed on the feminist use of both structuralist and poststructuralist theory. However, these divides are being challenged by scholars such as Derek Ryan, whose work strives to 'unsettle the perceived opposition between historical and theoretical approaches to Woolf's writings'.[30]

Although there are no book-length historicist readings of motherhood in Woolf's work there are scholars, both historicist and otherwise, who have written about Woolf and motherhood or Woolf and her own mother. As Emily Blair notes: 'A significant branch of Woolf studies has extensively examined Woolf's fictional representations of mothers through both mythological and psychoanalytic methodologies'.[31] While there is no separate section on motherhood in Hussey's *Virginia Woolf A to Z*, he gives several examples of ways in which scholars have analysed mothers in her writing.[32] Such scholars include Hermione Lee, whose influential biography charts Woolf's relationship with her mother and sister and her feelings about being child-free; Christine Froula, who writes insightfully about Woolf's mother characters; Kristin Czarnecki, who explores Woolf's relationship with the maternal through a comparative approach; and Marion Dell, who has looked at how Woolf was artistically influenced by her Victorian 'matriarchal' relatives Julia Margaret Cameron, Anny Ritchie and Julia Stephen.[33]

In recent decades both cultural history and literary scholarship have offered an increasingly contextualised view of women's lives in the first half of the twentieth century. As noted, one of the more significant changes during this period was in family size, which considerably decreased due to changing attitudes to women's domestic and professional lives and the growing acceptance of birth control. These changes were accompanied by new scientific and medical narratives. Accordingly, historicist research has examined contraception, women's sexuality, feminism and sexology.[34] Imperial expansion, commerce, and new technology also greatly affected women, as did the suffrage and cooperative movements. Woolf scholars have acknowledged the significance of these changes with interest expressed in a wide range of subjects such as trade, publishing, medical technology, and the details of Woolf's social activism.[35] Outside of Woolf studies, the historical and social aspects of motherhood have long been of scholarly interest. Twentieth-century European and American maternal politics, wartime motherhood both in Britain and abroad, and the effect that eugenic ideals and an increasingly ageist and consumerist culture had on motherhood have all drawn attention.[36]

Recently, the interdisciplinary nexus of scholarship on contemporary motherhood has been called maternal studies, motherhood studies or maternal feminism. Less historical in its perspective, maternal studies sits at the junction between psychoanalytic, feminist and gender studies. It grew out of early radical thinking about motherhood such as Simone de Beauvoir's *The Second Sex*; 'second-wave' feminist literary critics; 1970s and 1980s French feminist and poststructuralist theory (such as Julia Kristeva and Hélène Cixous); Sarah Ruddick's feminist philosophies on motherhood; and 1990's theories on queer and gender performance. Modern 'motherhood studies' have been championed in Canada by Andrea O'Reilly, who founded the Motherhood Initiative for Research and Community Involvement in 1998, as well as the associated *Journal of the Motherhood Initiative for Research and Community Involvement*. In England, 'maternal studies' have been established by Lisa Baraitser and the Department of Psychosocial Studies at Birkbeck University, who founded the Mapping Maternal Subjectivities, Identities and Ethics network and its associated online journal *Studies in the Maternal*.

While literary accounts of motherhood are included in maternal studies' interdisciplinary approach – the website for *Studies in the Maternal* lists 'representations of the maternal in literature' among its areas of interest and counts Rachel Bowlby as an international advisor – recent research in the area (as outlined by Samira Kawash in 2011) has focused on subjective views of motherhood, the place of motherhood in feminism and how contemporary critical thinking might change maternal practices.[37] One formal feature regularly observed in maternal scholarship is the author's subjective relationship to the material – these autoethnographic articles offer a sort of memoir or 'momoir', a testimony encased within the scholarly text. For example, while reviewing maternal studies literature from the 2000s, Kawash writes: 'Motherhood was on my mind too during the decade. I was hoping to have a baby, but my feminist reflexes were making me a little uncomfortable about what that would mean'. Similarly Tracey Jensen concludes her article 'Why Study the Maternal Now?' with a memory of 'when my five-year old deftly out-reasoned me: "That's your other name. Your real name is mummy"'.[38] While such language is not generally found within contemporary literary theory, it highlights a certain slippage towards the personal and subjective that often occurs in critical thinking about motherhood and that perhaps prompts the weight of psychoanalytic research found in maternity-focused Woolf scholarship.

The four chapters of this book seek to find a novel critical way of reading motherhood in Woolf's writing. They use Woolf's response to the maternal discourses surrounding WW1, the eugenics movement, the domestic realm of food preparation and the theories of psychoanalysis to elucidate her politics, feminism and artistic motivation. In the last decades, Woolf's pacifism and her unique contribution to war literature have earned well-merited critical attention, yet little has been written on the place of motherhood in her anti-war texts. The first chapter aims to address this by focusing on the way Woolf employed motherhood as a lens through which to investigate and condemn both war and war-making society. During WW1, motherhood, as Susan Grayzel has observed, was 'a major rhetorical tool with which debates about women and war were conducted'.[39] Government propaganda, feminist literature and the mainstream media bombarded the public with archetypal images of nationalistic mothers. Though Woolf was vocal about her antipathy to the patriarchal promotion of war, this public rhetoric laid an effective narrative device at her disposal. As motherhood became a way for the populace to speak about wartime femininity, so it became an effective way for Woolf, as a woman, to speak about war. Chapter 1 investigates Woolf's writing about wartime mothers by concentrating on three post-WW1 works: *Jacob's Room*, the short story 'A Society' and *Mrs Dalloway*. These works, written with the conflict still in recent memory, are different in terms of style and content, yet each uses maternal characters to investigate female endorsement of militarism. By comparing these characters, and highlighting a shared ethos in these diverse texts' maternal imagery, this chapter illustrates just how deeply Woolf felt motherhood had been made complicit in war-making.

Chapter 2 explores Woolf's complex engagement with eugenics, a multifaceted movement towards which she expressed both contention and agreement. By the beginning of the twentieth century eugenics was one of the most publicly debated subjects in Britain and its core topics – reproduction, gestational health and sterilisation – were intrinsically linked with childbearing. Woolf's responses to the movement were also mediated by deeply personal feelings about motherhood and her experience with private physicians. These feelings are at play when she uses maternal metaphors to trace a literary history of women's writing in *A Room of One's Own* and constructs this literary inheritance according to radical, feminist eugenic models. This chapter contextualises Woolf's eugenic thought by referencing a variety of sources including Leslie Stephen's writings about the dangers of eugenics, the professional opinions of Woolf's doctors, and the ideology of eugenic-supporting contemporaries such as Vita Sackville-West. It shows how Woolf's eugenic model for a literary canon can be read in its embryonic state in *Night and Day*, before analysing *A Room of One's Own*'s dialogue with the feminist eugenics texts of contraceptive campaigner Marie Carmichael Stopes.

While *Night and Day* and *A Room of One's Own* are chronologically and formally distant, they have a great deal in common. Both are discussions about creative inheritance and the transformation of social structure, both are concerned with women's restricted access to intellectual life, and both question the nature of reality and how to represent it in fiction. Both are also concerned with the conflict between women's romantic and creative lives ultimately foregrounding an artistic 'immortality' over a genetic one. There are even textual crossovers between the two, with *Night and Day*'s female characters exploring the prospect of rooms of their own and its protagonist, Katharine Hilbery, thinking the words 'in such a room one could work – one could have a life of one's own' (*ND* 229).

Chapter 3 investigates how Woolf used food as a way to access the material and performative aspects of motherhood. Woolf wrote about food with a passion that few other authors of her era matched, partly for aesthetic reasons, and partly because it was an excellent device for commenting on the lives of women. As domestic tasks such as childcare and food preparation rapidly transformed during Woolf's lifetime, they became the foci of changing class interactions and tension. Upper-class women used their unique mix of education and domestic knowledge to shape public welfare policy. Working-class women found power as consumers, effecting change at local and national levels through the Co-operative movement – a movement that Woolf was both active in and educated about. These public discourses, as well as private domestic anxieties, mean that where Woolf writes about food her texts are complicated by class tension.

Scenes concerning food, motherhood and class can be observed throughout Woolf's oeuvre. This chapter begins by looking at the class connotations of a number of scenes involving infant-feeding. It goes on to explore motherhood and food in *The Waves* and *The Years*. These two novels were written only five years apart and include three different women from rural homes who are from different classes, mother in different ways and are characterised through descriptions of meals or food. 'Memories of a Working Women's Guild' – Woolf's introductory letter to the Women's Co-operative Guild (WCG)'s collection of working-class women's memoirs – was also written in this period and is an excellent foil to the novels. It is one of Woolf's most controversial works, investigating the chasm between classes of women via an array of material differences, including food and body type. When read together, these three works shed light on Woolf's thoughts about the social aspect of mothering, class, and working-class women's contribution not just to culture but to art.

Chapter 4 turns to another school of thought that transformed public discourse in Woolf's lifetime – psychoanalysis. From the time of her marriage, Woolf's work and social life brought her into contact with those at the forefront of British psychoanalysis and it is well documented that she was sceptical about its theories.[40] However, in the 1930s, with fascism growing in Europe and the Second World War (WW2) looming, she began to look for new ways of understanding human nature. The wide-ranging cultural research she undertook for 'Professions for Women', *Three Guineas* and *The Years* saw her perusing contemporary pedagogic material that included psychoanalytic theory (such as the popular serialised textbook *The Science of Life* (1931)) and other more abstractly psychoanalytical sources (such as a Church of England report entitled *The Ministry of Women* (1935)). The outcome of this more detached introduction was twofold: she began to express an interest in Sigmund Freud's ideas about human instinct and group dynamics, and she became receptive to Melanie Klein's object-relations theories and their foregrounding of the formative effects of mother–child relationships. Using Woolf's late works, this chapter charts the changes in her attitude towards psychoanalytic theory. It begins by looking at how *Three Guineas'* investigation of fascism and war-making employs Freud's theories on gender and infant sexuality – including the Oedipus complex and castration complex – to understand patriarchal society's attitude towards women. It then turns to the character development in 'A Sketch of the Past' and *Between the Acts*, noting how both Freudian and Kleinian ideas of infant development can be found in the central place that mothers take in each character's narrative.

A recent trend in Woolf studies has been to concentrate on the ambivalence in her thinking, writing and actions. For example, the title of the collection *Contradictory Woolf* defines its essays' objectives and the papers in *Virginia Woolf: Twenty-First-Century Approaches* survey Woolf's 'unresolved dissonances, binaries and doubles, ruptured meanings, and oppositional factors, [. . .] ambivalence, antithesis and paradox'.[41] While motherhood is a powerful signifier in Woolf's writing it consistently emerges as something ambivalent. It is the device that motivates Mrs Ramsay to 'have liked always to have had a baby' while paradoxically stopping her from achieving her goal of setting up: 'A model dairy and a hospital' ('two things she would have liked to do, herself' she reflects: 'But how? With all these children?' (*TL* 64)). Similarly, in *A Room of One's Own* impregnation is deadly for Judith Shakespeare, yet it is the key to 'conceiving' a

18 *Virginia Woolf and Motherhood*

successful work of art. Ambiguity is characteristic of Woolf's writing about motherhood, it can be found in her earliest forays into fiction, with examples of doubt about childbearing emerging in short stories written well before she was married.[42] These stories illustrate Woolf's fears that childbearing profoundly compromised a woman's capacity to make art.

Woolf's diary and letters can also be ambiguous when dealing with the desire to be a mother. In 1908 she wrote to Violet Dickinson, 'I doubt that I shall ever have a baby. Its voice is too terrible, a senseless scream, like an ill omened cat' (*L1* 331), yet in a letter written to Leonard after he proposed, she twice stated how much she wanted children, writing, 'you'll be quite happy with him; and he will give you companionship, children, and a busy life' and 'I want everything – love, children, adventure, intimacy, work' (*L1* 496). Following the decision not to have children, while motherhood was often a source of pain it could also prove liberating. For example, when Leonard resigned from *The Nation and Athenaeum* Woolf noted in her diary: 'I'm amused at my own sense of liberation. [. . .] with £400 assured & no children, why imitate a limpet in order to enjoy a limpets safety?' (*D3* 70). Occasionally the decision not to have children even felt fitting, with Woolf remarking at the end of 1927,

> oddly enough I scarcely want children of my own now. This insatiable desire to write something before I die, this ravaging sense of the shortness & feverishness of life, make me cling, like a man on a rock, to my one anchor. (*D3* 167)

Gayle Letherby and Catherine Williams have written of the ambivalent emotions that accompany the decades-long, nebulous journey to being a non-mother.[43] When she was forty-six and reaching the end of this lengthy period, Woolf wondered with an insight that is, in itself, textually ambivalent, 'perhaps I have killed the feeling instinctively; as perhaps nature does' (*D3* 167).[44]

Later in the same diary entry, Woolf recognises her ability to 'dramatise myself as parent' (*D3* 167). Perhaps one of the most poignant examples of Woolf's literary skill can be seen in a passage about motherhood from *The Pargiters*, which describes a young Milly and Delia Pargiter:

> And both, as they stood at the window, had seen a woman pass, pushing a perambulator. The sight of the baby had stirred in each quite a different emotion. Milly had felt a curious, though quite

unanalyzed, desire to look at the baby, to hold it, to feel its body, to press her lips to the nape of its neck; whereas Delia had felt, also without being fully conscious of it, a vague uneasiness, as if some emotion were expected of her which, for some reason, some vaguely discreditable reason, she did not feel; and then, instead of following the perambulator, as her sister did, with her eyes, she turned and came back abruptly into the room, to exclaim a moment later, 'O my God,' as the thought struck her that she would never be allowed to go to Germany and study music. (*P* 36)

This passage is inherently political, contrasting the strictures of motherhood and Victorian domesticity with the creative promise of a talented woman. It is also deeply personal, highlighting impenetrable differences in human desires and expectations. In the wider context of the manuscript, the novel it would become, Woolf's personal life and the political landscape, this passage and others like it offer a new way to contextualise Woolf's work. The following chapters will attempt to undertake just such an exploration

Notes

1. In order to understand the evolution of Woolf's thinking about motherhood this book sees *Melymbrosia* not simply as a manuscript of *The Voyage Out* but as an important genetic step in Woolf's writing.
2. 'Wrapped in the Stars and Stripes: Virginia Woolf in the U.S.A', *The South Carolina Review*, 29.1 (1996), pp. 17–18.
3. Sandra M. Gilbert and Susan Gubar, *No Man's Land: The War of the Words* (New Haven, CT: Yale University Press, 1988), pp. 185, 198; Jane Marcus, *Virginia Woolf and the Languages of Patriarchy* (Bloomington: Indiana University Press, 1987), p. 120.
4. Though Woolf often uses the term 'childless', I have chosen to use non-mother because it is less freighted with moral assumptions. In other places I also use the terms child-free or without children.
5. For example, Ellen Bayuk Rosenman, *The Invisible Presence: Virginia Woolf and the Mother–Daughter Relationship* (Baton Rouge: Louisiana State University Press, 1986); Makiko Minow-Pinkney, *Virginia Woolf and the Problem of the Subject* (Brighton: Harvester, 1987), pp. 72–79; Patricia Moran, 'Virginia Woolf and the Scene of Writing', *Modern Fiction Studies*, 38.1 (1992), pp. 81–100.
6. 'Creativity and the Childbirth Metaphor: Gender Difference in Literary Discourse', *Feminist Studies*, 13.1 (1987), p. 49.
7. Ibid., pp. 65–67.
8. *Virginia Woolf and the Bloomsbury Avant-Garde* (New York: Columbia University Press, 2005), p. 191.

20 *Virginia Woolf and Motherhood*

9. *A Child of One's Own* (Oxford: Oxford University Press, 2013), p. 9.
10. In writing this Woolf anticipated the impediment facing maternal academia, wherein the personal encroaches upon the rational.
11. 'Reminiscences' is included in *Moments of Being*.
12. 'Mastering the Memoir: Woolf and the Family Legacy', *Modernism/modernity*, 10.1 (2003), p. 174.
13. *In the Reading Gaol: Postmodernity, Texts, and History* (Oxford: Blackwell, 1994), p. 207; *Ellipsis in English Literature: Signs of Omission* (Cambridge: Cambridge University Press, 2015), p. 153.
14. *A Literature of Their Own: British Women Novelists from Brontë to Lessing* (Princeton, NJ: Princeton University Press, 1977), p. 264.
15. Office of the Registrar-General, *The Census of Great Britain in 1851*, ed. Thomas Milner (London: Longman, Brown, Green, and Longmans, 1854), p. 4.
16. Ibid., pp. 36–37.
17. Jones notes Woolf's 'fractious relationship to the world of late-Victorian philanthropy' (*Virginia Woolf: Ambivalent Activist* (Edinburgh: Edinburgh University Press, 2016), p. 55, n2) and Radeva writes about the 'ways in which the discourse of philanthropy mediates women's relationship to the public sphere in Woolf's fiction' ('Re-visioning Philanthropy and Women's Roles: Virginia Woolf, Professionalization, and the Philanthropy Debates', in *Woolf Editing/Editing Woolf*, ed. Eleanor McNees and Sara Veglahn (Liverpool: Liverpool University Press, 2009), p. 206).
18. 'Womanly Duties: Maternalist Politics and the Origins of Welfare States in France, Germany, Great Britain, and the United States, 1880–1920', *The American Historical Review*, 95.4 (1990), p. 1079.
19. For example, a body of critical research focuses on the importance of maternalism during the founding of the welfare state: see Koven and Michel, 'Womanly Duties' and Susan Pedersen, *Family, Dependence, and the Origins of the Welfare State: Britain and France 1914–1945* (Cambridge: Cambridge University Press, 1993).
20. *Sisters of Charity; and, the Communion of Labour: Two Lectures on the Social Employments of Women* (London: Longman, Brown, Green, Longmans, and Roberts, 1859), p. 119.
21. For an example of how Woolf's contemporaries viewed maternalism, see Eleanor Rathbone, who also distanced herself from late-Victorian philanthropy, noting: 'There is so much futile prattle about child-welfare and the subject is so attractive to sentimentalists and amateurs that the real student tends to shy away from it ('The Remuneration of Women's Services', *The Economic Journal*, 27.105 (1917), p. 65).
22. *Sisters of Charity*, p. 135.
23. *Mom: The Transformation of Motherhood in Modern America* (Chicago: University of Chicago Press, 2010), p. 6; *Confronting Postmaternal Thinking: Feminism, Memory, and Care* (New York: Columbia University Press, 2012), p. 3.

Introduction 21

24. These two spheres of feminism and politics are arguably irreducible. As Maggie Humm has written: 'Woolf outlines in her writing a huge variety of political propositions all painted with a strong feminist hue' (*Feminisms: A Reader* (London: Harvester Wheatsheaf, 1992), p. 21).

25. See, for example, Beth Rigel Daugherty, 'Feminist Approaches', in *Palgrave Advances in Virginia Woolf Studies*, ed. Anna Snaith (Basingstoke: Palgrave Macmillan, 2007), pp. 98–124.

26. 'Historicising Woolf: Context Studies', in *Virginia Woolf in Context*, ed. Bryony Randall and Jane Goldman (Cambridge: Cambridge University Press, 2012), pp. 4, 8.

27. Hussey (ed.), *Virginia Woolf and War: Fiction, Reality, and Myth* (New York: Syracuse University Press, 1991); Levenback, *Virginia Woolf and the Great War* (New York: Syracuse University Press, 1999); Usui, 'The Female Victims of the War in *Mrs Dalloway*', in *Virginia Woolf and War: Fiction, Reality and Myth*, ed. Mark Hussey (New York: Syracuse University Press, 1991), pp. 151–63; Peach, 'Woolf and Eugenics', in *Virginia Woolf in Context*, eds. Bryony Randall and Jane Goldman (Cambridge: Cambridge University Press, 2012), pp. 439–48; Bradshaw, 'Eugenics: "They should certainly be killed"', in *A Concise Companion to Modernism*, ed. David Bradshaw (Oxford: Blackwell, 2003), pp. 34–55; Levy, *Servants of Desire* (New York: Peter Lang, 2010); Periyan, *The Politics of 1930s British Literature: Education, Class, Gender* (London: Bloomsbury Academic, 2018); Light, *Mrs Woolf and the Servants* (London: Penguin Books, 2008); Abel, *Virginia Woolf and the Fictions of Psychoanalysis* (Chicago: University of Chicago Press, 1989); Nicky Platt, 'When Freud Gets Useful: Retaining the Commonplace in Virginia Woolf's *Pointz Hall*', *Woolf Studies Annual*, 16 (2010).

28. *Virginia Woolf and the Real World* (Berkeley: University of California Press, 1986), p. 33.

29. 'Historical Approaches', in *Palgrave Advances in Virginia Woolf Studies*, ed. Anna Snaith (Basingstoke: Palgrave Macmillan, 2007), p. 170.

30. *Virginia Woolf and the Materiality of Theory* (Edinburgh: Edinburgh University Press, 2013), p. 4.

31. *Virginia Woolf and the Nineteenth-Century Domestic Novel* (Albany: State University of New York Press, 2007), p. 260, n46. For examples of psychoanalytic scholarship on motherhood see above at n. 4, for an example of mythological readings see: Eileen Barrett, 'Matriarchal Myth on a Patriarchal Stage: Virginia Woolf's *Between the Acts*', *Twentieth Century Literature*, 33.1 (1987), pp. 18–37.

32. *Virginia Woolf A–Z* (New York: Facts on File, 1995), pp. 31, 224–25, 253, 268, 315, 338, 393.

33. Lee, *Virginia Woolf* (London: Vintage, 1997); Froula, *Virginia Woolf and the Bloomsbury Avant-Garde*; Czarnecki, '"In my mind I saw my mother": Virginia Woolf, Zitkala-Ša, and Autobiography', in *Virginia Woolf and Her Female Contemporaries*, ed. Julie Vandivere and Megan

Hicks (Clemson, SC: Clemson University Press, 2016), pp. 143–50; Dell, *Virginia Woolf's Influential Forebears: Julia Margaret Cameron, Anny Thackeray Ritchie and Julia Prinsep Stephen* (Basingstoke: Palgrave Macmillan, 2015)

34. For Woolf and the contraceptive movement, see Christina Hauck, '"To escape the horror of family life": Virginia Woolf and the British Birth Control Debate', in *New Essays on Virginia Woolf*, ed. Helen Wussow (Dallas, TX: Contemporary Research, 1995), pp. 15–37. For a more general history, see Layne Parish Craig, *When Sex Changed: Birth Control Politics and Literature Between the World Wars* (New Brunswick, NJ: Rutgers University Press, 2013); and Lucy Bland, *Banishing the Beast: English Feminism and Sexual Morality 1885–1914* (London: Penguin Books, 1995).

35. A small example of these include Gregory Dekter, 'Perishable and Permanent: Industry, Commodity, and Society in *Mrs Dalloway* and *To the Lighthouse*', *Virginia Woolf Miscellany*, 88 (2016), p. 14; Alice Staveley, 'Marketing Virginia Woolf: Women, War, and Public Relations in *Three Guineas*', *Book History*, 12 (2009), pp. 295–339; Evelyn Chan, 'The Ethics and Aesthetics of Healing: Woolf, Medicine, and Professionalization', *Women's Studies*, 43:1 (2014), pp. 25–51; Sowon Park, 'Suffrage and Virginia Woolf: "The mass behind the single voice"', *The Review of English Studies*, 56.223 (2005), pp. 119–34; Jones, *Ambivalent Activist*.

36. For example, Ann Taylor Allen, *Feminism and Motherhood in Western Europe, 1890–1970* (Basingstoke: Palgrave Macmillan, 2005); Jane Lewis, *The Politics of Motherhood: Child and Maternal Welfare in England 1900–1939* (London: Croom Helm, 1980); Dana Cooper and Claire Phelan (eds), *Motherhood and War: International Perspectives* (Basingstoke: Palgrave Macmillan, 2014); Molly Ladd-Taylor, *Fixing the Poor: Eugenic Sterilization and Child Welfare in the Twentieth Century* (Baltimore. MD: Johns Hopkins University Press, 2017); Eileen Janes Yeo, 'The creation of "motherhood" and Women's responses in Britain and France, 1750–1914', *Women's History Review*, 8:2 (1999), pp. 201–18.

37. 'Focus and Scope', *Studies in the Maternal* <https://www.mamsie.bbk.ac.uk/submissions> [accessed 23 October 2019]; Samira Kawash, 'New Directions in Motherhood Studies', *Signs*, 36.4 (2011), pp. 969–1003.

38. 'New Directions', p. 969; 'Why Study the Maternal Now?', *Studies in the Maternal*, 1.1 (2009) <doi: http://doi.org/10.16995/sim.166> [accessed 22 October 2019], p. 3.

39. *Women's Identities at War: Gender, Motherhood, and Politics in Britain and France During the First World War* (Chapel Hill: University of North Carolina Press, 1999), p. 244.

40. See Lee, *Virginia Woolf*, p. 193 and Platt, 'When Freud Gets Useful', p. 157.

41. Derek Ryan and Stella Bolaki, 'Introduction', *Contradictory Woolf*, ed. Derek Ryan and Stella Bolaki (Liverpool: Liverpool University Press, 2012), p. ix; Jeanne Dubino et al., 'Introduction', *Virginia Woolf: Twenty-First-Century Approaches*, ed. Jeanne Dubino et al., p. 1.
42. For example, 'Phyllis and Rosamond' and 'The Journal of Mistress Joan Martyn', both written in 1906.
43. 'Non-Motherhood: Ambivalent Autobiographies', *Feminist Studies*, 25.3 (1999), pp. 719–28.
44. This paragraph represents just a small sample of the diary entries and letters that touch on motherhood. While many more will be explored in the following chapters, here is a further (limited) selection. *D1* 8; *D2* 72–73; *D2* 159; *D2* 221–22; *D3* 20; *D3* 195; *D3* 217; *D3* 283–84; *D3* 298; *D3* 168; *D4* 108; *D4* 333; *D5* 120; *D5* 305; *L1* 307; *L1* 309; *L1* 506; *L2* 137–38; *L2* 278; *L3* 110; *L3* 233; *L3* 236; *L3* 329; *L4* 119; *L4* 286; *L5* 57; *L5* 149; *L5* 404; *L6* 358.

Chapter 1

Motherhood and the Great War

Introduction

In 1924 Maine governor Percival Baxter went against the political grain and commissioned a woman sculptor, Bashka Paeff, to create a pacifist memorial for sailors and soldiers lost in WW1. The sculpture depicts a woman protectively shielding a child. Around them lie the bodies of young men, naked and non-partisan, victims of the conflict. Baxter was probably aware of what he was commissioning. Three years earlier Paeff had given an interview in which she had said of the war:

> After it is all done we are likely to make statues of soldier boys and sailor boys, in a kind of parade spirit, and set them up as if war were a fine thing. So we forget what suffering and horror it brought [. . .] we should set up memorials that would make us loathe war instead of admire it.[1]

As Paeff worked on her monument, Virginia Woolf was writing and editing the manuscript that would become *Mrs Dalloway*. This novel was to be her second to damn war, after the elegiac *Jacob's Room* published at the end of 1922. Like Paeff's bronze, Woolf's novels stood in contrast to the cultural norm. They exist as memorials that condemn war and its patriarchal origins – portraying tragic, empty loss, and creating a lasting reminder of the horror of such conflicts. All three works manifest prominent images of mothers to investigate their subject, reflecting a wartime trend that saw motherhood used as fuel for a variety of propaganda campaigns, both to promote war and to protest against it.

Many women embraced the ratification of war through images of motherhood, accepting this association as a way to strengthen their newfound social and political legitimacy. At the same time antithetical maternal images emerged in the pacifist movement, where women were depicted as innately peaceful due to their inherent maternal tendencies. Woolf was critical of both of these attempts to appropriate motherhood and included fictional mother figures in her wartime novels as a way to investigate idealised motherhood and maternal collusion, and to ask whether any real autonomy might be won by cooperating with, or attempting to effect change within, a patriarchal state.

Connections between Woolf's images of mothers, and war and peace, are often overlooked by scholars who write about her contribution to war literature. Yet her post-war novels recreate a moment when motherhood was the primary way to discuss issues related to women, be they political, economic or social. Using maternal characters and themes from *Jacob's Room*, *Mrs Dalloway* and the short story 'A Society', this chapter will investigate representations of the wartime exploitation of motherhood, to unveil a narrative thread that Woolf would return to throughout her literary career.

Manifestations of Motherhood in Pro-War Propaganda

The outbreak of the Great War was accompanied by great fluctuations in the status quo and the redefinition of communal functions such as gender roles. For women, this meant not only new economic and industrial responsibilities, but also the foregrounding of their reproductive duty as a civic obligation.[2] Investigating this phenomenon Susan Grayzel notes that in Britain's 'attempt to make it easier to raise [. . .] future soldiers, its self-interest in promoting motherhood was emphasized throughout the war'. This campaign penetrated public discourse. Grayzel points out that WW1 was

> the first war that allowed governments to take advantage of the mass media and mass culture of the early twentieth century [. . .] the first war shown in cinemas and presented to this more literate public through a vast array of newspapers, journals and popular literature.[3]

Such ubiquity allowed motherhood to be comprehensively regarded as women's patriotic duty, often comparable to enlistment. The media promotion of war and motherhood was particularly infuriating for Woolf. As a resolute pacifist and a non-mother with complex feelings towards maternity, a fundamental sense of alienation

26   *Virginia Woolf and Motherhood*

made her aware of the propaganda-spinning 'war machine'.[4] She understood the media's power not only to permit but also to encourage devastating conflicts and ideals, and she perceived how fiction influenced the fabric of society, especially when it was presented as fact. While Woolf was never shy of employing language to weave her own alternative cultural history, the overt establishment fallacy of *'dulce et decorum est'* angered her. She increasingly saw the press as a dominant, patriarchal influence, exemplified by the publisher Lord Northcliffe, whose paper, *The Times*, did 'all they can to insist upon the indispensability & delight of war. They magnify our victories to make our mouths water for more; they shout with joy when the Germans sink the Irish mail' (*D1* 200). The more the newspapers fêted war, the more anger Woolf expressed at the misinformation and general propaganda broadcast by what she would later colourfully refer to as 'our prostituted fact-purveyors' (*TG* 222).[5] And it was not just the pro-war press that she considered 'preposterous masculine fiction' (*L2* 76). Writing to Margaret Llewelyn Davies in 1917 of 'strong pacifist articles' in the 'local papers', Woolf concluded, 'how little one believes what anyone says now' (*L2* 178).

Woolf found the media as unsound as the war-gossip that spread among the general population, yet she had to depend on the unreliable sources available to her. In a letter to her sister Vanessa, on the day before WW1 was announced, she wrote:

> We are just (4 P.M.) off to Lewes to get a paper. There was none at breakfast this morning, but the postman brought rumours that 2 of our warships were sunk – however, when we did get papers we found that peace still exists [. . .] being Bank holiday of course makes us more remote from life than ever. (*L2* 50)

Reading the papers was already a daily ritual for the Woolfs but the war awarded this routine a sense of urgency. Neither the rumours nor the papers appeared to hold concrete facts and, like many civilians, Woolf experienced feelings of remoteness exacerbated by the reliance on a disingenuous press that distanced her from the truth of the conflict. Karen Levenback observes that Woolf 'seemed to suspect that the government and the press were engaged in a conspiracy aimed at hoodwinking the unthinking or searching young [. . .] into becoming players in the drama of war'.[6] This was as true for women as it was for men, with the government and press using idealised images of mothers to encourage them to join the war effort. Woolf saw this misappropriation of motherhood as a feature of a male-led society that nurtured violent conflict. The duplicity of this media indoctrination served to further her aversion to the war and her perturbance with the often oppressive, patriarchal culture she felt around her.

The ratification of motherhood was widespread. There were government sanctioned child- and healthcare initiatives – Grayzel cites cases such as the establishment of crèches, and labour agreements whereby factory workers could do progressively less taxing work as their pregnancies advanced.[7] The parliamentary recruiting committee – a cross-party body, led by the Prime Minister, which used local canvassing infrastructures as a means to promote enlistment – generated propaganda and posters that directly addressed mothers or showed them bravely seeing their men off to war.[8] And separation allowances – allotments of money made up of a portion of a soldier's pay matched by government funding – were controversially paid to wed and unwed mothers alike, proportional to the number of children they had.[9] Pro-maternal attitudes were not confined to those who represented government interests, but also manifested themselves in business, anti-war factions and general social commentary. Motherhood was promoted in commercial marketing, reports

Figure 1   Wright's coal tar soap advertisement. Reprinted with permission of Lornamead.

Figure 2 'Women of Britain Say "Go"' poster by E. J. Kealey (Parliamentary Recruiting Committee, 1915). Reprinted with permission of Imperial War Museums, London. © Imperial War Museum (Art.IWM PST 2763).

from charitable organizations, feminist literature, and by the public figures that composed the social narrative of the time. Pro-maternal propaganda found its way into daily life across a range of media. As well as posters, advertising, news and radio, pamphleting played an increasingly important role in wartime media – where people craved information, officials and civilians alike set to producing it.[10] The maternal ideal was so prevalent it even pervaded the literary magazines that Woolf read. The May 1915 edition of *The English Review* included an advertisement featuring a young boy, depicted in military uniform, reminding his mother to send soap to their man in the trenches.[11] And it was not merely the externally sourced marketing that promoted childbearing; an editorial in the same issue opines: 'There may yet come a time in this country, owing to the war, when motherhood will be a national duty'.[12]

A reasonable portion of the nationalistic copy about civic-minded mothers was created by women. In 1914, The Mothers' Union made an emotive attempt to include mothers in the war effort. They printed a pamphlet entitled *To British Mothers: How They Can Help Enlistment*. Notably authored by 'ONE OF THEM', it addresses 'MY SISTERS', damns mothers who are against the war and petitions women to be 'the right sort of Mother for Old England' by telling their sons: '*My boy, I don't want you to go, but if I were you I should go*'.[13] This nationalistic rhetoric endorsed violence and promoted a war that Woolf opposed. Moreover, as a non-mother at a time when the birth rate was decreasing and women were choosing not to have children, she must have sensed the limitations of material that directly petitioned mothers and posited them as the mainstay of British femininity. This literature excluded her, and those like her, from more than just a social group or collective; by focusing on motherhood, such rhetoric denied non-mothers a public voice. Although Woolf often wrote 'from the outsiders unsympathetic point of view' (*D1* 268), she was nevertheless a woman who spent much of her life seeking to make her opinions public. By 1914 she had two young nephews and was at the height of her childbearing years. Being without children would have amplified her sensitivity to the difference between herself and the women targeted by these works.

Feminist Pacifism, Suffrage and the Maternalist Language of War

Whether it was produced in support of or opposition to the war effort, speech that lionised motherhood to further public causes was fundamentally aligned with maternalism. Woolf had little sympathy for maternalists, having made up her mind that they, like many activists, were unrealistic and self-serving. This antipathy is exemplified in her early short story 'The Journal of Mistress Joan Martyn', written before the war, but featuring a prototypical pacifist-maternalist figure as the mother of the protagonist – a mother who 'rules us all' (*CSF* 46) with a

> theory of ownership; how, in these times, one is as the Ruler of a small island set in the midst of turbulent waters; how one must plant it and cultivate it; and drive roads through it, and fence it securely from the tides; and one day perhaps the waters will abate and this plot of ground will be ready to make part of a new world. Such is

30 *Virginia Woolf and Motherhood*

> her dream of what the future may bring to England [. . .] She bids me
> hope that I may live to see the whole of England thus solidly estab-
> lished; and if I do, I shall thank my mother, and other women like
> her. (*CSF* 59–60)

Woolf's opinion of such a vision can be seen in Joan's response, agreeing that her mother's utopian vision may be 'good; and we should
do right to wish it' (*CSF* 60) but instinctively finding it unrepresen-
tative of reality. The story's maternalist ideal – the establishment of
a peaceable nation, in accordance with the domestic values of 'my
mother, and other women like her', within the confines and conflicts
of an already established patriarchal system – is further undermined
by the death of Joan before she can wed. Joan's passing underlines
the problematic ethos of relying on motherhood as the sole feminine
agency of power within a patriarchy. Her failure to become a wife
and mother, despite extensive maternal guidance readying her for the
role, openly challenges the efficacy of maternalism.

During WW1 a number of feminist pacifist groups took an essentialist view of women, depicting them as inherently peaceable due
to their ability to nurture life.[14] In December 1914 radical feminist
Emmeline Pethick-Lawrence wrote a widely read article for the
popular American magazine *Harper's Weekly* that outlined the significance of women's participation in international relations, and in
particular the value of a maternal influence on diplomacy. Characteristic in its maternalist stance the article stated:

> It is vital to the deepest interests of the human race that the mother
> half of humanity should now be submitted into the ranks of the artic-
> ulate democracies of the world [. . .] The bedrock of humanity is
> motherhood. The solidarity of the world's motherhood, potential or
> otherwise, underlies all cleavages of nationality. Men have conflicting
> interests and ambitions. Women the world over, speaking broadly,
> have one passion and one vocation, and that is the creation and pres-
> ervation of human life [. . .] a denial of the necessity of war.[15]

Woolf saw Pethick-Lawrence at a 'Suffrage Rally' (*D1* 124) in King-
sway Hall in March 1918, recording her disillusion with the event
in her diary:

> The pure essence of either sex is a little disheartening. Moreover,
> whether it is a meeting of men or women, one can't help wondering
> why they do it. I get one satisfactory thrill from the sense of multitude;

then become disillusioned, finally bored & unable to listen to a word
[. . .] I watched Mrs Pethick-Lawrence rising & falling on her toes, as
if half her legs were made of rubber, throwing out her arms, opening
her hands, & thought very badly of this form of art. (*D1* 125)

Employing the 'pure essence of either sex', Pethick-Lawrence's
maternalist sermonising seems as fallacious as any patriarchal propaganda. Although feminist pacifists and female State sympathisers
were firm adversaries, both used maternal language to answer one
another. This rhetoric was universally serviceable. As Grayzel notes,

> both pacifists and patriots alike spoke for and with the voice of moth-
> ers – it became a primary way to talk about women during the war
> since it allowed for appeals to women across region, ethnicity, class
> and even nation.[16]

There was an additional reason that opposing pacifist and nationalist
factions shared a lexicon. Both parties, and the maternalist language
they used, had their roots in suffrage.

Scholars of the era have identified two main ways that suffragettes
reasoned for their right to the vote, the first, insisting upon women's
equality with men and the second, claiming a female moral superiority often associated with maternalism. Susan Kingsley Kent has
noted that, instead of choosing one of these approaches, separate factions of turn of the century feminists frequently 'espoused the tenets
of both strands as they demanded simultaneously equal rights and
moral reform'.[17] However, a distinctive difference between suffrage
groups could be seen in the advocacy of constitutional action versus
militancy. When the National Union of Women's Suffrage Societies (NUWSS) was formed in 1897 its president Millicent Fawcett
favoured peaceful campaigning methods. Disagreeing with this strategy, the Women's Social and Political Union (WSPU) split from the
NUWSS in 1903 and, under the leadership of Emmeline Pankhurst,
pursued more extreme tactics. Looking at female suffrage in Europe,
Ruth Rubio-Marín has noted:

> While most pursued suffrage through the means accorded by the
> political system, some – notably the suffragettes in the UK – were
> more radical in their methods. They [. . .] engaged in very uncon-
> ventional activities, which included arson and hunger strikes in
> prison, as expressions of what Mrs Pankhurst called a 'civil war'
> waged by women.[18]

32 *Virginia Woolf and Motherhood*

The WSPU became increasingly militant in the years leading up to WW1. Several prominent members disagreed with the extent of this physical force and formed splinter groups (including Pethick-Lawrence, who was ousted from the WSPU after a disagreement about arson, and helped found the less violent United Suffragists). When the war began, feminist groups were therefore already at odds with each other over the morality of aggressive action. What had begun as a domestic debate became an international question of the necessity of war. The idealistic divisions between the groups were enflamed; pacifists spoke out publicly against the war while the WSPU, now led by Christabel Pankhurst, became increasingly nationalistic, ceasing radical protests, renaming their periodical *Britannia* and publishing xenophobic and patriotic pro-war material.[19]

Feminism was so culturally influential that the media adoption of maternalist language resulted, at least in part, from the influence of these warring parties. As James Longenbach has argued, 'when the war finally came, its rhetoric was already in place, honed by the soldiers of modernism and suffrage'.[20] An example of the general uptake of such themes comes in the form of a 1916 pamphlet, 'A Mother's Answer to "A Common Soldier"', a tract that is often found in accounts of war propaganda due to its extreme nature. Originally a letter in *The Morning Post* – a paper Woolf did not buy regularly until 1921[21] – the pamphlet was incredibly popular, selling a staggering 75,000 copies in its first week.[22] Its author, a woman who called herself the 'Little Mother', claimed to opine:

> not what the Government thinks, not what the Pacifists think, but what the mothers of the British race think of our fighting men [. . .] a voice which demands to be heard, seeing that we play the most important part in the history of the world, for it is we who 'mother the men' who have to uphold the honour and traditions not only of our Empire but of the whole civilized world.

This language clearly displays its maternalist origins and calls to mind Woolf's pacifist objection (used in rather the opposite sense) in *Three Guineas*: where Woolf's 'outsider', finding 'that she has no good reason to ask her brother to fight on her behalf to protect "our" country', notes 'as a woman, I have no country. As a woman I want no country. As a woman my country is the whole world' (*TG* 234). Sounding remarkably like Pethick-Lawrence's article (despite their ideological differences), the leaflet declares: 'Women are created for

Motherhood and the Great War   33

the purpose of giving life, and men to take it'. And in reply to pacifist 'agitation', the writer of the letter states:

> we women, who demand to be heard, will tolerate no such cry as 'Peace! Peace!' where there is no peace [. . .] Send the Pacifists to us and we shall very soon show them, and show the world, that in our homes at least there shall be no 'sitting at home warm and cosy in the winter, cool and "comfy" in the summer'. There is only one temperature for the women of the British race, and that is white heat. With those who disgrace their sacred trust of motherhood we have nothing in common.

By speaking directly to the pacifists' sacrosanct maternity, the letter refutes their claim to a higher moral standing. However, it requires the reader to engage in a very high level of ethical identification. The original letter was printed complete with replies of support from the general populace and the Queen, some of which stretched the very boundaries of plausibility. One reply states:

> I have lost my two dear boys, but since I was shown the 'Little Mother's' beautiful letter a resignation too perfect to describe has calmed all my aching sorrow, and I would now gladly give my sons twice over. *A Bereaved Mother*.[23]

Unsurprisingly there was some debate over whether this letter was propaganda penned by a journalist; nevertheless, it gained wide circulation and was not unique. Suzanne Evans records several examples of stories, published in the allied countries' media, which follow this template.[24] Such accounts were another way in which the press distanced the domestic population from the truth of war.

Many civilians responded eagerly to this sort of propaganda while returning soldiers found it confusing and unbalanced. In his 1929 autobiography *Goodbye to All That*, WW1 soldier Robert Graves discusses the 'Little Mother' pamphlet noting: 'quotations from a single typical document of this time will be enough to show what we were facing'. Graves recounts how 'England looked strange to us returning soldiers. We could not understand the war-madness that ran wild everywhere, looking for a pseudo-military outlet. The civilians talked a foreign language; and it was newspaper language'.[25] Although it took some time for her to begin to comprehend the war, Woolf, like Graves, saw the wild jingoism of the press.[26] They

34   *Virginia Woolf and Motherhood*

encouraged a patriotic sentiment in the population that she found 'so revolting that I was nearly sick' (*L2* 57), and reduced women to a collection of conventional gender performances. In January 1919 Woolf wrote a short review in the *Times Literary Supplement* (*TLS*) entitled 'The War from the Street', beginning the piece with what she termed an 'important truth' known by each and every civilian:

> the history of the war is not and never will be written from our point of view. The suspicion that this applies to wars in the past has been much increased by living through four years almost entirely composed of what journalists call 'historic days'. (*E3* 3)

Woolf's prophecy was false; worried that people would 'soon forget all about the war, & the fruits of our victory will grow as dusty as ornaments under glass cases in lodging house drawing rooms' (*D1* 211), she would spend the rest of her life writing provocative war memorials from her own unique point of view. The conflict would shape and haunt her work and she would populate these war histories with mother figures, reflecting an area of contemporary society to which she was markedly sensitive.

Raising an Army: Mothering, the Great War and *Jacob's Room*

The distinctive focus on mothers in Woolf's war writing confirms she was uneasy about a rhetoric that engaged with such a highly emotive area of womanhood. Images of patriotic mothers giving birth for the war effort echo through Woolf's later novels and are perhaps captured best in a section reworked several times in the first experimental drafts of *The Waves*:

> A midwife, bundling up ~~such~~ whatever instruments as she had required [. . .] left the cottage [. . .] A son or daughter had been born [. . .] In this dim light one thing very easily suggested another. The creases of the table cloth might be waves endlessly sinking & falling, many mothers, & again many mothers, & behind them many more, endlessly sinking & falling, & each held up as ~~its~~ it raised its crest & flung itself on the shore, a child. Soon the beach was ~~writhing with~~ black with them. (*WH* 63)

The extent to which this image reflects the atmosphere of WW1 can be seen in a similar section of the 'Little Mother' letter:

We women pass on the human ammunition of 'only sons' to fill up the gaps, so that when the 'common soldier' looks back before going 'over the top' he may see the women of the British race at his heels, reliable, dependent, uncomplaining.[27]

Woolf's description reimagines going 'over the top' into a beach landing, tying the waves of the title to issues of feminism, patriotism and war. The image running through both passages, of the mothers of Britain silently sacrificing themselves to provide soldiers for the war machine, exposes the very heart of Woolf's antipathy to the wartime appropriation of motherhood. These maternal figures demonstrate her understanding of the sacrifice expected from women who stood to gain nothing in victory or loss, women who would continue to be acknowledged by their nations as little more than second-class citizens.

Though the institutionalisation of motherhood was not exclusive to times of war, it was certainly more pronounced. Correspondingly, the role of mother in Woolf's war literature is noticeably marked alongside a prominent critique of the patriarchal society that caused such conflict. In addition to outrage at the exploitation of motherhood, Woolf's interests lay in the ways women supported and cooperated with the war effort. Though she did not feel that patriarchy and matriarchy were gendered (rather that they encompassed a set of ideals that could be endorsed by either sex),[28] Woolf was surprised and dismayed at female involvement. A diary entry of 7 June 1918 displays her feelings on learning of women bomber pilots:

L. was told the other day that the raids are carried out by women. Women's bodies were found in the wrecked aeroplanes. They are smaller & lighter, & thus leave more room for bombs. Perhaps its sentimental, but the thought seems to me to add a particular touch of horror. (*D*1 153)

Woolf felt no great love for the idea that women were inherently peaceful yet she understood the war as a patriarchal enterprise and as such the idea of women participating troubled her. Marina MacKay writes that Woolf uses her WW1 fiction to 'diagnose the two problems of patriarchal culture: that it glorifies militaristic and materialistic models of masculinity [. . .] and that it renders women complicit in male violence'.[29] This complicity is elevated when cultural norms dictate that women's only public voice is as mothers, and thus their nurturing and motherly influences are exploited to further the patriarchal cause. Accordingly, women's support and

36   *Virginia Woolf and Motherhood*

participation combine with images of a patriotic mother to contribute a strong narrative thread to the first novel Woolf wrote that overtly deals with war themes, *Jacob's Room*.

Jacob's Room enacts a broad investigation into the way that culture moulds men, its daring modern form challenging the way that fiction traditionally examined such concepts. In his exploration of the novel, Alex Zwerdling describes it as 'Woolf's first consciously experimental novel; and it has remained her most baffling one: its narrative techniques are so innovative that they call attention to themselves'.[30] Taking into consideration Woolf's own admission that she was 'breaking with complete representation' (*L2* 569), a number of early critics considered the novel primarily a form of experiment.[31] Zwerdling suggests that the text, in its 'deliberately halting and fragmented style and [. . .] tone that is conspicuously impure',[32] is Woolf's attempt to minimise the dramatic and romantic adulation, not just of the glorious war dead, but all those who pass away young. Indeed, it is not despite but because of the novel's form that its sound damnation of society is so eloquent. It represents Woolf's successful break with the propagandistic form of the discourse of her time and her own attempt to write historical truth. The early chapters of *Jacob's Room* are an involved study of the way that society shapes young men into soldiers, highlighting the mother's role in shaping a war hero and her culpability in providing an upbringing rich in the patriarchal values of competition and violence. Even the name *Jacob's Room* is a clue to Woolf's intention, evoking the places that young men inhabit as they grow from child to adult, before taking ownership of the patriarchal domain by becoming 'fathers of families and directors of banks' (*JR* 133). Though scholars have noted the importance of architectural spaces within the novel,[33] few have observed the importance of the home and its influence on the main character as he moves from nursery to rooms at university, to lodgings in London and hotels in Greece. For Woolf the backbone of the novel was the domestic domain and its influence on Jacob. She wrote at the beginning of the first draft of the novel, while considering the novelty of her form: 'I think the main point is that it should be free. Yet what about the form? Let us suppose that the Room will hold it together' (*JRHD* 1).

Contrasted with the sophisticated, artistic rendering of Jacob Flanders – named for the battles of Ypres where so many young British men lost their lives – Elizabeth Flanders, Jacob's mother, is rather a caricature. Unlike *To the Lighthouse*'s Mrs Ramsay, she bears little resemblance to Woolf's own mother, nor is she endowed with the existential insecurity of Clarissa Dalloway. Despite her fundamental prominence in the text, scholars have tended to overlook Betty Flanders. Even Zwerdling – whose excellent treatment of *Jacob's Room* focuses on the historical context, and who notes that the reader is 'witnessing the preparation of cannon fodder' – largely ignores the significance of the childhood home in this process. Instead Zwerdling concentrates on Jacob's early manhood; what he terms the 'particular stage in a young man's life – the promising stage'.[34] Surprisingly, even critics who do reflect on Betty tend to ignore the resounding criticism of the patriarchal social system that she suggests and instead imbue her with the type of mythical maternal powers that Woolf rejected. Nancy Topping Bazin and Jane Hamovit Lauter consider *Jacob's Room* 'a war novel from a mother's perspective [. . .] To his mother, he is Jacob – who is too precious, too fragile, too sacred to be sacrificed'.[35] Sara Ruddick views Betty as a powerhouse of motherly love, noting: 'Her gaze and love are powerful. When tears come to her eyes, the mast of a ship wobbles'. She continues by describing Betty's largely discarded letters as a thread of maternal presence that suffuse the novel.[36] While Betty is singularly important for an understanding of the text it may be for reasons other than these critics have suggested. An intrinsic part of the nationalist system, she is the personification of 'war-mother', a woman who exists to nurture her soldier children for the benefit of the empire and to ready them for sacrifice. Betty's relationship with Jacob can be understood in terms of her affiliation to the values of patriarchy. Her relationships with men come under scrutiny in the early parts of the novel, giving a comprehensive view of her place in this society. Not only is Betty dependent on men because she is a widow of limited means, but she shows a proclivity towards a quintessentially patriarchal type of man.

Betty Flanders and Jane Harrison's 'post-matriarchal' Woman

Betty is 'post-matriarchal', a concept drawn from the work of academic Jane Harrison. Though it is difficult to pinpoint when she first learnt of the distinguished Greek scholar and anthropologist, Harrison had a significant impact on Woolf, and her thoughts on the formation of modern culture clarify the way that *Jacob's Room* relates to mothers and war.[37] Janet Case, Woolf's beloved Greek teacher, was highly influenced by Harrison and it seems likely that they discussed her work in their lessons, which began in 1902. The first letter in which Woolf mentions Harrison is dated 22 October 1904, and Harrison became more intimate with the Bloomsbury

38 Virginia Woolf and Motherhood

group in 1913 when she began living with the modernist poet Hope Mirrlees. The Woolfs' library contained Harrison's *Aspects, Aorists and the Classical Tripos* (1919), *Epilegomena to the Study of Greek Religion* (1921) and *Ancient Art and Ritual* (1912) – a 1923 Christmas gift to Virginia from the scholar herself.[38] Hogarth Press also published Harrison's *Reminiscences of a Student's Life* (1925) and her translation of *The Life of the Archpriest Avvakum by Himself* (1924). Two prominent works missing from this list are *Prolegomena to the Study of Greek Religion* (1903) and *Alpha and Omega* (1915), the latter collection including the essay *Peace with Patriotism*, a conceptual predecessor to *Three Guineas*. However, given Woolf's interests and erudite bookishness, the great esteem she held the anthropologist in, and the themes that span both of their writing, it seems plausible she had read the balance of Harrison's catalogue. In her 1920 letter to the *New Statesman* 'The Intellectual Status of Women', Woolf notes that women's intellect constantly grows, with each new century eclipsing the last, and uses Jane Harrison as one of those whose 'advance in intellectual power seems to me not only sensible but immense' (*D2* 339). Another mention of Harrison is found in *A Room of One's Own*, where Woolf's narrator, wandering into an almost Eden-like garden of learning in 'Oxbridge' spies 'a bent figure, formidable yet humble', and wonders, 'could it be the famous scholar, could it be J– H– herself?' (*AROO* 15).

Harrison's pre-Grecian models of feminine agricultural ritual, goddess narratives and chthonic fertility cults were particularly significant to Woolf's thinking on motherhood and patriarchy. In *Prolegomena* Harrison explains that religion is a mirror of culture, thus the evidence of goddess worship that lingered into early Greek art, mythology and religious practice reflected primitive civilisations' foregrounding of the mother. Harrison's work accompanied significant re-analysis and excavation of a number of Grecian artworks and pottery during the late nineteenth century. These artworks substantiated claims that pre-Grecian culture was matriarchal, especially when studied alongside goddess legends, which slowly receded from the fore as Grecian culture developed. *Prolegomena* explains that Grecian stories, 'deep rooted in matriarchy [. . .] look back to the days when the only relationship that could be proved, and that therefore was worth troubling about, was that through the mother'. In Harrison's model matriarchal culture came to an end through a slow transformation into a patriarchal society that domesticated and subjugated women. This morphing of civilisation evolved through religious dogma and narratives redressing the ancient mythology that went before. Harrison notes that the narratological development of a society refocusing can be seen in myths, which, in the case of Ancient Greece, represent the curtailing of women's hegemony over the political and agricultural realms, and man's growing social domination. She also suggests that the relationship between men and women changed when patriarchy swept women out of the public sphere and into the domestic one:

> The relationship of these early matriarchal, husbandless goddesses, whether Mother or Maid, to the male figures that accompany them is one altogether noble and womanly, though perhaps not what the modern mind holds to be feminine. It seems to halt somewhere between Mother and Lover, with a touch of the patron saint. Aloof from achievements themselves, they choose a local hero for their own to inspire and protect. They ask of him not that he should love or adore, but that he should do great deeds [. . .] With the coming of patriarchal conditions this high companionship ends. The women goddesses are sequestered to servile domesticity, they become abject and amorous.[39]

As men become dominant, they indulged in the type of manipulative, demanding behaviour that Woolf observed in her own father and subsequently wrote into many of her male characters. In response to this behaviour, women change and try out new submissive mannerisms. Harrison contextualises the manner in which many of Woolf's female characters indulge their men folk, beguiling and placating them in equal amounts.

In Harrison's theories post-matriarchal woman is desirous of man and responds to his domination. Accustomed to a certain level of subjugation she instinctively adopts patriarchal values and endorses them with her own behaviour until her very femininity depends on such performance. It would be wrong to suggest that all of the women in Woolf's literary universe respond to patriarchy in this way – her female characters are multifaceted and diverse; nonetheless Betty Flanders is an archetype of the post-matriarchal woman. Betty's response to her sons' aggressive bravado is an example of patriarchal endorsement:

> The rooster had been known to fly on her shoulder and peck her neck, so that now she carried a stick or took one of the children with her when she went to feed the fowls.
> 'Wouldn't you like my knife, mother?' said Archer [. . .]
> 'What a big knife for a small boy!' she said. She took it to please him. (*JR* 11)

Betty's response to her son's knife is so rife with double entendre it almost comes across as satire, and yet it reinforces her, and thus his,

40 Virginia Woolf and Motherhood

cultural values. Betty carries a stick or keeps a noisy child with her to deter the aggressive (male) rooster; Archer, reflexively male, proffers a killing tool that is offensive rather than defensive. Betty may not be a pacifist but as a woman her instincts tend towards to defence rather than attack; however, her learned response reinforces patriarchal values. Rewarded by his mother's admiration, Archer learns a stereotype which will aid him on the path of competition and violence; not only should boys play with knives, but also a bigger knife is always better. Later Betty amuses her sons by 'telling the story of the gunpowder explosion in which poor Mr Curnow had lost his eye' (*JR* 6). Endorsing the tale's violence in her retelling of it, Betty is 'aware all the time in the depths of her mind of some buried discomfort' (*JR* 6), however her unease is overridden by her devotion to such patriarchal narratives.

Woolf builds Betty's character with the type of stereotypical erraticism that patriarchal culture expects in its women:

> 'What did I ask you to remember?' she said.
> 'I don't know,' said Archer.
> 'Well, I don't know either,' said Betty, humorously and simply, and who shall deny that this blankness of mind, when combined with profusion, mother wit, old wives' tales, haphazard ways, moments of astonishing daring, humour, and sentimentality – who shall deny that in these respects every woman is nicer than any man? (*JR* 7)

Whether Betty is 'nicer than any man' remains to be seen, nevertheless her attributes enable her to be, by turn, forgetful, emotional, superstitious and full of excitable energy. Her 'niceties' are at odds with those qualities that allow men to get ahead in patriarchal society: book learning and rational unflappability. Through Betty's character Woolf examines how women in such a culture are confined by means of narrow clichés with negative connotations.

Having lost the autonomy afforded by a society reliant on her divine, fertility-related faculties, the post-matriarchal woman turns to champion patriarchal ideals. She is kept in her place both by a discourse that enforces social values and by a far more practical dependence on men for subsistence. Betty epitomises this reliance; her existence reveals a typical lack of fiscal autonomy:

> Elizabeth Flanders [. . .] a widow in her prime. She was half-way between forty and fifty. Years and sorrow between them; the death of Seabrook, her husband; three boys; poverty; a house on the outskirts of Scarborough; her brother, poor Morty's, downfall and possible demise – for where was he? what was he? (*JR* 10)

As a 'widow in her prime' Betty is defined through her dead husband; as a mother, she bears the burden of sustaining her children (who, as boys, must be educated). Paternal responsibility for Betty and her children is awarded to her closest male relative, heir to her as a part of her father's estate. In this case her brother Morty should support her, and his absence incriminates those laws of inheritance allegedly devised to protect women.

The framework for Betty's fiscal dependency is itself a reflection of a powerful religious narrative, albeit a modern descendent of those studied by Harrison. Early in the novel Mrs Jarvis, watching Mrs Flanders at church, thinks 'that marriage is a fortress and widows stray solitary in the open fields, picking up stones, gleaning a few golden straws, lonely, unprotected, poor creatures' (*JR* 3). Aptly summarised by the rector's wife, Woolf uses this reference to the Old Testament Book of Ruth to explore the patriarchal mythology of Judeo-Christianity. Like Betty, Ruth is a widow who has little in the way of security until Boaz, a member of her mother-in-law's family, claims her. Boaz seeks to marry Ruth out of a mixture of love, responsibility, pity and respect, but in order to make this legal she must be traded between male relations as an adjunct to a piece of land. Boaz's rights to Ruth are symbolised by the handing over of a worn sandal and she sleeps at his feet to show subjugation.

By drawing attention to the contemporary religious context of female dependence, Woolf establishes how the predicament of a lone, post-Victorian woman is a result of the type of cultural evolution that Harrison demonstrates. Betty is a mix of preference and compunction. This biblical allusion gives a historical context to women's lack of autonomy and establishes that Betty is, in many ways, ensnared by the workings of the patriarchal machine. However, notwithstanding this social and financial 'enslavement', the novel purposefully outlines Betty's options when it comes to choosing a partner and raising her sons. Social history traps Betty in the narrow, liminal position of a widow but, unlike Ruth, she chooses not to remarry, despite a proposal.

'An example for the boys': Seabrook Flanders and the Unknown Soldier

Betty's choice with regard to husbands, lovers and paternal role models reflects strongly on Jacob's upbringing. Her first husband is dead and she thinks of him abstractly, recalling him in a culturally prescribed way when she sees the cemetery or hears church bells.

42   *Virginia Woolf and Motherhood*

A description of his grave however, reveals more about her relationship with his memory:

> Seabrook lay six foot beneath, dead these many years; enclosed in three shells; the crevices sealed with lead, so that, had earth and wood been glass, doubtless his very face lay visible beneath, the face of a young man whiskered, shapely, who had gone out duck-shooting and refused to change his boots.
>
> 'Merchant of this city,' the tombstone said; though why Betty Flanders had chosen so to call him when, as many still remembered, he had only sat behind an office window for three months, and before that had broken horses, ridden to hounds, farmed a few fields, and run a little wild – well, she had to call him something. An example for the boys. (*JR* 10–11)

Betty's memorial to her husband – an irresponsible man who used to 'run a little wild' – is enlightening. Reimagining him as a man of industry, part of the patriarchal order, the gravestone leaves the Flanders boys a false but respectable example. Seabrook also lies in an inappropriate coffin that speaks of Betty's desire to glorify the dead. Triple-sealed caskets were very expensive and as such were popular among the rich in the Victorian era when lavish funerals were in vogue.[40] The discrepancy between this casket and the Flanders's financial resources suggests an outdated attitude towards death and a concern for appearances. By physically preserving Seabrook, Betty preserves the obsolescent. This, as well as her continued use of Victorian traditions, illustrates an unwavering endorsement of outmoded patriarchal values. Superfluous respect for the dead is a trait Woolf often employs for characters she wishes to denote as less modern, and Betty, with her advocacy of these patriarchal values, is immersed in a culture whose standards seem archaic.[41]

Contemporary readers would also have contrasted Mr Flanders's grave to that of his soldier sons or those who died in the fields bearing his name, young men who often fell unmarked in the mud or were left in mass graves.[42] Woolf had been writing *Jacob's Room* for four months when, on Armistice Day 1920, the Unknown Warrior was interred in his tomb in Westminster Abbey, an act of pro-war canonisation, ordered by the Prime Minister Lloyd George and realised with a large dose of pomp and ceremony. Woolf's diary provides her impression of the event:

> going down the Strand the night of the Cenotaph; such a lurid scene, like one in hell. A soundless street; no traffic; but people marching.

> Clear, cold, & windless. A bright light in the Strand; women cry-
> ing Remember the Glorious Dead, & holding out chrysanthemums.
> Always the sound of feet on the pavement. Faces bright & lurid [. . .]
> A ghastly procession of people in their sleep.[43] (*D2* 79–80)

This almost apocalyptic vision does little to commemorate those lost, but rather turns the procession of the living into a moment of chthonic terror. It is not the idea of remembrance that jars for Woolf – *Jacob's Room* is, after all, an attempt at a new form of eulogy – but, as with other modernist descents into hell, Woolf sees a parallel between wartime culture and a loss of spirituality or soul.[44] Given this hellish patriarchal ceremony conducted over the grave of an unknown man and the undetermined mass graves of the 'Glorious Dead', Betty's reimagination and false preservation of Seabrook seem almost obscene, and the respect given to the past outrageous com-pared to society's careless waste of young soldiers.

Critics have commented that Betty's grief, felt as both a wife and mother, frames the book and adds a gendered aspect to its narration. Suzanne Raitt notes that the text 'is focused through a specifically female yearning: through women's tears', while Sara Ruddick com-ments that Woolf 'feminises the perspective from which she reveals Jacob's life [. . .] framed by the hopes, works, vision and loss of his mother'.[45] While Betty's sorrow does bookend the novel it remains questionable whether this is an attempt to create a narrative of femi-nine grief through which to read conflict and loss. Given that Woolf would later publish *Three Guineas* as 'Women Must Weep' – a title that highlights women's prescribed place in war-mongering culture – it seems rather more likely this exaggerated womanly mourning is a critical comment on the place of female emotion in Woolf's society, and, more specifically, the post-war cult of maternal grief.[46] Grayzel investigates how the image of the grieving mother – 'a potent vehicle for the expression of collective memory and sorrow' – became the focus of national post-war commemoration:

> Not only did wartime and post-war efforts to provide spaces in which
> to mourn the dead highlight [. . .] the particular loss experienced by
> woman and mothers, but the monuments and rituals themselves also
> made the mourning mother a bearer of memory for the nation.[47]

Grayzel describes the inclusion of mother figures on war memorials, created, unlike Bashka Paeff's pacifist sculpture, as commemorations to those glorious dead who laid down their lives to defend national-istic and patriarchal ideals.

44   *Virginia Woolf and Motherhood*

The continued promotion of motherhood was an important part of post-war culture, and was designed to counteract the gender upheavals brought about by the establishment of peace. During the war motherhood had been endorsed in order to swell the birth rate and to generate patriotic support for the violent actions of the government. Nonetheless, the lack of men meant women were required to work in munitions factories or as land girls, as well as being responsible for their own finances. Many women experienced independence and fiscal security for the first time in their lives. At the end of the war these liberties represented a threat to patriarchal culture – as soldiers began to return there was a general fear that women would fight a return to their limited pre-war roles. By endorsing motherhood the State continued to encourage a higher birth rate, while also having the added benefit of strengthening Victorian ideals – recalling women to domesticity and overcoming any potential insurgence. Jessica Meyer has pointed out that returning soldiers were seen to be 'brutalised' and 'emasculated' by the trauma of fighting, and that it was believed there would be difficulties 'reintegrating men returning from war into anything other than a traditional understanding of gender, where they would neither threaten nor be threatened by women'.[48] But Woolf noted the inconsistencies inherent in asking women to work, and then taking this liberty away once the war was over. In *Three Guineas* the 'daughters of educated men' (*TG* 118) ask why being women, and having to give birth, did not 'incapacitate us from working in Whitehall, in fields and factories, when our country was in danger? To which the fathers replied: The war is over; we are in England now' (*TG* 269).

Dedicatory services that accompanied the unveiling of memorials were the ideal platforms for public displays of maternal grief. Such services were held up and down the country but the most highly publicised was the unveiling of the Cenotaph. The Cabinet Memorial Services Committee commissioned to oversee the Peace Day ceremony organised it with the spectacle of maternal mourners in mind, recommending that non-military members of the congregation for the burial service in Westminster Abbey be chosen from: '(a) Women who have lost husbands and sons or only son (b) Mothers who have lost all sons or only sons (c) Widows'.[49] Seating arrangements were to be determined in three classes: 'First Category: Women who have lost all their sons and their husband. Second: Women who have lost all their sons[.] Third: Widows who have lost their only son'.[50] The committee also requested: 'Accommodation for 1,500 <u>female</u> relatives in Government windows overlooking the Cenotaph and the route from the Cenotaph to the Abbey'.[51] These instructions marshalled the very public crowd of wives and mothers garishly portrayed by Woolf in her description of the day. In the light of Woolf's recognition of this spectacle, Betty's mourning takes on a new aspect. Woolf was accustomed to grief – she even associated the loss of her brother Thoby with that of Jacob – but she could not recognise it in these excessive displays. Like Betty crying over her husband's grave, these ceremonies invoked an idealised patriarchal standard of womanhood, and particularly motherhood. In addition, pretending to commemorate those who, once dead, can barely be remembered by the living, seemed the height of pretence. It is with respect to this hypocrisy that *Jacob's Room* stands as both social commentary and an alternative memorial.

Choosing a Father Figure: The Significance of Mr Floyd and Captain Barfoot

No matter how much of 'an example' Seabrook Flanders's tombstone promises to set, it is of little practical help when it comes to the job of lone parenting and Betty looks elsewhere for assistance, especially in guiding the wilful Jacob. Her brother is missing and can afford no advice; however, Betty receives a marriage proposal quite early in the novel from Mr Floyd, a member of the clergy, 'a nice man [. . .] such a scholar' (*JR* 15). When the proposal occurs, Betty is immediately confronted by an image of one of her sons which stops her from accepting. The text notes that she 'saw Johnny chasing the geese, and knew it was impossible for her to marry anyone' (*JR* 15). The rather extreme reaction of refusing a proposal because of some boyish aggression initially seems at odds with the earlier image of the knife and the rooster. Taken out of context one might wonder if, by raising the boys alone, Betty hopes to impart a calmer, more peaceful education, one foregrounding cooperation rather than competition, peace rather than violence. However, a closer look at the men in the Flanders's lives reveals an altogether different motive. Betty chooses to reinforce a strong patriarchal stereotype but she cannot 'marry anyone' because her preferred partner, Captain Barfoot, is already married and thus unavailable. Indeed, it might be said that Betty's primary concern is to harness her sons' raw male energy and mould it into a functioning part of patriarchal society rather than allowing it to be squandered by way of a 'wild-goose' chase.

The novel is quite clear in its suggestion that Betty and Mr Floyd are mismatched. If Betty is a post-matriarchal (indeed patriarchal) woman then Mr Floyd is a matriarchal man. Betty is friends with

46   *Virginia Woolf and Motherhood*

Mr Floyd's mother – indeed she finds his proposal note in the hall 'when she came back from having tea with old Mrs Floyd' (*JR* 14). There may be some suggestion that this association holds Betty even higher in Mr Floyd's esteem; in other words, he chooses Betty, in part, because his mother likes her and he respects his mother. However, the pair's incompatibility becomes apparent in a short flash-forward featuring Mr Floyd's cat Topaz – whom the Flanders have inherited (Topaz shares Mr Floyd's foremost physical characteristic of red-headedness):

> 'Dear me,' said Mrs Flanders, when she read in the *Scarborough and Harrogate Courier* that the Rev. Andrew Floyd, etc., etc., had been made Principal of Maresfield House, 'that must be our Mr Floyd.' [. . .]
> Mrs Flanders got up and went over to the fender and stroked Topaz on the neck behind the ears.
> 'Poor Topaz,' she said (for Mr Floyd's kitten was now a very old cat, a little mangy behind the ears, and one of these days would have to be killed).
> 'Poor old Topaz,' said Mrs Flanders, as he stretched himself out in the sun, and she smiled, thinking how she had had him gelded, and how she did not like red hair in men. Smiling, she went into the kitchen. (*JR* 16–17)

The ambiguous use of the pronoun 'him' in the final sentence allows the symbolically spayed Topaz to symbolise the matriarchal Principal. Betty rejects and emasculates Mr Floyd who, as a passive intellectual, is lacking patriarchal vigour.[52] As an educator – always in the service of culture but never as its master – Betty encourages Mr Floyd to help in her sons' early schooling by teaching them Latin, a proficiency all educated young men need to learn in order achieve their full potential. Yet he is only there as an implement for her usage and remains unsuitable husband material, ultimately marrying a more progressive woman and whiling away his days with a daughter rather than sons and feeding the ducks on Hampstead Heath.

When Mr Floyd proposes, Betty is, in fact, already in a long-term relationship with archetypal patriarchal figure Captain Barfoot. Barfoot offers Betty both guidance on her sons' educations, and also the opportunity to be reflected in the eyes of the patriarchy as a sexual object. The Captain is 'lame and wanted two fingers on the left hand, having served his country' (*JR* 18), something Sarah Cole has observed as constituting 'an almost unique physical symbol in Woolf's works, which strenuously avoid almost any inclusion of physical scarring and deformation of its primary characters'.

Comparing Barfoot to *The Years'* Colonel Abel Pargiter who 'had lost his two fingers of the right hand in the Mutiny' (*Y* 10), Cole has noted how their military action 'exemplifies the mid-Victorian violence spree around the world' concluding, 'Abel [. . .] was no WW1 conscript or deluded volunteer, no victim in the sense that Woolf's generation understood the soldiers of their era to be'.[53] The same is true of Barfoot whose disability marks him out as a man of violence, both received and performed, and who represents colonial aggression in a way that Jacob and his brothers do not.

A lengthier description of Barfoot explores his significance as a symbol of patriarchal culture:

> There was something rigid about him. Did he think? Probably the same thoughts again and again. But were they 'nice' thoughts, interesting thoughts? He was a man with a temper; tenacious, faithful. Women would have felt, 'Here is law. Here is order. Therefore we must cherish this man. He is on the Bridge at night,' and, handing him his cup, or whatever it might be, would run on to visions of shipwreck and disaster, in which all the passengers come tumbling from their cabins, and there is the captain, buttoned in his pea-jacket, matched with the storm, vanquished by it but by none other. 'Yet I have a soul,' Mrs Jarvis would bethink her, as Captain Barfoot suddenly blew his nose in a great red bandanna handkerchief, 'and it's the man's stupidity that's the cause of this, and the storm's my storm as well as his' . . . so Mrs Jarvis would bethink her when the Captain dropped in to see them [. . .] But Betty Flanders thought nothing of the kind. (*JR* 21)

Barfoot's 'rigid', repetitive, unoriginal thoughts indicate his attachment to an old corrupt belief system. His masculinity makes women think of the patriarchal law and order that Woolf derided, while 'Visions of shipwreck and disaster' suggest the ruin of an aggressive imperial society closed off from new ideas and the outside world. The Captain, as a definitive patriarchal figure, makes a vain attempt to use his obsolete principles to do battle with nature. In this passage Woolf makes little attempt at veiled symbolism. The Captain stands for patriarchy and the danger and blind violence it brings to mankind. Mrs Jarvis, who provides a searching, passionate voice throughout the novel, understands that 'man's stupidity' has caused war – a storm that besieges them all – however Betty's 'abject and amorous' nature keeps her captivated by the Captain.[54]

For his part, Barfoot uses his relationship with Betty to fulfil the obligations of a true paterfamilias. As the ladies of Scarborough point out: 'A man likes to have a son – that we know' (*JR* 10) (this assertion replacing several pages in the novel's draft where the locals and narrator speculate about why the Captain likes to visit with Betty even though 'he does not wish to marry' her (*JRHD* 16)). Without sons of his own the Captain is unable to fully realise his paternal role, to educate and steer. At a time when divorce was difficult and extramarital affairs more a source of gossip than taboo, Betty and the Captain form a curiously orthodox couple. As historian Gertrude Himmelfarb has noted: 'Those caught up in an irregular situation of this kind tried, as far as they possibly could, to 'regularize' it, to contain it within its conventional form, to domesticate it and normalize it'.[55] In this fashion Betty Flanders and Captain Barfoot maintain a conventional and domestic relationship, with her boys' education as its main focus. Indeed, although the relationship spans several decades, the novel only records one conversation between Betty and the Captain, and this specifically concerns Jacob's further education. With Barfoot maintaining that there is 'nothing better than to send a boy to one of the universities' (*JR* 22), mother and male role model collaborate to determine that: 'Jacob Flanders, therefore, went up to Cambridge in October, 1906' (*JR* 22).

In her essay '*Jacob's Room* as Comedy', Judy Little depicts the young Flanders as an 'orphan' and notes: 'No one takes charge of Jacob's education [. . .] No one cares enough about Jacob's development either to help or hinder him'.[56] This observation is not only incorrect but it also undermines the value Woolf attaches to the traditional education chosen for Jacob, her observations on British men of a certain class, and her complex relationship with the university system, and in particular Cambridge. In *Three Guineas* Woolf explains how such an education encourages 'competition and jealousy – emotions which, as we need scarcely draw upon biography to prove, nor ask psychology to show, have their share in encouraging a disposition towards war' (*TG* 138). This opinion strongly recalls Jane Harrison, who, in *Peace with Patriotism*, writes:

> our whole education, our public school system is based on [. . .] neck-to-neck competition in work and in games. We teach our children to work, not that they may do their best for the sheer love of the thing done, but that they may do better than somebody else [. . .] If children are so reared can we wonder that grown men are at war?[57]

Years later, in 'A Sketch of the Past', Woolf would recall a successful cousin and ask:

> What [. . .] would Herbert Fisher have been without Winchester, New College and the Cabinet? What would have been his shape had he not been stamped and moulded by the patriarchal machinery? Every one of our male relations was shot into that machine and came out at the other end, at the age of sixty or so, a Headmaster, an Admiral, a Cabinet Minister, a Judge. (*MB* 155)

Here Woolf notes the way men are 'stamped and moulded' by their academic and professional surroundings – on meeting the great force and presence of patriarchy they become an expression of space and form. If this statement foregrounds the public and overlooks the private pieces of the patriarchal machine, it is not due to Woolf's ignorance of the fundamental importance mothering (and other forms of parenting) had to play in such a society. *Jacob's Room* depicts the first and perhaps most important stage of this process, the home environment that first moulds a boy. The novel shows how a co-parental decision to send Jacob to Cambridge pulls the trigger that 'shoots' him into the heart of the machine.

Mr Floyd's proposal offers Betty the option of providing an earnest, congenial academic as a standard, but by preferring Captain Flanders as her aide and abettor she shows her partiality towards the system of patriarchy and war-mongering. Under the guidance of Captain Barfoot Jacob matures into a certain type of man, a different man to the one he would have become under Mr Floyd. These two Jacobs are worlds apart, a fact impressed upon the reader when Mr Floyd sights the adult Jacob in the street and: 'he was so tall; so unconscious; such a fine young fellow' (*JR* 153) 'that Mr Floyd did not like to stop him' (*JR* 16). This meeting can be found twice, once near the beginning of the novel and also a few pages before the end. In such a sparingly sketched novel an image must warrant special significance to be described twice. Given that the first mention occurs when Betty must choose between Mr Floyd and Captain Barfoot and thus decide how to raise her boys, and the second is the last time Jacob is seen alive, it seems that Betty's choice is not only significant for Jacob but is arguably his life's most formative event.

'To produce good people and good books': 'A Society' and 'The Intellectual Status of Women'

It is significant that, despite her age, Betty's relationship with Captain Barfoot enables her to maintain her social status as a sexual object.

50   *Virginia Woolf and Motherhood*

Although the draft version mentions that Betty partly declines Mr Floyd due to a growing disinterest in 'copulation' (*JRHD* 14) the final novel describes how 'the attentions of the Captain – all ripened Betty Flanders, enlarged her figure, tinged her face with jollity, and flooded her eyes for no reason that any one could see perhaps three times a day' (*JR* 10). In response to her lover, Betty wears the traditional features of a fertile maid, a blushed cheek, quick emotions and the ability to ripen or grow like so much fecund fruit. In his company she becomes relevant – restored to the sexual and reproductive prime of a patriarchal stereotype. While Woolf understood that during wartime mothers accessed citizenship through their wombs, she also perceived how much they lost by doing so. In the first draft of *Jacob's Room*, Betty glances at one of her sons and is afforded the sentiment: '"I'm younger than I thought," – & sorrow, & pride too' (*JRHD* 7). As the most valuable woman in a patriarchal country is the one who gives birth to soldiers, Betty's fertility is bittersweet, signifying both fulfilment and loss.

Further insight into the place of motherhood in the lives of wartime women can be found in the short story 'A Society', which Woolf produced two months into writing the first draft of *Jacob's Room*. 'A Society' combines Woolf's disavowal of WW1 with a maternity narrative, highlighting just how deeply Woolf felt the role of mother was enmeshed with the patriarchal system and the roots of conflict. The short story examines motherhood rather differently to *Jacob's Room*. Where the novel takes a bleak view of the patriarchal commandeering of motherhood and judges conformist mothers equally accountable within the system of dominance and subordination, 'A Society' views childbearing and -raising as a form of blinkering – women are not drawn to patriarchal violence and strength, but rather blind to it. The story depicts a gathering of young women who, innocently musing on the virtuosity of men, discover that they have been misinformed and that society, with all its creative, scientific and political progress, is not quite as evolved as they have been led to believe. They have 'taken it for granted that it was a woman's duty to spend her youth in bearing children' (*CSF* 125) having 'gone on all these ages supposing that men were equally industrious, and that their works were of equal merit' (*CSF* 125). But, distracted by childbearing, the women have overlooked calamitous failings in culture and civilisation, allowing men a freedom that has been used to the disadvantage of all.

A tongue-in-cheek commentary on how female ignorance enables patriarchy, 'A Society' appears incongruously conventional within the innovative collection *Monday or Tuesday* (1921). At the end of her life, Woolf chose not to include the piece in a retrospective anthology, a decision that Susan Dick has attributed to the story's conventional style, limited scope, and the fact that it reflected 'with striking immediacy the historical and cultural context in which it was written'.[58] Dick also suggests that Woolf may have felt she had written the story's argument more succinctly in the feminist polemic *A Room of One's Own* and *Three Guineas*, which incorporate many of the themes of 'A Society', as well as its central premise of 'a society of outsiders' (*TG* 235).

The story was initially a distraction during a low point in the writing of *Jacob's Room*. Although Woolf felt that dealing with such issues diverted from her programme of artistic testimony and the new form she was creating, she was compelled to finish and publish it. The story provides a sarcastic, feminist commentary on contemporary British culture that Woolf may have found too pressing to ignore. Dick submits that 'A Society' was written both as a response to Arnold Bennett's book *Our Women* and to a Desmond MacCarthy review of the same. The book had enraged Woolf, who noted in her diary that she had begun 'making up a paper upon Women, as a counterblast to Mr Bennett's adverse views' (*D2* 69).[59] MacCarthy's review, published in the *New Statesman* on 2 October 1920 and written under the pen name the 'Affable Hawk', endorsed Bennett's opinion that 'women are inferior to men in intellectual power, especially in that kind of power which is described as creative', and incorporated such generalities as: 'on the whole intellect is a masculine speciality'.[60] In response Woolf sent two acerbic letters to the *New Statesman* summing up her anger at the defamation of women's intellect, and arguing that it was a lack of 'education and liberty' (*D2* 342) that impeded female creative expression. Echoing the reasoning of the short story, Woolf's second letter to the *New Statesman*, titled 'The Intellectual Status of Women', points out that women 'have brought forth the entire population of the universe. This occupation has taken much time and strength. It has also brought them into subjection to men' (*D2* 341-42).

Like her candid letters, 'A Society' offers insight into Woolf's feelings on subjugated motherhood. The group in the story presupposes 'that the objects of life were to produce good people and good books' (*CSF* 126). In order to find out whether men do either they take a vow of chastity and decide to abstain from motherhood, agreeing: 'Before we bring another child into the world we must swear that we will find out what the world is like' (*CSF* 125).[61] Though the vow of

52   Virginia Woolf and Motherhood

chastity is broken (and one of the group, Castalia, has a daughter, Ann), the group's investigation into the arts, the military, academia, science and law, reveals the extent of the decline in male intellect. The relationship between this decline and war is established by Woolf's *New Statesman* letters, where she wryly observed that:

> though women have every reason to hope that the intellect of the male sex is steadily diminishing, it would be unwise, until they have more evidence than the great war and the great peace supply, to announce it as a fact. (*D2* 339)

In keeping with this sentiment, damnation and derision of war-mongering can be found throughout 'A Society'. The narrative begins several months before the war first breaks out, the women meet to discuss their findings on the day it is declared, and the final scene is set on 28 June 1919 when the Treaty of Versailles officially ended the state of war between Germany and the Allies. In the story the declaration of war is met with the following conversation:

> 'War! War! War! Declaration of War!' men were shouting in the street below.
> We looked at each other in horror.
> 'What war?' we cried. 'What war?' We remembered, too late, that we had never thought of sending anyone to the House of Commons. We had forgotten all about it. We turned to Poll, who had reached the history shelves in the London Library, and asked her to enlighten us.
> 'Why,' we cried, 'do men go to war?'
> 'Sometimes for one reason, sometimes for another,' she replied calmly. 'In 1760, for example – ' The shouts outside drowned her words. 'Again in 1797 – in 1804 – It was the Austrians in 1866 – 1870 was the Franco-Prussian – In 1900 on the other hand – '
> 'But it's now 1914!' we cut her short.
> 'Ah, I don't know what they're going to war for now,' she admitted.
> (*CSF* 133–34)

Revealing Woolf's pejorative opinion of the facts held by the 'history shelves in the London Library', the story presents war as foremost among the destructive and incomprehensible patriarchal forces.[62] Dick suggests that the unvisited House of Commons reminds readers that 'in 1914 women could neither vote nor stand for election to Parliament'.[63] This prompt only serves to further emphasise the idea that men are predominantly to blame for the calamity, reinforcing this point of difference between the short story and *Jacob's Room*.

Peace Day, the Paris Peace Conference and The Second International Conference of Women

In addition to targeting war and making a comedy of its destructive power, 'A Society' adds a new dimension to Woolf's thoughts on militarism, using irony to engage with the thorny issue of peace creation (denoted in the *New Statesman* letters as 'the great peace supply' (*D2* 339)). The condemnation of peace-making is an important extension of Woolf's pacifism, reflecting national and international unease with the Allies' negotiation strategy for the capitulation of Germany and Russia. Her feelings about the peace being forged at the end of WW1 are expanded in several diary entries concerning 19 July 1919. This date marked Peace Day, the centrepiece of a collection of celebrations organised by the foreign secretary Lord Curzon. The entries begin with a clear indication of Woolf's antipathy to the event: 'One ought to say something about Peace day, I suppose, though whether it is worth taking a new nib for that purpose I don't know' (*D1* 292). What follows are two rather long and negative descriptions of the celebration highlighting her disillusionment, alongside feelings of infantilisation and a horror of the uniformity of herd-mentality. Woolf's discomfort also emerges in the form of class bias, and she registers the event as 'a servant's festival; something got up to pacify and placate "the people"' (*D1* 292). Recording that she feels 'a little mean at writing so lugubriously; since we're all supposed to keep up the belief that we're glad and enjoying ourselves' (*D1* 293), Woolf's despondency about the 'horrid fraud' (*D1* 293) is that of a woman who feels little hope for her society in light of the new found peace.

The negative sentiments in this diary entry are tied to Woolf's understanding of the loss the war had caused. She dwells on the gloomy weather,[64] and an even gloomier set of attendees, writing: 'It was a melancholy thing to see the incurable soldiers lying in bed at the Star & Garter with their backs to us, smoking cigarettes and waiting for the noise to be over. We were children to be amused' (*D1* 294). The emotion that Woolf projects upon these soldiers shows her certainty of their terrible misuse and spotlights the futile damage she observes in their injury. Without even speaking to these men she

54   *Virginia Woolf and Motherhood*

taps into a sentiment held by many returning soldiers. Peace Day was denounced by members of the public as well as established groups such as the Ex-Servicemen's Federation, whose East Anglia branch boycotted the parade due to its glorification of military action, with one official stating:

> Our pals died to kill militarism, not to establish that here. We have had militarism burned into us, and we hate it [. . .] The Norwich branch of the federation, which consists of nearer 4,000 men than 3,000, has decided that they will take no part in the celebration of this mock peace.[65]

These soldiers substantiate Woolf's diary entries, yet the feelings of unease provoked by the celebrations were not solely due to the glorification of military force. The 'mock peace' mentioned by the Ex-Servicemen's Federation and denoted by Woolf's ironic 'great peace supply' also refers to the Allies' much-maligned peace process.

In condemning the peace process, Woolf makes an argument that is very much marked by its time – and one that echoed through many factions of society. At the end of WW1 the victors met in Paris to negotiate, among themselves, the terms of their victory. Although this was named the Paris Peace Conference, the exclusion of Germany and Russia, as well as the insistence of the Allies on a full admission of German guilt and untenable reparations, convinced many that the peace was a dangerous one, most likely leading to resentment, poverty and ultimately more violence. Woolf's opinion is consistent with others in her set. In his book *The Economic Consequences of the Peace* (1920) John Maynard Keynes made a strong argument against the economic penalties incurred by Russia and Germany. In 1922, Leonard Woolf stood for parliament on a platform of international cooperation, trade and disarmament and called for the revision of the Versailles Treaty. In addition, Hope Mirrlees's poem *Paris*, published by the Hogarth Press in 1920, was written in the city in 1919 and, as Melissa Boyde notes, 'alludes disparagingly to elements of the Paris peace conference'.[66]

Before the conference had even begun many sceptics pointed out the danger that lay in the ruling powers' inability to form a balanced and cooperative response. In her *Harper's Weekly* article Emmeline Pethick-Lawrence asserted:

> If the same people who by secret diplomacies brought war upon Europe, without the consent, without even the knowledge of their

respective democracies, settle in the same way the conditions of peace, then the new peace will once again be the prelude of the new war.[67]

Like many feminists from all sides of the globe, Pethick-Lawrence's appeal for a democratic process incorporated a call for a female presence at the Peace Conference, but this was not to be. Undeterred, a large number of feminist organisations came together to hold a concurrent congress, The Second International Conference of Women. These activists seized the opportunities afforded to them by a unique moment in history, fighting for an autonomous voice while pointing out the flaws in the Allies' peace offer. The women's conference reflected its maternalist origins, with resolutions recognising that 'women's service to the world not only as wage earners but as mothers and homemakers is an essential factor in the building up of the world's peace'.[68]

Although its values and methods were not synonymous with her own, and her support for it was questionable,[69] Woolf had much in common with the conference. The questions that the attendees debated were also issues with which she wrangled, with many openly asking whether societies that create war could be trusted to create peace. 'A Society' and the *New Statesman* letters also asked a rather more subversive question: in a society without gender equality, could a conflict-free period labelled 'peace' be any more constructive than that termed 'war'. Woolf remained dubious of all proclamations and negotiations regarding 'peace' and faced these concerns in 'A Society', substituting a conference of feminist activists for a group of curious and sometimes infuriated young women. Like many feminists, Woolf's group ceases its activity for the duration of the war, reconvening on Peace Day, when the unilateral peace treaty forces them to come to an alarming conclusion about the future of society. In a satirical twist one of the group suggests that the only way to save the race is to

> devise a method by which men may bear children! It is our only chance. For unless we provide them with some innocent occupation [. . .] we shall perish beneath the fruits of their unbridled activity; and not a human being will survive to know that there once was Shakespeare! (*CSF* 135)

Use of the word 'innocent' hints at a different image of motherhood than the one portrayed by *Jacob's Room*, where mothers are condemned for their involvement in raising war-mongering sons. Instead,

56 *Virginia Woolf and Motherhood*

'A Society' parodies the maternalist claim that being a mother means having an inherently peaceable nature. The comic suggestion that some devastating, future conflict might mean the end of humankind, also reflects the widely held concern that war would be once more on the horizon for Europe. The story's divinatory nature can be seen in some of the character names. Castalia's mythological namesake was changed into a fountain famed for giving prophetesses visions of the future, while, in the *Agamemnon* by Aeschylus, Cassandra spurned Apollo and was punished with torturous insights that no one believed.[70]

'The maternal instinct subdued': Forsaking Motherhood for the Greater Good

The suggestion that men bear children is an unsubtle mockery which works all the better for underplaying childbirth and motherhood almost as much as it derides war-making. Maternalists imagined maternity as a divine institution above such mockery, but Woolf struggled to regard it as such. Drawing on her discomfort with motherhood, and provoked by Bennett and MacCarthy's oppressive male-intellectualism, Woolf created this parallel between maternity and soldiering to mock both. During WW2 she would return to this comparison in a rather more sober essay entitled 'Thoughts on Peace in an Air Raid', a text which finds a parallel between the instincts that drive men to war and women to motherhood.[71] Analogising war with maternity is not inherently unusual – such metaphors were common in both contemporary and historical narratives.[72] However, written from the pacifist perspective, the parallel suggests something destructive about motherhood (not unlike Betty's childrearing).

Although the prediction of doom in 'A Society' would become a devastating reality by the time of 'Thoughts on Peace', Woolf's letters to MacCarthy predict a more hopeful future. They voice her conviction that women might be able to improve themselves given the right conditions, and explain how this can come about:

> it is not education only that is needed. It is that women should have liberty of experience; that they should differ from men without fear and express their difference openly [. . .] that all activity of the mind should be so encouraged that there will always be in existence a nucleus of women who think, invent, imagine, and create as freely as men do, and with as little fear of ridicule and condescension. (*D2* 342)

Motherhood and the Great War **57**

There is, of course, the question of whether these creative, intellectual women have children. Do they 'go on bearing children, but [. . .] in twos and threes, not in tens and twelves' (*AROO* 101), or do they create and remain child-free (like Austen, the Brontës and Eliot)? Susan Dick suggests that the assembly in 'A Society' may represent this 'nucleus of women', and though the society are investigators rather than creators, the investigative process does give them access to the self-expression and freedom of understanding that Woolf recommends.[73] By introducing the idea of chastity, the story openly questions whether women could 'think, invent, imagine, and create as freely as men do' as mothers. However, Castalia gains the 'liberty of experience' when she loses her chastity and becomes pregnant: a point made clear when one of the women states, 'chastity is nothing but ignorance – a most discreditable state of mind. We should admit only the unchaste to our society' (*CSF* 130). With chastity rejected, and Castalia installed as president of the society, the women see a leap forward in their worldly knowledge. Nonetheless the question remains whether mothering curbs women's development and if it is better to stay child-free. The group grapple with this difficulty but come to no firm conclusion:

> 'supposing [. . .] that women still wish to bear children – '
> 'Of course we wish to bear children!' cried Castalia, impatiently. Jane rapped the table.
> 'That is the very point we are met to consider,' she said. 'For five years we have been trying to find out whether we are justified in continuing the human race. Castalia has anticipated our decision. But it remains for the rest of us to make up our minds.' (*CSF* 130–31)

The problem is too universal to yield an answer, leaving only clues and associations to allow the reader to draw their own conclusions.

Despite the tangled associations that come with bearing children – the, perhaps inadvertent, support of nationalism, the pain when these children are used up by the state and the loss of innovation that comes with having a nursery as one's primary creative space – Castalia's pregnancy is a positive episode in an otherwise rather pessimistic story (notwithstanding its comedic appeal). Though Woolf proposes childbearing as the reason for centuries of women's subjugation and lack of creative influence, in 'A Society' having a child is not necessarily shown as a morally or artistically poor choice. Looking at the child's gender rather than the process of giving birth may elucidate this discrepancy. At the very beginning of the story Jane asks: 'Why

58   *Virginia Woolf and Motherhood*

[. . .] if men write such rubbish as this, should our mothers have wasted their youth in bringing them into the world?' (*CSF* 125). If mothers waste their youth bringing *men* into the world, correspondingly it seems they only regret their sons and not their daughters. This generalisation may seem rather sweeping but it finds support in *Jacob's Room* and Woolf's wider canon. From Betty Flanders's three sons and her involvement in their violent and competitive upbringing, to Mr Floyd's peaceful family with one daughter, *Jacob's Room* uses sons and daughters to imply certain attitudes in their parents, appointing them either for the patriarchy or for free intellectual debate.[74] In the case of Castalia and her daughter Ann, it appears that giving birth to girls leads to a fostering of matriarchy, enabling a retrospective thread of creativity and strength, and a narratological signal of the ability to 'think back through our mothers' (*AROO* 69) that Woolf imagines in *A Room of One's Own*.

Ultimately, in a world where being able to choose the sex of a child would have been the stuff of eugenic dreams, Woolf's investigation into childbirth lends itself to two clear directives – women deserve the right to explore and experience, and the liberty to choose.[75] These, however, remain impossible in a society that perverts the concept of childbearing, affording it the status of a nationally ordained production line for soldiers. When the women interview their male acquaintances to ask, 'why does your family grow?', they are met with the answer: 'Their wives wished that too, or perhaps it was the British Empire' (*CSF* 132). The men's ambiguous understanding of their wives' aspirations, their expectation that these desires match those of the State, is a clear indictment of the lack of autonomy British women enjoy in marriage. Whether wilfully or naively, these husbands compound the patriarchal oppression of their wives, who are subject to both domestic tyranny and ignorance, and national laws intended to preserve their dependency and obedience. (Indeed, it was only in 1923, two years after Woolf wrote 'A Society', that the Matrimonial Causes Act gave women and men equal rights regarding divorce and thus far greater equality in marriage.)

By using a group of women who are different to the maternal character she paints in *Jacob's Room*, Woolf uses 'A Society' to explore another aspect of the relationship between motherhood and war. Castalia underlines this with a lament for an ignorant bliss that brings Betty Flanders to mind:

> 'If we hadn't learnt to read,' she said bitterly, 'we might still have been bearing children in ignorance and that I believe was the happiest

life after all. I know what you're going to say about war [. . .] and the horror of bearing children to see them killed, but our mothers did it, and their mothers, and their mothers before them. And *they* didn't complain.' (*CSF* 134)

Woolf and her contemporaries knew that their foremothers did not have sufficient public (or indeed private) voice to make their feelings known – they 'didn't complain' because they *couldn't* complain. Ironic statements such as this illustrate Woolf's campaign against passive compliance. An attempt to awaken both men and women to the danger of accepting gender roles mandated by a State that disregarded not only the lives of its enemies, but also its own citizens.

'Unmaternal' and Post-Maternal Moments in *Mrs Dalloway*

Despite both texts' preoccupation with war, Woolf avoids putting forward a soldier's point of view in *Jacob's Room* or 'A Society', instead maintaining her distance from images of battle. The single, brief description of warfare that is included in *Jacob's Room* is detached:

The battleships ray out over the North Sea, keeping their stations accurately apart. At a given signal all the guns are trained on a target which (the master gunner counts the seconds, watch in hand – at the sixth he looks up) flames into splinters. With equal nonchalance a dozen young men in the prime of life descend with composed faces into the depths of the sea; and there impassively (though with perfect mastery of machinery) suffocate uncomplainingly together. Like blocks of tin soldiers the army covers the cornfield, moves up the hillside, stops, reels slightly this way and that, and falls flat, save that, through field glasses, it can be seen that one or two pieces still agitate up and down like fragments of broken match-stick.

These actions, together with the incessant commerce of banks, laboratories, chancellories, and houses of business, are the strokes which oar the world forward, they say. And they are dealt by men as smoothly sculptured as the impassive policeman at Ludgate Circus. (*JR* 136)

Words like 'nonchalance', the repetition of 'impassive', and the comparison of soldiers to machines suggest a detached inhumanity for this self-proclaimed progressive society. This language also maintains

60 Virginia Woolf and Motherhood

the novel's distance from images of war, consistent with the perspective of a civilian. Woolf had no practical experience of battle and thus could not describe it, she may have also deliberately disengaged from images of combat, since to position both herself and the reader within the conflict, no matter how fictitious, would be to memorialise a patriarchal activity she condemned. However, six years after the war ended Woolf did chose to include the interior monologue of returned soldier Septimus Warren Smith in *Mrs Dalloway* and used this perspective to further negotiate the relationship between war and motherhood.

Similar to *Jacob's Room* in its pacifist outlook, *Mrs Dalloway* takes its starting point from the post- rather than pre-war moment. Elements of the earlier novel's detachment from war linger in the form of Septimus's post-traumatic disorder and the irrational sense of dispassion he experiences when thinking of battle:

> when Evans was killed, just before the Armistice, in Italy, Septimus, far from showing any emotion or recognising that here was the end of a friendship, congratulated himself upon feeling very little and very reasonably [. . .] He was right there. The last shells missed him. He watched them explode with indifference. (*MD* 94–95)

By emphasising Septimus's indifference, his sense that 'something failed him; he could not feel' (*MD* 95), Woolf participates in a debate on 'shell-shock' – a newly diagnosed illness which had been controversial and mismanaged. Woolf may have based some of this characterisation on her brother-in-law Philip Woolf, who was injured by a shell that also killed his brother Cecil. After visiting Philip in hospital, Woolf noted in her diary: 'I can imagine that he is puzzled why he doesn't feel more' (*D1* 92). Focusing on Septimus's disengagement, the novel draws attention to the lasting damage of the war, the underlying ills of society and the bleakness that accompanies the new peace.

Septimus's detachment is even more effective when contrasted with Clarissa Dalloway's post-war feelings. She appears joyful, out walking and revelling in:

> what she loved; life; London; this moment of June.
> For it was the middle of June. The War was over, except for some one like Mrs Foxcroft at the Embassy last night eating her heart out because that nice boy was killed and now the old Manor House must go to a cousin; or Lady Bexborough who opened a bazaar, they said,

with the telegram in her hand, John, her favourite, killed; but it was over; thank Heaven – over. It was June. The King and Queen were at the Palace. And everywhere, though it was still so early, there was a beating, a stirring of galloping ponies, tapping of cricket bats; Lords, Ascot, Ranelagh and all the rest of it. (*MD* 4–5)

It is mid-June 1923, the soldiers have returned and the inequitable Treaty of Versailles is in place. Weighed against Woolf's gloomy post-war diary entries, Clarissa's joy appears injudicious. The same is true of patriarchal society's easy return to pleasure-seeking activities – the nonchalant resumption of sports that were (and are) the domain of upper-class men: cricket at Lords, racing at Ascot and sailing at Ranelagh. Starkly contrasting with Septimus's irreparable damage, Clarissa's flippancy serves to emphasise the alacrity of communal, post-war amnesia and highlights the continued responsibility to examine and condemn the war-mongers. Clarissa's happiness is also at odds with Mrs Foxcroft and Lady Bexborough's grief, their inclusion signposting that, despite the general desire to move on, the image of the mourning mother was still an important part of post-war culture and remained an important way for Woolf to explore and criticise society. Indeed, later in the text, Woolf shows how affective this image was, describing:

Little Mr Bowley, who had rooms in the Albany and was sealed with wax over the deeper sources of life but could be unsealed suddenly, inappropriately, sentimentally, by this sort of thing – poor women waiting to see the Queen go past – poor women, nice little children, orphans, widows, the War – tut – tut – actually had tears in his eyes. (*MD* 21)

The effect not just of war widows, but of mothers and children in general, can be seen clearly through Mr Bowley, a middle-class 'man in the street' who Woolf chose to represent the everyman not just in *Mrs Dalloway*, but also in a scene in *Jacob's Room*.

Motherhood, or more specifically non-motherhood, appears throughout *Mrs Dalloway*, forming one of the central themes of the novel. Although she is a thoughtful mistress and supportive wife, Clarissa Dalloway is 'unmaternal' (*MD* 209). She is emotionally and physically distant from her seventeen-year-old daughter Elizabeth, and alienated by Elizabeth's looks which are 'an Oriental mystery' (*MD* 134). As a mother of a single daughter, Clarissa is contrasted with a series of characters who fortify the national effort:

62   Virginia Woolf and Motherhood

Mrs Foxcroft and Lady Bexborough, Sally Seton, who prides herself on her 'five enormous boys' (*MD* 188), and the well-bred party guests with their 'six sons at Eton' (*MD* 208). At a time when war made mothers valuable to society, Woolf uses her female protagonist's personal, social and biological distance from motherhood as part of her endeavour 'to criticise the social system, & to show it at work, at its most intense' (*D2* 248).

Clarissa is what age theorist Margaret Morganroth Gullette describes as a 'post-maternal' character – 'a mother who, having stayed home to raise her children, had come to the "end" of her childrearing years and still retained many years of "surplus" life to "fill"'.[76] Clarissa is also menopausal and so physically post-maternal.[77] Her menopause is initially revealed in the short story 'Mrs Dalloway in Bond Street' in a scene where Hugh Whitbread mentions that his wife is: 'Out of sorts', and Clarissa reflects: 'Of course [. . .] Milly is about my age fifty – fifty-two. So it is probably *that*' (*CSF* 153). Although this line was edited out of the final novel, the consequences of Clarissa's menopause are still outlined in the following passage:

> But often now this body she wore (she stopped to look at a Dutch picture), this body, with all its capacities, seemed nothing – nothing at all. She had the oddest sense of being herself invisible; unseen; unknown; there being no more marrying, no more having of children now, but only this astonishing and rather solemn progress with the rest of them, up Bond Street, this being Mrs Dalloway; not even Clarissa any more; this being Mrs Richard Dalloway. (*MD* 11)

As a post-fertile woman in a patriarchy which primarily values women for their childbearing abilities, Clarissa is denied selfhood and rendered 'invisible'. Walking up the prominent shopping thoroughfare of Bond Street there appears something funereal about her 'solemn progress' towards non-existence. Immediately before this moment Clarissa wishes she could be more integral to society. She imagines herself 'slow and stately; rather large; interested in politics like a man; with a country house; very dignified, very sincere' (*MD* 11). In seeking to become a recognisable part of society Clarissa particularly yearns to resemble 'the woman she admired most, Lady Bexborough, opening the bazaar' (*MD* 10) (indeed Clarissa's admiration for Lady Bexborough is repeated at intervals throughout the novel). While this approbation is partly class-related, Lady Bexborough is first identified as a grieving mother, suggesting that Clarissa does not simply wish that she were still serviceably fertile, but that she could be as valuable to society as an archetypal war mother.

'Not old yet': Shopping, Internal Time and the Ageing Woman

Consumerist culture represented a significant pastime and preoccupation for women of the upper-middle class and it is not by chance that Clarissa's menopausal, existential crisis occurs amid the high-end Bond Street shops. Cynthia Port has explored how 'changing economic theories of accumulation and consumption, shifts in population, the emergence of gerontology [. . .] and the evolving status of women' led to a blossoming culture of anxiety about ageing among women in the 1920s and 1930s, explaining Clarissa's feelings of invisibility among the exclusive clothes, books and art.[78] However, this feeling is paradoxical given how the media of the age paid undue attention not only to the desirability of youth but also to the subject of the 'ageing' woman. Throughout the novel several people gaze at Clarissa, from the first few paragraphs when Scrope Purvis deems her 'vivacious, though she was over fifty, and grown very white since her illness' (*MD* 4), until the last lines when Peter Walsh sees Clarissa and becomes filled with 'extraordinary excitement' (*MD* 213). The reunion of contemporaries Peter and Clarissa offers some commentary on the social stigma attached to women's ageing, with Peter thinking 'she's grown older' twice in rapid succession while Clarissa reflects that he is: 'Exactly the same [. . .] a little thinner, dryer, perhaps, but he looks awfully well, and just the same' (*MD* 44). Other women, predominantly older, are also observed throughout the novel. During her party, Clarissa watches an old woman in the house opposite. Acknowledging some mystical quality in the woman, the 'privacy of the soul' (*MD* 139), Clarissa finds power, and even triumph, in her own situation. In a scene which shows how early the objectification of women begins, Richard Dalloway watches his own daughter Elizabeth and wonders: 'Who is that lovely girl? (*MD* 212). And Peter Walsh and Rezia Smith observe an elderly 'battered woman' (*MD* 89) on the street who, when she sings, becomes a symbol of an ancient, fertile creativity more powerful and infinite than the childbearing around which patriarchal society shapes its feminine ideals. In attaining this level of mystical 'earth-mother', this older woman manages to negate the gazes of those around her.[79] Her song lyrics – 'if some one should see, what matter they?' – refer to being observed and overcoming the stigma attached, and as she sings the narrator observes how 'all peering inquisitive eyes seemed blotted out, and the passing generations – the pavement was crowded with bustling middle-class people – vanished' (*MD* 90).

64   *Virginia Woolf and Motherhood*

Clarissa's age and the end of her fertility are also directly related to the novel's leitmotif of time. Several scholars have written on the important theme of time within *Mrs Dalloway*. Paul Ricoeur, for example, has outlined two categories of time within the novel: what he calls 'monumental time' and 'internal time'. 'Monumental time' concerns not only the audible expressions of time itself – Big Ben sounding a 'warning, musical; then the hour, irrevocable' (*MD* 4, 128), and 'the clocks of Harley Street' 'Shredding and slicing, dividing and subdividing' (*MD* 112) – but also the 'sense of proportion' (*MD* 109) of 'figures of authority and power' such as Sir William Bradshaw. Without directly focusing on Mrs Dalloway's menopause, Ricoeur places 'internal time', or 'the living time experienced by Clarissa and Septimus' in contrast with this 'monumental time'.[80] Time is a term closely aligned with cultural concepts of menopause and women's cycles. Though the expression 'biological clock' was not in use when Woolf was writing *Mrs Dalloway,* she would later refer to her menopause as her 'time of life' (*L6* 60) or 'T of L' (*D5* 64) and worried that it might be 'a difficult & even dangerous time' (*D3* 254). Clarissa's memories of pre-menopause also show a conflict between the fluid circular time of a woman's cycle and the linear organisation of patriarchal culture. In 'Mrs Dalloway in Bond Street', Clarissa recalls her physical abilities as subject to the state of her menstrual cycle (or time of the month). Thinking of those intervals when she and her friends 'couldn't ride' and wondering: 'How then could women sit in Parliament? How could they do things with men?' (*CSF* 153), Clarissa introduces a set of prohibitions, based on biology and imposed by patriarchal culture, which bar women from participating in the operation of 'monumental time'.

Clarissa's lived time is associated with her thoughts and memories; there is, as *Orlando*'s narrator notes, an 'extraordinary discrepancy between time on the clock and time in the mind' (*O* 68). Clarissa's lived time is reflected in feelings of agelessness: 'She felt very young; at the same time unspeakably aged' (*MD* 8), 'Like a nun withdrawing, or a child exploring' (*MD* 33). The inclusion of the image of the nun draws attention to the sexlessness or non-fertility of such stages of life. Clarissa experiences shock when confronted with the reality of her biological age. For example, seeing herself from Peter's perspective:

> would she see him thinking when he came back, that she had grown older? It was true. Since her illness she had turned almost white.
>   Laying her brooch on the table, she had a sudden spasm, as if, while she mused, the icy claws had had the chance to fix in her.

She was not old yet. She had just broken into her fifty-second year. Months and months of it were still untouched. June, July, August! Each still remained almost whole, and, as if to catch the falling drop, Clarissa (crossing to the dressing-table) plunged into the very heart of the moment, transfixed it, there – the moment of this June morning on which was the pressure of all the other mornings, seeing the glass, the dressing-table, and all the bottles afresh, collecting the whole of her at one point. (*MD* 39–40)

Observing herself in the mirror, Clarissa longs for time to stop, the dressing table with its age-defying creams further proving Woolf's awareness of the way that consumer culture played on older women's images.

That Clarissa sometimes enjoys the trappings of consumerism – buying tonics to stop an ageing against which she, at times, rebels – calls attention to the ambiguities and complexities of her character.[81] Her independence, her instinctive ability to fight for self-determination and her empathy for Septimus contrasts with her admiration for the British class structure and her sometimes enthusiastic embrace of traditional female behaviours. Woolf herself felt some uncertainty about her capricious protagonist, worrying that the novel's strong form and narrative may be let down by: 'The doubtful point [. . .] the character of Mrs Dalloway. It may be too stiff, too glittering & tinsely' (*D2* 272). After its publication, Woolf recalled a letter from Lytton Strachey echoing these reservations, and pointing out 'some discrepancy in Clarissa herself': not only that 'she is disagreeable & limited, but that I alternatively laugh at her, & cover her, very remarkably, with myself' (*D3* 32). Agreeing with this assessment, Woolf records in her diary how, even after publication, 'some distaste for her persisted' but notes, 'one must dislike people in art without its mattering' (*D3* 32). Many of Clarissa's frivolous qualities come from Kitty Lushington Maxse, a family friend who acted as a mother figure after the death of Julia Stephen. Kitty helped Woolf and her sister enter society and was particularly critical of Woolf's artistic aspirations.[82] Clarissa Dalloway's first incarnation in *The Voyage Out* is 'almost Kitty verbatim' (*L1* 349) but, in a bid to realise her ambitions to write a social critique Woolf gave her final rendering of Clarissa memories and self-awareness, writing of this process in her diary: 'I dig out beautiful caves behind my characters; I think that gives exactly what I want; humanity, humour, depth' (*D2* 263). Indeed, Clarissa's vulnerabilities could be said to be part of what makes her such a compelling heroine. Interestingly, Kitty had

66 *Virginia Woolf and Motherhood*

no children of her own, so even as early as *The Voyage Out* Woolf's decision to give Clarissa a child marks a narrative ploy to comment upon motherhood in society.

'That woman's gift': *Mrs Dalloway*'s Menopause and Party Making

Clarissa appears disinterested in the specifics of everyday politics – when confronted with her husband's political enthusiasm she reflects; 'people would say, "Clarissa Dalloway is spoilt." She cared much more for her roses than for the Armenians' (*MD* 131–32). This trait recalls Leonard Woolf's assertion that Virginia was 'the least political animal that has lived since Aristotle invented the definition'.[83] Yet it seems incongruous to evaluate a woman's activism from her disinterest in (or in Woolf's case dislike for) the everyday acts of an administrative body that dismissed her sex. Though her feminist politics are not as forthright as Woolf's, Clarissa's rebellion does materialise in her desire to live, to continue 'stretching [. . .] absorbing, as in the youthful years, the colours, salts, tones of existence, so that she filled the room she entered' (*MD* 33). She achieves this through party-making, an act that confronts the patriarchy's image of an ageing, infertile woman and regains, albeit temporarily, her status as a valued member of society. Not all scholars agree that Clarissa's party is a radical undertaking – Makiko Minow-Pinkney finds it an act of complicity, noting that she 'accepts the role prescribed by the paternal law, becoming "the perfect hostess"'.[84] Certainly there is some tension here since party-giving does not subvert gender or social stereotypes. Not only does Peter mock Clarissa for being 'the perfect hostess' (*MD* 8, 67), but she struggles to 'imagine Peter or Richard taking the trouble to give a party for no reason whatever' (*MD* 133).

A key to interpreting Clarissa's party as a form of creative, menopausal rebellion can be found in Woolf's 1929 diary:

> I am 47 [. . .] will there not be the change of life? And may that not be a difficult & even dangerous time? Obviously one can get over it by facing it with common sense – that it is a natural process; that one can lie out here & read; that one's faculties will be the same afterwards; that one has nothing to worry about in one sense – I've written some interesting books, can make money, can afford a holiday – Oh no; one has nothing to bother about; & these curious intervals in life – I've had many – are the most fruitful artistically – one becomes fertilised. (*D3* 254)

The association between the menopause and an enhanced mental 'fertility' is unusual, running counter to medical theories which usually warned that menopause might lead to physical or mental infirmity – Leslie Hankins has noted of this entry that Woolf 'both internalized the cultural assumptions of a "dangerous age" of menopausal madness and revised those assumptions to envision menopause as a fertile interlude with creative potential'.[85] Interestingly the entry that immediately follows this considers the end of Vanessa's years of maternal caretaking:

> Angelica goes to school for the first time today I think; & I daresay Nessa is crying to herself – one of the emotions I shall never know – a child, one's last child – going to school, & so ending the 21 years of Nessa's children – a great stretch of life; how much fuller than I can guess – Imagine all the private scenes, the quarrels, the happinesses, the moments of excitement & change, as they grew up. And now, rather sublimely she ends her childhood years in a studio alone, going back, perhaps rather sadly to the life she would have liked best of all once, to be a painter on her own. (*D3* 254–55)

Contrasted with the creative freedom that Woolf foresees in her own menopause, Bell's melancholy post-maternal return to art suggests that women who are innately maternal, or who choose procreativity as a life path, risk forfeiting the joy of creating art. Compared with Vanessa's sadness, Clarissa's determination to love and enjoy life, and pursue it through her party, reconfirms her 'unmaternal' disposition. The party gives Clarissa a radically different way to express her 'extraordinary gift, that woman's gift, of making a world of her own wherever she happened to be' (*MD* 83).

Somewhat mystical, Clarissa's capacity to make 'a world of her own' is related to Woolf's talent for writing, and the maternal ability to create an entirely new being. In *The Hours* draft, Clarissa's gathering demonstrates 'that persistent sense of life [. . .] and instinct for bringing together, the creative instinct' (*H* 197). And when contemplating why she wants to give a party in the final version, Clarissa thinks:

> Here was So-and-so in South Kensington; some one up in Bayswater; and somebody else, say, in Mayfair. And she felt quite continuously a sense of their existence; and she felt what a waste; and she felt what a pity; and she felt if only they could be brought together; so she did it. And it was an offering; to combine, to create; but to whom?
>
> An offering for the sake of offering, perhaps. Anyhow, it was her gift. Nothing else had she of the slightest importance; could not

68   *Virginia Woolf and Motherhood*

> think, write, even play the piano. She muddled Armenians and Turks;
> loved success; hated discomfort; must be liked; talked oceans of non-
> sense: and to this day, ask her what the Equator was, and she did not
> know. (*MD* 133–34)

Clarissa repeatedly links her lack of formal education to her 'gift'.[86] By allowing this gift to thrive despite the strictures of patriarchal society, Woolf gives her protagonist, and the novel itself, a seed of the mystical, fertile femininity that Harrison saw in pre-Grecian matriarchal society (and which Woolf illustrates with her elderly 'battered' woman performing 'the pageant of the universe' (*MD* 89)). In line with Clarissa's 'tinsely' character, her act of bringing people together is tempered by her sentimental devotion to the British class system and her admiration of the aristocracy. An ironic moment occurs when Clarissa imagines herself welcoming her guests in the same manner that guests are welcomed at Buckingham Palace. Bryony Randall notes that Woolf 'admired, as well as satirised, the successful hostess', and the party reflects this fact, with moments of climactic exhilaration tempered by failed conversation and interactions that highlight the gathering's rigid social hierarchy. However, the success of the party is somewhat immaterial. Ultimately, it is Clarissa who benefits from her own victory – as Randall notes 'of all Woolf's hostesses, it is Mrs Dalloway who is most deeply implicated in, and potentially fulfilled by, her own creative act'.[87]

That Clarissa reaches some sort of climactic success at her party can be substantiated by tracing the repetitions of a phrase from *Cymbeline*: 'Fear no more the heat o' the sun/ Nor the furious winter's rages' (*MD* 10); an allusion which initially represents loss but comes to denote acceptance, and finally triumph in adversity. Tracing this arc also establishes Clarissa's bond with Septimus, who plays an important part in the novel's dialogue about motherhood and war. The first time Clarissa reads these lines it leads her to think of Lady Bexborough and how: 'This late age of the world's experience had bred in them all, all men and women, a well of tears' (*MD* 10). It is interesting that Woolf does not discriminate between the weeping women and their male counterparts here but instead establishes a cross-gender connection that will bear out in the relationship between Clarissa and Septimus. The second iteration – 'Fear no more the heat o' the sun' (*MD* 32) – occurs when Lady Bruton snubs Clarissa by not inviting her to lunch. Clarissa's fears about her declining social status – 'the dwindling of life' (*MD* 32) – lead to profound feelings of loss connected to her age and failing fertility.

At this moment, Clarissa fears 'time itself' (*MD* 32), she is a 'nun' unable to 'dispel a virginity preserved through childbirth which clung to her like a sheet' (*MD* 33–34) – an image that reinforces her 'unmaternal' demeanour.

The phrase is repeated a third time when Clarissa is: 'Quiet [. . .] calm, content' (*MD* 43), fixing a party dress which falls in waves across her lap. The text paints a picture in which 'waves' become a metronome for Clarissa's internal time:

> So on a summer's day waves collect, overbalance, and fall; collect and fall; and the whole world seems to be saying 'that is all' more and more ponderously, until even the heart in the body which lies in the sun on the beach says too, That is all. Fear no more, says the heart. Fear no more, says the heart, committing its burden to some sea, which sighs collectively for all sorrows, and renews, begins, collects, lets fall. And the body alone listens to the passing bee; the wave breaking; the dog barking, far away barking and barking. (*MD* 43)

Allowing the body's internal time to move into the foreground, Clarissa is at one with her environment instead of fighting against it. Here the quote ceases to be a lament about the passing of an age or ageing but instead commits 'its burden to' the sea of internal time and becomes an instruction – 'Fear no more'. Margaret Morganroth Gullette has pointed out that the rise of consumer culture in the early twentieth century led to a 'decline ideology' in which women learned to identify with the products they consumed and discarded, eventually seeing themselves as entities which deteriorate.[88] This scene acknowledges and rebukes such ideology, with Clarissa remembering dressmaker Sally Parker, now retired, whose 'dresses were never queer. You could wear them at Hatfield; at Buckingham Palace' (*MD* 43). By fixing Sally's dress instead of buying a new one, Clarissa verifies the worth of things which are older.

The final two repetitions tie Clarissa and Septimus together. The fourth occurs in Septimus's stream of consciousness, at the beginning of the scene in which he kills himself. Like Clarissa, Septimus is 'bathing, floating, on the top of the waves, while far away on shore he heard dogs barking and barking far away' (*MD* 153). His 'insanity' means that he is at one with nature and empowered to liberate himself from those championing 'monumental time'. The final repetition occurs at the novel's climax, when Clarissa imagines Septimus's death and watches the old woman opposite. At this moment she has overcome society's limited view of post-maternal women and gained complete

70 *Virginia Woolf and Motherhood*

control of her 'gift' (*MD* 134). This success is, of course, only momentary, Elfi Bettinger has noted of Clarissa that: 'Throughout the day, her mood swings from exhilaration and ecstasy to resignation. Her bodily self-perception [. . .] relates to the loss of fertility', and it is true that the cycle of empowerment seen with these allusions is a temporary triumph.[89] Nonetheless even if just for a moment Clarissa does overcome the strictures society places on her to exist boldly – no longer fearing the heat of the sun – in a way that has nothing to do with maternity, and especially the maternity of a war-mother.

'One cannot bring children into a world like this': Septimus Smith's Feminised Rebellion

While Clarissa battles the cultural stigma of being a post-maternal woman, Septimus complements her actions not only by committing suicide, but by turning away from reproduction. Where 'unmaternal' Clarissa subverts social standards of femininity, Woolf feminises Septimus, intensifying his status as an outsider in a society that was, as Zwerdling has noted, 'dedicated to covering up the stains and ignoring the major and minor tremors that threaten its existence'.[90] Apart from the wave-like internal time that Septimus shares with Clarissa he has many feminine traits. He openly cries in public (*MD* 23) and he helps his wife design a hat – taking pride and pleasure in a creative process that is traditionally not only performed by women, but for women. In addition, Septimus's character may have queer elements. Several scholars have read his relationship with Evans as romantic and suggested a certain feminine quality to his character.[91] Septimus's gender is also subverted by his 'shell-shock'. Initially the illness was explained as an effect of trauma on the eardrum, caused by being too near an exploding shell, but by the end of the war it came to be associated with female hysteria. According to historian George L. Mosse, 'war was regarded as a true test of manliness'. Men afflicted with 'shell-shock' 'were thought to be effeminate, they endangered the clear distinction between genders which was generally regarded as an essential cement of society'.[92] Even suicide, an act at least twice as prevalent among men, can arguably be seen as emasculating. Reading nineteenth-century cultural representations of suicide, Margaret Higonnet has contended that such statistics 'directly conflict with our mythic vision of suicide as feminine'.[93] Indeed, Woolf originally envisioned the novel's suicide to be Clarissa herself, emulating the death of Kitty Lushington Maxse, who – though it had never been established as a suicide – had fallen to her death not through a window but over an upstairs banister.

Grayzel notes that during the war: 'Contrasted with soldiering, the dominant, gender-specific role that was explicitly denied to them, women evaded their duty not by refusing to fight, but by refusing to produce future fighters'.[94] Although he has already been to war, by refusing to reproduce Septimus adopts a specifically feminine form of defiance against the patriarchy. As a man, Septimus's struggle against childbirth is not a struggle with instinct (society does not suggest he must feel an innate compulsion to have children), or autonomy (the choice to have a baby remains his own), nor is it a struggle with creativity itself (child-making and art-making generally need not be mutually exclusive paths for men), instead it is an effect of his aversion to his war-making society. In 'The Prime Minister', one of the short stories completed before Woolf wrote *Mrs Dalloway*, Septimus's madness has a different focus. Instead of dwelling on procreation, he imagines himself as a messianic figure sacrificed for the sins of his war-mongering civilisation, even while doubting that this civilisation can be saved (*CSF* 321–22). The Septimus of the short story is already antagonistic towards the patriarchy, but by introducing his resistance to procreation the novel reinforces the link between childbirth and war as well as strengthening the connection between Septimus and Clarissa. Woolf was not alone in imagining that soldiers might reject procreation after seeing war. For example, in 1916 feminist and social reformer Evelyn Greville Warwick suggested – in a book that spoke out against the war and the government and labelled the press 'the greatest distorting medium in the world' – that after the war, many a surviving soldier 'will hesitate to become a father lest his sons have to take their place in time to come on the fields of war'.[95]

Septimus's hostility towards reproduction is contrasted against his wife Lurezia's desperate and lonely desire for a baby. Rezia tells her husband of five years 'she must have children' (*MD* 97), '*She* could not grow old and have no children!' (*MD* 99), while Septimus thinks: 'One cannot bring children into a world like this. One cannot perpetuate suffering, or increase the breed of these lustful animals' (*MD* 98). The circumstances of Rezia's yearning serve to further reinforce the gravity of the British Empire's rapaciousness. Masami Usui notes that 'Lucrezia is one of the war brides who were brought to Britain as a symbol of male triumph, power, egotism and romanticism [. . .] she is oppressed as a woman and as a foreigner'.[96] Septimus meets and marries Rezia in Milan, the city he was billeted in when peace was announced, and Merry Pawlowski argues that this is a response

72 Virginia Woolf and Motherhood

to Mussolini who shaped his 'fascist ideology to support his view of the place of women in the state, taking them as his "brides" and encouraging them to bear children for Italy'.[97] Whether Woolf was comparing England to the increasingly chauvinistic Italy or damning it in its own right, the character of Lucrezia Warren Smith exemplifies women's internalisation of patriarchal obligations. Despite living in a State that claims authority over her person, dominates her with inequality and treats her as an unwanted outsider, Rezia clings to the deep-rooted belief that she cannot be whole unless she bears a little soldier to protect and serve the national ideals. By imbuing Rezia with solitude and desolation, Woolf almost seems to mourn the patriarchal pollution of childbirth. When Rezia pleads 'she must have a boy. She must have a son like Septimus' (*MD* 97–98) the reader, having seen the confusion and distress in Septimus's mind, wonders how deep-rooted the perversion of this desire runs, how any woman could long to have a son in a world so dangerous to his sex. Having faced the danger of battle, Septimus refuses to support the militaristic regime by reproducing. Given how Woolf portrays patriarchal society as inherently 'mad', the decision not to have a child seems rational despite the clinical classification of Septimus's psychological disorder. As Molly Hite notes: 'Septimus's emphasis may be extreme, but we are in a novel where, as we have seen, the "proportion" ascribed to medically defined normality is explicitly called oppressive and even murderous'.[98]

Woolf employs the works of Shakespeare, and particularly *Antony and Cleopatra*, in Septimus's case against giving his wife a baby. Septimus contends that: 'Love between man and woman was repulsive to Shakespeare. The business of copulation was filth to him before the end' (*MD* 97). In much the same way that childbearing is commandeered as civil duty, Woolf shows that even Shakespeare's work – composed in the name of art and individualism – can be usurped by the patriarchy and used to promote militarism. Thus *Antony and Cleopatra*, written, according to Woolf, 'without hate, without bitterness, without fear, without protest, without preaching' (*AROO* 61) could be framed in such a way as to lead a man to war. Having originally learnt the classics (and fallen a little in love) 'with Miss Isabel Pole, lecturing in the Waterloo Road upon Shakespeare' (*MD* 93), Septimus goes 'to France to save an England which consisted almost entirely of Shakespeare's plays and Miss Isabel Pole in a green dress walking in a square' (*MD* 94).

Though naïve notions of protecting art and love lure Septimus to the front, he is utterly changed by his experience of battle. Septimus feels that the war has 'taught him. It was sublime' (*MD* 95). This shift in understanding is focused on Shakespeare and reproduction. Septimus feels:

> That boy's business of the intoxication of language [. . .] had shrivelled utterly. How Shakespeare loathed humanity – the putting on of clothes, the getting of children, the sordidity of the mouth and the belly! This was now revealed to Septimus; the message hidden in the beauty of words. (*MD* 97)

With the horror of battle behaving as a catalyst, the art that sends Septimus to war becomes the very argument he uses against having children. Woolf's choice of *Antony and Cleopatra* is, of course, deliberate; it is a work that pits the masculine against the feminine, patriarchy against matriarchy and links fertility with death. The play is full of imagery of motherhood, war and destruction.[99] Cleopatra, synonymous with Egypt, represents the feminine principle contrasting with the masculinity of Rome and Mark Antony. When Cleopatra is taken prisoner by Rome, the emperor Octavian Caesar repeatedly lies to her, assuring her of his honourable intentions. Knowing that she is doomed to the indignity of being escorted through the streets in Caesar's victory parade, Cleopatra takes her own life as her last form of resistance. Cleopatra's death is an example of Higonnet's 'mythic vision' of feminine suicide. Michael Payne explains how the relationship between destruction and fertility builds to a climax so that when Cleopatra 'puts the asp to her breast and says quietly to Charmian: "Dost thou not see my baby at my breast, / That sucks the nurse asleep?" (V.ii.311–13) the experience of death has become [. . .] maternal'.[100] Since Caesar has also promised to murder Cleopatra's children if she kills herself, bringing an end to her genetic line, these last words highlight how the immortal and mystical powers of fertility that constitute motherhood are consumed and perverted by the paternal state.

Septimus emulates Cleopatra's suicide with his own, with Woolf writing Septimus's death as the last stand in a long struggle against the 'good intentions' and patriarchal rationale of his inherently immoral doctors. Struggling to free himself from their strictures, Septimus is forced to escape using the last available option:

> Holmes was coming upstairs. Holmes would burst open the door. Holmes would say 'In a funk, eh?' Holmes would get him. But no; not Holmes; not Bradshaw. Getting up rather unsteadily, hopping

74   *Virginia Woolf and Motherhood*

indeed from foot to foot, he considered Mrs Filmer's nice clean bread knife with 'Bread' carved on the handle. Ah, but one mustn't spoil that. The gas fire? But it was too late now. Holmes was coming. Razors he might have got, but Rezia, who always did that sort of thing, had packed them. There remained only the window, the large Bloomsbury-lodging house window, the tiresome, the troublesome, and rather melodramatic business of opening the window and throwing himself out. (*MD* 163)

Septimus does not desire death. He kills himself to defy the medical establishment, men whose rationale and rules represent all that is most harmful and base about the patriarchy, and whose tyranny denied Woolf the chance to have children of her own. Septimus's suicide is not only 'defiance' (*MD* 202), but the most complete form of self-fulfilment for a man held captive by a society that is plagued by the patriarchal madness of war and peace.

Hearing about Septimus's death at her party, Clarissa's response initially seems the very epitome of a 'tinsely' reaction. Sounding flippant, she is 'glad that he had done it; thrown it away [. . .] He made her feel the beauty; made her feel the fun'.[101] In the draft version of this scene Woolf elucidates this moment with the explanation 'she felt no pity for the young man who had killed himself; nor for his wife; nor for herself; nothing but pride; nothing but joy' (*H* 399) and in an even earlier draft allows Clarissa herself to muse 'why did she feel no pity, no not a scrap for the young man who had killed himself' (*H* 398). These excerpts may have been removed during Woolf's editing process to allow the reader to come to their own conclusions about the connection between the two characters. In fact, Septimus's death allows Clarissa to connect her party – an event which has consumed her thoughts for most of the novel despite being belittled by the men in her life – to an act of defiance. In the draft Woolf complements Clarissa's feelings of being alive with the sentiment 'she would go back & she would fight Sir William Bradshaw [. . .] She must go back; ~~she must~~ breast her enemy; she, ~~must~~ take her rose, Never would she submit – never, never!' (*H* 399). Though the defiant tone of this text is moderated in the final version – it becomes 'she must go back. She must assemble' (*MD* 204) – the battle metaphor remains. This is especially interesting in a work that denounces war and brings to mind Leonard Woolf's book *The War for Peace* (1940).[102] The image of 'taking her rose' is also intriguing. Elisa Kay Sparks has written of Woolf's extensive symbolic use of flowers, especially roses, and has noted that *Mrs Dalloway* is 'the most floral of all Woolf's novels'.[103] In the book, Peter Walsh pictures new social freedoms as the dissolution of a 'pyramidal accumulation', which, in past generations, 'had pressed; weighed them down, the women especially, like those flowers Clarissa's Aunt Helena used to press between sheets of grey blotting-paper' (*MD* 178). By taking back her roses Clarissa is overcoming the stricture put on women, but there is more to this image. Here and elsewhere in Woolf's works roses are an intimation of health, the colour in a woman's cheeks, for example. They also symbolise menses, suggesting that Clarissa must re-join the party – and do battle – to lay claim to her own body, sexuality and femininity: a womanliness that is set quite apart from the bearing of children. This reading is supported in the text by Mrs Dempster who has given up her roses, her figure and her feet to married life. A similar reference also occurs in *The Years*, where Mrs Malone tells her daughter Kitty, who is looking pale after a tiring day, to go to bed, explaining 'I don't like to see your roses fade' (*Y* 60).[104]

Molly Hite has explored 'the tonal ambivalence' of Clarissa's feelings after Septimus's suicide, noting how

> the problem of how to take Clarissa nags at even very nuanced readings [. . .] different ways of reading *Mrs Dalloway* indicate how a lack of authoritative tonal cues can lead to conflicting interpretations of a character and even an entire novel.

Examples of divergent readings of this moment include viewing Clarissa's reaction as a symptom of her 'class privilege', and interpreting it as 'the summit of her character development'.[105] Some clarity might be offered by examining the genesis of the novel. Woolf changed her plans to end the narrative with Clarissa's suicide very soon after starting writing, linking the party to Septimus's death and noting: 'All must bear finally upon the party at the end; which expresses life, in every variety & full of conviction: while S. dies' (*H* 415). Thus, not only do Clarissa and Septimus share a bond from being on the liminal edges of society, but Woolf kills Septimus so that Clarissa (and her party) might thrive. This accomplishes Woolf's plan 'to give life & death' (*D2* 248) in the novel, a thematic coupling which aligns closely with the subversive images of motherhood and war, not only in *Mrs Dalloway*, but also in *Jacob's Room*. In both novels, motherhood during times of war is seen not as life-giving, but as a route to death. While Jacob's death is as purposeless and empty as his shoes – nullifying Betty's lifelong maternal labour – Septimus's death offers 'unmaternal' Clarissa vitality. It also eliminates the physical presence

76 *Virginia Woolf and Motherhood*

of war from the novel, and puts an end to the prospect of a new generation of soldiers 'like Septimus'. Ultimately, in her 'unmaternal' existence Clarissa becomes the answer to the war-mother in Woolf's earlier work. The joy she experiences at Septimus's death lies in sharp contrast to Betty's tears at the end of *Jacob's Room*.

Woolf initially perceived WW1 as 'a stage of suffering [. . .] where any expression save the barest is intolerable' (*E2* 270). But, by connecting the conflict to her own personal trauma – the loss of her brother Thoby to the death of a soldier in *Jacob's Room*, and her own psychosis to the point of view of a 'shell-shocked' soldier in *Mrs Dalloway* – she eventually brought a powerful, feminine voice to bear witness to the domestic experience of war. Within these novels, Woolf turns to motherhood as a way to express her frustration with a culture that restricted women's freedom and yet expected loyalty and sacrifice in return. These narratives of motherhood and war also intersect with other contemporary issues, and one of the more striking is eugenics – a movement which is to be investigated in the following chapter. The rise of eugenics is closely linked to wartime rhetoric, it initially garnered significant popular interest and support following the early losses of the Second Boer War (1899–1902) when reports emerged that large numbers of soldiers were not healthy enough to perform their duties. Fears about the health of the working-class population and concern about the falling birth rate, led to apprehension about the 'decline' of the general population. During WW1 the newly defined condition of 'shell-shock' became a part of this public eugenic rhetoric and Woolf engaged with these discussions through the character of Septimus Smith.

Many eugenicists believed that physical features were the means to understanding character – Francis Galton, for example, was a keen gatherer of physiognomic data, setting up his first anthropometric laboratory in the 1880s. Throughout her writing Woolf's attention to eyes, mouths, foreheads and hands participate in and question eugenic language and she describes Septimus's features accordingly:

> To look at, he might have been a clerk, but of the better sort; for he wore brown boots; his hands were educated; so, too, his profile – his angular, big-nosed, intelligent, sensitive profile; but not his lips altogether, for they were loose; and his eyes (as eyes tend to be), eyes merely; hazel, large; so that he was, on the whole, a border case, neither one thing nor the other. (*MD* 92)

Septimus's appearance is ambiguous. Aspects of his profile speak to an artist's sensitivity, but, as Donald Childs points out, 'hereditary taint' can be read into his loose lips (a feature shared with a 'female vagrant' (*MD* 127) that Richard Dalloway passes on his walk through Green Park).[106] The 'hereditary taint' hinted at by Septimus's profile is accentuated by his 'shell-shock', an illness which some doctors suspected showed 'weakness, instability or defect of the nervous system'.[107] Woolf related Septimus's post-traumatic stress disorder to her own mental illness, an association that made sense given that most of her eugenic-minded doctors also treated veterans.[108] Furthermore she used Septimus's treatment to investigate the relationship between her own eugenic profile and her doctors' recommendations that she avoid motherhood. Interestingly, while *Mrs Dalloway* depicts these doctors in a hostile light, Woolf also shows some interest in eugenic theories pertaining to the 'healthiest' or 'fittest' way for humans to reproduce. The following chapter investigates how she combined these ideas with maternal metaphors to create her own theory about the way texts perpetuate themselves.

Notes

1. Bashka Paeff, quoted in M. J. Curl, 'Boston Artists and Sculptors Talk of Their Work and Ideals: IX – Bashka Paeff', *The Sunday Herald*, 6 February 1921, p. 6.
2. For more on the promotion of motherhood during war, see Nancy Huston, 'The Matrix of War: Mothers and Heroes', in *The Female Body in Western Culture: Contemporary Perspectives*, ed. Susan Rubin Suleiman (Cambridge, MA: Harvard University Press, 1985), pp. 120–36, and D. A. Boxwell, 'The (M)Other Battle of World War One: The Maternal Politics of Pacifism in Rose Macaulay's *Non-Combatants and Others*', *Tulsa Studies in Women's Literature*, 12 (1993), pp. 85–101.
3. *Women's Identities at War*, pp. 110, 244.
4. For more on Woolf's pacifism, see Paula Maggio, 'Taking up Her Pen for World Peace: Virginia Woolf, Feminist Pacifist. Or Not?', in *Virginia Woolf: Writing the World*, ed. Pamela Caughie and Diana Swanson (Liverpool: Liverpool University Press, 2015), pp. 37–42.
5. For Woolf's opinion of the press during times of war, see Judith Allen, *Virginia Woolf and the Politics of Language* (Edinburgh: Edinburgh University Press, 2010); particularly chapter 6, 'Virginia Woolf, "Patriotism" and "our prostituted fact-purveyors"', pp. 97–112.
6. 'Virginia Woolf's "War in the Village" and "War from the Street"', in *Virginia Woolf and War: Fiction, Reality and Myth*, ed. Mark Hussey (New York: Syracuse University Press, 1991), p. 43.

78 *Virginia Woolf and Motherhood*

7. *Women's Identities at War*, p. 116.
8. See Sarah Drewery, 'Recruitment and Fundraising Posters, World War One', *Liddell Hart Centre for Military Archives, King's College London* (2008) <http://www.kcl.ac.uk/lhcma/summary/xr30-001.shtml> [accessed 8 May 2013].
9. For examples of the separation allowance arguments of the time, see Eleanor Rathbone, 'Separation Allowances: I', *Common Cause*, 7.359 (1915), pp. 611–12 and 'Separation Allowances: An Experiment in the State Endowment of Maternity II', *Common Cause*, 7.362 (1916), pp. 648–49.
10. Jane Potter, *Boys in Khaki, Girls in Print* (Oxford: Oxford University Press, 2005), pp. 52–55.
11. Wright's coal tar soap advertisement, *The English Review*, May 1915, p. xi.
12. Austin Harrison, 'For the Unborn', *The English Review*, 20 May 1915, p. 236.
13. Mothers' Union, *To British Mothers: How They Can Help Enlistment* (London: Mothers' Union, 1914).
14. The *Encyclopedia of Motherhood* defines maternal essentialism in the following way:

> the notion that all women naturally possess innate female qualities that drive them to pursue maternal goals above all others. These essentialist notions go beyond the obvious biological fact that women physically give birth, and assume that women are genetically destined to be responsible for childcare and, by extension, most domestic duties. (Myrl Coulter, 'Essentialism and Mothering', *Encyclopedia of Motherhood*, 3 vols, ed. Andrea O'Reilly (Los Angeles: Sage, 2010), I, pp. 357–58)

Maternalist pacifism assumed women were genetically predisposed not only to care for children but to universally nurture mankind.
15. 'Motherhood and War', *Harper's Weekly*, 5 December 1914, p. 542 <https://babel.hathitrust.org/cgi/pt?id=mdp.39015033848030&view=1up&seq=612> [accessed 19 July 2013].
16. *Women's Identities at War*, p. 2.
17. *Sex and Suffrage in Britain 1860–1914* (Princeton, NJ: Princeton University Press, 1987), p. 169.
18. 'The Achievement of Female Suffrage in Europe: On Women's Citizenship', *International Journal of Constitutional Law*, 12.1 (2014), p. 12.
19. In her 1914 pamphlet 'Women and the War' Christabel Pankhurst wrote: 'Urgently do the women of the W.S.P.U. reinforce the appeal for new recruits for the new Army [. . .] We think that, as militant women, we may perhaps be able to do something to rouse the spirit of militancy in men'. (*Women's Writing of the First World War: An Anthology*, ed. Angela K. Smith (Manchester: Manchester University Press, 2000), pp. 71–72). Also see Les Garner, *Stepping Stones to Women's*

Liberty: Feminist Ideas in the Women's Suffrage Movement 1900–1918 (Madison, NJ: Fairleigh Dickinson University Press, 1984), p. 55, and Susan Kingsley Kent, Making Peace: The Reconstruction of Gender in Interwar Britain (Princeton, NJ: Princeton University Press, 1993), particularly chapter 4 'The Vote: Sex and Suffrage in Britain 1916–1918', pp. 74–96.

20. 'The Women and Men of 1914', in Arms and the Woman: War, Gender and Literary Representation, ed. Helen Cooper, Adrienne Munich and Susan Squier (Chapel Hill: University of North Carolina Press, 1989), p. 98.

21. On 10 August 1921, Woolf announced in her diary: 'I have changed the Daily News for the Morning Post' (D2 127).

22. Suzanne Evans, Mothers of Heroes, Mothers of Martyrs: World War I and the Politics of Grief (Montreal: McGill-Queen's University Press, 2007), p. 88.

23. 'A Mother's Answer to "A Common Soldier"', The Morning Post, 14 August 1916, quoted in Robert Graves, Goodbye to All That (London: Penguin, 2000), pp. 189–91.

24. Mothers of Heroes, Mothers of Martyrs, pp. 86–88.

25. Goodbye to All That (London: Penguin, 2000), p. 188.

26. Karen Levenback has argued that, for Woolf, 'Rupert Brooke's death seems the pivotal event that moved the war into the real world' ('Virginia Woolf's "War in the Village"', p. 44).

27. 'A Mother's Answer to "A Common Soldier"', quoted in Graves, p. 189.

28. Patricia Cramer, 'Virginia Woolf's Matriarchal Family of Origins in Between the Acts', Twentieth Century Literature, 39.2 (1993), pp. 171–76; Susan Kingsley Kent, Sex and Suffrage in Britain 1860–1914 (Princeton, NJ; Princeton University Press, 1987), p. 169. Kingsley Kent makes the argument that, much like Woolf, many suffragettes did not see gender as sex but as a cultural construction.

29. 'The Lunacy of Men, the Idiocy of Women: Woolf, West, and War', NWSA Journal, 15.3 (2003), p. 124.

30. 'Jacob's Room: Woolf's Satiric Elegy', ELH, 48.4 (1981), p. 894.

31. For example: David Daiches, Virginia Woolf (New York: New Directions, 1963), pp. 61–62; Michael Rosenthal, Virginia Woolf (London: Routledge & Kegan Paul, 1979), pp. 75–78.

32. 'Jacob's Room: Woolf's Satiric Elegy', pp. 911–12.

33. For example, Allyson Booth, Postcards from the Trenches: Negotiating the Space between Modernism and the First World War (New York: Oxford University Press, 1996), p. 43, and Amy E. Elkins, 'Old Pages and New Readings in Virginia Woolf's Orlando', Tulsa Studies in Women's Literature, 29.1 (2010), p. 131.

34. 'Jacob's Room: Woolf's Satiric Elegy', pp. 65–66.

35. 'Woolf's Keen Sensitivity to War', in Virginia Woolf and War: Fiction, Reality and Myth, ed. Mark Hussey (New York: Syracuse University Press, 1991), p. 16.

80 *Virginia Woolf and Motherhood*

36. 'Private Brother, Public World', in *New Feminist Essays on Virginia Woolf*, ed. Jane Marcus (Lincoln: University of Nebraska Press, 1981), p. 198.

37. There has been a wealth of research into Harrison's influence on Woolf. Sandra Shattuck wrote an early investigation into Harrison's *Ancient Art and Ritual* and Woolf's *Between the Acts* ('The Stage of Scholarship: Crossing the Bridge from Harrison to Woolf', in *Virginia Woolf and Bloomsbury: A Centenary Celebration*, ed. Jane Marcus (Indianapolis: Indiana University Press, 1987), pp. 278–98), while Patricia Cramer's article investigating group dynamics in *Between the Acts* takes a closer look at the way that Woolf explores matriarchal and patriarchal cultural influences ('Virginia Woolf's Matriarchal Family of Origins in *Between the Acts*'). In addition, Martha C. Carpentier's *Ritual, Myth and the Modernist Text: The Influence of Jane Ellen Harrison on Joyce, Eliot and Woolf* (London: Routledge, 2013), covers Harrison's influence on the modernist literature of Joyce, Eliot and Woolf. Jean Mills's more recent book length study, *Virginia Woolf, Jane Ellen Harrison, and the Spirit of Modern Classicism*, 're-examines the origins and sources of Virginia Woolf's intellectual, literary, and political views by decisively positioning her work in dialogue with the theories and practices of [. . .] Harrison' ((Columbus: Ohio State University Press, 2014), p. 1). Particularly relevant to this study (where I will later demonstrate that *Jacob's Room* builds on Harrison's work to investigate the role Jacob's mother plays in his education) is Kathryn Holland's assertion that 'Woolf repeatedly refers to Harrison in her arguments about women's agency within and outside of educational institutions' ('Late Victorian and Modern Feminist Intertexts: The Strachey Women in *A Room of One's Own* and *Three Guineas*', *Tulsa Studies in Women's Literature*, 32.1 (2013), p. 82).

38. *Catalogue of Books from the Library of Leonard and Virginia Woolf: Taken from Monks House, Rodmell, Sussex and 24 Victoria Square, London and now in the Possession of Washington State University Pullman, U.S.A.* (Brighton: Holleyman & Treacher, 1975), V/s, II, p. 3.

39. *Prolegomena to the Study of Greek Religion*, 2nd edn (Cambridge: Cambridge University Press, 1903; repr. 1908), pp. 246, 273.

40. For information on the culture of death in the Victorian era, see Julie-Marie Strange, *Death, Grief and Poverty in Britain, 1870–1914*. (Cambridge: Cambridge University Press, 2005).

41. The dead culture, usually Victorian, is represented by pictures of relatives, old furniture or books. Mrs Hilbery in *Night and Day*, for example, keeps a museum of family relics and frets over portraits of deceased relatives in broken frames.

42. Joanna Bourke, *Dismembering the Male: Men's Bodies, Britain, and the Great War* (Chicago: University of Chicago Press, 1996), p. 215.

43. The chrysanthemum, here held as a flower of mourning, also brings to mind the purple aster described at the beginning of *Jacob's Room*,

both coming from the genus Asteraceae. In the draft of the novel Betty places the flower beside Jacob's bed and Woolf describes the petals falling 'down- down' (*JRHD* 4), in a prophetic image forewarning Jacob's death. Elisa Kay Sparks also discusses purple flowers as a symbol of death in *Jacob's Room* ('"Everything tended to set itself in a garden": Virginia Woolf's Literary and Quotidian Flowers: A Bar-Graphical Approach', in *Virginia Woolf and the Natural World*, ed. Kristin Czarnecki and Carrie Rohman (Liverpool: Liverpool University Press, 2011), pp. 48–49).

44. For example, the 'Unreal City's parade of soldiers in T. S. Eliot's *The Waste Land*, which Ferner Nuhn has described as 'one of a series of poetic "descents into hell"' (*The Wind Blew from the East* (New York: Harper & Brothers, 1942), p. 222), and of which Paul Lewis has noted: 'In *The Waste Land*, mankind is already in the pit, already enflamed by lust, boredom, and spiritual collapse' ('Life by Water: Characterization and Salvation in *The Waste Land*', *Mosaic*, 11.4 (1978), p. 90).

45. Suzanne Raitt, 'Virginia Woolf's Early Novels: Finding a Voice', in *The Cambridge Companion to Virginia Woolf*, ed. Sue Roe and Susan Sellers (Cambridge: Cambridge University Press, 2000), p. 44. Sara Ruddick, 'Private Brother, Public World', p. 197. In addition, see Nancy Topping Bazin and Jane Hamovit Lauter's 'Woolf's Keen Sensitivity to War', p. 15.

46. In 1938 Woolf published an early version of *Three Guineas* as a pair of articles in *The Atlantic*. While the first article was simply called 'Women Must Weep' the second article had an expanded title: 'Women Must Weep – Or Unite Against War', thus offering unity and opposition as an alternative to women's proscribed wartime grieving.

47. *Women's Identities at War*, pp. 10, 226.

48. '"Not Septimus now": Wives of Disabled Veterans and Cultural Memory of the First World War in Britain', *Women's History Review*, 13.1 (2004), p. 119, also see Adam Stanley, 'Hearth, Home, and Steering Wheel: Gender and Modernity in France After the Great War', *The Historian*, 66.2 (2004), p. 233. This is also related to the discourse of 'shell-shock', which will be discussed later.

49. Maurice Hankey, 'Recommendations of the Committee (3rd Revise)', Cabinet Memorial Services (November 11th) Committee, *The National Archives*, Public Works Record, Public Records Office, CAB 24/114/65 (5 November 1920), p. 10.

50. 'Letter from L. Storr (Secretary of Memorial Services Committee) to J. T. Davies', document F/23/3/20, David Lloyd George Papers, *House of Lords Record Office*, London (28 October 1920), quoted in Grayzel, *Women's Identities at War*, p. 230.

51. Hankey, 'Recommendations of the Committee', p. 10.

52. Jane Marcus views Betty's gelded cat as representing her female autonomy and independence, but we shall see that this is emphatically not the case: see 'Liberty, Sorority, Misogyny', in *The Representation of Women in Fiction*, ed. C. Heilbrun and M. Higonnet (Baltimore, MD: Johns Hopkins, 1983), p. 62.

82 *Virginia Woolf and Motherhood*

53. *At the Violet Hour: Modernism and Violence in England and Ireland* (Oxford: Oxford University Press, 2012), pp. 257–58.
54. The final novel mentions nothing of Mrs Jarvis's children, giving the novel very little in the way of progressive mothering. But in the draft Woolf writes a scene where the rector's wife walks on the moor connecting with nature and reading Shelley. In this scene Woolf writes:

> Mrs Jarvis, *though she had two children*, was the sort of woman to lose her faith, or worse, ~~to be~~ not to lose her faith, ~~but~~ not to leave her husband, not to read any book through, & yet to go on walking alone, looking at the moon, & feeling [. . .] that ~~there is a spirit of the universe~~. (*JRHD* 22, my emphasis)

Despite having borne her clergyman husband's children and complied with society's wish to make her a mother, Mrs Jarvis is still incapable of conforming.
55. 'In Defense of the Victorians', *Wilson Quarterly*, 12.3 (1976), p. 92.
56. '*Jacob's Room* as Comedy: Woolf's Parodic Bildungsroman', in *New Feminist Essays on Virginia Woolf*, ed. Jane Marcus (Lincoln: University of Nebraska Press, 1981), pp. 109–10.
57. *Peace with Patriotism* (Cambridge: Deighton Bell, 1915), p. 25.
58. '"What fools we were!": Virginia Woolf's "A Society"', *Twentieth Century Literature*, 33.1 (1987), p. 51.
59. Beth Rigel Daugherty's article 'The Whole Contention Between Mr Bennett and Mrs Woolf, Revised' explores the dialogue between Woolf and Bennett, and her motivations to respond to his book (in *Virginia Woolf: Centennial Essays*, ed. Elaine K. Ginsberg and Laura Moss Gottlieb (Troy, NY: Whitston, 1983), pp. 269–94).
60. 'Current Literature: Books in General', *New Statesman*, 2 October 1920, p. 704. *A Room*'s attention to how certain male writers view women's intellect as inferior highlights the continued relevance of this exchange to Woolf.
61. This idea remains, though somewhat altered, in *Three Guineas* where Woolf notes: 'There is of course one essential that the educated woman can supply: children. And one method by which she can help to prevent war is to refuse to bear children' (*TG* 275).
62. The introduction to *Three Guineas* echoes this endeavour by examining several different men's opinions as to why war was necessary, including Wilfred Owen, The Lord Chief Justice, the Scarborough Conference of educated men, the Bournemouth Conference of working men, a soldier and members of the clergy.
63. '"What fools we were!"', p. 58.
64. In 'A Society' Woolf describes Peace Day with: 'The rain was falling and interfered no doubt with the proper explosion of the fireworks' (*CSF* 136). This could be taken straight from her diary where the rain leaves her 'in no doubt that any remaining festivities are to be completely quenched' (*D1* 294).

Motherhood and the Great War 83

65. Quoted in Eric Homberger, 'The Story of the Cenotaph', *Times Literary Supplement*, 12 November 1976, pp. 1429–30.

66. 'The Poet and the Ghosts are Walking the Streets: Hope Mirrless – Life and Poetry', *Hecate*, 35.1–2 (2009), p. 31. Woolf was particularly familiar with the poem since, as Julia Briggs notes, it 'was the single most difficult task [she] ever undertook as a printer', not only did she set the type but also 'spent an annoying afternoon making two further corrections by hand in each of 160 copies' (*Reading Virginia Woolf* (Edinburgh: Edinburgh University Press, 2006), pp. 83–84).

67. 'Motherhood and War', p. 542.

68. Delegates of Second International Conference of Women, 'Resolutions of the Zürich Congress 1919' (Geneva: Women's International League for Peace and Freedom, 1919) <http://www.ja1325.org/PDFs/Resolutions%20of%20the%20WILPF%20Zurich%20Congress%201919.pdf> [accessed 12 January 2013], p. 4.

69. On Peace Day Woolf wrote in her diary:

> It seems to me more & more clear that the only honest people are the artists, & that these social reformers & philanthropists get so out of hand, & harbor so many discreditable desires under the disguise of loving their kind, that in the end there's more to find fault with in them than in us. (*D1* 293)

70. For more on this, see Emily Dalgarno, 'Virginia Woolf: Translation and "Iterability"', *The Yearbook of English Studies*, 36.1 (2006), pp. 145–56, and Yopie Prins, '"OTOTOTOI": Virginia Woolf and "The Naked Cry" of Cassandra', in *Agamemnon in Performance 458 BC to AD 2004*, ed. Fiona Macintosh et al. (Oxford: Oxford University Press, 2005), pp. 163–85.

71. For more on this essay, see Chapter 4, pp. 237–39.

72. See Huston, 'The Matrix of War: Mothers and Heroes', p. 127, and Boxwell, 'The (M)Other Battle', p. 85.

73. 'What fools we were!', p. 54.

74. There are other places this can be observed in Woolf's earlier fiction, some of which will be discussed later; for example, Clarissa Dalloway and her single daughter compared with Sally Seton and her five sons.

75. There are undertones of birth control advocacy here; birth control will be discussed in the following chapter on eugenics.

76. 'Inventing the "Postmaternal" Woman, 1898–1927: Idle, Unwanted, and Out of a Job', *Feminist Studies*, 21.2 (1995), p. 221.

77. Elizabeth Hirsh has also explored Clarissa's menopause: 'Mrs Dalloway's Menopause: Encrypting the Female Life Course', in *Woolf in the Real World*, ed. Karen V. Kukil (Clemson, SC: Clemson University Press, 2005), pp. 76–81.

78. '"Ages are the stuff!": The Traffic in Ages in Interwar Britain', *NWSA Journal*, 18.1 (2006), p. 138. Consumer culture was increasingly important for all classes of society and an investigation into working-class

84   *Virginia Woolf and Motherhood*

women and the Co-Operative Women's Guild will be conducted in Chapter 3. For consumer culture in Woolf, see also Kathryn Simpson, *Gifts, Markets and Economies of Desire in Virginia Woolf* (London: Palgrave Macmillan, 2009), especially chapter 2 'Queering the Market: "Mrs Dalloway in Bond Street", *Mrs Dalloway* and "The Hours"' pp. 50–84.

79. 'Earth-Mother' is a phrase that Jane Harrison repeatedly uses in her work. See, for example, *Prolegomena*, pp. 263–76.

80. *Time and Narrative*, 3 vols, trans. Kathleen McLaughlin and David Pellauer (Chicago: University of Chicago Press, 1984–88), II (1985), pp. 106–08. See also Bryony Randall, *Modernism, Daily Time and Everyday Life* (Cambridge: Cambridge University Press, 2007; repr. 2011), pp. 159–61.

81. Many scholars have explored Clarissa's multifaceted character: see, for example, Alex Zwerdling, '*Mrs Dalloway* and the Social System', *PMLA*, 92.1 (1977), pp. 78–79, and Molly Hite, 'Tonal Cues and Uncertain Values: Affect and Ethics in *Mrs Dalloway*', *Narrative*, 18.3 (2010), pp. 267–68.

82. For more on Lushington Maxse see Christine Froula, '*Mrs Dalloway*'s Postwar Elegy: Women, War, and the Art of Mourning', *Modernism/ modernity*, 9.1 (2002), pp. 125–63.

83. Leonard Woolf, *Downhill All the Way* (New York: Harcourt Brace Jovanovich, 1975), p. 27.

84. *Virginia Woolf and the Problem of the Subject* (Brighton: Harvester, 1987), p. 72.

85. '"To kindle and illuminate": Woolf's Hot Flashes Against Ageism – Challenges for Cinema', in *Virginia Woolf and Her Influences*, ed. Jeanette McVickers and Laura Davies (New York: Pace University Press, 1998), p. 26.

86. Another example being:

> How she had got through life on the few twigs of knowledge Fräulein Daniels gave them she could not think. She knew nothing; no language, no history; she scarcely read a book now, except memoirs in bed [. . .] Her only gift was knowing people almost by instinct. (*MD* 9)

87. 'Virginia Woolf's Idea of a Party', in *The Modernist Party*, ed. Kate McLoughlin (Edinburgh: Edinburgh University Press, 2013), pp. 106–07.

88. *Declining to Decline: Cultural Combat and the Politics of the Midlife* (Charlottesville and London: University Press of Virginia, 1997), pp. 181–83.

89. '"The journey, not the arrival, matters" – Virginia Woolf and Ageing', *Journal of Aging, Humanities, and the Arts*, 1.3–4 (2007), p. 181.

90. '*Mrs Dalloway* and the Social System', p. 72.

91. For example: Bonnie Kime Scott, 'The Word Split Its Husk: Woolf's Double Vision of Modernist Language', *Modern Fiction Studies*, 34.3 (1988), p. 378; Kimberly Engdahl Coates, 'Virginia Woolf's Queer Time and Place: Wartime London and a World Aslant', in *Queer Bloomsbury*, ed. Brenda Helt and Madelyn Detloff (Edinburgh: Edinburgh University Press, 2016), pp. 283–84.

92. Mosse, 'Shell-Shock as a Social Disease', *Journal of Contemporary History*, 35.1 (2000), pp. 102, 103.

93. Higonnet, 'Suicide: Representations of the Feminine in the Nineteenth Century', *Poetics Today*, 6.1/2 (1985), p. 104.

94. *Women's Identities at War*, p. 2.

95. *A Woman and the War* (London: Chapman & Hall, 1916), pp. v, 131.

96. 'The Female Victims of the War in *Mrs Dalloway*', pp. 151–52.

97. *Virginia Woolf and Fascism* (Basingstoke: Palgrave Macmillan, 2001), p. 8. This is a rather surprising reference given that Mussolini only came into power in 1922 and Woolf does not mention his pronatalism in her writing until *A Room* in 1929 (or in her letters or diary until 1933).

98. 'Tonal Cues and Uncertain Values', p. 265.

99. For more on fertility imagery within the play, see David Kaula, 'The Time Sense of *Antony and Cleopatra*', *Shakespeare Quarterly*, 15.3 (1964), p. 212.

100. 'Erotic Irony and Polarity in *Antony and Cleopatra*', *Shakespeare Quarterly*, 24.3 (1973), p. 270.

101. Virginia Woolf, *Mrs Dalloway* (New York: Harcourt, 2002), p. 186. Due to last-minute editing this line was not included in the British (Hogarth Press) first edition of *Mrs Dalloway* but can be found in the American (Harcourt, Brace) first edition, both of which were published simultaneously. The British version reads: 'She felt glad that he had done it; thrown it away while they went on living' (204). For more on the two versions' differences see E. F. Shields, 'The American Edition of *Mrs Dalloway*', *Studies in Bibliography*, 27 (1974), pp. 171–72.

102. Christine Froula has explored the concept of 'thinking as fighting' among Bloomsbury group members ('*Bloomsbury Avant-Garde*', p. 5).

103. '"Everything tended to set itself in a garden"', p. 49.

104. Elizabeth Hirsh also discusses this symbolism in 'Mrs Dalloway's Menopause', pp. 77–78.

105. 'Tonal Cues and Uncertain Values', pp. 253–54.

106. *Modernism and Eugenics* pp. 52–53. Septimus also appears to have an interest in eugenics. Woolf records him 'devouring [. . .] Darwin, [. . .] and Bernard Shaw' (*MD* 93), both key reading for lay eugenicists.

107. Committee of Enquiry into 'Shell-Shock', 'Report of the War Office Committee of Enquiry into "Shell-Shock"' (London: War Office, 1922), p. 95.

108. The 1920 War Office Committee of Enquiry into 'shell-shock' involved two of Woolf's specialists, Maurice Craig (as one of the committee members), and Henry Head (as a witness).

Chapter 2

Motherhood and Eugenics

Introduction

In April 1928, during an intimate dinner, John Maynard Keynes explained to Virginia Woolf that: 'There are two royal stocks in England [. . .] from which all intellect descends' (*D3* 181). Recording the dinner in her diary, Woolf presented these thoughts as a mark of Keynes's 'remarkable mind', which was, 'working always, on Russia, Bolshevists, glands, genealogies' (*D3* 181). Keynes was director of the Eugenics Society from 1937 to 1944, and the eugenic nature of his comment is characteristic both of his beliefs and of its time. Its sympathetic reception by Woolf is also not unusual, for she was open to eugenic ideas, sometimes adopting them for her own literary purposes. Woolf and Keynes accepted their intellectual superiority, embracing a shared membership of the society they were discussing, but a shadow hung over their eugenic profiles because neither had children. Since 'breeding' strong, healthy children was a key tenet of every branch of the eugenics community, society's acceptance of eugenic principles would compel Woolf to find some other way to validate her reproductive choices and bequeath her talent. She achieved this by repurposing eugenics; turning it into a theory of literary legacy that used reproductive models to explain how canons are created.

In recent years the topic of eugenics has gained attention among Woolf scholars, with Donald Childs arguing that:

> In Woolf's case, the language of eugenics moves from conversations in the consulting rooms and at the dinner tables of her doctors into both her fiction and, ultimately, her feminist theorization of woman's imagination in *A Room of One's Own*.

Childs uses textual and biographical evidence to support his claim that Woolf was supportive of both positive and negative eugenics.[1]

By contrast, David Bradshaw claims that 'Woolf *satirizes* the hereditarian mindset as part of her more general opposition to patriarchy'.[2] In answer to both, Linden Peach notes that within Woolf's writings, eugenics 'constitutes part of their diverse range of contemporary cultural allusions' providing 'a discourse which assisted Woolf's thinking about heredity' and a 'vocabulary which Woolf employed occasionally unquestioningly and sometimes critically'.[3] This chapter will attempt to further elucidate these nuances, focusing on eugenics not as a single, unified school of thought but as a collection of different – sometimes antagonistic – doctrines. It will help to clarify Woolf's relationship with eugenics by taking a closer look at the figures in her life who supported, or disputed, eugenic thought.

Part of the reason that scholars have disagreed on Woolf's relationship with eugenics is because of the multiplicity of eugenic beliefs, with Richard Overy describing the movement as 'a broad church whose congregation sang loudly if discordantly'.[4] This allowed Woolf to internalise and expound certain aspects of the doctrine while simultaneously treating the Eugenics Society, and its reliance on traditionalist patriarchal structures, with characteristic irony. But interpreting Woolf's rejection of certain factions of the eugenics movement as an unequivocal rejection of eugenics itself is to dismiss unorthodox voices such as Marie Stopes and her American counterpart Margaret Sanger, leaders of the birth control movement, a lobby based on eugenic principles that drove an immense and enduring social revolution. This alternate type of 'feminist eugenics' concentrated on the emancipation of women, and its influence over Woolf merits recognition.[5]

Eugenic theory was never purely abstract. Whether it manifested as science or was used within birth control rhetoric, it was always a hypothesis upon which a large number of people wanted to build a social model for birthing humans. Thus it is of no surprise that when Woolf engages with eugenics, issues of motherhood appear. Eugenics are notably present in *Night and Day*, written after the Woolfs had decided not to have children, and in *A Room of One's Own*, where Woolf appropriates Stopes's emphasis on the part that ideal parents play in the creation of ideal babies, and translates it seamlessly into her directive on the hereditary dynamics involved in producing ideal texts.

'A sample of heredity': Leslie and Virginia Stephen

The popularity of eugenics was coincident with Woolf's life so that, by the time she was writing, it had become an important civic science, deeply entrenched within the medical profession and influential

88   *Virginia Woolf and Motherhood*

over parliamentary policy. The term 'eugenics' was coined in 1883 by Charles Darwin's cousin Frances Galton and, in an era when science was becoming popularised, his theories quickly captured the public's interest, remaining prevalent until WW2 when the Nazis extreme use of eugenic principles caused it to fall from public favour. In the Victorian era, family had become the epicentre of British culture and Galton formulated his ideas for eugenics when thinking about talented people not as individuals but rather as products of a gifted lineage or family group. His research, as noted by Woolf in *Night and Day*, attempted:

> to prove that intellect is a possession which can be tossed from one member of a certain group to another almost indefinitely, and with apparent certainty that the brilliant gift will be safely caught and held by nine out of ten of the privileged race. (*ND* 26)

Galton was also interested in how to propagate mental or physical ability and speculated on how humans could be bred like animals, and selected 'to produce a highly-gifted race of men by judicious marriages during several consecutive generations'.[6]

The first and largest eugenics organisation in Britain was the Eugenics Education Society (EES), which was formed in 1907, renamed the Eugenics Society in 1924, and reached a peak in paid membership during the early 1930s. Initially, Galton and his Society were interested in so-called positive eugenics – promoting unions between 'fit' individuals and inspiring them to have additional children. However, as they grew in influence British eugenicists began to embrace the negative eugenics that could be seen in America and other parts of Europe. This meant reducing the birth rate in what were considered 'undesirable' parts of society, segregating the mentally ill and advocating for legal sterilisation of those who were judged beyond cure. Consequently, the Society backed a variety of public policies: standardisation in the definition and treatment of the mentally ill, greater powers to institutionalise (and thus suppress) the 'unfit', welfare and healthcare for young families, compulsory instruction in eugenic hygiene and pre-marital counselling. Influential eugenicists disagreed about the technical aspects of how inheritance worked and how to go about achieving their aims. For example, when Galton died in 1911 a quarrel erupted between his protégé Karl Pearson, who continued to promote and study Galton's 'biometrics', and the Eugenics Society, which expressed a preference for Mendelian genetics.[7] Despite these clashes, eugenics thrived, with significant reductions in child mortality arguably being one of the most important legacies of this era. Along with war, feminism and the labour movement, eugenics was influential during a period when the structure of society was rapidly changing. Consequently, it was one of the lenses through which Woolf viewed society and her place in it, contemplating eugenic ideas in her work and using eugenic language to describe her fictional worlds.

Hereditary theory was an intrinsic part of Woolf's general consciousness. Indeed, when she was born her godfather James Russell Lowell sent the family a poem bearing the sentiment: 'I simply wish the child to be, A sample of heredity'.[8] Julia Stephen came from a family renowned for their beauty and Leslie boasted an intellectual ancestry that attracted the interest of Galton himself. In 1869 the Stephen family was included in *Hereditary Genius*, Galton's foremost book on pedigree, which catalogued outstanding contributors to various social institutions such as government, science, the arts or law.[9] Woolf's great-grandfather, grandfather, great-uncle, father and uncle are listed in the chapter 'Literary Men'. As the heir to the family's literary legacy, the young Virginia Stephen grew up in the shadow of these 'men of genius' and their pedigree was a mainstay of the ancestral stories that fabricated her identity. As *Night and Day*'s semi-autobiographical heroine observes; 'The quality of her birth oozed into Katharine's consciousness from a dozen different sources as soon as she was able to perceive anything' (*ND* 27). This 'quality' was part of Woolf's ontology; it informed her understanding of her biology, intellectual capacity and place in society – as Hermione Lee notes 'it was a powerful ingredient [. . .] in her definition of herself'[10] – yet Woolf also questioned the notion of 'genius in the Victorian sense' because it was a classification reserved almost exclusively for men who 'were like the prophets' (*MB* 118). Woman, on the other hand, had so many domestic duties that she could 'never get her genius expressed whole and entire' (*AROO* 63). While Woolf was familiar with the concept of heritability and interested in the social context of Darwinian evolution (and the inevitable change and momentum this implied) she was averse to Galton's rigid patriarchal Victorianism, an ideology that endeavoured only to conserve the status quo. Her views were most likely influenced by Leslie Stephen, who wrote a good deal about the social implications of evolutionary theory, but was wary of the emerging hereditary science that would become Galtonian eugenics.

In the introduction to *The Science of Ethics* – Stephen's book on the 'philosophy of evolution' published the year Woolf was born – he acknowledged 'the great intellectual debt' he owed to Darwin and the

Origin of Species.[11] In accordance with this statement Katherine Hill finds that Stephen was 'one of the first English thinkers to embrace and support Darwin's discoveries'. Hill notes that 'Evolution is [. . .] the cornerstone of Stephen's system of thought', not only in *The Science of Ethics* – but in 'other philosophical works' such as 1904's *English Literature and Society in the Eighteenth Century*.[12] An important tract to add to this list is 'Heredity', a paper that Stephen gave in the winter of 1894/5 to the Ethical Societies of London, and later published as part of his book *Social Rights and Duties*. Woolf inherited both *The Science of Ethics* and *Social Rights and Duties* from her father and they remained in the Woolfs' library until Leonard's death.[13] The former was a particularly meaningful text, with Woolf noting in a letter that although Stephen's *History of English Thought* 'is generally felt to be his most important work [. . .] he told me that he was most interested himself in *The Science of Ethics*' (E5 591). Since the subject of heredity was of personal interest to Woolf that it seems likely that she was familiar with her father's views. Indeed, the similarities between Stephen's convictions and her own further suggest that his thoughts went some way towards shaping hers.

The Science of Ethics* was Stephen's first attempt at applying evolutionary theory to human ethics. It expresses serious concerns about pseudo-scientific hereditary theory and its departure from Darwinian logic. Using such headings as 'Imperfection of science generally', 'Hopeless complexity of the problem of individual conduct' and 'Even average conduct too complex for calculation', the book presents a compelling argument against the impractical, idealistic aspects of Galton's ideals, noting that for the eugenic 'man of Science':

> Progress means approximation to some utopia in which our natures will be so improved that we shall always sympathise with each other, and society be so happily constituted that the conduct which gives to any man the greatest chance of happiness will give it an equal advantage to his neighbours. Such speculations are legitimate. They may be useful in defining an end towards which all well-wishers to their fellows may desire to act [. . .] Yet it does not solve the difficulty for us. Speculations about the future of society are rash [. . .] Progress means a stage of evolution. Evolution from the earliest to the latest stages means a continuous process of adjustment, which is always determined by the fact that at any existing stage the adjustment is imperfect. Complete equilibrium [. . .] would therefore mean, not perhaps stagnation, but a cessation of progress, an attainment of the highest arc of the curve, after which we would only expect descent.[14]

Stephen observes that in their pursuit of primacy, hereditary scientists abandoned common sense. Their utopian plots adopted the rationale of philosophers, theologians and artists, but from an empirical standpoint evolution could have no idyllic end point and neither could humanity.

'Heredity' goes on to question the significance of new discoveries about inheritance. Referencing Galton, it looks at the dangerous rhetoric surrounding early eugenic theory and argues that scientific progress should not lead men to assume that they are doomed to a genetic fate. Stephen reasons that, no matter his disposition, man has accountability for his actions, responsibility to better himself and an obligation to create opportunities for others through education and employment. He ends the address by observing an 'undeniable fact':

> that the difference between a civilised man and a barbarian, between the highest types of modern life and the apparently irreclaimable brutes who are exhibited in our police-courts, is not dependent upon the mark of the beast irreclaimably fixed upon them at their birth; but to certain later influences, which may or may not be brought to bear upon them effectually [. . .] I think that the doctrine of heredity is sometimes interpreted in such a way as to suggest the hopelessness or at least the extreme difficulty of introducing any sensible improvement within any limited time; and what I have tried to urge is that, if properly understood, it does not in the least degree tend to justify such forebodings, or to imply that we are to abandon ourselves to a demoralising fatalism.[15]

This foregrounding of nurture situates Stephen at the beginning of a history of diverse anti-eugenic voices that included contemporaries of Woolf such as authors G. K. Chesterton and Hilaire Belloc. Pointing to the difference between empirical science and the rather public discussions of eugenics that relied heavily on rhetoric, 'Heredity' highlights the conjecture that was gathering around social Darwinism. Although eugenics was still relatively obscure, Stephen recognised that Galton and his contemporaries lacked the type of data that would lend empirical proof to their theories (something their prolific and often well-known experimentation would attempt to address).[16] This led to a reliance on selective observations and emotive social theory until eventually speculation and fear-mongering became a mainstay of the eugenics movement, strengthening it as a populist political and social force.

Though eugenics was still in its infancy, Stephen showed a considerable understanding of the dangers of the hereditary sciences.

92   *Virginia Woolf and Motherhood*

'Heredity' is an interesting opinion piece in the history of eugenic debate because, while it clearly disagreed with pre-determinism and warned against the dangers of using hereditary arguments to resolve social issues, it also advocated for the betterment of mankind through public education and welfare, principles which would, by necessity, be embraced by eugenicists in the ensuing decades. If the core principles of eugenics focused on pre-birth – conception and the production of babies – its activists also lay behind many social initiatives that sprung up in the early twentieth century. Michael Freeden has described eugenics as an example of 'the social-reformist tendencies of early-twentieth-century British political thought', and eugenicists were largely responsible for the welfare programmes that helped reduce childhood mortality. It made practical sense to improve the lifestyles of the lower classes, who made up the majority of the reproductive population, and schemes such as clean milk and mother-and-child visits allowed the working class poor to enjoy greater health and resources.[17]

Stephen's progressive philosophical discussions embrace the concept of social evolution while criticising Galton's theories. These opinions are echoed in Woolf's writing, which explores social progress while also taking a cynical view of the material advantages of good birth, thus disrupting socio-scientific theories. Stephen's thoughts on these issues paved the way for Woolf to take an interest in the arguments that played out in the eugenic arena, while granting her the confidence to mock those she found blinkered or self-serving. Laid out during Woolf's – and the eugenic movement's – earliest years, his ideas were part of a wider context that led his daughter to question heredity so keenly that she wrote *Night and Day*, and later *A Room of One's Own*, to unravel her intellectual inheritance and explore the place of modernity in a world of hereditary theory. These works use maternal metaphors, substituting books for babies as a way of influencing and evolving culture and thus society.

Woolf's Doctors and the Question of Babies

To further understand how eugenics shape themes of motherhood in Woolf's works it is necessary to review her treatment by doctors that, in the words of *Mrs Dalloway*, 'forbade childbirth, penalised despair' (*MD* 109). As a newly married woman Woolf was at the centre of – although perhaps not fully engaged in – a debate over her own reproductive future. This debate occurred just as eugenic values were being institutionalised within the medical community and catching the public's imagination. In the summer of 1912, less than a fortnight before Leonard and Virginia were married, London hosted the First International Eugenics Congress. In the following years the Woolfs would consult several eugenic doctors (including Congress attendees T. B. Hyslop and George Savage), not only on the question of whether Virginia should have children but also on her treatment during the traumatic and prolonged breakdown that followed this decision.[18]

Both before and after their marriage Leonard visited a series of mental health specialists to discuss the question of children. In his autobiography he recalled:

> We both wanted to have children, but the more I saw the dangerous effect of any strain or stress upon her, the more I began to doubt whether she would be able to stand the strain and stress of childbearing. I went and consulted Sir George Savage; he brushed my doubts aside. But now my doubts about Sir George Savage were added to my doubts about Virginia's health. There seemed to be more of a man of the world ('Do her a world of good, my dear fellow, do her a world of good!') in his opinion than of the mental specialist. So I went off and consulted two other well known doctors, Maurice Craig and T. B. Hyslop, and also the lady who ran the mental nursing home where Virginia had several times stayed. They confirmed my fears and were strongly against her having children. We followed their advice.[19]

Frederic Spotts notes that Leonard's diary and correspondence confirm that he consulted specialists in a somewhat different order to the one he recalled:

> he first saw Dr Maurice Craig [. . .] and Jean Thomas, proprietor of the nursing home where Virginia had stayed during earlier breakdowns. Both considered it too risky. He later consulted Dr Maurice Wright [. . .] and George Savage [. . .] They were in favour. And finally he spoke to Dr T. B. Hyslop [. . .] who advised putting off a decision for eighteen months.[20]

Roger Poole is one of several scholars who suggest that Leonard's decision may have been motivated by the 'popular belief, among certain circles of eugenics theorists, that people with histories (or family histories) of mental disease should not be allowed to have children'.[21] This argument is not substantiated by Leonard, whose writing on the subject only mentions his concerns for Woolf's health and not the effect on any potential children. However, in addition to

94 Virginia Woolf and Motherhood

Virginia's breakdowns, Leonard had been declared unfit for military service (by Drs Craig and Wright) because of a tremor which was severe enough that:

> When he drank tea or coffee, or a glass of wine, he would arrange a handkerchief or table napkin carefully round the back of his neck and draw the cup or glass up to his lips to avoid slopping the contents on his hostess's damask cloth.[22]

There was also the question of racial mixing, with Leonard's Judaism marking him out as 'other' to his group of intellectual friends. However, it is difficult to say whether this actually played into his decision. *Hereditary Genius* is in praise of Jews 'who appear to be rich in families of high intellectual breeds', and other eugenic voices such as Sidney Webb – with whom Leonard had both social and professional associations – did not disapprove of Jews procreating as long as their numbers stayed proportional to the general population.[23] Virginia did seem to draw links between her own mental instability and Leonard's 'otherness' – in a pre-engagement letter outlining her hopes and fears about marriage, her concerns moved swiftly from one to the other: 'Possibly, your being a Jew comes in also at this point. You seem so foreign. And then I am fearfully unstable' (*L1* 496). However she did not reject the idea of children because of Leonard's religion, just as she did not reject motherhood because of her own mental illness.[24]

Whether Leonard's decision was eugenic in nature or not, his clinicians' opinions were unavoidably so. Poole observes that T. B. Hyslop in particular was a hard-line eugenicist and notes 'it was to him, precisely, that Leonard went to get a medical opinion on the advisability of Virginia having children'[25] Hyslop, a campaigner for the 1913 Mental Deficiency Act, could be fanatical – in 1905 he gave a paper at the 73rd Annual Meeting of the British Medical Association in which he asserted,

> the removal of woman from her natural sphere of domesticity to that of mental labour not only renders her less fit to maintain the virility of the race, but it renders her prone to degenerate and initiate a downward trend which gathers impetus in her progeny [. . .] the more our women aspire to exercising their nervous and mental functions so they become not only less virile, but also less capable of generating healthy stock. Now not only is this a question concerning the virility of the race, but it has very direct bearings upon the

increase of nervous instability. In fact, the higher women strive to hold the torch of intellect, the dimmer the rays of light for the vision of their progeny.[26]

Hyslop's opinions did not go unchallenged; even at the meeting they elicited a number of questioning responses, with some contemporaries finding his 'general strictures' on women too severe.[27] Nonetheless these views were well within the boundaries of what was both acceptable and respectable within the medical profession.

All of Woolf's psychiatrists held eugenic opinions on reproduction. In 1910, in a paper entitled 'Discussion on Insanity and Marriage', George Savage attempted to define who should be prevented from marrying and reproducing. In lieu of 'practical legislation' Savage offers some advice on 'which marriage should be hindered or prevented' noting with particular relevance to Woolf, that although:

> certain persons who have suffered from a degree of mental disorder which may be classed as insanity may yet recover and marry with no real increase of risk to their partner or their children [. . .] In no case should it be allowed where there is a history of periodical recurrences, and it is certain that there is very grave risk in those cases of adolescents who at puberty and with adolescence have periods of depression and buoyancy.[28]

Savage treated Woolf from her childhood until her marriage; he was responsible for her care for her first three breakdowns and he knew that she had manic symptoms recurring from puberty. Why then did he declare that marriage and children would: 'Do her a world of good'?[29] Indeed, looking at Spotts's note it seems that all of Woolf's doctors were more open to the idea of Woolf having children than Leonard later recalled. Hyslop only recommended 'putting off a decision for eighteen months' by which time Virginia was in the depths of what is widely recognised as her most severe breakdown and a pregnancy could no longer be considered.

It is interesting to reflect on why a group of eugenic doctors might have encouraged the Woolfs – a man with a tremor and a woman with a recurrent mental illness – to have a child. To begin with, negative eugenics were largely directed towards the working class, and class dictated much of how Savage, Hyslop and Craig diagnosed and treated Woolf. When he first saw her as a teenager Savage diagnosed Woolf with neurasthenia, an illness identified in the 1860s by George Miller Beard as, 'frequently associated with superior intellect, and with

96   *Virginia Woolf and Motherhood*

a strong and active emotional nature [. . .] the civilized, refined, and educated, rather than of the barbarous and low-born and untrained'.[30] In a 1911 article in *The Medical Magazine*, Savage described neurasthenia as a diverse set of symptoms that inhabited the mysterious mental terrain between health and mental illness. The diagnosis was a way to label without stigmatising, a wonderful tool for his upper-class patients and a word that had, Savage noted, 'been a great comfort both to doctors and to the friends of patients'.[31] The breadth of this catch-all diagnosis even allowed Savage to recommend childbearing to Woolf despite stating, in 'Insanity and Marriage', that he 'would speak equally strongly against marriage as relief for so-called neurasthenia'.[32]

In addition, Woolf was a writer, a career considered appropriate for women and not considered mental labour in the same vein as science, politics or law. As the descendant of those great men of letters featured in *Hereditary Genius*, Woolf's doctors may have considered her genes worthy of handing down, and may have worried that not enough women of her intellect and class were reproducing. Indeed, Galton asserted that women from 'eminent' families were only half as likely to bear children as ordinary women, partly ascribing this to the fact that,

> the aunts, sisters, and daughters of eminent men do not marry, on the average, so frequently as other women. They would be likely not to marry so much or so soon as other women, because they would be accustomed to a higher form of culture and intellectual and moral tone in their family circle, than they could easily find elsewhere [. . .] one portion of them would certainly be of a dogmatic and self-asserting type, and therefore unattractive to men, and others would fail to attract, owing to their having shy, odd manners, often met with in young persons of genius, which are disadvantageous to the matrimonial chances of young women.[33]

Given eugenic fears about the reduced birth rate in Woolf's class, and the 'eminent' status of her family, there would have needed to be a degree of certainty that childbearing would prove dangerous to keep her doctors from recommending it.

Woolf's excitability could also be attributed directly to her talents since it was commonly held that madness was related to genius. As Galton notes:

> there is a large residuum of evidence which points to a painfully close relation between the two [. . .] I have been surprised at finding how

often insanity or idiocy has appeared among the near relatives of exceptionally able men. Those who are over eager and extremely active in mind must often possess brains that are more excitable and peculiar than is consistent with soundness. They are likely to become crazy at times, and perhaps to break down altogether.[34]

This belief that madness and genius were somehow linked was more than just a widely held notion, it was a personal conviction. Writing about Woolf in his autobiography, Leonard quotes Dryden's *Absalom and Achitophel*: 'Great wits are sure to madness near allied'.[35] And Virginia saw an innate connection between her hereditary nervous illness and her family's literary talents – a judgement that makes yet more sense in light of Thomas Caramagno's assertion that Savage had given Leslie the same clinical diagnosis of neurasthenia.[36] In 1930, when Woolf was feeling unwell with one of the many ailments she associated with her condition, she wrote to Ethel Smyth:

But – oh damn these medical details! – this influenza has a special poison for what is called the nervous system; and mine being a second hand one, used by my father and his father to dictate dispatches and write books with – how I wish they had hunted and fished instead! – I have to treat it like a pampered pug dog, and lie still directly my head aches [. . .] To think that my father's philosophy and the Dictionary of National Biography cost me this! (*L4* 144–45)

Woolf clearly felt that her forefathers' writing had exacerbated her poor mental health like some sort of acquired characteristic, but it also came attached to a talent she could devote her life to, something that frequently saved her from the distress of not having children and repeatedly made her question whether motherhood was right for her. And since neurasthenia affected both genders equally, Woolf's diagnosis helped confirm that her literary prowess, as a complement to her illness, came down to her through the masculine line. Accordingly, her doctors treated her with a sense of sensitivity to her brilliance. In the midst of her 1913 breakdown Dr Maurice Wright wrote to Leonard: 'It is terribly sad to see so fine a mind as Mrs Woolf's lose balance, but I do hope time & rest will restore the stability again'.[37]

It is unclear how much involvement Woolf had in the decision not to have a baby. Her doctors met and corresponded with Leonard, and it does not appear that she discussed it with Jean Thomas, whom she sometimes saw socially. In early 1913, Vanessa wrote to both Woolfs about the subject. In her letter to Leonard she was ambiguous, at first

98 *Virginia Woolf and Motherhood*

agreeing with his decision, noting 'I had for some time been thinking so more and more definitely myself', but then adding that a baby might be possible if Virginia avoided excitement, and finally concluding: 'I think on the whole almost any amount of temporary boredom *is* worthwhile for the sake of having children'. To Virginia she wrote 'I expect on the whole by waiting a bit and being careful enough you could have one with very little risk [. . .] Jean told me she thought it very likely that a baby would be very good for you', and later 'I shouldn't worry about the baby question. One can never really settle these matters beforehand [. . .] I wonder why Leonard has gradually come to think child bearing so dangerous'.[38] Leonard may have been less than forthright with Woolf, who, in April 1913, wrote to Violet Dickinson: 'We aren't going to have a baby, but we want to have one, and 6 months in the country or so is said to be necessary first' (*L2* 23). Nonetheless he never wavered in his decision to avoid children. Perhaps he even saw it as a necessary evil to protect her intellect – which he greatly respected and valued – rather than merely seeing her as the potential mother of a male genius. Hermione Lee suggests the anger that Woolf exhibited towards Leonard during her subsequent breakdown was due to his decision, but if Woolf held Leonard culpable for their not having children her writing shows little evidence of it. Instead, she blamed herself – 'my own fault' (*D5* 107) – and her doctors.[39] Through *Mrs Dalloway*'s Septimus Smith, Woolf angrily fictionalised her treatment by doctors whose negative eugenics 'forbade childbirth'. Woolf and Septimus share not only a diagnosis but also a treatment plan – 'rest in bed; rest in solitude; silence and rest; rest without friends, without books, without messages; six months' rest' (*MD* 108). Layne Parish Craig has observed that this six-month rest enforces a separation that blocks Septimus and his wife Rezia from conceiving a child.[40] Septimus's recommended six months of sexual separation in 'a delightful home down in the country' (*MD* 106) also bears a striking resemblance to the '6 months in the country' Woolf mentioned to Dickinson.

'The life which they had given her': The Genetic Inheritance of Katharine Hilbery

Though Woolf's mental health would go on to be stable for long periods of time Leonard did not change his mind about whether they should have children. This state of affairs added impetus to Woolf's exploration of what it meant to remain child-free – especially in a world where eugenics and heredity were prominent. Maternal metaphors were a useful tool in this inquiry and they can be seen in *Night and Day*, a book written in the aftermath of Leonard's decision and Woolf's breakdown. Traditional eugenic theory is prominent in *Night and Day*. Early on in the novel protagonist Katharine Hilbery is accused 'of belonging to one of the most distinguished families in England, and if any one will take the trouble to consult Mr Galton's 'Hereditary Genius,' he will find that this assertion is not far from the truth' (*ND* 26). Woolf's use of *Hereditary Genius* offers a quick and comprehensive indication of Katharine's station and shows how much Galton's list of 'eminent' people had entered public awareness. In keeping with Leslie Stephen's rejection of eugenics, Galton's analysis is immediately subverted:

> English society being what it is, no very great merit is required, once you bear a well-known name, to put you into a position where it is easier on the whole to be eminent than obscure. And if this is true of the sons, even the daughters, even in the nineteenth century, are apt to become people of importance – philanthropists and educationalists if they are spinsters, and the wives of distinguished men if they marry. (*ND* 26)

Woolf's exposé of this society shows her dislike of Galton's gender bias.[41] It is as a member of this society – where female roles are limited by values that both come from the past and are maintained by modern 'science' – that Katharine must make the central decision of the novel's romantic plot, who and indeed whether to marry.

The Hilberys live a cosseted existence, perpetuating a status quo based on nepotistic principles:

> The Hilberys, as the saying is, 'knew every one,' and that arrogant claim was certainly upheld by the number of houses which, within a certain area, lit their lamps at night, opened their doors after 3 p.m., and admitted the Hilberys to their dining-rooms, say, once a month. An indefinable freedom and authority of manner, shared by most of the people who lived in these houses, seemed to indicate that whether it was a question of art, music, or government, they were well within the gates, and could smile indulgently at the vast mass of humanity which is forced to wait and struggle, and pay for entrance with common coin at the door. (*ND* 309)

Born into knowledge, taste and policy-making, Woolf's characters silently collude with the pseudo-scientific establishment while the 'vast mass of humanity' is kept shut out. Under these circumstances

100 *Virginia Woolf and Motherhood*

Galtonian eugenics offers not a logical, scientific explanation for the social strata, but a tool to maintain them. Michael Bulmer notes that Galton was aware that objections might be levelled against his work because it dealt with persons of social and material advantage, and argued that:

> By restricting his attention to the open professions of literature and science, as contrasted with the more closed professions of statesman-ship and generalship [. . .] he had excluded the effect of social position and had isolated the effect of heredity in this calculation.[42]

The deep irony with which Woolf treats Galton in *Night and Day* shows that she did not agree with this claim. Although it is important to note that despite its denunciation of Galton, *Night and Day* does not reject hereditary science outright, but engages with and examines it.

As the only grandchild of Richard Alardyce – a man so monumental that he is signified throughout the novel as simply 'the poet' (*ND* 27) – Katharine's heritage is more 'eminent' than most. Woolf based Alardyce on Leslie Stephen's first father-in-law, William Makepeace Thackeray.[43] Where members of the Stephen family were writers of note, Thackeray was canonical. This exceptional heritage is a boon *and* a disadvantage to Katharine, who is 'the companion of those giant men, of their own lineage' (*ND* 9), while also finding that:

> The glorious past, in which men and women grew to unexampled size, intruded too much upon the present, and dwarfed it too consistently, to be altogether encouraging to one forced to make her experiment in living when the great age was dead. (*ND* 29)

This complicated version of heredity is a rich vein of enquiry for the novel. As with Woolf, who questioned what it meant to be the carrier of a literary talent that had predominantly favoured the men in her family, Katharine is a young woman grappling with making her mark, searching the legacy of her ancestors and her 'share in the life which they had given her, the life which they had lived' (*ND* 272). By changing Katharine's passion from the family trade of literature to mathematics and astronomy, Woolf is able to question the true nature of an intellect that changes profoundly as it randomly skips generations and genders. In addition, Katharine's gifts are impeded by persistent nineteenth-century attitudes that limit her academic pursuits. As the live-at-home daughter of an educated man – that 'very great profession which has, as yet, no title and very little recognition' (*ND* 33) – writing is permitted but access to mathematics is checked.[44] Both

Katharine's hereditary status and her desire for intellectual freedom are the driving factors behind her romantic decisions and add impetus to the novel's marriage plot.

Love and Eugenics in Gardens: *Night and Day* at Kew and the Zoo

Night and Day's interest in the hereditary science and the related fields of botany and ethology, is both serious and mocking, a fact illustrated by Mary Datchet's amusement when she discovers that Ralph Denham is a keen amateur hereditarian. Like Galton, Ralph knows 'as much about breeding bulldogs as any man in England and has 'a collection of wild flowers found near London'. He also regularly visits 'old Miss Trotter at Ealing, who was an authority upon the science of Heraldry' (*ND* 105).[45] Elsewhere in the novel Ralph rejects the works of anti-eugenic authors Chesterton and Belloc in favour of eugenicist George Bernard Shaw. Despite Mary's amusement, this interest does not mark Ralph out as a disagreeable character. Indeed, he has the good humour to join in with Mary's laughter. More generally, his curiosity regarding the hereditary sciences (like Woolf's) translates into an interest in the levelling potential of social Darwinism, and Ralph endeavours, though not always successfully, to conduct egalitarian friendships with women. There are interpretations of *Night and Day* that dispute this reading of Ralph's character, nonetheless this chapter agrees with Ian Blyth when he calls Ralph an 'outsider' who cultivates 'a studied "indifference" to the conventions of family and social life', and aspires to 'somehow find a way of "living differently"'.[46] I would build on this argument by suggesting that the reader is shown repeatedly how, despite his human fallibility, Ralph is interested in the mechanics of friendship between men and women. For example, he thinks deeply about how he should speak with Mary, the result being that while generally:

> she was accustomed to find young men very ready to talk about themselves, and had come to listen to them as one listens to children, without any thought of herself [. . .] with Ralph, she had very little of this maternal feeling, and, in consequence, a much keener sense of her own individuality. (*ND* 106)

With no role models to follow and no clear understanding of the relationship between love and marriage (something held in common between all of the novel's characters) Ralph is unsure of how

102   *Virginia Woolf and Motherhood*

to conduct this friendship. He frequently thinks about what he can share with Mary, and he proposes to her without really meaning it. Nonetheless, as a man who wants to explore truth and reality with all of his acquaintances regardless of gender, Ralph is different from those characters Woolf based on her father, men who needed women to be – like Patmore's 'Angel' – 'intensely sympathetic', 'immensely charming' and 'utterly unselfish' (*E6* 480). This interaction is also fascinating for its glimpse into Mary's 'maternal feeling', a theme that will be discussed later.

Elsewhere, *Night and Day* proves how conversant Woolf was with the hereditary sciences, demonstrating an informed knowledge of Galton and Darwin with direct references to some of their better-known experiments. There are scenes set at Kew Gardens and London Zoo – both sites for experiments by Galton. Through the satire which is one of the formal aspects of the text, Woolf uses these scenes as opportunities to contrast the realities of human courting behaviour with theories of eugenic breeding, theories which, at their core, supposed human relations could be modelled on plant and animal reproduction. At Kew Ralph teaches Katharine how plants are:

> in the first instance, bulbs or seeds, and later, living things endowed with sex, and pores, and susceptibilities which adapted themselves by all manner of ingenious devices to live and beget life, and could be fashioned squat or tapering, flame-coloured or pale, pure or spotted, by processes which might reveal the secrets of human existence. (*ND* 281)

Woolf was aware of botany's relevance to eugenics. Aside from having a keen mind and eclectic interests, she was directly connected to this world through Leonard's brother-in-law, the influential botanist Robert Heath Lock, whose popular textbook *Recent Progress in the Study of Variation, Heredity, and Evolution*, was one of the first to cover Mendelian inheritance and eugenics.[47] Many biologists believed that experiments in plant breeding were the best tool they had for expounding the human reproductive process. Sweet peas found particular favour because of their relatively short life cycles and the ease with which scientists could select for individual characteristics. With no time to follow sufficient consecutive generations of humans, floral experimentation was used to provide more immediate insight into the transmission of hereditary attributes. Indeed, when Darwin suggested that Galton work with sweet peas in the 1870s, the resulting experimental crops were grown both at Kew, and in Darwin's own garden.[48]

While welcoming advances in scientific knowledge, critics of eugenics pointed out the absurdity in directly equating plant and human reproduction. In 1914 H. Fielding-Hall wrote in *The Atlantic*:

> Man's body has developed in many thousands of years from being an animal, and in many ten thousands of years from being a plant; [. . .] There seems no objection to Eugenists classing themselves with cabbages and dogs and cats, but does the rest of the world accept this for itself?[49]

In *Night and Day* Woolf puts forward a similar case. While Katharine is fascinated when Ralph describes to her 'how science felt not quite blindly for the law that ruled their endless variations', she also observes how: 'A law that might be inscrutable but was certainly omnipotent appealed to her at the moment, because she could find nothing like it in possession of human lives' (ND 281). While Katharine wants to believe in this scientific fairy-tale, she is sceptical because

> Circumstances had long forced her, as they force most women in the flower of youth, to consider, painfully and minutely, all that part of life which is conspicuously without order; she had had to consider moods and wishes, degrees of liking or disliking, and their effect upon the destiny of people dear to her. (*ND* 281)

Katharine's reservation about hereditary science's bold use of botany ties in with Woolf's unique feminism. Quite apart from the disparity between human and plant lives, Katharine's criticism of Galton's eugenic ideology is that it has been envisioned by a pair of male eyes. The order sought and imposed by patriarchal science has little to do with the domestic lives of young women, which proceed according to a set of highly evolved and intricately wrought social contracts that no amount of botany could ever begin to untangle.[50] Galton's assumption that 'the secrets of human existence' could be determined by the knowledge gleaned from growing and counting crops of sweet peas and then delineated by a set of fractions and equations seems especially inane when contrasted with Katharine's own abstract (almost mystical) mathematics, a science that resolutely 'hasn't got to do with human beings' (*ND* 163).

Night and Day does not simply reject patriarchal, eugenic ideology, instead the novel makes a much more dynamic move by proposing its

104 Virginia Woolf and Motherhood

own theory of social evolution. Focusing on mating and marriage, this alternative to eugenics still separates society into distinctive groups and suggests that these groups refrain from mixing, but in the novel these strata are determined by social characteristics – how progressive an individual's views are – rather than physical or intellectual qualities. The novel's young characters are divided into 'visionaries', capable of leading society into a new age, and 'old guards', who chose to continue under fading social rubrics. Woolf reiterates Ralph and Katharine's visionary status by imbuing their narratives with trance-like moments – moments which, Ann-Marie Priest notes, are triggered by a 'longing to escape from a socially constructed identity that is oppressive'.[51] Both characters also continually look in or out of windows seeking to see things from a new perspective. The pair encourage each other in their window gazing – the text notes that when Katharine visits Ralph, and he urges her to experience his view of London: 'The sight of her gazing from his window gave him a peculiar satisfaction' (*ND* 322).

As with a traditional social evolutionary system, social progress in the novel is threatened by mixing between the progressive and traditional groups. The seeds of this segregation can be seen in the chapter set at London Zoo, where progressive Katharine's first engagement to conservative William Rodney – 'A man naturally alive to the conventions of society' and 'strictly conventional where women were concerned' (*ND* 206–07) – is giving way to a new relationship with forward-thinking Ralph. The Zoo is a fitting place for the novel's 'love rectangle' (Ralph, William, Katharine and her cousin Cassandra Ottoway) to woo each other. In this setting human courting seems both contiguous to, but also separate from, the animals, which, within their contrived environments, create 'an atmosphere in which human beings tended to look pale and to fall silent' (*ND* 313). The Zoo's links to the hereditary sciences are overt. Cassandra chooses it as a destination because she 'had once trifled with the psychology of animals, and still knew something about inherited characteristics' (*ND* 310). These words might have caused contemporary readers to think once again of Galton – the father of behavioural genetics – who even coined the phrase 'nature and nurture'.[52]

In the setting of the Zoo, which invokes and interrogates behavioural studies, Katharine and Ralph are shown to be each other's counterpart while William finds his equal in Cassandra. Finding herself walking alone with William, Cassandra's

> manner became immediately different, as if, for the first time, she felt consciously womanly, and as if William might conceivably wish

Motherhood and Eugenics   105

later on to confide in her. She forgot all about the psychology of animals, and the recurrence of blue eyes and brown, and became instantly engrossed in her feelings as a woman who could administer consolation. (*ND* 311)

Cassandra's behaviour shows her susceptibility to becoming a domestic 'angel'. It also raises questions over why someone with scientific leanings (Cassandra is also an amateur sericulturist) might choose to participate in restrictive gender performances. In her exploration of Lepidoptera in Woolf's writing, Rachel Sarsfield has compared the symbolism of the 'lately emerged and semi-conscious' (*ND* 312) butterfly that Katharine sees at the zoo with Cassandra's silkworms, insects that die within their chrysalises. Katharine, like the butterfly, is awakening to a new world, while Cassandra is 'securely committed to the patriarchal thread which cocoons and envelops her in the past'.[53] Christina Alt argues that, by encouraging her cousin to forfeit her scientific pursuits and silkworms in favour of William, Katharine sacrifices 'Cassandra to convention [. . .] as a means of safeguarding her own independence'.[54] However, since Cassandra's scientific interests are linked directly to eugenics – like sweet pea trials, eye-colour inheritance particularly appealed to early eugenicists because it was easy to gather significant amounts of human data over several generations – it is also possible that she is predisposed to the conservative eugenic belief that a woman's principal function is procreation.[55] Indeed, Donald MacKenzie observes that women were 'highly represented in the EES [Eugenics Education Society] (forming, for example, a majority of its total members in 1913)'.[56] Given the diversity of eugenic beliefs it is perfectly possible that Cassandra and Ralph might both have an interest in heredity but divergent social values.

At the zoo, the spontaneous emotions the couples feel for each other – despite Katharine and Ralph's class differences[57] – both confirm the integrity of Woolf's pairings, and bring doubt to Galton's plan to forcibly pair off humans and 'breed' them according to the strategies of animal husbandry. The problem is not simply an innate bestiality encoded in human sexual conduct – Woolf is clear that her humans are different to the animals they observe – rather, Galton has misjudged the path of human evolution. Eugenicists cannot expect perfection according to a schema modelled on an antiquated status quo that subjugates women, instead civilisation has reached a moment where gender equality represents the next step forward. By the end of the book, William and Cassandra form a marriage where a flattering wife submits to her husband (and, one speculates, produces

106 *Virginia Woolf and Motherhood*

empire-expanding children), while Ralph and Katharine create a liberal progressive union which exerts a far greater influence over society by producing books. Woolf uses the couples as a foil against each other but her real interest lies with Katharine and Ralph, the pair she sees evolving towards a future emerging 'more splendid than ever from this construction of the present' (*ND* 432). This evolution is decidedly Darwinian; Katharine pictures William as 'a wretched misanthropical ape' (*ND* 314), while the feelings between them inhabit 'some horrible swamp of her nature where the primeval struggle between man and woman still rages' (*ND* 314). Brutish William 'isn't kind to animals', misunderstanding one 'creature's secluded disposition and nocturnal habits' (*ND* 313) as he would have misunderstood Katharine's (Cassandra acts similarly, gently prodding 'some Oriental hog [. . .] with the point of her umbrella' (*ND* 311)). Conversely, Ralph's receptive disposition, his ability to empathise, means that he treats animals and women with respect.

William is also intellectually incompatible with Katharine. Lamenting his poetic-but-talentless disposition he admits to her: 'If I could write [. . .] I shouldn't bother you to marry me then' (*ND* 52). William lacks the ability to 'do something worth while; [. . .] write a book' (*ND* 230), and so he requires a woman's body to satisfy his creative ambitions. William also believes a woman's creative potential is predicated on babies – when speaking to Katharine of marriage he states: 'Why, you're nothing at all without it; you're only half alive; using only half your faculties' (*ND* 52). This misogynistic statement recalls Galton who notes: 'there exists no criterion for a just comparison of the natural ability of the different sexes [. . .] A mother transmits masculine peculiarities to her male child, which she does not and cannot possess'.[58] For William and Galton, women are not only incapable of fully exploiting the gifts they inherited from their fathers and grandfathers, they are also compelled to reproduce to make use of their 'faculties'.

Katharine Hilbery, Ralph Denham and the Social Evolution of Marriage

Happily, Katharine *is* interested in exploring the social and hereditary impact of exercising her intellect. This investigation is tied together with *Night and Day*'s study of love, and its conclusion that a balanced heterosexual relationship with Ralph will be both mutually beneficial – fostering diligence and productivity in both – and socially progressive. Due to *Night and Day*'s tonal ambivalence, readings of this relationship vary. For example, Priest finds that:

> Katharine's fantasy of another mode of identity is re-appropriated by patriarchy through the discourse of romantic love – a discourse that seems at first to enable her to create the fluid, unconfined, reciprocal self she longs for but which turns out to be simply an expert means of returning that self to the service of patriarchy.[59]

Similarly, Julia Briggs reads 'post-romantic' cynicism in the text, noting that Woolf's ploy of 'endowing both its lovers with full subjectivity creates a potential for division and disharmony that carries with it tragic implications'.[60] Yet, other scholars have seen Katharine's movement from Rodney to Denham as an example of personal development. In the first book-length work on Woolf, Winifred Holtby perceived the marriage as a moment of self-discovery and sovereignty for both – 'the union was complete, a union not so much of a man with a woman, as of a man with himself, a woman with herself'.[61] More recently, Elizabeth Cooley has seen *Night and Day* as 'the story of a young woman's growth beyond the societal order to an individual order that allows honesty of expression and freedom for desire', wherein Katharine emerges 'not subordinate but equal to her male counterpart'.[62]

Reading Katharine and Ralph's relationship as progressive does not ignore the text's anxiety or uncertainty about love and marriage, since these are not mutually exclusive properties. A useful insight into Woolf's feelings about the novel's romantic pairs can be found in her enthusiastic response to an unsigned *TLS* review that summarised *Night and Day*'s love story in the following way:

> Could we fully understand the love affairs of William Rodney and Cassandra Otway, of Mary Datchet and Katharine Hilbery and Ralph Denham – and especially of the last two – then we should understand a great deal more than we do of the age we live in [. . .] we come to see in the mind's eye the long rows of volumes that might be written on the truths about society and human development which Mrs Woolf has been so careful to refrain from mentioning in the novel, built on them though it be. There, at any rate, is Katharine, rooted in the Victorian era and shooting up into the untried future; now asking William Rodney to keep her safely in the sure comfort of her origin; now dreading and daring with Ralph Denham, her true partner in the adventure of life. These two, coming together after goodness knows what of queer reluctance and fear and fantasy, are going, at least, to

108 *Virginia Woolf and Motherhood*

make their lives something that shall be true. They are going to be honestly themselves. We foresee for them a hard and glorious time.[63]

Not only did this reviewer recognise a mixture of hope and apprehension in *Night and Day*'s central relationship, acknowledging it could be both 'hard' *and* 'glorious', but, in the novel's marriage plot, they also recognised Woolf's deep-seated interest in 'human development' or social evolution.

Woolf's approval of this review – 'high praise; and intelligent too' (*D1* 308) – indicates that she appreciated its analysis of her narrative. Another clue to her intentions for *Night and Day*'s marriage plot might be found in a diary entry about Leonard's first reading of the book:

> L finds the philosophy very melancholy [. . .] Yet if one is to deal with people on a large scale & say what one thinks, how can one avoid melancholy? I don't admit to being hopeless though – only the spectacle is a profoundly strange one; & as the current answers don't do, one has to grope for a new one; & the process of discarding the old, when one is by no means certain what to put in their place, is a sad one. (*D1* 259)

The Victorian standards for relationships were unviable by the end of WW1 but rather than feeling 'hopeless' Woolf used *Night and Day* to endow modern romantic interactions with potential. Woolf's new relationship model did not emulate concomitant eugenic schemes whose objectives were generally utopic (though Woolf *would* attempt to base the writing of literature on such a model in *A Room of One's Own*), but it does recall Darwinian evolution where, as Leslie Stephen noted, 'at any existing stage the adjustment is imperfect'.[64]

In a Galtonian scheme Katharine and Ralph would not be an ideal match, she is from a 'gifted' Chelsea dynasty and he is from a middle-class Highgate family who have 'never done anything to be proud of' (*ND* 11) (to reiterate these distinctions the novel introduces a Highgate-exiled uncle of Katharine, 'Poor John, or the fool of the family', of whom it is noted: 'The other boys were so brilliant, and he could never pass his examinations' (*ND* 124)). The match highlights the flaws in Galton's proposals for recommending unions based not just on physical health, but on a family history of achievement. Katharine and Ralph's creative relationship is 'consummated' in a scene that suggests a future of equality and intellectual engagement. When they finally share their work with one another, ideas that had been profoundly private before, the moment verges on the sexual, with Katharine experiencing 'half shame' – a word that is also repeated eight times in quick succession in *Moments of Being* when Woolf recalls being molested by her half-brother Gerald Duckworth – 'and half the prelude to profound rejoicing' (*ND* 419) – a phrase that prefigures the celebration of *A Room of One's Own*'s intellectual nuptials. Having shared their work the pair experience moments of intellectual rapture. Not only does Katharine find that 'the immense riddle was answered; the problem had been solved; she held in her hands for one brief moment the globe which we spend our lives in trying to shape, round, whole, and entire from the confusion of chaos' (*ND* 428), but both share 'the same sense of the impending future, vast, mysterious, infinitely stored with undeveloped shapes which each would unwrap for the other to behold' (*ND* 420). After completing each other's visions Katharine and Ralph predicate their relationship not on babies, the principal objective of any eugenic marriage, but on 'Books [. . .] to be written' (*ND* 432). In its final paragraphs *Night and Day* subverts the image of a happy young couple planning a family home to be filled with children – instead:

> since books must be written in rooms, and rooms must have hangings, and outside the windows there must be land, and an horizon to that land, and trees perhaps, and a hill, they sketched a habitation for themselves upon the outline of great offices in the Strand and continued to make an account of the future upon the omnibus which took them towards Chelsea. (*ND* 432)

Wending their way home Katharine and Ralph plan their future residence. This place of sanctuary is not designed to hold a 'fourth generation' who might carry on their bloodlines but is instead a rural writer's retreat, rooms of their own.

Books or Babies: The Young Women of *Night and Day*

In the resolving romantic narrative Katharine is contrasted not only with Cassandra but also with Mary Datchet, who conquers heartbreaking rejection by Ralph. Although Mary does not find love, she does achieve personal growth over the course of the narrative; moving from an unpaid administrative position in a somewhat ridiculous women's suffrage group to an intellectually challenging, salaried role with Mr Basnett's 'Society for the Education of Democracy'

110   *Virginia Woolf and Motherhood*

(a society which, Clara Jones notes, echoes the People's Suffrage Federation – an adult suffrage organisation that Woolf supported and volunteered for).[65] What is particularly interesting about Mary is her maternal disposition and how this contrasts with Katharine's disinterest in maternity. As previously noted, Mary experiences a 'maternal feeling' when talking to her male acquaintances. She is also motherly towards her younger brother. In one scene Ralph watches Mary stroke her brother's hair 'much as though he were a child' (*ND* 160) and both then, and later, he longs for her to do the same for him (this is a decidedly non-romantic desire with Ralph wishing 'her arms would hold him like his mother's' (*ND* 191)). At work Mary shows 'gentleness and strength, an indefinable promise of soft maternity blending with her evident fitness for honest labour' (*ND* 138). There is a touch of the maternalist campaigner in this description and later Mary tells Katharine and Basnett 'you can't limit work [. . .] No one works harder than a woman with little children' to which Basnett replies 'It's precisely the women with babies we want to get hold of' (*ND* 303). But, while the comedy in Basnett's reply exposes the irony with which Woolf viewed maternalist campaigners, maternalism is not Mary's primary motivation for thinking of motherhood. By 'giving her youth' to 'the cause' (*ND* 69) Mary is relinquishing a domestic role that would suit her and which she seems to desire. One of Mary's workmates, Mrs Seal, feels 'uneasy' about Mary abandoning marriage to work, noting how young she is and 'full of the promise of womanhood' (*ND* 221). And Mary herself feels that by rejecting marriage to Ralph, and choosing work, she is 'not quite "in the running" for life' (*ND* 222) and has 'seen her future turned from one of infinite promise to one of barrenness' (*ND* 333).

It is interesting to consider why Woolf writes so much about Mary's maternal tendencies only to let them go unsatisfied. It could be argued that Mary's capacity for maternity is what *makes* her most unsuitable for marriage. By entering into a marriage, even with Ralph, Mary would most likely be tempted to become a mother and forsake a single life which she finds fulfilling. At the beginning of the novel Woolf writes:

> There were few mornings when Mary did not look up, as she bent to lace her boots, and [. . .] breathed some sigh of thankfulness that her life provided her with such moments of pure enjoyment [. . .] to get so much pleasure from simple things, such as eating one's breakfast alone in a room which had nice colours in it, clean from the skirting of the boards to the corners of the ceiling, seemed to suit her so thoroughly

that she used at first to hunt about for some one to apologize to, or for some flaw in the situation. She had now been six months in London, and she could find no flaw, but that, as she invariably concluded by the time her boots were laced, was solely and entirely due to the fact that she had her work. (*ND* 61)

Becoming enmeshed in domesticity would rob Mary of the 'contentment' (*ND* 61) that her independence provides. Keeping Mary single could even be said to be part of Woolf's alternative eugenics. Since Mary is inclined to embrace motherhood and lose both her autonomy and her ability to influence society, Woolf takes this option away, inflicting some pain but exploring the possibility of a more rewarding vocation.

This reading can be supported by considering Katharine as a foil to Mary. Katharine refuses to use 'the usual feminine amenities' (*ND* 7) to keep men happy, not only in conversation, but also in domestic affairs. When visiting both William and her cousin Henry, she 'forces' them 'to act the part generally taken by women' (*ND* 165). It is not that Katharine is manly – although she does exhibit the odd masculine 'gesture' (*ND* 112) or 'attitude' (*ND* 241) – rather she embodies 'the manly [. . .] sides of the feminine nature' (*ND* 290). Katharine never appears as a maternal presence. Though William pictures her as 'a perfect mother – a mother of sons' he immediately begins 'to have his doubts on this point' (*ND* 206). And once Cassandra is engaged to William it becomes obvious how little interest Katharine has in becoming a mother during the following exchange:

'I hope we shall have a great many children,' said Cassandra. 'He loves children.'
This remark made Katharine realize the depths of their intimacy better than any other words could have done [. . .] She had known William for years, and she had never once guessed that he loved children. (*ND* 369)

Katharine fails to see William's desire for children not because he is unwilling to share this intimacy with her but because his aspiration is so dissimilar to her own. Katharine's non-maternal nature is defined in contrast to Cassandra's and Mary's. In one scene Mary watches Katharine serve tea and, 'thinking of Katharine as one who would soon be married [. . .] maternal airs filled Mary's mind'. However, Mary is merely reading her own attitudes in Katharine's actions. Moments later Mary corrects this error and recognises that

112   *Virginia Woolf and Motherhood*

Katharine's conduct and character are, in actual fact, 'not altogether in the maternal spirit' (*ND* 145).

By matching up Katharine and Ralph rather than Mary and Ralph, Woolf not only allows Katharine, and indeed, Ralph, a space in which to nurture their intellectual 'gifts' but enables Mary to continue being a young woman of purpose who not only 'intended to earn [. . .] her own living' (*ND* 36) but realises this dream. There is some question over how to evaluate the conclusion to Katharine and Mary's narratives. Given the text's tonal ambivalence it is difficult to say whether by remaining single (and not having children) Mary has chosen an inferior path, or whether she has 'conquered' (*ND* 333) something by giving up Ralph. Feminist readings, that view Katharine's marriage to Ralph as a submission to patriarchy, see Mary as the vicarious fulfilment, as Briggs writes, of 'Katharine's desire for power and independence'.[66] Sowon Park finds that 'Mary offers Katharine a glimpse of what she might hold if she succeeds in breaking free from the groaning inheritance of her grand literary predecessor'.[67] But reading Mary's situation as superior to Katharine's assumes that Woolf identifies with Mary, foregrounding her passion for social reform over Katharine's inherited 'gifts' and enthusiasm for mathematics.

Though the text is ambiguous, by reading *Night and Day* as a forerunner of *A Room of One's Own* there is a case to be made that, while Mary's work is a useful substitute for love, it is not equal with the creative potential of Katharine Hilbery (or Virginia Woolf) – women who venture into progressive marriages which act as fertile environments for creative offspring. Katharine considers that 'a world entrusted to the guardianship of Mary Datchet and Mr Basnett seemed to her a good world, although not a romantic or beautiful place' (*ND* 304). Performed high up in her flat, where she sits alone, 'impersonal and serene', making 'plans for the good of a world that none of them were ever to know' (*ND* 431), Mary's work is not valued as art. Some proof that Woolf saw Mary's choice as second-best can be found in the well-received *TLS* review, which noted: 'Mary Datchet, missing what she most wanted in life, works out for herself something that is as true, though not nearly so exciting as the adventure of Katharine and Ralph'.[68] Ultimately, the text's tonal ambivalence resists settled readings. Whether they are intended to be hierarchical or not, Katharine and Mary explore different ways for women to live in a changing world and the shifting narrative allows each woman's choices and outcomes to constantly unsettle the other's.

Read unironically, Katharine and Ralph's love can, temporarily, rivet 'together of the shattered fragments of the world' (*ND* 412) and their intellectual pursuits thrive on these moments of visionary wholeness. *Night and Day* champions the heterosexual union – as Mrs Hilbery states (and Katharine concurs), marriage is, 'the most *interesting* life' (*ND* 179, emphasis in original).[69] This reading is supported by Woolf's personal writing; for example, this diary entry, which describes the appeal of everyday life with Leonard:

> I was glad to come home, & feel my real life coming back again – I mean life here with L. Solitary is not quite the right word; one's personality seems to echo out across space, when he's not there to enclose all one's vibrations. This is not very intelligibly written; but the feeling itself is a strange one – as if marriage were a completing of the instrument, & the sound of one alone penetrates as if it were a violin robbed of its orchestra or piano. (*D1* 70)

Written while writing *Night and Day*, after five years of marriage and a severe breakdown, this passage shows that Woolf could find her marriage complementary and soothing. In this vision, written after several days observing Vanessa and her young sons, marriage emerges as a muse, or space of creative harmony.

Leonard helped with other aspects of the writing process, such as dealing with a work's critical reception. In 1934 when, during a party, the author Rose Macaulay inadvertently revealed her sensitivity to critics, Woolf noted: 'She is a ravaged sensitive old hack – as I should be, no doubt, save for L' (*D4* 250). The attraction of marriage would remain a feature of Woolf's life, and she would write to Vita Sackville-West some eight years later; 'in all London, you and I alone like being married' (*L3* 221). It is perhaps partly this feeling of marriage being right – a feeling Woolf continued to have even while carrying on an emotional affair with a woman – that led her to foreground heterosexual interactions in *A Room of One's Own*'s literary maternal metaphor.

'They should certainly be killed': Woolf and Eugenics

Nigel Nicolson has noted that Woolf's breakdowns, though frequently attributed to the strains of writing and the anticipated reception of her novels, more often occurred after times of emotional upheaval; for example, the deaths of her mother, half-sister, brother, and her

114 *Virginia Woolf and Motherhood*

father.[70] The idea that Woolf's breakdowns were related to the writing process can perhaps be traced to Leonard who wrote in his autobiography, 'it is significant that, whenever she finished a book, she was in a state of mental exhaustion and for weeks in danger of a breakdown'.[71] While these claims need not necessarily negate each other, the intense depression that followed her marriage to Leonard and the decision not to have children fits with Nicolson's observation. Indeed, in the case of *Night and Day* the book resulted from the breakdown. Some years later Woolf recalled how:

> After being ill and suffering every form and variety of nightmare and extravagant intensity of perception [. . .] I was so tremblingly afraid of my own insanity that I wrote *Night and Day* mainly to prove to my own satisfaction that I could keep entirely off that dangerous ground. (*L4* 231)

Her most famous eugenic reflection transpired at this time, in a 1915 diary entry where she adopted a surprisingly normative voice:

> On the towpath we met & had to pass a long line of imbeciles. The first was a very tall young man, just queer enough to look twice at, but no more; the second shuffled, & looked aside; & then one realised that every one in that long line was a miserable ineffective shuffling idiotic creature, with no forehead, or no chin, & an imbecile grin, or a wild suspicious stare. It was perfectly horrible. They should certainly be killed. (*D1* 13)

This oft-quoted extract uses the eugenic language of the Mental Deficiency Act, which, when it first passed two years earlier, legislated a classification system for the mentally ill consisting of four categories: idiots, imbeciles, feeble-minded and moral defectives.

Hermione Lee tempers the brutality of this passage with a reminder that 'eugenics were standard terms' and a belief that: 'This violent endorsement of an extreme theory of eugenics, written between two very severe breakdowns, must be understood as expressing her dread and horror of what she thought of as her own loss of control'.[72] Despite the courageous act of self-sufficiency that *Night and Day* represented. Woolf still feared that madness could strike at any time. While the diary entry is an 'endorsement' of negative eugenics, it is also true that Woolf recognised her own fragility in this group, and their image stayed with her. Writing *Mrs Dalloway* in 1923, she recreated this experience for Septimus Smith:

once a maimed file of lunatics being exercised or displayed for the diversion of the populace (who laughed aloud), ambled and nodded and grinned past him, in the Tottenham Court Road, each half apologetically, yet triumphantly, inflicting his hopeless woe. And would *he* go mad? (*MD* 98, emphasis in original)

The reflexive disgust of the first quote – 'They should certainly be killed' – is directed inward in the second – 'would *he* go mad?' The latter portrays a more considered representation of the author's anxiety over her mental stability and eugenic profile.

Though she was contemptuous of the patriarchal cronyism of Galton and the Eugenics Society, Woolf lived in a eugenic world and sometimes expressed eugenic sentiments. Eugenics was popular among her upper-middle-class, intellectual and artist friends and, while she often reasoned that privilege and education played a significant role in achievement, she did not entirely reject eugenic models of intellectual supremacy. Woolf's understanding of contemporary eugenics came from many places. Donald Childs notes that her doctors were a 'likely source of her knowledge' – especially the dinners she took at George Savage's home – but the Woolfs had many other links with the eugenic community. Eugenics had a universal appeal and was popular among liberal intellectuals, socialists *and* the conservative right wing.[73] John Maynard Keynes was perhaps the most prominent eugenicist among Woolf's acquaintances. In 1911, as a fellow at Cambridge, he helped found the university's Eugenics Society and acted as its treasurer for several years. Later, after completing a stint as director of the London Eugenics Society (from 1937 until 1944), Keynes noted eugenics to be 'the most important, significant and, I would add, genuine branch of sociology which exists'.[74] Keynes was also a firm supporter of women's rights and, in 1923, briefly took on the vice-presidency of Marie Stopes's Society for Constructive Birth Control and Racial Progress.[75]

Many of Woolf's more eugenically minded acquaintances were associates of Leonard. In the early 1910s Leonard met Sidney and Beatrice Webb and became a committed member of the Fabian Society. The Webbs, along with fellow Fabian George Bernard Shaw, were enthusiastic supporters of the eugenics movement, and between 1909 and 1910 the Fabian Society convened a 'Biology' group that devoted a portion of its time to examining eugenic theory.[76] In June 1916 the Woolfs joined the Webbs and Bernard Shaws for a weekend in the country. On a walk through the woods Virginia noted that the company 'all talked so incessantly upon so many different subjects that

116   *Virginia Woolf and Motherhood*

I never saw a single tree' (*L2* 101). Though it is conjecture, it is not difficult to imagine that some of this conversation covered the group's shared passion for eugenics. While it would be wrong to suggest that Virginia had great friends among Leonard's work associates, her connection with the Webbs and Bernard Shaws rendered another opportunity for her to be kept abreast of the state of modern eugenics.

Woolf was also frequently exposed to eugenic opinion in her reading matter. For example *The Nation and Athenaeum* – which was committed to bringing 'literature, art and science' to its readers.[77] It was so incredibly popular among Woolf's circle that Vanessa once complained to Roger Fry:

> It seems to me like a drug. Everyone reads it and discusses it in and out and there's always a lot of gossip about each article or review – one is quite out of it if one hasn't seen it for some weeks.[78]

Woolf was frequently published in *The Nation*, and when Keynes bought the weekly periodical in 1923, he appointed Leonard as literary editor, a role that Leonard occupied until 1930. These seven years represented a fertile period for eugenics in British culture and *The Nation* published many eugenic articles. One such example is Vera Brittain's 'Our Malthusian Middle-Classes', a feminist, pro-contraceptive discussion of the falling birth rate which contrasts the middle class's eugenic desire for more children with the dangers of economic instability. Brittain calls into question the claim that the falling birth rate is due to, 'the "selfishness" of modern young parents, and particularly young wives [. . .] the loss of the maternal instinct, the superior attractions of a career, feminism, the love of comfort, and a cowardly shrinking from the pain and peril of childbirth'. How, she wonders, can her contemporaries bring up an abundance of children with 'decency and order [. . .] beauty and affection [. . .] to leaven the national lump of mediocrity and inefficiency', when they cannot afford to maintain a civilised lifestyle. She continues to ask; 'Are we really working for eugenic birth control if we persuade our few thoroughly civilized individuals to descend even a little towards the standard of the slum-dweller?'[79]

'Family histories': The Eugenic Influence of Vita Sackville West

Whether or not Woolf read Brittain's article, its general eugenic tone was one she would certainly have encountered in her personal and professional reading. In 1924 Hogarth Press added Vita Sackville-West to their stable, publishing *Seducers in Ecuador*. Sackville-West had already written several explicitly eugenic books. Her first novel *Heritage* (1919) contemplates human mate selection and the nature and perpetuation of hereditary taint, references 'moral eugenics' and fictionalises an experiment by Galton.[80] *The Dragon in Shallow Waters* (1921) begins by describing two malevolent and physically disabled brothers born from a father 'whom everybody had known as a rake, and who never ought to have married, much less begotten children'.[81] Woolf knew about Sackville-West's eugenic inclinations and, because of Sackville-West's aristocratic heritage and the loss of her childhood home Knole though the laws of primogeniture, Woolf associated her with modes of inheritance that were both biological and fiscal. After their first meeting, Woolf asked for a copy of Sackville-West's book *Knole and the Sackvilles*, remarking: 'There is nothing I enjoy more than family histories' (*L3* 1). A fascination for Sackville-West's eventful life and intriguing bloodline would find its way into Woolf's unconventional biography *Orlando*. Like Vita, Orlando is made up of a variety of heritages – French nobility, Spanish gypsy, with 'grains of the Kentish or Sussex earth' added by 'a certain grandmother' who 'had worn a smock and carried milkpails' (*O* 20). Orlando is also more than a collection of bloods, he/she is the incarnate expression of centuries of British history. The very first time Woolf visited Knole she had a vision of a living past that explains Orlando's extraordinary existence:

> All the centuries seemed lit up, the past expressive, articulate; not dumb & forgotten; but a crowd of people stood behind, not dead at all; not remarkable; fair faced, long limbed; affable; & so we reach the days of Elizabeth quite easily. (*D3* 125)

In a way Orlando is an embodiment of her ancestors *and* the great house, a blend of biological and cultural heritage that stretches back into history.

In making *Orlando* a fictional biography of Sackville-West, Woolf continued a practice she had engaged in since childhood when she first began peopling her stories with family and friends. This fictionalising was mutual – in 1925 Woolf famously proposed to Sackville-West, 'if you'll make me up, I'll make you' (*L3* 214) – and in both their private correspondence and their novels the two artists traded portrayals of each other. Several scholars have written on this interaction, with Ellen Hawke noting that 'recreating each other's personalities had been an essential part of their correspondence', and Joanne Trautmann

118   *Virginia Woolf and Motherhood*

comparing Woolf's writing practice to *The Waves'* Bernard, who uses his friends as 'copy' (a word that Vita used about herself with regard to *Orlando*).[82] Vita, for her part, reinvented Woolf in a way that the other two people closest to her – Leonard and Vanessa – did not.[83] The image of herself that Woolf saw reflected in her lover's eyes was feminine and strong – much more empowering than the 'frigid' virgin created by her Bloomsbury friends.[84] With Sackville-West, Woolf could reclaim those parts of herself that the death of her mother had made difficult to acknowledge. Louise DeSalvo notes of the relationship: 'An index of its positive effect for Virginia Woolf is that she, who so detested mirrors throughout her life, bought herself an antique mirror when she went to France with Vita'.[85] Sackville-West challenged Woolf's picture of herself as a flawed example of femininity, seeing her instead as a complete woman; as womanly, even, as Julia had been. Vita's response to *To the Lighthouse* was to ask Woolf: 'I wonder if you know how like Mrs Ramsay you are yourself'?[86] Though Woolf somewhat brushed off the question – responding: 'I don't know if I'm like Mrs Ramsay: as my mother died when I was 13 probably it is a child's view of her' (*L3* 374) – she welcomed the connotation. Indeed, Woolf had previously written to Vita: 'I'm not cold; not a humbug; not weakly; not sentimental. What I am; I want you to tell me' (*L3* 233).

Unsurprisingly, Woolf and Sackville-West's idealised versions of each other reflected their principles. For Woolf, this meant foregrounding artistic generation over biological motherhood, amplifying Sackville-West's role as an author and minimising descriptions of her as a mother. *Orlando* does have a birth scene that is written with creative fanfare, but this event adds nothing to the novel's plot and the baby is not mentioned again.[87] This contrasts with the task of writing a successful piece of art, something that takes Orlando a lifetime. While the absence of the baby could be read as a comment on the limited interaction that upper-class women had with their children, Woolf's decision to create a strong female artist rather than a maternal figure also reflects her feelings about her subject. Writing was a significant part of their relationship. They discussed, encouraged and appraised each other's work, and Vita was one of the select few to whom Woolf sent each new novel, keenly awaiting feedback. In addition, Woolf had observed that Sackville-West was fairly un-maternal, 'a little cold & offhand with her boys' (*D3* 52), and knew how Vita enjoyed long periods of solitude every day, using them to write and take care of her gardens. Nigel Nicolson noted of his mother:

Motherhood and Eugenics   119

To us, her children, she felt distant affection. Babies were an interruption, a reminder of duty, of her place in the home, a reminder of their innocence compared to her guilt, a reminder, even, of maternity, which by then [. . .] she found distasteful.[88]

Interestingly, one of the few criticisms that Sackville-West had of *Orlando* was that her namesake marries and becomes a mother; writing to her husband Harold Nicolson that Woolf had:

slightly confused the issues in making Orlando 1) marry, 2) have a child. Shelmerdine does not really contribute anything either to Orlando's character or to the problems of the story [. . .] and as for the child it contributes less than nothing, but even strikes rather a false note. Marriage & motherhood would either modify or destroy Orlando, as a character: they do neither.[89]

The strong wording of this letter ('either modify or destroy') suggests that Sackville-West was more affected by motherhood than Woolf acknowledged, but these emotions may have gone unrecognised or uncommunicated because of Woolf's position as a non-mother.

In private Woolf evaluated Sackville-West's ability as an author in relation to her maternity. In the early stage of their mutual admiration she was deeply impressed by Sackville-West's ability to write despite the responsibilities of motherhood, noting in her diary (about *Seducers in Ecuador*):

she has shed the old verbiage, & come to terms with some sort of glimmer of art; so I think; & indeed, I rather marvel at her skill, & sensibility; for is she not mother, wife, great lady, hostess, as well as scribbling? (*D2* 313)

However, with the first flush of adoration over, Woolf's opinion of Sackville-West's work changed. Lacking some 'central transparency' (*L3* 302), it failed as art, was like 'a schoolboys essay' (*L6* 185), or even simply 'not [. . .] very good' (*D3* 306). Where she had seen amazing competence, Woolf now saw unfulfilled potential, and again she attributed this failure to Sackville-West's domestic situation, her having two 'sons, one Eton, one Oxford, which explains why she has to spin those sleepwalking servant girl novels' (*L5* 266).[90]

For her part, Sackville-West fictionalised the Woolfs as Viola and Leonard Anquetil in her 1932 book *Family History*. Viola is the insightful heart of a well-adjusted household, with two happy,

120   *Virginia Woolf and Motherhood*

healthy and intelligent children (one son and one daughter). While giving her fictional Virginia children was clearly important, this rather idyllic family group also shows how pro-contraceptive Sackville-West's eugenics were: she did not believe in unlimited reproduction or women being solely dedicated to childbearing and rearing. In 1929 Sackville-West and her husband Harold Nicolson had a profoundly progressive radio debate about marriage that clearly denoted them as eugenicists and supporters of birth control, with Sackville-West at one point noting that she, 'didn't think we were setting out to discuss marriage from the biological point of view, though I admit it is an important one'. During the discussion Sackville-West argued that marriage and childbearing can turn women into 'a sort of appendage', with men predisposed to 'imagine that marriage is a condition which will contribute to *your* growth at the expense of *our* vitality'. With both recognising the importance of reproduction and acknowledging women's right to work, they went on to formulate a revolutionary plan – a series of nurseries freeing women to enter the workforce. These nurseries, imagined in typically eugenic fashion, would result in 'a caste of intellectuals, bred, if not born, in the purple of the crèche'.[91]

While Sackville-West and Woolf shared many interests, eugenics has not traditionally been viewed as one of those commonalities. Nonetheless there are several feminist eugenic standards they both upheld. They shared an interest in feminine bloodlines and non-patrilineal modes of inheritance (Sackville-West's efforts to 'think back' through her mother led to *Pepita* (1937), a biography of her grandmother and mother), they both believed in reduced childbearing not only because, as artists, they needed to dedicate themselves to their work, but also because they understood the need for women's autonomy in every walk of life. Both were also in heterosexual marriages that they, for the most part, enjoyed, and, I would argue, both advocated for heterosexual unions in their work. These shared ideals reflected one of the most influential movements of their age – Marie Stopes's contraceptive crusade. In fact, when Harold Nicolson read *Married Love*, Stopes's 1918 book on sexual desire, he wrote and insisted that Vita read it.[92]

In the book *Vita and Virginia*, which includes a chapter on Sackville-West's 'moral eugenics', Suzanne Raitt suggests that Sackville-West became more liberal under Woolf's influence, but this change may well have involved a mutual cultivation of feminist eugenic ideals.[93] During their 1928 trip to France – during which Vita noted 'V. is curiously feminist [. . .] Says that women stimulate her imagination' – the

Motherhood and Eugenics   121

pair had a conversation that stuck in Sackville-West's mind. In her diary she described it as a discussion about 'science & religion [. . .] and the ultimate principle',[94] but after Woolf's death she revisited the memory, noting:

> what I remember most vividly is one night when a superb thunderstorm broke over Vezelay and we sat in darkness while the flashes intermittently lit up her face. She was, I think, a little frightened, and perhaps that drove her to speak with a deeper seriousness than I had ever heard her use before of immortality and personal survival after death.[95]

Science, religion, the ultimate principle, immortality and personal survival after death are all topics that related in some way to Woolf's interpretation of eugenics and reproduction, and it is not unfathomable to reason that these friends had been talking about a topic they had both expressed a thoughtful, creative interest in. Both had written about their family histories and knew they came from well-known hereditary lines. Through her children, Sackville-West continued her aristocratic lineage and achieved genetic immortality; Woolf, on the other hand, continued her family's literary tradition and believed a certain type of immortality could be guaranteed by making art.

Woolf's notion of authorial immortality may have been borrowed from Leslie Stephen, who speaks of 'the immortal Thomas', 'the immortal George Eliot' and 'the immortal Goethe' in his letters.[96] Woolf also shared her thoughts on writing as a form of immortality with her friends, relating such a conversation in her diary:

> Lytton, Mary, Clive, came here yesterday, discussed immortality; & I find my bid for it is as letter writer. What about poor Jacob then? [. . .] Lytton gave me a lesson in simplicity. If anyone has a right to talk of immortality he has with his 9 editions. (D2 63–64)

Although she speaks of '9 editions' this immortality proved tricky to calculate, with a later diary entry suggesting that it could not be evaluated through sales and even questioning whether it was related to popularity or longevity. Comparing *Night and Day* with Strachey's *Queen Victoria*, she wrote:

> He's sold, so they say, 5,000 copies this week, & another edition is printing. I have sold just 300. Well, but that doesn't prove my immortality, as I insinuate. The truth is I have no notion of my standing, or of Lytton's. One ought to write more of this occasion,

122 *Virginia Woolf and Motherhood*

since I suppose in 20 years' time the publication of *Queen Victoria* will be thought an important matter; but these things aren't important to us. (*D2* 110)

Even though it was intangible, Woolf still wondered about the details of authorial immortality. With a mystical writing style that advocated for women's autonomy and cooperative, respectful relationships between the sexes, Marie Stopes gave Woolf the perfect framework on which to explore such theories.

Eugenic Feminism and Marie Carmichael Stopes

Marie Stopes's birth control movement was impossible to ignore. It affected every part of society and transformed the moral tone of the nation. In *Mrs Dalloway* Peter Walsh observes this transformation:

Those five years – 1918 to 1923 – had been [. . .] somehow very important. People looked different [. . .] On board ship coming home there were lots of young men and girls – Betty and Bertie he remembered in particular – carrying on quite openly; the old mother sitting and watching them with her knitting, cool as a cucumber. The girl would stand still and powder her nose in front of every one. And they weren't engaged; just having a good time; no feelings hurt on either side. As hard as nails she was – Betty What'shername – ; but a thorough good sort. She would make a very good wife at thirty – she would marry when it suited her to marry; marry some rich man and live in a large house near Manchester. (*MD* 78–79)

'Those five years' which were so significant for British sexual liberty represent a moment when the public were ready for change. Ellen Holtzman has noted that: 'The stresses of the First World War [. . .] caused people to grow more interested in experiencing pleasure than in controlling themselves'. Holtzman describes how: 'Changing attitudes toward personal pleasure', alongside 'early twentieth-century feminist gains, and the need for a new female role [. . .] combined to make Stopes's sexual ideal particularly attractive to her women readers'.[97] Certainly *Married Love*, published by Stopes in 1918, was immediately popular, selling 2,000 copies within a fortnight and going through seven editions in the first year of publication.[98] In 1921 Stopes founded the Society for Constructive Birth Control and Racial Progress and set up her first birth control clinic in Holloway. By 1923 – the year *Mrs Dalloway* was set – contraception, and Stopes, were established as cultural phenomena. In the same year, Woolf noted in a letter to Molly MacCarthy:

> I've been talking to the younger generation all afternoon. They are like crude hard green apples: no halo, mildew, or blight. Seduced at 15, life has no holes or corners for them. I admire, but deplore. Such an old maid, they make me feel. 'And how do you manage not – not – not to have children?' I ask. 'Oh, we read Mary Stopes of course.' Figure to yourself my dear Molly – before taking their virginity, the young men of our time produce marked copies of Stopes! (L3 6)

Layne Parish Craig calls the tone of this letter 'somewhat exaggerated', noting that Woolf 'was after all eleven years into a childless marriage with Leonard'.[99] While it is questionable how sexually active the Woolfs were, and thus how much they practised birth control methods, Virginia knew of contraception before they were married. In 1908 Vanessa sent her an entertaining letter reporting 'wildly improper' conversations she was having with friends about: 'Different methods of stopping children and the joys of married life'. Bell, who already had one baby, explained that she hoped to 'get some useful tips from Mrs Raven-Hill as to the best methods of checking one's family and I mean to make use of the dance at Devizes for the purpose' although, she jokingly continues, 'since she is very deaf I shall probably cause a scandal'.[100] Given the amusement such conversations had already provided it makes sense that the shocked tone in Woolf's letter to MacCarthy is produced for comical effect. It is worth noting that the letter pokes fun at both the 'younger generation' and Woolf herself rather than Stopes's work or values.

Though they would not meet in person until years later, Woolf would come to see Stopes as more than just the face of the birth control movement. She recognised and found inspiration in Stopes's eugenic utopian model of procreation, using it as a template for her argument about 'the effect of tradition and of the lack of tradition upon the mind of a writer' (AROO 70).[101] In A Room of One's Own, Woolf both positions Stopes as a champion of the changing landscape of women's sexual and professional autonomy, and also makes an example of her fiction as an important midpoint in the evolution of female literature. Stopes falls somewhere between 'the fiery imagination, the wild poetry, the brilliant wit, the brooding wisdom of her great predecessors, Lady Winchilsea, Charlotte Brontë, Emily Brontë, Jane Austen and George Eliot' (AROO 83) and the 'great' female 'poets' of the future (AROO 102).

124   *Virginia Woolf and Motherhood*

Stopes herself was primarily a eugenicist, and did not initially set out to champion contraceptives. She wrote *Married Love* to help women find sexual satisfaction in marriage and briefly referenced contraception simply as a means to an end. However, much of the response that the book received was from women desperate for more practical contraceptive advice. Stopes went on to write *Wise Parenthood* (1922); a guide to birth control that primarily recommended the rubber cap and quinine suppositories. Richard Soloway notes that Stopes initially advised that a simple visit to the chemist or doctor would avail a woman of this paraphernalia. However, as it became clear that contraceptives were far from readily available, she moved to open a birth control clinic with the backing of her businessman husband Humphrey Roe. Soloway explains that Stopes was hopeful that the 'public authorities [. . .] would recognise the benefits to public health and racial improvement that would result from the establishment of similar ante-natal clinics and welfare centres throughout the country'.[102]

Birth control advocacy was a natural extension of Stopes's eugenic beliefs. Like Woolf, Galton was an acquaintance of Stopes's father and she knew of his work from a young age. She joined the Eugenics Society in 1912 and remained a member until her death when she bequeathed it no less than the sum of her life's work in the form of her clinics, her library and a large legacy. Despite this, conventional eugenicists were reserved about Stopes, who could be a difficult character to deal with and provoked countless arguments with both the Eugenics Society and other bodies working in the contraceptive field.[103] It did not help that eugenic thinkers initially worried that falling birth rates among the wealthy and educated – populations whose growth they most desired – suggested that contraceptives were dysgenic.[104] Relations between Stopes and the Eugenics Society remained strained even as public interest compelled the Society to take more initiative in the area, such as investing in the experimental spermicide Volpar. For her part, Stopes saw contraceptives as an integral part of eugenic progress. She embraced both positive eugenics – promoting sexual harmony, spaced births and happy, healthy mothers – and negative – recommending legislation for enforcing sterilisation in the 'hopelessly rotten and racially diseased'.[105]

In 1923, when Stopes was involved in a well-publicised libel case against Dr Halliday Sutherland, the court transcripts showed her eugenic objectives. When asked: 'Is the reduction of the birth rate any part at all of your campaign?' Stopes responded: 'Not reduction

Motherhood and Eugenics   125

in the total birth rate, but reduction in the birth rate at the wrong part and increase of the birth rate at the right end of the social scale'. And when questioned about the primary objective of her Society, Stopes replied that it was

> to counteract the steady evil which has been growing for many years of the reduction of the birth rate on the part of the wise, thrifty, well contented and generally sound members of our community; and the reckless breeding of the C3 end, the semi-feeble-minded, the careless, who are proportionately increasing because of the slowing of the birth rate at the other end of the scale. It was in order to try to right that grave social danger that I embarked on this work.[106]

In line with these ambitions, Stopes opened her clinics in poorer areas and invented a diaphragm called the Pro-Race cap, as well as birth control suppositories labelled Racial Solubles. Though Stopes's life-long work lionised motherhood it was ultimately her belief that: 'The power of parenthood ought no longer to be exercised by *all*, however inferior, as an "individual right". It is profoundly a duty and a privilege, and it is essentially the concern of the whole community' (*RM* 211–12, emphasis in original). In 1918, when the parliamentary committee the National Council of Public Morals set up a National Birth Rate Commission to investigate 'problems of population', Stopes was asked to be a member. She proved to be militant, recommending compulsory health certification before marriage, eugenic education in schools and enforced sterilisation for 'hopelessly bad cases, bad through inherent disease, or drunkenness, or character'.[107]

While she was an unreserved supporter of the Eugenics Society, Stopes's values were not always in line with orthodox eugenic ideals. Deborah Cohen has highlighted Stopes's clinical practice of treating all married women regardless of class, social standing or even family size. Cohen includes the following story that Stopes used to explain her policy:

> [O]ne of the first women who came to me said she had two children and she must have help. She couldn't have any more. And so I said to her: 'Oh but you know two children is not so very many. I think if you are well as you look you ought to have three, don't you? What about having one more? And then come back to us?' Well, she talked for a little while; she nearly cried, and I found out her history in detail. She had been six other times pregnant; every time a natural abortion took place the fourth or fifth month, and the last time because her drunken husband had kicked her where the child lay.[108]

126 *Virginia Woolf and Motherhood*

While Stopes believed that the 'miserable, the degenerate, the utterly wretched in body and mind, who when reproducing multiply the misery and evil of the world' (*RM* 224), predominantly came from the poorest sector of society, she advocated for all women, arguing that the 'rejuvenescence and reform of the race' (*RM* 216) would only occur if all classes embraced smaller families with babies who were wanted and cared for.[109] Believing that all sections of society deserved, and would benefit from, control over their fertility, she wrote *Married Love* and *Wise Parenthood* for a middle- and upper-class readership, in addition to publishing a more affordable pamphlet entitled 'A Letter to Working Mothers: On How to Have Healthy Children and Avoid Weakening Pregnancies' (1919).

Besides being an advocate for contraception, Stopes was a feminist who encouraged women to enter the professions. Before moving into the realm of sexology she had a successful career as a palaeobotanist. In *Radiant Motherhood* she challenges the 'narrow vision' of 'leading doctors and others [. . .] that the whole capability of the individual mother should be devoted solely to contributing to her children' (*RM* 158). Stopes continues by explaining that

> the individual woman, normal or better than the average, *should* use her intellect for her individual gain in creative work; not only because of its value to the age and community in which she lives, but also for the inheritance she may thus give her children and so that when her children are grown up they may find in their mother not only the kind attendant of their youth, but their equal in achievement. With a woman of capacities perhaps still exceptional, but by no means so rare as some men writers would like to pretend, the pursuit of her work or profession and honourable achievement in it is not at all incompatible with but is highly beneficial to her motherhood. (*RM* 159)

The value of intellectual inheritance articulated by Stopes also finds expression, albeit with less reliance on biological maternity, in Woolf's *A Room of One's Own*, and will be discussed below. Stopes's feminist attitude was part of her own 'intellectual inheritance' – her mother was Charlotte Carmichael Stopes, an enthusiastic supporter of women's suffrage who wrote *British Freewomen: Their Historical Privilege* (1894) (a text that Laura Mayhall describes as: 'Perhaps the single most influential text in casting women's struggle for the vote within the radical narrative of loss, resistance, and recovery').[110] As well as being a committed suffragist, Carmichael Stopes was a member of the Rational Dress Society, clothing herself (and Marie) according to their standards. The Society objected to

> any fashion in dress that either deforms the figure, impedes the movements of the body, or in any way tends to injure the health [. . .] the wearing of tightly-fitting corsets; of high-heeled or narrow-toed boots and shoes; of heavily-weighted skirts, as rendering healthy exercise almost impossible; and of all tie-down cloaks or other garments impeding on the movements of the arms [. . .] crinolines or crinolettes of any kind as ugly and deforming.[111]

Stephanie Green relates how, in 1889, just before Marie turned nine, Charlotte attracted 'widespread press attention [. . .] after staging a programme coup at the annual meeting of the British Association for the Advancement of Science'.[112] During this 'coup', Carmichael Stopes presented an unsanctioned, but reportedly popular, panel on the 'Psychological and Physiological Aspects of Women's Dress'. While it seems highly unlikely that Woolf read the *Rational Dress Society's Gazette* (it only ran from April 1888 until July 1889) one article of particular interest questions, 'the true state of intelligence of a creature which deliberately loads itself with quantities of useless material around its legs, in spite of discomfort and danger, without any object in view, beyond the object of copying one another?'[113] Woolf engages in similar debates about women's clothing in *Orlando*, where her newly female protagonist observes that: 'skirts are plaguey things to have about one's heels [. . .] the stuff (flowered paduasoy) is the loveliest in the world [. . .] Could I, however, leap overboard and swim in clothes like these?' (*O* 109).

'Scientific, social, aesthetic': Stopes, Class and Contraception

Despite holding many parallel beliefs, Woolf and Stopes engaged with public life in very different ways. Like her mother, Stopes wanted to work within existing power structures – she believed in the efficacy of legislation, sitting on government committees and inviting politicians to chair her public meetings. Woolf mistrusted political activity, as she mistrusted patriarchal culture in general (in *A Room of One's Own* she would explain that women 'reformers' are as responsible for bringing 'about a state of sex-consciousness' (*AROO* 93) as their male counterparts).[114] Notwithstanding their different approaches,

128   *Virginia Woolf and Motherhood*

Woolf and Stopes both expressed pejorative views of the working class and poor while also advocating for those groups. Both also wanted women (predominantly middle- and upper-class women) to be free to obtain intellectual fulfillment. Woolf understood that the autonomy Stopes offered was crucial to women's art of any sort. By empowering the individual, the contraceptive movement stood in contrast to the broad patriarchal nationalism displayed by the Eugenics Society, wherein women were little more than baby-making machines. Stopes may have appealed to Woolf *because* her eugenics differed so vastly from Galton's. Like Woolf, Stopes had no particular interest in 'men of genius'. *Love's Creation* argues against elitism and patriarchy, denouncing

> the supposition that [. . .] the weakest must go to the wall, that a strong, successful, rich man is good to carry on the human race, that the material success of the few is all that matters. It is *not* all that matters.[115]

This stance advocates for the working class but it is also feminist. Since women were traditionally seen as the weaker sex and had historically been unable to earn money or inherit property, it was important for activists such as Stopes to disrupt arguments suggesting that strength, success and wealth equalled genetic or cultural value. The same was true for her mother, who, in *British Freewomen*, countered patriarchal opinions about the limits on women's capacity for fiscal and social responsibility by providing historical examples of female self-rule.[116]

There are other reasons to suggest that Woolf saw how the birth control movement had the potential to change the social landscape and transform women's lives. The Woolfs had been involved in Margaret Llewelyn-Davies's Women's Co-operative Guild (WCG) since 1912, when reforming maternity care was among its primary objectives. It was Virginia who, in 1914, encouraged Llewelyn-Davies to publish *Maternity: Letters from Working Women*, a collection of missives that made clear the danger of repeat motherhood in deprived circumstances. Not only are these letters reminiscent of Stopes's story about her early patient with two children and a history of miscarriages but, in *Radiant Motherhood*, Stopes actually quotes from *Maternity*, calling it a 'poignant book' (*RM* 177n). Inspired by the WCG's collection, Stopes went on to publish her own book of letters from working-class mothers, *Mother England* (1929). In these

Motherhood and Eugenics   **129**

letters women not only describe the twin burdens of poverty and repeat maternity, but ask for contraceptive advice.

Like Stopes, Woolf valued birth control as a safe, hygienic and affordable form of family limitation for working-class women. In a deleted scene from the holograph draft of *The Years*, written in 1933 but set in 1910, Woolf looks back to the days before birth control was available:

> 'Look at those wretched little children' said Rose, looking down into the street.
> 'Stop them, then' said Maggie. 'Stop them having children.'
> 'But you cant' said Rose.
> 'Oh nonsense, my dear Rose,' said Elvira. 'What you do is this: you ring a bell in Harley Street. Sir John at home? Step this way ma'am. Now Sir John, you say, casting your eyes this way & that way, the fact of the matter is, ~~my husband~~' whereupon you blush. Most inadvisable, most inadvisable, he says, the welfare of the human race – sacrifice, private interests – ~~three~~ six words on half a sheet of paper. ~~A tip.~~ [In the margin: Three guineas in his left hand]. Out you go – well that's all. What I mean is, in plain language, ~~if that woman~~ Maggie ~~says she wont have a child~~, she wont [have] a child [. . .] 'We wouldnt have children if we didnt want them,' said Maggie.
> '~~You wouldn't be allowed~~ But you cant say that in public' said Rose. 'You can say that here, to me, in private' [. . .] 'but how is that woman down there going to Harley Street? with three guineas?'
> 'Well then, publish it in the Times' said Elvira [. . .]
> 'D'you never take anything seriously Elvira?' said Rose. '~~It's against the law~~'.[117]

The doctor protects the 'welfare of the human race' in a eugenic fashion, offering abortions so that disadvantaged children – those born too close together or later children in an already large family – might not be born. While Maggie acknowledges that Harley Street abortions are not a viable or affordable option for the women down in the street, those women's chance at controlling their own reproductive lives changed as birth control methods became accessible.[118]

This passage highlights not only an important social change that had occurred in the intervening years, but also the classist and eugenic impetus for this change. In addition, Woolf appreciated how birth control gave wealthier women greater autonomy over their intellectual and professional lives. She saw first-hand the difference between her somewhat liberated contemporaries – Vanessa or Vita – and the yoke of maternity that burdened her own mother and quickly killed Stella. She explores this in *To the Lighthouse*, where, not only must Mrs Ramsay placate and support her husband, but she must sacrifice herself through fecundity:

> It was sympathy he wanted, to be assured of his genius, first of all, and then to be taken within the circle of life, warmed and soothed, to have his senses restored to him, his barrenness made fertile, all the rooms of the house made full of life – the drawing-room; behind the drawing-room the kitchen; above the kitchen the bedrooms; and beyond them the nurseries; they must be furnished, they must be filled with life.

The text goes on to note how draining all this life-giving was: 'all her strength flaring up to be drunk and quenched [. . .] So boasting of her capacity to surround and protect, there was scarcely a shell of herself left for her to know herself by; all was so lavished and spent' (*TL* 43–44). Given how harmful repeat motherhood was, it makes sense that the three guineas previously set aside for abortions became the title of Woolf's polemic on 'the sexual life' (*D4* 6) of professional women. With the birth control movement changing life for women, this money was now free to improve other areas of society.

The increased freedom that came with voluntary motherhood and fewer children fitted in with the aspirations for womankind expressed in *A Room of One's Own*. Stopes plays a central role in the text's campaign for the creation of a female literary tradition, a movement that is predicated upon a post-contraceptive world in which women can 'go on bearing children, but, so they say, in twos and threes, not in tens and twelves' (*AROO* 101).[119] Early on in *A Room*, the narrator explains how excess childbearing has taken its toll on women's achievements:

> Making a fortune and bearing thirteen children – no human being could stand it. Consider the facts, we said. First there are nine months before the baby is born. Then the baby is born. Then there are three or four months spent in feeding the baby. After the baby is fed there are certainly five years spent in playing with the baby. You cannot, it seems, let children run about the streets. (*AROO* 20)

Women cannot achieve under the pressure of excessive maternity, which leaves them time-, resources- and space-poor. Childbearing must be curbed before acquiring a room, £500 and the time to enjoy

Motherhood and Eugenics 131

them. And Woolf's contemporary reader would have implicitly associated this pro-contraceptive argument with a public crusade that saw Stopes as its established figurehead.

Something that may have further galvanised Woolf with regard to Stopes is the slew of sensational censorship cases that erupted in the interwar period. Three of the most important – against James Joyce's *Ulysses* (banned in 1922), Radclyffe Hall's *The Well of Loneliness* and D. H. Lawrence's *Lady Chatterley's Lover* (both banned in 1928) – prompted the Woolfs to start an anti-censorship campaign. In April 1929, only a month after her 'Women and Fiction' lectures were published in US magazine *The Forum*, and exactly the time she began to edit them into the final form they would take for *A Room*, Woolf contributed an essay to a series entitled 'The Censorship of Books'. In this essay she commented:

> There can be no doubt that books fall, in respect of indecency, into two classes. There are books written, published and sold with the object of causing pleasure or corruption by means of their indecency [. . .] There are others whose indecency is not the object of the book, but incidental to some other purpose – scientific, social, aesthetic – on the writer's part. The police magistrate's power should be definitely limited to the suppression of books which are sold as pornography to people who seek out and enjoy pornography. The others should be left alone. Any man or woman of average intelligence and culture knows the difference between the two kinds of book and has no difficulty in distinguishing one from the other. (*E5* 36)

Though Stopes's books were never confiscated, banned or censored, the very public Halliday libel trial addressed charges of obscenity against her works.[120] By championing Stopes's writing during a time of literary censorship, *A Room* proves that Woolf associated Stopes's writing with something more than titillation; writing with a 'purpose – scientific, social, aesthetic'.

Marie Stopes and Procreative Pleasure in *A Room of One's Own*

While this chapter contends that *A Room of One's Own* thoroughly engages with Stopes's writing and ideas, this has been disputed in the past. Although Donald Childs, Jane Marcus and Anna Snaith have noted that Marie Stopes is present in the text under the pseudonym

132   *Virginia Woolf and Motherhood*

Mary Carmichael, with Stopes's newly published novel *Love's Creation* appearing under the alternative title 'Life's Adventure', some critics temper these assertions. Christina Alt argues that that the difference between Marie Stopes and the woman whom Woolf calls Mary Carmichael has been too easily put to one side, and Celia Marshik even goes so far as to call Mary Carmichael 'fictional'.[121] Alt also points out that the two friendly women scientists Woolf describes in *A Room* do not exist in *Love's Creation* – instead only one woman enters a room full of rather hostile men.

Woolf does misrepresent Carmichael, describing her as 'an unknown girl writing her first novel in a bed-sitting-room, without enough of those desirable things, time, money and idleness' (*AROO* 85), when, in fact, Stopes was supported by a very wealthy husband and had numerous 'rooms of her own' in which to work. However, the rest of the text's discrepancies are easily resolved. *Love's Creation* was originally published under Stopes's mother's maiden name – Carmichael – to draw a line between her scientific writing and this foray into creative literature. Thus all early editions bear this name, as do any coexistent reviews. Andre Gerard also notes that Marie Stopes often went by the name Mrs Carmichael in public and that this may well have been how Woolf knew her at the time.[122] So, in fact, Carmichael *is* the correct surname name of the author. It is also possible that Woolf used the name Carmichael because it was a name that Stopes shared with her mother. In addition to being a feminist and suffragist, Charlotte Carmichael Stopes was a Shakespeare scholar who had written several biographies of the poet that explored his family life, including the lives of his sister Joan and daughter Judith, who are amalgamated into a single fictional figure that Woolf uses to further her arguments about women poets.[123] In addition, Woolf's letter to Molly MacCarthy (quoted above) refers to Stopes as Mary, so the inaccurate first name could have been playfulness or a longstanding error – although it is more likely to be a continuation of *A Room*'s allusion to the four Marys.

Woolf points out, several times, that 'Life's Adventure' is Carmichael's first novel, a fact taken from *Love's Creation*'s original publisher's note which read:

> The public will be interested to learn that this first novel is by an author already world-famous for other works. She is taking a pen name for her fiction so that readers may not be confused and find themselves in possession of a type of book different from that they expect [. . .] 'Marie Carmichael' is really another facet of Dr Marie Stopes. (*LC* 2)

Motherhood and Eugenics   133

The narrative differences between *Love's Creation* and 'Life's Adventure' can be explained by the fact that Woolf had already written the section on the unnamed book by an anonymous author *before* she added Mary Carmichael to the text. Carmichael and 'Life's Adventure' were non-fictional additions that fleshed out Woolf's feminist narrative about two female scientists who liked each other. In the final version of the text Carmichael figures before Chloe and Olivia, but in the manuscript the unnamed author and the story of Chloe and Olivia make their appearance in an undated section that appears to have been written before any mention of Carmichael. In fact, Carmichael's inclusion in Woolf's draft can be dated to between 22 and 25 March 1929.[124] Since *Love's Creation* was published in 1928 Woolf must have read it before the end of March 1929 and found that its feminist, pro-contraceptive, evolutionary ethics chimed with the story of the hereditary female canon she was trying to tell.

Beyond their joint aspirations for women's liberation through contraception, *Love's Creation* and *A Room of One's Own* share an interest in evolution – Stopes of the biological/organic sort and Woolf of the artistic/intellectual – with both borrowing freely from each other's discipline. In *Love's Creation* scientist Kenneth Harvey hones a theory of Darwinian proportions that is heavily influenced by evolutionary and eugenic principles. Like Galton and other empirically focused social scientists of the time, Kenneth maintains that his theory will result in 'an enlargement of our scientific conceptions, but at the same time that it will change all our social problems and everything else: then we may have an era of *healthiness*' (*LC* 135, emphasis in original). In *A Room* Woolf investigates the evolution of women's writing and the measures required to ensure a healthier future for the canon. Her metaphors are organic, depicting texts as intellectual offspring birthed from the parent books of previous generations. Texts become carriers for a hereditary social code and reading and writing become transmissive so that, 'when one takes a sentence of Coleridge into the mind, it explodes and gives birth to all kinds of other ideas [. . .] it has the secret of perpetual life' (*AROO* 91). This can also be true for middlebrow fiction such as 'Life's Adventure' which, Woolf asserts, must be read 'as if it were the last volume in a fairly long series, continuing all those other books that I have been glancing at [. . .] For books continue each other' (*AROO* 72).

After the point where Carmichael was added to the narrative of *A Room* her influence becomes ubiquitous. One of the most notable examples of this is the depiction of artistic creation as a pleasurable procreative act, what Shelley Saguaro calls 'Woolf's sexual allegory

134   *Virginia Woolf and Motherhood*

of the nuptials of the "androgynous mind"'.[125] Donald Childs high-lights the difference between the 'understanding of sexual intercourse as having an exclusively procreative function' – a particularly eugenic viewpoint – and Stopes's linking of conception and sexual gratifica-tion. In the eyes of many eugenicists Stopes's attention to pleasure endowed sexual intercourse with an alternative 'immoral' motivation. Childs suggests that Woolf (as a eugenicist) was morally offended by Stopes's work, even if she 'admired the technological sophistication' of contraception.[126] However, while Woolf's letter to MacCarthy uses humour to explore the generational difference between an older, more reserved attitude to sex and a new relaxed stance, the incorporation of sexual pleasure in *A Room*'s scene of literary creation, and the excitement she exhibited when 'conceiving' 'an entire new book [. . .] about the sexual life of women' (*D4* 6), suggest that Woolf saw cre-ative possibilities in such ideas. Indeed, Layne Parish Craig notes that not only did Stopes purposefully align herself with British sexologists like Havelock Ellis and Edward Carpenter (two of *Married Love*'s epigraphs are Carpenter quotes) but that this 'codevelopment of the politics of birth control and sexuality [. . .] would have provided con-text and acceptance for the narratives of sexuality Woolf explores'.[127]

Stopes maintained that sexual pleasure and compatibility were vital to the production of eugenically sound babies; a view that is central to the plot of *Love's Creation*. One of the novel's protagonists – a beautiful and maternal young woman named Rose Amber – loses two pregnancies in her first marriage because she is 'drained by' the 'too constant passion' (*LC* 123) of her husband, a man who lacks self-control and is ignorant of women's sexual needs. In addition to exhausting Rose Amber without rousing the emotions considered essential to the creation of a healthy child, this man is dysgenic. He is indifferent to whether he passes on his genetic code and eventually reveals that he does not much care about having children because 'my father's line can very well be continued by the children of my younger brother' (*LC* 137). It is essential to the eugenic romance of *Love's Creation* that this character dies. When he does, Rose Amber remarries, creating a eugenically appropriate and sexually compat-ible union. Not only is her new husband (scientist Kenneth) 'healthy and so beautifully straight' (*LC* 8), but he also understands that his 'strength and self-control' (*LC* 182) are fundamental to their mar-riage's sexual success. To this end he promises she 'never need fear that we shall not go *together* – even to the innermost experiences' (*LC* 182, emphasis in original). Finally able to 'experience and understand the thrilling joys of the body' (*LC* 122), the couple are free to dedicate themselves to parenthood.

Motherhood and Eugenics   135

This idea of sexual harmony also pervades Chapter VI of *A Room*, where Woolf's sexual metaphors link the act of writing with the act of intercourse. Woolf writes:

> Some collaboration has to take place in the mind between the woman and the man before the art of creation can be accomplished. Some marriage of opposites has to be consummated [. . .] Not a wheel must grate, not a light glimmer. The curtains must be close drawn. The writer, I thought, once his experience is over, must lie back and let his mind celebrate its nuptials in darkness. (*AROO* 94)

There are two factors fundamental to the success of this (pro)creative act: heterosexuality and enjoyment. Woolf insists that the best writing comes from heterosexual pleasure because 'the union of man and woman makes for the greatest satisfaction, the most complete happiness' (*AROO* 88). This image is redolent of Stopes's eugenic sexual ideal – a paring necessary to make perfect babies as well as perfect texts. For Stopes, such conditions, facilitated by judiciously used contraception, would result in well-spaced and well-desired babies, ultimately leading to a rapid improvement in humankind. For Woolf, the same conditions would spark new books into life in the brains of well-read women.

Woolf's heterosexual union of the mind is complex and at turns contradictory. The heterosexual creative act does not, necessarily, promote a heteronormative existence. She argues that the best creative mind – a mind that 'is fully fertilized and uses all its faculties' (*AROO* 89) – is androgynous, containing both masculine and feminine attributes in order to support its procreative act. Barbara Fassler, who has investigated various sexologists' influence on the Bloomsbury group, has noted that this argument fits with 'a common belief that to be artistic one must have the unique combination of masculine and feminine elements found in hermaphrodites and homosexuals'.[128] This idea was shared by contemporary thinkers such as Havelock Ellis and Sigmund Freud, and can be found in art ranging from the ancient Greek (*The Symposium*) to modern poetry (Rainer Maria Rilke, *Book of Hours*). In *A Room* Woolf attributes the theory to Coleridge, noting: 'when he said that a great mind is androgynous [. . .] He meant, perhaps, that the androgynous mind is resonant and porous; that it transmits emotion without impediment; that it is naturally creative, incandescent and undivided' (*AROO* 89). Woolf goes on to list Coleridge, Shakespeare, Keats, Sterne, Cowper and Lamb as examples of androgynous authors, Shelley as 'sexless', Milton and Ben Jonson as 'too [. . .] male' and Proust as 'wholly

136   *Virginia Woolf and Motherhood*

androgynous, if not perhaps a little too much of a woman'. Interestingly, at this point (perhaps under the influence of the more gender-traditional Stopes) Woolf adopts a voice that is rather conventional. She notes at the end of this list of *male* authors, that 'without some mixture of the kind the intellect seems to predominate' (*AROO* 93), and thus implies that the masculine side of the brain is responsible for rationality, and the female side for emotion.

'The Third Generation': The Utopian Eugenics of *Love's Creation* and *A Room of One's Own*

In *A Room* Woolf acknowledges *Love's Creation*'s eugenic nature, noting of Stopes's novel: 'I am going to get the hang of her sentences first, I said, before I load my memory with blue eyes and brown and the relationship that there may be between Chloe and Roger' (*AROO* 73). The eugenic nature of the reference to blue and brown eyes is unmistakeable given Woolf's previous use of the terms, but it is also accurate – *Love's Creation* does include several references to the eye colour of its protagonists and their potential offspring.[129] Similarly, Woolf's adaptation of Darwinian inheritance to the literary canon adopts eugenic fears about an increasingly 'unfit' population. Like those eugenicists who used the losses of the Boer War to argue that the general population was declining, *A Room* notes a literary decline that sees 'some of the finest works of our greatest living writers fall upon deaf ears. Do what she will a woman cannot find in them that fountain of perpetual life' (*AROO* 92). This literary decline is echoed by Stopes, who writes in *Radiant Motherhood*:

> our artists have in recent years tended ever more and more to forget that the highest form of art should also be infectious. Goodness, beauty and prophetic vision have as strong a contagious quality as disease if they are embodied in a form rendered vital by the mating of truth and beauty. (*RM* 220)

Woolf and Stopes agree that art is handed down from generation to generation. For both this contemporary decline in artistic potency is due to a lack of sexual unity, whether between 'truth and beauty' or 'the two sides of the mind' (*AROO* 91). Woolf likens reading some living authors to 'eavesdropping at some purely masculine orgy' and of the uber-patriarchy of fascist Italy, where 'one can hardly fail to be

Motherhood and Eugenics 137

impressed [. . .] by the sense of unmitigated masculinity' (*AROO* 92), she wonders:

> whether poetry can come of an incubator. Poetry ought to have a mother as well as a father. The Fascist poem, one may fear, will be a horrid little abortion such as one sees in a glass jar in the museum of some county town. (*AROO* 93)

This language is particularly strong – though this image of abortion bears less resemblance to the morally ambiguous actions of *The Years*' deleted doctor, and rather more to a spontaneous (if unnatural) miscarriage. Stopes, for her part, did not entirely dismiss abortion when medically necessary, but called it, along with infanticide, 'the early and more barbarous equivalents of contraception'.[130]

Despite the worrying trend of living writers who 'lack suggestive power' and produce deformed, inviable offspring, both Woolf and Stopes are optimistic about the future, consoling themselves 'with the reflection that this is perhaps a passing phase' (*AROO* 93). A recurring theme in Stopes's work is the notion of being within two generations of the perfect human race – the grandparents of greatness. In *Radiant Motherhood* Stopes anticipates that 'by a second generation all should be already far on the highway to new and wonderful powers, which are to-day almost unsuspected' (*RM* 218). She repeatedly notes how excited she is to meet these 'grandchildren belonging to a generation so wonderful, so endowed and so improved out of recognition' (*RM* 216–17). In 1921, at a meeting that was intended to whip up public support for birth control, she stated that widespread adoption of her sexual recommendations – both contraceptive and procreative – would lead to an

> entirely new type of human creature, stepping into a future so beautiful, so full of the real joy of self-expression and understanding that we here today may look upon our grandchildren and think almost that the gods have descended to walk upon the earth.[131]

Love's Creation reiterates the pre-eminence of this third generation, with Kenneth repeatedly stating that his own worth lies in the fact that his scientific ideas, as well as his genetic strength, are only likely to be fully realised in his grandchildren. Kenneth twice explains that he 'may only be the Focus-Changer's grandfather' (*LC* 118, 182–83) finally asking Rose Amber: 'I fear I'm only the epoch-maker's *grandfather*! How long can you love a man whose only claim to greatness

138 *Virginia Woolf and Motherhood*

is that he will be a grandfather?' (*LC* 183, emphasis in original). He also observes that Erasmus Darwin's work was a precursor to his grandson Charles's theory of evolution noting, even 'Darwin drove into our silly heads the idea which had been hovering in the minds of his grandfather and *lots* of other people'.

For Woolf – who briefly intended to call *Night and Day* 'The Third Generation' (*D1* 19) – this perfection of a future generation translates into the promise that, given the ideal environment (time, money, leisure, a room of one's own, freedom from oppressive motherhood and access to reading matter possessing 'the secret of perpetual life' (*AROO* 92)) a female poet of Shakespearian worth will arrive in 100 years. Indeed, this utopian prediction is inspired by Carmichael's novel:

> Give her another hundred years, I concluded, reading the last chapter [. . .] give her a room of her own and five hundred a year, let her speak her mind and leave out half that she now puts in, and she will write a better book one of these days. She will be a poet, I said, putting *Life's Adventure*, by Mary Carmichael, at the end of the shelf, in another hundred years' time. (*AROO* 85)

By giving Stopes the opportunity to fulfil her promise in the form of a poetess descendant, Woolf shows her sensitivity to *Love's Creation*'s story and its eugenic ideas.

One of the reasons Woolf adopts Stopes as a figurehead for eugenic, literary maternity is because *Love's Creation* not only prescribes biological parenthood but also embraces forms of intellectual inheritance. Kenneth has a grand theory of 'super-consciousness' – an almost mystical concept of social unity that posits a universal mind among all humans. Kenneth hypothesises that each

> consciousness, definite, comprehensive, though limited, ultimately subserves a greater super-consciousness; my life, fleeting and trivial, definitely fits into a greater life, as the cells of my body are doing within me in my own life. These cells are replaced as they individually die, but through them I retain the very memory of incidents in my life long past. So may I as a unit vessel, the brain cell perhaps, of this larger more complex super-consciousness hand on remembered beauty. (*LC* 149)

This idea chimes well with Woolf's claim in *Moments of Being* that: 'Behind the cotton wool is hidden a pattern; that we – I mean all human beings – are connected with this; that the whole world is a work of art; that we are parts of the work of art' (*MB* 85). While each author's metaphor remains consistent with their area of interest – Woolf: art and Stopes: biology – both depict a universal social-consciousness whose fundamental drive is aesthetic. Both *Love's Creation* and *A Room* borrow freely from each other's domains, the mixing of scientific and artistic language and ideas adding cultural and historic context to both (and also corroborating the prevalence and significance of pseudo-scientific language at the time). Stopes makes frequent reference to intellectual or 'spiritual' inheritance. In one scene, Kenneth asserts that, if not his biological children, then one of his 'spiritual children, will [. . .] turn the wheel that guides the focus of mankind' (*LC* 148). Correspondingly, Woolf takes her argument for literary inspiration into the realm of heredity. When she uses art to negate her childfree status and stake a claim to 'immortality', she is given licence by the fact that eugenicist Stopes accepts that inheritance, in the very best of human endeavours, can be 'spiritual' rather than organic.

From *Night and Day* – which concentrates on the ideal domestic setting in which to create texts – to *A Room of One's Own* – which focuses on the intellectual atmosphere that fertilises them – Woolf's focus on the healthiest way to 'birth' a text is eugenic. In *A Room*, Woolf uses class-focused eugenic language to make her argument about the inequality inherent in a stratified, patriarchal system. She declares: 'genius like Shakespeare's is not born among labouring, uneducated, servile people. It was not born in England among the Saxons and the Britons. It is not born to-day among the working classes' (*AROO* 44). This language exposes the character of a movement that not only embraced class-bias, but was class-based. Donald MacKenzie's research shows that both the leadership and the membership of the EES were almost exclusively middle-class professionals.[132] In *Three Guineas* the narrator discusses membership of this class, stating that she comes 'of what, in this hybrid age when, though birth is mixed, classes still remain fixed, it is convenient to call the educated class' (*TG* 118). This idea of 'mixed' birth within a traditional class structure recalls William Rodney and Ralph Denham – men who have achieved equal status through education and employment, despite being born into families with different class histories.

For middle-class professionals who had come from humbler backgrounds, part of the appeal of eugenics was its meritocratic ideals – the belief that people of intelligence and aptitude would thrive under

140 *Virginia Woolf and Motherhood*

the correct social conditions.[133] Clare Hanson explains this ideal in the following way;

> the aim of the meritocracy is not equality but 'equality of opportunity' [. . .] the meritocracy is a society in which it is alleged (by the elite) that everyone is given a fair opportunity to find the role for which he or she is suited.[134]

This meritocracy had limits – in a eugenic utopia an individual's role would still be dictated by social class. A tension can be located in Woolf's thinking in the juxtaposition between texts where she publicly recognises the discrimination offered by a society in which inequality begins before birth, and those where she falls to class-bias (for example, calling *Mrs Dalloway*'s Doris Kilman 'degradingly poor' (*MD* 135)). This tension will be investigated in the next chapter through Woolf's literary representations of food and motherhood.

When, in *Three Guineas*, Woolf argues for a maternal wage (something that working-class organisations such as the WCG also supported), she does so as a professional middle-class woman with a eugenic voice. She insists that a woman from her class 'must make it her business to press for a living wage in all the professions now open to her sex' and that 'above all she must press for a wage to be paid by the State legally to *the mothers of educated men*' (my emphasis). 'Consider', Woolf entreats, 'what effect this would have upon the birth-rate, in the very class where the birth-rate is falling, in the very class where births are desirable – the educated class' (*TG* 236). Woolf is not interested in universal maternity payments, but in intellectual emancipation for women of her class. Nonetheless, to make her arguments she borrows the rhetoric widely used in the appeal for working-class women's maternity endowments, testifying to the 'poverty' and 'hardships' (*TG* 236) of childbearing for upper middle-class women. In popular debates such arguments often revolved around food.[135] Those campaigning for maternity endowments for poor women argued that such imbursements would allow women to feed themselves and their children better, and thus 'safeguard' against the 'permanent enfeeblement of the nation's stock'.[136] In one 1914 tract on the living expenses and lifestyle of the working-class, pro-family endowment writer (and Fabian) Maud Pember Reeves found that men used around 35 per cent of the weekly budget on weekday dinners compared with 5 per cent for their wives and children. Pember Reeves notes that due to 'the pressure of circumstances' the working-class wife must feed her husband 'sufficiently and make what is over do for herself and the children'.[137] Woolf's comparison of the meals at Oxbridge men's and women's colleges in *A Room* borrows from such family endowment narratives, but repurposes them to suit a text about the educated middle class. By reading moments such as this alongside other maternal discourses of the time it is possible to highlight how nexuses of food and motherhood in Woolf's writing uncover class-based tensions that ofen cannot be resolved.

Notes

1. *Modernism and Eugenics: Woolf, Eliot, Yeats and the Culture of Degeneration* (Cambridge: Cambridge University Press, 2001), pp. 14, 22.
2. 'Eugenics: "They should certainly be killed"', in *A Concise Companion to Modernism,* ed. David Bradshaw (Oxford: Blackwell, 2003), p. 50. Emphasis in original.
3. 'Woolf and Eugenics', p. 439.
4. *The Morbid Age: Britain and the Crisis of Civilisation, 1919–1939* (London: Allen Lane, 2009), p. 106.
5. Whether this type of feminist eugenics requires the term 'unorthodox' itself deserves some discussion. While the public face of eugenics was somewhat patriarchal, feminists were always an integral part of the movement. Indeed, the Eugenics Education Society was founded when Sybil Neville-Rolfe, a social reformer who strongly believed in the dual use of contraceptives and positive eugenic principles, approached Francis Galton with her proposal for an organisation dedicated to bringing reproductive hygiene to the general population. Neville-Rolfe worked with prostitutes and unmarried mothers, founded the Imperial Society for Promoting Sex Education, and argued that: 'The popularization of the use of relatively effective contraceptive methods has given to those with sufficient intelligence [. . .] a long step towards personal, social and economic freedom' (*Social Biology and Welfare* (London: George Allen & Unwin, 1949), p. 305). For more on feminists within the Eugenics Society, see Ann Taylor Allen, 'Feminism and Eugenics in Germany and Britain, 1900–1940: A Comparative Perspective', *German Studies Review*, 23.3 (2000), p. 480; and Michael Freeden, 'Eugenics and Progressive Thought: A Study in Ideological Affinity', *The Historical Journal*, 22.3 (1979), pp. 645–71.
6. *Hereditary Genius: An Inquiry into its Laws and Consequences* (London: Macmillan, 1869), p. 1.
7. Overy, *The Morbid Age*, p. 105.
8. James Russell Lowell, 1882, quoted in Frederic Maitland, *The Life and Letters of Leslie Stephen* (London: Duckworth 1906), pp. 318–19.

142 *Virginia Woolf and Motherhood*

9. Leslie Stephen and Frances Galton also knew each other, having climbed Col du Geant together in 1857 (Maitland, *The Life and Letters of Leslie Stephen*, p. 81). Woolf read (or planned to read) *Hereditary Genius* in January 1905 (*PA* 221).
10. *Virginia Woolf*, p. 55.
11. *The Science of Ethics* (London: Smith, Elder, 1882), pp. viii, v–vi.
12. 'Virginia Woolf and Leslie Stephen', p. 355.
13. *Catalogue of Books from the Library of Leonard and Virginia Woolf*, V/s, I, 39, 57.
14. *The Science of Ethics*, pp. 443–44.
15. *Social Rights and Duties: Addresses to Ethical Societies* (London: Swan Sonnenschein, 1896), pp. 52–54.
16. Galton was so driven to create this empirical data that he ended up making several important contributions to the world of statistics. See Ruth Schwartz Cowan, 'Francis Galton's Statistical Ideas: The Influence of Eugenics', *Isis*, 63.4 (1972), pp. 509–10.
17. 'Eugenics and Progressive Thought', p. 645.
18. 'Memoranda', *British Journal of Inebriety*, 10 (1912), pp. 105–14 and *Report of Proceedings of the First International Eugenics Congress, Held at the University of London, July 24th to 30th, 1912* (*Problems in Eugenics*, vol. II) (London: The Eugenics Education Society, 1912).
19. *Beginning Again* (New York: Harcourt Brace Jovanovich, 1975), p. 82.
20. *Letters of Leonard Woolf* (New York: Harcourt Brace Jovanovich, 1989), p. 181, n. 3.
21. *The Unknown Virginia Woolf* (Brighton: Harvester, 1982), p. 121. Also see Craig, *When Sex Changed*, p. 51; Childs, *Modernism and Eugenics*, p. 29; and Victoria Glendinning, *Leonard Woolf: A Biography* (London: Simon & Schuster, 2006), pp. 148–49.
22. 'Cecil Woolf Remembers Leonard Woolf', *Virginia Woolf Miscellany*, 72 (2007), p. 10.
23. *Hereditary Genius*, p. 4. See Webb, *The Decline in the Birth-Rate* (London: The Fabian Society, 1907): this tract is often misread and misquoted as recommending limitations on the Jewish population.
24. There is a considerable body of work on Woolf's attitude towards Jews and Judaism: see, for example, Briggs, *Reading Virginia Woolf*, pp. 178–81.
25. *The Unknown Virginia Woolf*, p. 121.
26. T. B. Hyslop, 'A Discussion on Occupation and Environment as Causative Factors of Insanity', *British Medical Journal*, 2.2337 (1905), p. 942.
27. Ibid., p. 944.
28. 'Discussion on Insanity and Marriage', *British Medical Journal*, 2.2599 (1910), pp. 1242–43.
29. This phrase is Leonard Woolf quoting Savage (*Beginning Again*, p. 82).
30. *American Nervousness: Its Causes and Consequences, a Supplement to Nervous Exhaustion (Neurasthenia)* (New York: G. P. Putnam, 1881), p. 26.

Motherhood and Eugenics   143

31. 'A Lecture on Neurasthenia and Mental Disorders', *The Medical Magazine*, 20 (1911), p. 620.
32. 'Discussion on Insanity and Marriage', p. 1243.
33. *Hereditary Genius*, p. 328.
34. Ibid., pp. ix–x.
35. *Beginning Again*, p. 32.
36. *The Flight of the Mind: Virginia Woolf's Art and Manic-Depressive Illness* (London: University of California Press, 1992), p. 11.
37. Spotts (ed.), *Letters of Leonard Woolf*, p. 192.
38. Quoted in Lee, *Virginia Woolf*, p. 335.
39. *Virginia Woolf*, p. 334.
40. *When Sex Changed*, p. 69.
41. For Galton's view on the intellectual inferiority of women, see Allen Buss, 'Galton and Sex Differences: An Historical Note', *Journal of the History of the Behavioral Sciences*, 12 (1976), pp. 283–85. Buss warns behavioural scientists against taking an unquestioning stance on Galton's work on the psychology of sex differences, asking them to keep in mind how Galton's belief 'that women were inferior (not just different!) to men was not confined to physical traits' (p. 284).
42. 'The Development of Francis Galton's Ideas on the Mechanism of Heredity', *Journal of the History of Biology*, 32.2 (1999), p. 266.
43. It is interesting to note that Woolf bases both of her semi-autobiographical protagonist's parents on the Stephen side of the family, effectively disregarding any hereditary input her mother and the maternal side of the family may have had in her intellectual make-up.
44. Although Galton presents a list of Woolf's fore*fathers* in his survey of the Stephen family's literary prowess, Leslie Stephen felt writing was a woman's occupation, noting once in a letter about Thoby: 'I don't want him to be an author. That is a thing for ladies and Ginia will do well in that line' (quoted in Hill, 'Virginia Woolf and Leslie Stephen', p. 351). Woolf echoes this sentiment in 'Professions for Women': 'Writing was a reputable and harmless occupation. The family peace was not broken by the scratching of a pen' (*E6* 479).
45. While both dogs and flowers were keen interests of Galton's, I have not been able to find any proof he was interested in heraldry; however, it is clear from the beginning of *Flush*, where Woolf compares the positive and negative breeding techniques of the Spaniel Club with 'The Heralds College [. . .] attempt to preserve the purity of the human family' (*F* 7), that she associated the discipline of heraldry with eugenics.
46. 'Do Not Feed the Birds: *Night and Day* and the Defence of the Realm Act', in *Contradictory Woolf*, ed. Derek Ryan and Stella Bolaki (Liverpool: Liverpool University Press, 2012), p. 280. For an example of an article that disagrees with this reading, see Hussey, 'Refractions of Desire: The Early Fiction of Virginia and Leonard Woolf', *Modern Fiction Studies*, 38.1 (1992), pp. 127–46.

144 *Virginia Woolf and Motherhood*

47. Originally published in 1906 with a chapter on 'Mendelism', *Recent Progress* was expanded to include eugenics in 1909. See Walter Garstang, review of Robert Heath Lock *Recent Progress in the Study of Variation, Heredity, and Evolution*. Second Edition (1909), *The Eugenics Review*, 1.3 (1909), pp. 210–12.
48. Schwartz Cowan, 'Francis Galton's Statistical Ideas', pp. 516–17.
49. 'Eugenics and Common Sense', *The Atlantic*, September 1914, pp. 349–50.
50. Woolf's desire to overthrow social expectations can be seen in *Night and Day*'s subtle connections with radical feminism. For example, Michael Whitworth points out that the orchid houses and refreshment pavilion at Kew – both of which Katherine and Ralph visit – were the site of two separate militant suffragist attacks in February 1913 (Whitworth, 'Introduction', in Virginia Woolf, *Night and Day*, ed. Michael Whitworth (Cambridge: Cambridge University Press, 2018), p. 657, EN 350: 36, 359: 7).
51. 'Between Being and Nothingness: The "Astonishing Precipice" of Virginia Woolf's *Night and Day*', *Journal of Modern Literature*, 26.2 (2003), p. 68.
52. R. Plomin, *Genetics and Experience: The Interplay between Nature and Nurture* (Thousand Oaks, CA: Sage, 1994), p. 3.
53. 'Cassandra's Worms: Unravelling the Threads of Virginia Woolf's Lepidoptera Imagery', *Hungarian Journal of English and American Studies*, 9.1 (2003), p. 111.
54. *Virginia Woolf and the Study of Nature* (Cambridge: Cambridge University Press, 2010), p. 113.
55. In 1886, Galton published 'Family Likeness in Eye-Colour' (*Nature*, 34 (1886), p. 137), while in 1907 the eugenic zoologist Charles Davenport and his embryologist wife Gertrude Davenport announced their finding that eye colour was inherited in the Mendelian fashion ('Heredity of Eye Color in Man', *Science*, 26 (1907), pp. 589–92).
56. 'Eugenics in Britain', *Social Studies of Science*, 6.3/4 (1976), p. 505.
57. There is a significant body of scholarly work that examines class in *Night and Day* which is beyond the scope of this chapter. For Rodney as an 'appropriate match' for Katharine, see Randy Malamud, 'Splitting the Husks: Woolf's Modernist Language in *Night and Day*', *South Central Review*, 6.1 (1989), p. 35; for a comparison of Ralph's class and Leonard's Judaism, see Hussey, 'Refractions of Desire', p. 130, and for an interesting examination of Leonard's class, see Cecil Woolf, 'Cecil Woolf Remembers Leonard Woolf', pp. 9–10, and Freema Gottlieb, 'Leonard Woolf's Attitudes to his Jewish Background and to Judaism', *Transactions & Miscellanies*, 25 (1973–75), pp. 25–37.
58. *Hereditary Genius*, p. 62.
59. 'Between Being and Nothingness', p. 66.
60. *Reading Virginia Woolf*, p. 49.
61. *Virginia Woolf: A Critical Memoir* (London: Continuum International, 2007), p. 93.
62. 'Discovering the "Enchanted Region": A Revisionary Reading of *Night and Day*', *CEA Critic*, 54.3 (1992), pp. 15–16.

Motherhood and Eugenics   145

63. Review of Virginia Woolf, *Night and Day*, *Times Literary Supplement*, 30 October 1919, p. 607.
64. *The Science of Ethics*, p. 444.
65. *Ambivalent Activist*, p. 87.
66. *Reading Virginia Woolf*, p. 54.
67. 'Suffrage and Virginia Woolf', p. 127.
68. Review of *Night and Day*, p. 607.
69. Critics have disagreed about Mrs Hilbery's role in Katharine's coming of age. Priest sees her 'as an agent of the patriarchy' who forces her daughter into a marriage she does not want ('Between Being and Nothingness', p. 79), while Cooley records how she acts as a catalyst for positive change and maturation, helping Katharine learn 'the importance of matriarchal – rather than patriarchal – guidance' ('Discovering the "Enchanted Region"', p. 15). For all Mrs Hilbery's work-shy, socially oblivious chaos, I would contend that she is a liberating, intuitive, positive force in the book. As she says of herself: 'I'm quite a large bit of the fool, but the fools in Shakespeare say all the clever things' (*ND* 260). In *Virginia Woolf's Influential Forebears*, Marion Dell discusses how Woolf based Mrs Hilbery on Anne Ritchie, Leslie's sister-in-law through his first wife and daughter of William Makepeace Thackeray (pp. 33–35).
70. *L2* xvi.
71. *Beginning Again*, p. 81.
72. *Virginia Woolf*, p. 188.
73. *Modernism and Eugenics*, p. 28.
74. 'Opening Remarks: The Galton Lecture', *The Eugenics Review*, 38 (1946), p. 40.
75. Keynes quickly resigned, losing patience with Stopes's trying ways, but he continued to champion birth control. Richard Davenport-Hines, *Universal Man: The Seven Lives of John Maynard Keynes* (London: William Collins, 2015), p. 242.
76. Charles Webster (ed.), *Biology, Medicine and Society 1840–1940* (Cambridge: Cambridge University Press, 2009), p. 231.
77. Dickie Spurgeon, 'The Athenaeum', in *British Literary Magazines: The Romantic Age, 1789–1836*, ed. Alvin Sullivan (Westport, CT: Greenwood, 1989), p. 22.
78. Quoted in Lee, *Virginia Woolf*, p. 447.
79. 'Our Malthusian Middle-Classes', *The Nation and Athenaeum*, 7 May 1927, pp. 140–41. While Brittain wrote the article as a woman who favoured birth control – recommending it for the wider good as well as her own benefit – Marie Stopes responded to this mention of 'eugenic birth control' as insinuating that the birth control means she advocated were dysgenic. Stopes wrote to both the magazine and Keynes personally to register her disappointment with the article. Keynes tersely replied that he wished 'the various Birth Control Organizations would not spend so much time scrapping with one another! It tends to sap public confidence in all of them alike' (quoted in John Toye, *Keynes on Population* (Oxford: Oxford University Press, 2000), p. 185).

146 *Virginia Woolf and Motherhood*

80. *Heritage* (London: William Collins, 1919), p. 5.
81. *The Dragon in Shallow Waters* (London: G. P. Putnam's, 1921), p. 6.
82. Bernard says to fellow writer Neville: 'let me then create you. (You have done as much for me)' (*W* 63). Ellen Hawke, 'Woolf's "Magical Garden of Women"', in *New Feminist Essays on Virginia Woolf*, ed. Jane Marcus (Lincoln, NE: University of Nebraska Press, 1981), p. 53; Joanne Trautmann, *The Jessamy Brides: The Friendship of Virginia Woolf and V. Sackville-West*, Penn State Studies, No. 36 (University Park: Pennsylvania State University Press, 1973), p. 38.
83. Leonard 'made up' his wife in *The Wise Virgins*, a portrait that paints her as beautiful, intelligent and independent but also depicts her as someone a-feminine, to whom marriage and childbearing would not come naturally (Virginia's character is told by her sister, 'You are such an impossible person. You weren't made for marriage, you weren't made for a husband and children and middle-aged domesticity' ((New Haven, CT: Yale University Press, 2007), p. 97)). Victoria Glendinning notes that when the novel was published Virginia did not read it for several months because she was in the middle of her worst breakdown. While Glendinning states that it might have been coincidental, she also notes how Virginia relapsed two weeks after reading it (*Leonard Woolf: A Biography*, pp. 190–91).
84. For more on Woolf's reputation as 'frigid' and 'virginal', see Lee, *Virginia Woolf*, pp. 244, 331.
85. 'Lighting the Cave: The Relationship Between Vita Sackville-West and Virginia Woolf', *Signs*, 8.2 (1982), p. 199.
86. *The Letters of Vita Sackville-West to Virginia Woolf*, ed. Louise DeSalvo (San Francisco: Cleis, 2004), p. 171.
87. It is worth noting that during the birth the reader is transported to Kew Gardens with Woolf likening Orlando's gestation to 'bulbs, hairy and red, thrust into the earth in October; flowering now' (*O* 203).
88. *Portrait of a Marriage* (London: Weidenfeld and Nicolson, 1973), p. 144.
89. Quoted in Madeline Moore, '*Orlando*: An Edition of the Manuscript', *Twentieth Century Literature*, 25.3/4 (1979), p. 349.
90. This opinion is especially interesting given how much Woolf personally and financially benefited from Sackville-West's novels. For more on this, see DeSalvo, 'Lighting the Cave', p. 201, and Stephen Barkway, '"Oh Lord what it is to publish a best seller": The Woolfs' Professional Relationship with Vita Sackville-West', in *Leonard and Virginia Woolf, The Hogarth Press and the Networks of Modernism*, ed. Helen Southworth (Edinburgh: Edinburgh University Press, 2010), pp. 234–59. It is also interesting to compare Woolf's comments to a passage from Leslie Stephen's *Studies of a Biographer* about the writer Margaret Oliphant: 'She resigned her chance of [. . .] fame because she wished to send her sons to Eton' (4 vols (London: Duckworth, 1898–1902), IV (1902), p. 48). For more on the fascinating relationship between Oliphant and Woolf, see Blair, *Virginia Woolf and the Nineteenth-Century Domestic Novel*.

Motherhood and Eugenics **147**

91. Vita Sackville-West and Harold Nicolson, 'Marriage', *Listener*, 26 June 1929, 1.24, pp. 899–900.
92. In *Vita: The Life of Vita Sackville-West* ((New York: Knopf, 1983), p. 99) Though Victoria Glendinning quotes from Nicolson's 1920 letter about *Married Love*, she misidentifies Stopes's *Married Love* (1918) as Theodoor Van de Velde's *Ideal Marriage* (1926).
93. *Vita and Virginia: The Work and Friendship of V. Sackville-West and Virginia Woolf* (Oxford: Oxford University Press, 1993), p. 90.
94. John Henry Stape (ed.), *Virginia Woolf: Interviews and Recollections* (Basingstoke: Macmillan, 1995), p. 35.
95. Joan Russell Noble (ed.), *Recollections of Virginia Woolf by Her Contemporaries* (London: Cardinal, 1989), p. 166.
96. Maitland, *The Life and Letters of Leslie Stephen*, pp. 240, 294, 307.
97. Ellen M. Holtzman, 'The Pursuit of Married Love: Women's Attitudes toward Sexuality and Marriage in Great Britain, 1918–1939', *Journal of Social History*, 16.2 (1982), p. 41.
98. Soloway, 'Marie Stopes, Eugenics and the Birth Control Movement', in *Marie Stopes, Eugenics and the Birth Control Movement: Proceedings of a Conference Organized by The Galton Institute, London, 1996*, ed. Robert A Peel (London: The Galton Institute, 1997), p. 52.
99. *When Sex Changed*, p. 1. In addition, this letter is somewhat misleading since, as Holtzman notes, married women were as likely to read Stopes as young men ('The Pursuit of Married Love', p. 41).
100. *Selected Letters of Vanessa Bell*, ed. Regina Marler with an introduction by Quentin Bell (London: Bloomsbury, 1993), p. 61.
101. The only recorded meeting between Stopes and Woolf was on Woolf's 57th birthday. Anne Olivier Bell notes that it was likely Stopes visited to elicit support for a petition to get Lord Alfred Douglas a civil list pension (*D5* 202n).
102. 'Marie Stopes, Eugenics and the Birth Control Movement', pp. 52–53.
103. Ibid., pp. 58–59.
104. It is important to note that British eugenicists were not, for the most part, trying to suppress the lower classes but hoped to improve every part of society, while maintaining the existing class system.
105. *Radiant Motherhood: A Book for Those Who are Creating the Future* (hereafter *RM*) (London: G. P. Putnam, 1920), p. 223. Further page references will be given within the main text.
106. Muriel Box (ed.), *The Trial of Marie Stopes* (London: A Femina Book, 1967), pp. 76–77.
107. National Birth-Rate Commission. *Problems of Population and Parenthood: Being the Second Report of and the Chief Evidence Taken by the National Birth-Rate Commission, 1918–20* (London: Chapman and Hall, 1920), pp. 200, 133.
108. 'Private Lives in Public Spaces: Marie Stopes, the Mothers' Clinics and the Practice of Contraception', *History Workshop Journal*, 33.1 (1992), p. 101.

148   *Virginia Woolf and Motherhood*

109. This attitude of putting both women's choice (and babies' health) first was emblematic of the contraceptive movement on both sides of the Atlantic.

110. 'Defining Militancy: Radical Protest, the Constitutional Idiom, and Women's Suffrage in Britain, 1908–1909', *The Journal of British Studies*, 39.3 (2000), p. 350.

111. *Rational Dress Society's Gazette*, April 1888, p. 1.

112. *The Public Lives of Charlotte and Marie Stopes* (Abingdon: Routledge, 2016), p. 2.

113. 'Dangers of Women's Dress', *Rational Dress Society's Gazette*, April 1888, p. 3.

114. Woolf's stance on political activism brings to mind Clarissa Dalloway's belief that: 'the veriest frumps, the most dejected of miseries sitting on doorsteps (drink their downfall) [. . .] can't be dealt with [. . .] by Acts of Parliament for that very reason: they love life' (*MD* 4).

115. Stopes, *Love's Creation* (hereafter *LC*) (London: John Bale, 1928; repr. Eastbourne: Sussex Academic, 2012), p. 150. Further page references will be given within the main text.

116. The first half of *British Freewomen* lists the property, titles and public offices of a number of 'Royal Women', 'Noblewomen', 'County Women' and 'Freewomen' from the medieval period onward (London: Swan Sonnenschein, 1894).

117. Quoted in Lee, *Virginia Woolf*, pp. 335–36.

118. In 'Marie C. Stopes and the Popularization of Birth Control Technology' Peter Neushul gives one example of the affordability of Stopes's birth control methods, explaining of sponges: 'The low price [. . .] pleased Stopes, who noted that "with the non-rubber 'Clinocap' sponge, all a woman needs to spend is 1s. 3d. to last her for an indefinite number of years"' (*Technology and Culture*, 39.2 (1998), p. 254).

119. It is important to note that in order to destabilise extant social structures Woolf embraces ambiguity even in the case of contraception. Donald Childs points to two ironic points in this statement – 'first, that women must continue to respect their biological functions, and second, that women must respect what "they say" – "the economists are saying that Mrs Seaton has had too many children"' (*Modernism and Eugenics*, p. 71). Woolf further probes pro-contraceptive narratives by noting that, had Mrs Seton been at liberty to have an intellectual or commercial life, Mary 'would never have come into existence at all' (*AROO* 20).

120. Stopes did have a play, *Vectia*, banned from being performed at the Royal Court Theatre in 1923 but the slot for the production was filled with another of her own, contraceptive-themed, plays which opened to excellent reviews.

121. Childs, *Modernism and Eugneics*, p. 69; Marcus, *Virginia Woolf and the Languages of Patriarchy* (Bloomington: Indiana University Press, 1987), p. 175; Snaith, '*A Room of One's Own*', in *The Literary*

Encyclopedia (2001) <https://www.litencyc.com/php/sworks.php?rec= true&UID=7038> [accessed 2 October 2019]; Alt, *Virginia Woolf and the Study of Nature*, p. 115; Marshik, 'Thinking Back Through Copyright', in *Modernism & Copyright*, ed. Paul K. Saint-Amour (Oxford: Oxford University Press, 2011), p. 72.

122. Andre Gerard, 'Blog #55: A Tendentious Lighthouse: Virginia Woolf and Marie Carmichael Stopes' <http://patremoirpress.com/blog/?p=629> [accessed 12 March 2018].

123. There is no proof Woolf read Stopes's biographies, which included a book specifically on *Shakespeare's Family* (1901). *A Room* does refer to Sir Sidney Lee's *A Life of William Shakespeare* (1898) and Lee also wrote the substantial entry on Shakespeare in the *DNB*, whose editorship he inherited from Leslie Stephen in 1891. (It is worth noting that Charlotte Stopes was also a contributor to the *DNB*.)

124. See pp. 113–14, 129 in Virginia Woolf, *Women & Fiction: The Manuscript Versions of A Room of One's Own*, transcr. and ed. S. P. Rosenbaum (Oxford: Blackwell, 1992).

125. Saguaro '"Something that would stand for the conception": The Inseminating World in the Last Writings of Virginia Woolf', *Green Letters: Studies in Ecocriticism*, 17.2 (2013), p. 109.

126. *Modernism and Eugenics*, p. 71.

127. *When Sex Changed*, pp. 62–63.

128. 'Theories of Homosexuality as Sources of Bloomsbury's Androgyny', *Signs*, 5.2 (1979), p. 250.

129. For example: 'Blue-eyed babies are *so* sweet,' whispered Rose Amber [. . .] her clear brown eyes looking deep into the older woman's. 'You must have a blue-eyed daughter-in-law so as to make certain that Kenneth's babies are blue-eyed like himself' (*LC* 140).

130. *Contraception* (London: John Bale, 1923), p. 242.

131. Stopes et al., *Queen's Hall Meeting on Constructive Birth Control: Speeches and Impressions* (London: G. P. Putnam, 1921).

132. 'Eugenics in Britain', pp. 503–05.

133. Many of the EES Council members whom MacKenzie lists had come up in the world through hard work and talent. For example, Havelock Ellis was the son of a sea captain, Sir Edward William Brabrook the son of a warehouse manager, Sir John Alexander Cockburn the son of a farmer, and Professor Ernest William MacBride the son of a linen manufacturer (ibid., pp. 523–27).

134. *Eugenics, Literature, and Culture in Post-War Britain* (Abingdon: Routledge, 2013), p. 19.

135. For some examples, see Pedersen, *Family, Dependence, and the Origins of the Welfare State*, pp. 159–60.

136. Rathbone, 'The Remuneration of Women's Services', p. 55.

137. *Round About a Pound a Week* (London: G. Bell, 1914), p. 156.

Chapter 3

Motherhood and Food

Introduction

In his posthumous profile of Woolf, the writer E. M. Forster particularly highlights her accomplishment with regard to those

> passages which describe eating. They are invariably good. They are a sharp reminder that here is a woman who is alert sensuously. She had an enlightened greediness which gentlemen themselves might envy, and which few masculine writers have expressed [. . .] when Virginia Woolf mentions nice things they go right into our mouth, so far as the edibility of print permits. We taste their deliciousness: the great dish of *Boeuf en Daube* which forms the centre of the dinner of union in *To the Lighthouse*, the dinner which exhales affection and poetry and loveliness, so that all the characters see the best in one another at last and for a moment [. . .] Such a dinner cannot be built on a statement beneath a dish-cover which the novelist is too indifferent or incompetent to remove [. . .] The *Boeuf en Daube*, which had taken the cook three days to make and had worried Mrs Ramsay as she did her hair, stands before us.[1]

The dinner that Forster describes is an expression of Mrs Ramsay's maternal power, her ability to nourish and to combine guests in an almost mystical moment of bringing together. However, this maternal act holds within it layers of class commentary and concern. Systems of unequal effort and reward are reflected by a dinner that has taken Mildred the cook 'three days to make', but has 'worried Mrs Ramsay as she did her hair'. Forster's sensory identification with the scene draws attention to an important difference between Woolf and her male contemporaries (a difference which he notices but does not attempt to explain). What Forster omits is that Woolf did not solely include food for its aesthetic value, nor were her literary meals meant only to portray the pleasure found in eating. Instead, understanding that the preparation and service of food held a particular place in women's lives, Woolf was interested in using it as a vehicle to explore broader cultural, economic and political connotations.

Alice Lowe has observed that Woolf used 'food imagery to describe people, to demonstrate character and to set a stage'.[2] Reflecting food's position as an intensely visceral part of the human experience, Woolf's epicurean writing spans a wide variety of situations and a range of vivid emotions. Food is offered as nourishment, as a catalyst for group adhesion, to highlight social difference, and to capture class, existential dread and even sexual desire. Despite a history of criticism focusing on the times Woolf was ill – when, as Leonard noted, 'one of the most troublesome symptoms of her breakdowns was a refusal to eat' – the prevalence of food in Woolf's novels has recently produced a rich vein of historicist research.[3] Francesca Orestano and Jans Ondaatje Rolls have unearthed the recipes she might have followed and the cooking utensils and appliances she might have used.[4] And looking outside of Woolf's dietary habits, scholars such as Janine Utell and Vicki Tromanhauser have examined her literary use of food to reflect public discourses on topics such as mourning, war and class.[5] This chapter continues this investigative path by looking at the relationship between food and motherhood in Woolf's writing.

Food is always an important aspect of social practice, often occupying a central place in tradition or rituals. For the upper-class women of Woolf's era, food culture was bound up with gender and class, with food growing, preparation and service all being activities that involved inter-class interactions. Though Julia Stephen may have directed the contents of meals and kept the household accounts, none of the Stephen family would have envisaged spending time within the kitchen, 'a dark insanitary place' (*MB* 123) that was the domain of the cook and kitchen maids. However, the economic hardships and shortages of two World Wars, the increase in women entering the workforce (and therefore reduction of those going into domestic service) and burgeoning bohemianism, meant that Woolf's generation was the first in which women of her social class needed to learn how to prepare food for themselves.[6] Contesting her sentiment 'we think back through our mothers if we are women' (*AROO* 69), Woolf was among these women learning new domestic practices. By the time she was an adult, she could do something her mother could not – prepare simple meals and bake capably. As Woolf famously notes, change arrived 'in or about December, 1910' not only 'in the character of

152   *Virginia Woolf and Motherhood*

one's cook' (*E3* 421–22) but also in the character of the mistresses who suddenly found themselves in the kitchen.

Food was also important because of its political significance. Maternalist rhetoric held that Victorian women, with their unique mix of education and domestic knowledge, were considered the perfect candidates for shaping public welfare policy. Although upper-class women never cooked for themselves, nutrition and food preparation were spheres of feminine knowledge that gave them the opportunity to influence public discourse. In *To the Lighthouse* Mrs Ramsay engages in the type of philanthropic activism that typified such campaigns. She speaks of a trio of maternalist concerns – 'hospitals and drains and the dairy' (*TL* 64) – all directly related to real life efforts to lower infant mortality.[7] In contrast to this, Woolf was a committed member of the Women's Co-operative Guild (WCG), an organisation that originated in 'Mothers' Meetings' (*E5* 187) for working-class women who wanted to use more than their basket-power to effect change. Unlike the philanthropic maternalism of Mrs Ramsay, the Guild was built on egalitarian participation and, with the Woolfs' great friend Margaret Llewelyn Davies as its president, grew into an organisation of considerable political influence. Or, as Woolf phrased it in 1930 – 'from debating questions of butter and bacon, working women at their weekly meetings have to consider the relations of one great nation to another' (*E5* 188).

Food was a natural instrument through which Woolf could understand and describe maternity. Not only did a woman's domestic responsibilities include the household shopping, budgeting and cooking (even if by proxy), but one of the primary acts of motherhood is feeding a baby. However, the rigorous social order of caretaking roles within the upper-class household, and the way that mothering differed considerably between classes, caused Woolf's literary approach to motherhood through food to be tempered by questions of class – with cooking, eating and corporeality being used to differentiate between mothers from different backgrounds. Woolf wrote about food to expose women's 'infinitely obscure lives' (*AROO* 81) yet she was aware of her own limitations. Even though she directly associated working-class women with motherhood and cookery, she could not fictionalise their domestic routines. She explored this failure of her imagination when she most inventively used food to investigate class and motherhood – in *The Waves*, 'Memories of a Working Women's Guild' and *The Years*.

This chapter will begin with an examination of the class and cultural anxieties that inhabit Woolf's fictional and personal writing about infant-feeding. It will then survey these three primary texts, all written in the six-year period from 1929 to 1935. *The Waves* is perhaps the most food-filled novel from Woolf's canon, portraying Susan as an archetypal mother whose productivity is measured through a steady output of food and babies. *The Waves*' engagement with food and motherhood is examined through the lens of the writing of Otto Weininger, Malthusian theory, the Great Depression and contemporary population debates. Susan's narrative is also studied for its notable lack of interactions with working-class domestic staff. Written at the same time as *The Waves*, 'Memories of a Working Women's Guild' explores Woolf's inability to imagine working-class mothers' lives through their food choices. Finally, in *The Years*, Woolf compares mothers from different classes through a pair of meals, and in doing so experiments with representing the working-class mother who had been obscured in the previous two texts.

Infant-Feeding, Milk and Class at the Turn of the Twentieth Century

Biologically, milk is the first food a human baby needs, with the maternal touch and gaze during feeding forming the primary bond between mother and child.[8] In Woolf's time milk was a central component of the British diet. It was an important topic in maternalist discourse and also played a role in healing a variety of diseases (for example, Julia Stephen writes that 'a milk diet' was recommended: 'For any affection of the bladder').[9] Gregory Dekter argues that during Woolf's lifetime, the 'social value of milk cannot be overemphasized'.[10] During the nineteenth century, as more people moved from rural to urban living, cow's milk had to travel larger distances and became increasingly contaminated, both naturally by milk-borne diseases, as well as artificially through the addition of materials such as chalk, boric acid and water. Diarrhoea from tainted milk was a common cause of childhood morbidity and the purity of milk was a topic that created widespread anxiety. Megumi Kato notes that 'a glance at the *British Medical Journal* at the beginning of [the twentieth] century will show how much milk was discussed in Medical discourse'. Kato explains that:

> The milk problem was deeply rooted in the 'ideology of motherhood' in late Victorian and Edwardian Britain. In this ideological climate the improvement of maternity, child-rearing, and infant health was pursued as a national agenda [. . .] Solving the milk problem was crucial for the future of the race.[11]

154   Virginia Woolf and Motherhood

Given the social concern over milk, and the eugenic tenor of the rhetoric around the topic, it is unsurprising not only how often moments of bottle and breastfeeding can be seen in Woolf's writing, but also the class subtext that accompanies them.

Then, as now, breastfeeding was an active choice that could denote privilege. Maternal breastfeeding (as opposed to wet-nursing) was generally accepted as the healthiest way to feed a baby, and both Julia Stephen and Vanessa Bell breastfed their children – though Stephen had to stop feeding the infant Virginia after ten weeks.[12] Research suggests that the majority of mothers did breastfeed, but the experience varied between upper-class mothers, whose babies would be brought to them at a preordained time by nurses and taken away immediately afterwards, and lower-middle-class housewives, who were responsible for all their babies' needs.[13] Working women also wanted to breastfeed, not only for their babies' health but because, as Peter Atkins has observed, 'it was the cheapest option and [. . .] reduced their chance of conceiving another child'.[14] However, women from the lower classes often stopped prematurely because they had to go out to work or were too malnourished to maintain an adequate milk supply.

While maternal breastfeeding remained in high regard, other parallel forms of infant nutrition changed significantly during Woolf's life. Up until the late nineteenth century wet-nursing had been popular, but the practice declined due to innovations in bottle-feeding and formula. In 1899 the first Infants' Milk Depot opened. This centre cleaned, nutritionally balanced and distributed fresh bottled milk for babies, recommending a feeding schedule still widely used today.[15] While the change from wet-nursing to medically endorsed bottle-feeding was culturally significant, both systems were complicated by class. Professional wet nurses were working class and could earn a fair salary, but they often left their own babies in baby-farms to be fed – typically by hand – by much poorer women. Since hand-feeding was less nutritious and sanitary a significant number of these babies died. Indeed, a slew of court cases in the second half of the nineteenth century revealed that some baby-farmers were taking sizeable fees and then abandoning or killing their charges. One particularly sensational 1870 infanticide case – that of baby-farmer Margaret Waters – elicited so much public outrage that it eventually led to the Infant Life Protection Act of 1872.

Class issues were intrinsic to a system where the health of a baby was jeopardised by its mother's employment. In addition, with upper-class babies dependent on the bodies of working-class women, moralist, classist and eugenic rhetoric emerged that questioned the nurses' integrity and the quality of their care, as well as speculating about adverse developmental effects on the babies they tended. Even Mrs Beeton's 1861 *Book of Household Management* warned new mothers to 'remember with gentleness the order of society from which our nurses are drawn'. Beeton advocated closely monitoring such things as what the wet-nurses ate, and what home remedies they gave their charges; arguing that among such working-class women 'conscientiousness and good faith [. . .] are, unfortunately, very rare'.[16] This was ironic given that upper-class women also unknowingly gave their babies all manner of dangerous substances. Vanessa Bell, for example, wrote to Roger Fry about the 'grey powders' she was giving Angelica – grey powders being a popular concoction of chalk and mercury.[17]

As wet-nursing declined and baby-farming came under strict regulation, women of all classes adopted bottle-feeding as a viable and healthy alternative. Woolf was aware of the postulated benefits of bottle-feeding and displayed this in *The Voyage Out* when Mrs Thornbury reads aloud, and provides a commentary on, a passage from a gossipy letter that states: 'Eleanor certainly looked more like herself than I've seen her since the winter. She has put Baby on three bottles now, which I'm sure is wise (I'm sure it is too), and so gets better nights' (*VO* 163). Even though the text satirises the letter and Mrs Thornbury's opinion, this passage not only shows Woolf's knowledge of bottle-feeding rhetoric but also acknowledges the proprietorial attitude extended towards maternal bodies and baby-feeding. Women of all classes bottle-fed, yet the practice still had classist connotations. This was possibly because the milk depots driving innovation in this area – part of the larger maternalist, philanthropic milk hygiene movement Mrs Ramsay finds so engaging – explicitly targeted working-class women. Woolf acknowledges this class-bias in *Melymbrosia* when a higher-class passenger, a Miss Löbstein, bored by too many days at sea, is able to distract herself with the benevolent care of a passenger in steerage, who has given birth so unexpectedly that 'the baby had no clothes and the mother had no milk' (*M* 105).

Woolf connected this type of dairy philanthropy with her mother. Kato and Dekter both observe how Mrs Ramsay is politicised by opinions on milk that explicitly tie her to maternalist discourses. Mrs Ramsay's desire to start both a 'model dairy *and* a hospital' (*TL* 64, my emphasis) can also be linked to Julia Stephen's interest in milk hygiene and nursing. In the essay 'Notes from Sick Rooms', Julia

156   *Virginia Woolf and Motherhood*

explains the importance of sterility for a patient ordered to follow a milk diet:

> The nurse must see the milkman herself and impress on him the importance of sweet fresh milk from one cow being always brought. When brought she must empty the milk into a flat pan [. . .] this pan must be placed in a cool place, and must be well scalded each time it is emptied.[18]

Although Stephen's advice was eminently sensible at a time when milk-borne diseases were rife, her dedication to the vocation of nursing is not acknowledged in Mrs Ramsay's narrative. Instead, the Ramsay children laugh at their mother's impassioned argument about milk and healthcare, suggesting that Woolf judged Stephen's nursing the same way she judged maternalist philanthropy: as outdated, patronising to the working class and a way to exploit women's labour while denying them access to a system of commerce and ownership. This unpaid, upper-class maternalist rhetoric stood in stark contrast to Woolf's belief in women's professional status (and the empowerment that came with payment for services rendered), and her experience of the WCG's working-class activism.

Despite her anti-maternalist stance, classist sentiments continued in Woolf's work, especially where she writes about food. Alison Light has suggested that this is *because* she did not have the moral assuredness that came with the Victorian mistress/maid, philanthropist/ needy dualism:

> In the 1900s Julia's daughters rapidly sloughed off their charitable duties [. . .] But philanthropy had made sense of being a mistress. It was a way of managing the differences, the emotional housekeeping, which kept the tensions between rich and poor women under control. When she came to run her own household, Virginia Woolf had neither the confidence of the maternal role nor the faith in fellowship with the poor [. . .] Stripped bare of the flummery, the fine words and good intentions, all that remained was the nakedness of caste feeling.[19]

Woolf was uncomfortable with the often highly charged interactions she had with her maids and cooks and considered the system of keeping live-at-home domestics outdated, referring to it as 'a fine rubbish heap left by our parents to be swept' (*D3* 220). Some who knew her well felt that this discomfort was related to not being a mother. Angus Davidson, for example, compared Woolf to Bell and alleged:

'Much of the difference in their attitude to life may have been due to Vanessa's having produced a family. She was more calm and composed, also more practical'.[20]

That mistress-hood had historically been aligned with motherhood can also be seen in Julia Stephen's essay 'The Servant Question'. In this essay Stephen explores the duty of care that a mistress owes the girls that worked in her house, describing maids as 'women who of all others should receive from us most care and for whose welfare we are responsible'. Stephen equates the homes of mothers and mistresses – asking of those who live out: 'Where are these girls to spend the night? It is clear that [. . .] to live out of their mistresses' home will not mean to live in their mothers''. She maintains that a mistress should care for and supervise her charges, body and soul; yet, though she challenges the idea that this mistress–servant interaction might be demeaning (and was known for her own successful relationships with her domestic staff[21]), she struggles to lay to rest those class tensions that she denies. The essay finally acquiesces that 'the closer' the tie becomes between mistress and maid, *the easier it will be to bear*'.[22] In *To the Lighthouse* Woolf explores the inequality of this mistress–maid relationship. Megumi Kato notes how housekeeper Mrs McNab 'associates Mrs Ramsay with milk, because Mrs Ramsay often kept a plate of milk soup for her'. 'The gesture of giving precious milk to a poor maid', Kato explains, 'implies the hierarchical power relationship of the two persons'. Using milk to illustrate this gesture also highlights how the system maternalises the mistress and infantilises the maid (even when the maid is significantly older than her employer).[23]

Bach or Breastfeeding: Classism, Colonialism and Creativity in Woolf's Early Writing

Infant feeding – especially breastfeeding – emerges as an unsettling act in some of Woolf's earlier works. In particular, 'The Journal of Mistress Joan Martyn' and *The Voyage Out* bring class, gender and race together to weigh art against motherhood through the image of a breastfeeding mother. In 'Mistress Joan' a nursing labourer's wife, in a cottage 'more like the burrow of some rabbit on the heath than the house of a man' (*CSF* 52), appears to Joan as so poor she is hardly human:

> There was but a rotten log on which a woman sat, nursing a baby. She looked at us, not with fright, but with distrust and dislike written clear

in her eyes; and she clasped her child more closely. Anthony spoke to her as he would have spoken to some animal who had strong claws and a wicked eye. He stood over her, and his great boot seemed ready to crush her. But she did not move or speak; and I doubt whether she could have spoken, or whether snarling and howling was her only language. (*CSF* 53)

Initially the scene seems to suggest that breastfeeding one's own child is somehow less 'civilised' or an act for the lower classes to perform (an idea that is supported by the appearance in the text of 'Old Anne', Joan and her mother's old nurse, who also may have fed her charges). Joan sees the woman as an animalistic, unclassifiable 'pest' (*CSF* 53). An older Woolf would perhaps have created more irony out of this scene, using comedy to make Anthony, the chief steward, a problematic patriarchal figure, but humour is absent from this account. Though Joan sees Anthony as 'crass' she nonetheless values him – he is 'faithful' and has taught her about the land, which she loves (*CSF* 51). Indeed, Anthony is connected with the bucolic innocence and 'childlike [. . .] clear vision' (*CSF* 52) that Joan associates with remaining unmarried. Instead, the breastfeeding scene is a moment of irreconcilable conflict. Joan cannot and does not identify with this inhuman being – aside from her alienating poverty the labourer's wife is pre-linguistic, whereas Joan is one of the 'few women in Norfolk' (*CSF* 61) who can read and write. Yet the woman, as a breastfeeding mother, also represents a possible future for Joan, who had been contemplating marriage and motherhood in the scene immediately prior.

The absence of satirical markers means it is difficult to know how to read the nursing mother.[24] However there is a similar, though less ambivalent, scene in *The Voyage Out* which offers the opportunity of a comparative reading. In this passage Rachel Vinrace and Terence Hewet visit a village where they exchange gazes with a breastfeeding indigenous woman:

As she drew apart her shawl and uncovered her breast to the lips of her baby, the eyes of a woman never left their faces, although they moved uneasily under her stare, and finally turned away, rather than stand there looking at her any longer. (*VO* 269)

Like the labourer's wife, the village mother's eyes remain on her visitors; however, this scene is unambiguous in highlighting the class and imperial issues at play in the meeting. Unlike Joan and Anthony, the

English visitors in *The Voyage Out* are 'ugly and unnatural' (*VO* 269) in their surroundings and become increasingly more uncomfortable. Looking at the villagers Rachel feels a sense of foreboding. 'Peaceful, and even beautiful at first', the women in the village, most fully represented in the figure of the nursing mother, quickly make her 'feel very cold and melancholy' (*VO* 269). By using motherhood as a narrative device, these scenes draw parallels between patriarchal conquest and imperial colonisation, ratifying Anna Snaith's observation that 'Woolf's anti-imperialism is inseparable from her feminism'.[25]

Mark Wollaeger has contextualised this scene against the backdrop of a European craze for picture postcards of foreign indigenous peoples and imperial exhibitions in London that reconstructed entire 'native' villages. While postcards of bare-chested women hovered at the periphery of what was acceptable in British culture – Wollaeger notes how one postcard-censoring strategy 'covered naked women with white powder and posed them as classical statuary' – those of nursing mothers were appreciated because they presented 'images of far-flung domesticity'.[26] Breastfeeding was a respectable undertaking, although, as Marilyn Yalom notes, breastfeeding in public was a mark of coarseness that was likely to be observed 'in such public places as parks and railroads, especially among the popular classes'.[27] Wollaeger argues that the 'circulation of such postcards [. . .] both reinforced and undermined the imperial stereotypes that Rachel must negotiate as she follows English culture out into the world and attempts to establish her identity'.[28] This identity is challenged when she encounters the breastfeeding woman. Like Mistress Joan, Rachel – who is newly engaged and at the beginning of a journey into motherhood – is compared and contrasted with the nursing mother. The earlier version of this scene in *Melymbrosia* sees Rachel trying to identify with the indigenous mothers, thinking 'that her own happiness would have made it easy for her' (*M* 305). Despite her intentions, however, the women remain profoundly 'other':

> Their faces were an oily brown, and this perhaps explained why they did not look like faces; they seemed neither old nor young, neither clever malicious women, or sweet sympathetic women; they seemed more like fruit hung high up in their own forest trees. She owned that she knew nothing about them. (*M* 305)

Rachel's dissociation from the women is so complete they do not even have the self-determination of animals but are 'like fruit hung high up' ready for consumption.

Figure 3 'A Native Woman and Child'. Black-and-white postcard, July 1908, photographer unknown, printed by P. S. & Co., Cape Town. Reprinted with permission of Beinecke Rare Book & Manuscript Library, Yale University.

One of the interesting features of both scenes is the strength and antipathy of the mothers' gazes. These looks can be read in light of Derek Ryan's work on the gaze in *Flush* – where a 'close domestic and co-evolutionary relationship' is signified by sympathetic gazes between Flush and Elizabeth Barrett Browning. In contrast, Rachel and Joan's inability to share, or identify with, the gazes offered by their breast-feeding counterparts shows how detached each set of women is. Far from being what Ryan calls an 'invitation to trespass [. . .] divides', these moments of unsustainable eye-contact highlight the gulf between cultures, between coloniser and colonised, and between mother and non-mother.[29] There is also a complete lack of verbal communication between the women – not only because of a language barrier, but also because of the labourer's wife and indigenous women's inability to articulate. Like the silent mother in 'Mistress Joan', the woman and her fellow villagers are 'far far beyond the plunge of speech [. . .] if they spoke, it was to cry some harsh unintelligible cry' (*VO* 269). Using an example from *The Years*, Anna Snaith illustrates how the links that Woolf 'forges between colonialism and patriarchy [. . .] perform a kind of silencing'. As victims of both colonial and patriarchal suppression, the mothers in these scenes remain silent. Snaith notes that 'Woolf both critiques this inability to "hear" otherness but also perpetuates it via a lack of alternative narratological perspectives'.[30] As shown by the labourer's wife in 'Mistress Joan', this inability to explore 'otherness' is as much a problem of class as it is of race, and, as will be seen later, is something that Woolf acknowledged and tried to confront in her later work.

Another aspect of the disconnection between Rachel and Joan and the mothers they observe is in their creative outputs. As a writer (Joan) and a musician (Rachel), Woolf's protagonists struggle to identify with these women whose productivity is found in their breastmilk and babies (and, in *The Voyage Out*, the functional straw baskets that the reader imagines they have made since time immemorial). Both texts posit marriage and motherhood in opposition to the creative drives. In 'Mistress Joan' this contrast is doubled – not only does Joan's father tell her in anticipation of her marriage: 'Well then Joan, you must keep your writing [. . .] or rather, I must keep it for you. For you are going to leave us' (*CSF* 61), but also Rosamond Merridew, the researcher whose narrative frames the diary, notes that she has 'exchanged a husband and a family and a house' (*CSF* 33) for her research and writing. In *Melymbrosia*, the following passage occurs after Rachel (who has become disengaged from a conversation Helen Ambrose and Clarissa Dalloway are having about motherhood), starts to play the piano:

> She played well. Of half the young ladies in Kensington that might be said without adding as one added in Rachel's case, that they were born to play. They were born for a thousand other reasons; to marry, to nurse, to ride, to fill the world; music, with painting and a knowledge of English history, was like a tiny tin sword [. . .] to fight the world with, if other weapons failed.[31] (*M* 65–66)

In this passage not only are 'playing' and 'nursing' directly contrasted, but the creative arts (and a knowledge of history) are devices that make social pressure on young women easier to bear. However, this creative freedom is also part of a vicious circle, for when the young ladies of Kensington play

> a certain discontent would come over them. 'One does have to sacrifice a lot for children doesn't one?' they would complain. But how triumphantly the sum balanced on the right side! There were lights in all the windows; one heard children crying in the nursery, as one opened the front door. (*M* 66)

162 *Virginia Woolf and Motherhood*

Written at a time when Woolf still thought she might have children, this passage, alongside 'Mistress Joan', offers the earliest examples of Woolf's juxtaposition of motherhood and art.[32] The sarcastic treatment of the joy that might be found in marriage and motherhood is reiterated later in the text: 'You've a free soul!' Terence tells Rachel: 'To you time will make no difference, or marriage or anything else' (*M* 288). As a representative of the patriarchy that seeks to subjugate Rachel – a fate which she (and Joan) ultimately die to evade – Terence's words are dubious. Written for satirical effect, they suggest that Woolf may have been apprehensive about marriage as she edited *The Voyage Out* and became engaged to Leonard.

Woolf uses the breastfeeding women in 'Mistress Joan' and *The Voyage Out* as part of her engagement with evolutionary discourses. Elsewhere in *Melymbrosia*, Rachel ironically recalls that: 'Women [. . .] are more common than men; and Darwin says they are nearer the cow' (*M* 28). By tying breastfeeding to Darwin, Woolf highlights the devolutionary connotations and creative consequences of women's obligation to nurse, turning breastmilk – a foodstuff with incredibly high social currency – into something exploitative. Another example of devolutionary breastfeeding can be seen in *Jacob's Room*. Here, a gaggle of Greek women 'as jolly as sand-martins in the heat, quarrelling, scolding, suckling their babies' speak perfectly well but provide a point of humdrum, physical difference to the archaeological and intellectual grandeur of the Parthenon in whose shadow they are both bird-like and distinctly simian – 'crying to a child to come and have the insects picked from its head' (*JR* 154). These animated women, directly descended from and contrasted with one of the most important relics of an ancient dead culture (a culture which was incredibly important as a foundation to Woolf's art) recalls Leslie Stephen's argument that man is shaped by his society and not his genes. Set against the firing of warship guns at the moment Jacob dies, these women evoke melancholy, but they also illustrate humanity's (perhaps foolish) desire to carry on come what may, the inexorability of the maternal instinct, and the disparity between raising children and making art.

The 'mothers of Pimlico': Infant Feeding and Class in *Mrs Dalloway*

Another reference to breastfeeding can be seen in *Mrs Dalloway*, which returns to the image of the nursing mother to make a further class-fuelled comment on war. As she walks across St James's Park,

Clarissa Dalloway observes the 'mothers of Pimlico' giving 'suck to their young' (*MD* 7) as comfortably as if they were by their 'own fender' (*MD* 21). The combination of this public act and their place of residence confirms Sarah Bletchley and Emily Coates as lower-middle-class. To emphasise these class connotations the text describes how they amuse themselves while they sit and feed, comparing their own lives with 'the housemaids, the innumerable housemaids, the bedrooms, the innumerable bedrooms' (*MD* 21) of Buckingham Palace. A later scene is even more explicit about the class associations involved in public infant feeding, following Richard Dalloway, 'crossing the Green Park and observing with pleasure how in the shade of the trees whole families, poor families, were sprawling; children kicking up their legs; sucking milk; paper bags thrown about' (*MD* 127).

Language is not absent but it is obfuscated for these Pimlico mothers as they attempt to read the skywriting appearing above them. Where others read the word 'Kreemo', Coates sees an advertisement for 'Glaxo' baby formula (*MD* 22). Despite its brief and ambiguous mention, 'Glaxo' brings with it a wealth of associations with both imperial trade and Mrs Ramsay's maternalist discussion 'of real butter and clean milk' (*TL* 112). Glaxo was created by Joseph Nathan & Co., a New Zealand butter company that became successful in the 1890s, when fortnightly, refrigerated steamers began transporting perishable goods from New Zealand to England. Butter was one of the more important imports from the colonies, as well as being central to the French style of cooking enjoyed by Woolf and the Bloomsbury set.[33] Although the business was already profitable, the Nathan family wanted to find a commercial use for all their skimmed milk waste and so, in 1903, they bought the patents to the Just-Hatmaker process, a new and revolutionary drying method that retained the nutritional value of milk without spoiling it. Originally marketed as a replacement for fresh (yet dirty) household milk, this powder was rather unsuccessful, but in 1906 the company changed its strategy and rebranded the formula as 'Glaxo', a milk intended for babies. The Nathan family then sponsored infant-feeding trials in London, and by the end of 1907 five milk depots had opened in Sheffield to supply mothers with dried rather than fresh milk. The method was a huge step forward in curbing infant mortality – in one 1911 diarrhoea outbreak in Rotherham it was recorded that, of 240 babies fed Glaxo, only one died, but out of 160 babies fed by other means 37 died. In 1913, Glaxo embarked on a major advertising campaign that was so prolific that by 1915 *Advertising World* noted 'it is not exaggeration to say that every mother at least knows about Glaxo', and in 1917 the Ministry of Food contracted Glaxo to supply all local authority infant welfare centres with its milk.[34] Indeed, even non-mothers like Woolf knew about Glaxo. In their history of the company Richard Davenport-Hines and Judy Slinn use *Mrs Dalloway* as proof of 'the pervasiveness of its advertising'.[35] This advertising certainly involved postcards of the sort that Wollaeger writes about, and possibly even included the latest form of marketing – skywriting.

Mrs Coates's association with Glaxo is another class signifier. The infant welfare centres serviced the working-class community, and the government bought Glaxo milk at a reduced price and passed it on to mothers at cost, making these contracts more meaningful to the company for their effect on its brand name than their profitability. There are also eugenic connotations. As they stare at the skywriting, dreaming of bottled formula, the mirroring between mother and child, – 'Mrs Coates [. . .] gazing straight up, and her baby, lying stiff

Figure 4   Glaxo 'Builds Bonnie Babies' poster (1918). 'Medical Advertisement from Days Past'. Reprinted with permission of Waiuku Museum, Waiuku.

Motherhood and Food 165

Figure 5   Glaxo 'Remembrance' poster. *Illustrated London News*, 25 January 1919, p. 19. Reprinted with permission of Illustrated London News Ltd/ Mary Evans Picture Library.

and white in her arms, gazed straight up' (*MD* 22) – brings to mind discussions about the role that breastfeeding played in inheritance of class traits.[36] Seen through Clarissa Dalloway's eyes these nursing mothers are a pleasurable sight, ensuring the continuation of the British way of life; however, the subtext reveals a working-class woman carrying a pallid corpse-like infant, losing all animation under the influence of corporate marketing. Not only was Glaxo advertising widespread, it was particularly vocal in its support of the empire and war effort. One 1918 magazine advertisement read: 'As it Builds Bonnie Babies so it Builds Soldiers for the Empire'. Another post-war 1919 full-page newspaper commercial entitled 'Remembrance' was particularly reminiscent of British government-sponsored memorials, with its idyllic pictures of mothers and children. The ubiquity of this type of non-government, pro-war rhetoric – what Wollaeger calls 'the propaganda of everyday life'[37] – must have affected Woolf, and her dislike of the war and those that supported the war effort,

166   *Virginia Woolf and Motherhood*

led her to draw parallels between Glaxo's fantasy soldiers of tomorrow and the corpse-like Pimlico babies.

Woolf also made several personal references to breastfeeding that can shed light on her fictional nursing mothers. During WW1, when Vanessa Bell had just given birth to an as-yet-unnamed daughter and was desperately searching for a nanny, Woolf commiserated:

> I see you say that you *are* getting very tired. I'm sure its a desperate thing to attempt both feeding and nursing – All those ounces are sucked off you, though I'm very glad they go to Susanna – still – What a hellish business it all is! (*L2* 334, emphasis in original)

With sympathy (or perhaps distaste), Woolf frames breastfeeding as physically depleting and the baby's hunger as parasitic. The 'desperate' 'hellish business' of *'feeding and nursing'* like a working-class mother – with no nanny to carry off, change, burp and settle the baby – takes up Bell's energy and the valuable time she could be using to create art. Woolf also used these torturous connotations in letters, connecting breastfeeding to her own working woes. In 1923 she complained to Barbara Bagenal that 'the Press is worse than 6 children at breast simultaneously' (*L3* 55), and in 1927, when Woolf found herself coerced into 'Phases of Fiction', she called it 'that bloody book which Dadie and Leonard extort, drop by drop, from my breast' (*L3* 436). It is important to note that antipathy to breastfeeding was not a common trope in contemporary fiction. In Naomi Mitchison's *The Corn King and The Spring Queen* (1931), a breastfeeding scene is filled with sensual pleasure, with both baby and nursing mother laughing as 'He lay across her belly and thighs, heavy and utterly alive'.[38] This joyful act gives something to the mother as well as the baby, who is entirely different to the corpse-like baby Coates. Indeed, a glance at the happy mother in the postcard above shows a more typical view of breastfeeding, whose positive associations in the eyes of the general public are echoed in Clarissa's joy at the sight of the 'mothers of Pimlico'. Nonetheless, reading deeper, Woolf's breastfeeding scenes reveal yet more examples of places in her writing that signal motherhood both as a drive that is perverse and self-defeating, and also as a way that women are made subservient to the patriarchy.

The Waves, Food and Motherhood

Of all of Woolf's characters the drive to mother is represented most fully in the character of Susan in *The Waves* – a character who is also closely related to food. *The Waves* is also arguably Woolf's most sustenance-filled novel. Within the book meals are nexus points bringing each life-stage into focus, and allowing the characters to constantly renegotiate (and often reiterate) their relationships with each other and the world around them. Janine Utell has observed how within Woolf's work, and especially in *The Waves*, 'food and being are intimately connected [. . .] this renders food and meals ideal vehicles for Woolf to consider being and its end, death'. Since, as Allie Glenny and Vicki Tromanhauser have pointed out, food imagery also relates to motherhood, Utell's conclusion should be expanded to include another significant aspect of the human life cycle – procreation – with the drive to produce, reproduce and nurture finding expression in the character of Susan.[39]

When planning *The Waves*, Woolf wrote that she was ready to create 'in a very few strokes the essentials of a person's character. It should be done boldly, almost as caricature' (*D3* 300). She achieved this end with an experimental 'play-poem' structure, in which interspersed monologues allowed the novel's six protagonists to emerge slowly and create what Sangham MacDuff has called 'a composite whole [. . .] which is both unified and discrete'.[40] Form and characterisation are intrinsically linked in the novel, with Woolf – influenced by the works of that 'famous scholar' (*AROO* 15) Jane Harrison – merging her modernist sensibilities with aspects of ancient Greek drama. Rowena Fowler has noted how 'Woolf absorbed from Harrison insights about the way Greek ritual conventions embody archetypal emotions and states of mind'.[41] Taking ancient Greek choral forms and applying experimental techniques to them, Woolf built *The Waves*' characters in a way that was radical and new. By combining these two diverse models she created an atmosphere that was collective, and also, to use Leonard Woolf's words, 'purely psychological and highly introspective'.[42]

Susan Gorsky has observed that *The Waves*, 'defines human and literary character as simultaneously archetype and individual'.[43] Within the novel Bernard explains that the characters look 'to that which is beyond and outside our own predicament; to that which is symbolic, and thus perhaps permanent, if there is any permanence in our sleeping, eating, breathing, so animal, so spiritual and tumultuous lives' (*W* 191). *The Waves*' visionary characters manage to achieve an elusive duality: they are ancient yet new, collective yet individual, 'symbolic' but also entrenched in humanity. Pam Morris notes that on the corporeal side of this split Woolf's 'vision of transient human life [. . .] offers a compassionate transcendence that is rooted in materiality rather than idealism'.[44] Food, with its various symbolic functions and cultural significance, is a fitting vehicle with which to explore the

168 *Virginia Woolf and Motherhood*

physical aspects of this transaction. It is an everyday item that provides the reader with some key to the more ethereal questions that the book confronts.

Within this scheme, Susan is an archetypal mother who embodies the culture and drives of maternity. As mistress of the kitchen, garden and field, she is baker, jam-maker, fruit and vegetable grower, and substitute mother to abandoned lambs. Motherhood is especially significant in *The Waves* because it is bound up with the novel's origin. Of particular importance to the novel's genesis is a letter exchange between Woolf and Vanessa Bell that occurred in the spring of 1927. At the time Woolf was already contemplating writing her next 'very serious, mystical, poetical work' (*D3* 131), though it would be another two years before she would begin a first draft. The pertinent conversation began when Woolf, who was enjoying a trip through Italy with Leonard, wrote to Bell of a dream she had had in which Duncan Grant had impregnated their mutual friend Dora Carrington:

> I dreamt all night of Duncan and Carrington. She asked him to get her with child, which he did. This was so vivid that I woke and asked Leonard if he would think it a compliment should Bea ask the same of him. But alas – my dream is gone like smoke; Carrington bears none of Duncan's children within her, I'm sure. Aint it odd how all the flowers of female youth will die with their buds unopened – Carrington, Alix, Frances. (*L3* 362–63)

Whether she was prompted to reply because Woolf had described Duncan impregnating another woman, because she was touched by the image of their friends' wasted fertility (Carrington, Alix Strachey and Frances Marshall/Partridge were all child-free at the time), or in response to Woolf's carefree jaunt through Italy – made so much easier because it necessitated no logistics or childcare – Bell countered by asking: 'I wonder how you'd really like the problem of children added to your existence. I don't feel at all equal to it myself' (*L3* 365). The day after receiving this question Woolf wrote a considered response:

> I'm sure [. . .] that I should make a vile mother. For one thing (though I try to hide this from you) I slightly distrust or suspect the maternal passion. It is obviously immeasurable and unscrupulous. You would fry us all to cinders to give Angelica a days pleasure, without knowing it. You are a mere tool in the hands of passion. Other mothers are much worse and I've no doubt I should be worst of all [. . .] In fact what you feel about marriage I feel about motherhood, except that of the two relations motherhood seems to me the most destructive and

limiting. But no doubt I'm merely trying to make a case for myself: there's some truth in [it] though; I don't like profound instincts – not in human relationships. (*L3* 365–66)

Though Woolf tempered her argument with a self-effacing reference to her own non-motherhood, these views, stated plainly, bear out what she had been writing about motherhood in her fiction (two weeks later, when *To the Lighthouse* was published, Bell would read it and comment on the accuracy of Woolf's portrait of their mother).

Woolf knew that this description of motherhood as self-centred and damaging – a view that countered the pacifist, essentialist vision of mothers – might be inflammatory, adding 'I have tried to be as annoying as possible – to drop a little salt on Dolphin's snout so that she may spit columns of fury into the air' (*L3* 366). However in her reply, a long letter about motherhood and *Lepidoptera* which was a significant inspiration for *The Waves*,[45] Bell seemed to have understood and even agreed with Woolf, calling the 'maternal instinct [. . .] one of the worst of the passions, animal and remorseless'. This suggested that Woolf's feelings, rather than being eccentric, marginal notions, may have been an opinion shared by her bohemian friends and contemporaries. Furthermore, Bell urged Woolf to 'write a book about the maternal instinct'.[46] In response, Woolf took Bell's image of a moth's dangerous attraction to the lights of her room and, through the character of Susan, used it to explore this notion of motherhood as passionate and destructive.

Virginia Woolf and the Gender Theory of Otto Weininger

Although 'unscrupulous' and 'remorseless' were radical ways to describe mothers in the early twentieth century, Woolf and Bell were not alone in their views. One unorthodox but popular philosopher who put forward an account of motherhood as unprincipled and obsessive was Otto Weininger, an associate of Sigmund Freud who was well known by the contemporary British sexologists Woolf read, such as Havelock Ellis. Weininger was a divisive figure many branded sexist and anti-Semitic; nonetheless, his arguments were enjoyed by some of Woolf's friends.[47] In his renowned 1903 book *Sex & Character* Weininger developed a theory of sex – based on a constantly shifting set of gender traits – that had much in common with Woolf's work. Several scholars have written on Weininger's influence over

170 *Virginia Woolf and Motherhood*

Bloomsbury and, more specifically, Woolf. Jesse Wolfe, for instance, argues that Clarissa Dalloway 'exemplifies Weininger's theory of permanent bisexuality'.[48] With respect to motherhood, Weininger has many similar ideas to Woolf. Susan in particular, embodies his argument that mothers often become blinkered by their focus on their genetic issue. Similar to Woolf's claim that motherhood is 'destructive and limiting' (*L3* 366), Weininger explains, a mother's 'interest in her own child may become all-absorbing and make her narrow, blind, and unjust'.[49]

Though there is no proof that Woolf read *Sex & Character* she was certainly familiar with its theory. The review that 'Affable Hawk' (Desmond MacCarthy) wrote of Arnold Bennett's *Our Women* also examined *Sex & Character*, finding it 'an honest, wild book, full of ingenious, highly questionable reasoning, insight and unfairness'. In the review, MacCarthy briefly and coherently outlined Weininger's book, noting:

> It began with a general characterisation of Woman, 'W,' which was then divided into two main types, the Courtesan and the Mother, differentiated by their preoccupation with lovers or with children. It ended with discourse upon abnormal types of women and a definition of hysteria as 'the organic mendacity of women.' In every human being there were mixed the two elements, 'M.' (Man) and 'W.' (Woman) [. . .] To 'M.' Weininger attributed all the admirable moral and intellectual qualities and to 'W.' all the bad ones. Women therefore came out badly, for there was by hypothesis more 'W.' in them than in the great majority of men.[50]

While this section of text is shorter than MacCarthy's critique of Bennett, it is significantly longer than a brief final paragraph which reviews Orlo Williams's *The Good Englishwoman*. Yet in her reply Woolf only mentions Bennett and Williams, writing:

> I am unable to face the depression and the loss of self respect which Mr Arnold Bennett's blame and Mr Orlo Williams' praise [. . .] would certainly cause me if I read their books in the bulk. I taste them, therefore, in sips at the hands of reviewers. (*D2* 339)

It is curious that Woolf does not reference Weininger, but it is difficult to say whether she had not yet heard of and thus had not formed an opinion on him or whether she had already been introduced to his ideas and felt disinclined to refute his work.[51] Accepting that she had a relatively higher proportion of 'M' than most women might have made sense of Woolf's discomfort with traditionally feminine roles like mother, homemaker and mistress. It also might have explained how she had inherited her father's tradition of writing and why, as a child, 'she, on the whole, preferred' him.[52]

It is important to note that Weininger was not arguing the same case as Bennett, Williams and MacCarthy. Where they believed women were biologically incapable of intellectual achievement, Weininger offered specific examples to explain women's genius in terms of the male and female principles he had outlined. For Weininger, woman possessed genius 'in direct proportion to the amount of maleness in her' (*SC* 64), and women authors wrote under male pseudonyms not merely because it was difficult to publish as a woman, but because it gave 'expression to the inherent maleness they feel' (*SC* 68). This is not to suggest that Weininger's works were not misogynistic – he still claimed that 'not a single woman in the history of thought, not even the most manlike [. . .] can be truthfully compared with men of fifth or sixth-rate genius [. . .] if we eliminate hysterical visionaries' (*SC* 69). However, Weininger's writing appealed to Woolf's contemporaries because it corresponded with certain beliefs they had about themselves, as well as theories they held about art. Woolf included Weiningerian ideas in her theories about the creation of art in *A Room of One's Own* where she wrote:

> I went on amateurishly to sketch a plan of the soul so that in each of us two powers preside, one male, one female; and in the man's brain the man predominates over the woman, and in the woman's brain the woman predominates over the man. The normal and comfortable state of being is that when the two live in harmony together, spiritually co-operating. (*AROO* 88)

However, while Woolf allowed that in any given sex one gender might predominate over the other, she differed from Weininger by not making any sex intellectually superior to the other.

Weininger also argued that artists were often homosexual, an idea that was popular among many of the artists and thinkers that associated with the Bloomsbury group, and may have helped Woolf explain her 'sapphic' tendencies.[53] Indeed, Woolf became versed in Weininger's thinking through Vita Sackville-West, who had owned a 'heavily annotated' copy of Weininger's book since at least 1918 and considered his explanation of gender key to understanding her own psyche. Sackville-West continued to be influenced by *Sex & Character* throughout the 1920s and 1930s, referencing him in her 1929

172   *Virginia Woolf and Motherhood*

BBC broadcast 'Marriage' and a 1933 article entitled 'Our Future Beckons'. Barbara Fassler has explained how Sackville-West used Weininger's theories to explore her own life story:

> Weininger [. . .] maintained that, since a person can be only one sex at a time, the homosexual would swing wildly between masculinity and femininity [. . .] In 1920, the 28-year-old Sackville-West used such a construct to explain her own nature. In her autobiographical sketch of that year, she traced the alternating stages in her own life: after a very tomboyish childhood and an adolescent lesbian relationship, her marriage to Harold Nicolson 'brought out all the feminine' in her. She took pains with her appearance, socialized as the charming young diplomat's wife, and had two children. Then, one day in 1918, when Harold was away, some newly ordered breeches came for Vita in the mail. Donning this unaccustomed clothing, she ran over the fields in glorious abandon. That day she and her friend Violet Keppel began a passionate love affair. Vita looked upon that day as the emergence of the long-buried masculine side of her character, referring to the 'well-known theory' that there are some persons 'in whom masculine and feminine elements alternately preponderate'.[54]

Woolf did not read Sackville-West's autobiography, *Portrait of a Marriage*, which was only published posthumously.[55] Nonetheless, the best proof that she had absorbed this Weiningerian life history in other ways can be found in *Orlando*, a book that not only tells the story of a character who changed sex in the middle of a 300-year-long life, but that continually blurs and complicates the experience of gender and sexual orientation. In *Orlando*, Woolf repeatedly depicts sartorial gender shifts like the one described by Sackville-West. Clothing affects the disposition of the wearer from the opening line: 'He – for there could be no doubt of his sex, though the fashion of the time did something to disguise it' (*O* 11) – to the moment when the recently female Orlando first wears 'the dress of a young Englishwoman of rank' (*O* 108) and is struck by what it means to be female. As the text notes, 'it is clothes that wear us and not we them [. . .] they mould our hearts, our brains, our tongues to their liking' (*O* 132). *Orlando* also incorporates Sackville-West's theory of 'alternate preponderance', which – as Fassler points out – was taken directly from Weininger. In *Sex & Character* Weininger explains that, 'every human being varies or oscillates between the maleness and the femaleness of his constitution' (*SC* 54) – an idea echoed in *Orlando*, which notes: 'Different though the sexes are, they intermix. In every human being a vacillation from one sex to the other takes place' (*O* 132–33).

Courtesan, Mother, Hysteric: Weiningerian Archetypes in *The Waves*

Parallels between *The Waves* and Weininger's work – especially in their analysis of motherhood – invite us to also read this later novel with a Weiningerian framework in mind. Although Woolf was thinking about *The Waves* before she began writing *Orlando* 'at the top of my speed' (*D3* 131), it was only once she started to have more concrete formal ideas that her three female protagonists began to fall into Weiningerian categories. As MacCarthy had noted, Weininger separated woman into two 'normal' archetypes, 'the Courtesan and the Mother' – both of which exist, to varying degrees, in all but the most stereotypical women – and, the 'abnormal type, the hysterical woman' (*SC* vi). Reading *The Waves* through this theory Jinny falls into the category of 'Courtesan' – leaping from man to man and settling with no one; Susan can be read as a 'Mother' because she is motivated solely by the drive to procreate; and Rhoda – who has 'no face' (*W* 23, 31, 91, 98, 171) – might be compared to a 'hysteric' (Rhoda's traumatic alterity gives her the freedom to criticise society). While *Sex & Character* offers a useful counterpart for *The Waves* there are notable differences between the two texts. In particular, Weininger does not concentrate on the possessive quality of motherhood – a trait that is central to Susan's character.

As with Weininger's 'Mother' – who, in childhood, is already 'devoted to dolls' and 'attentive to children' (*SC* 219) – Susan's nurturing, possessiveness and monomania mark her out from early on in the novel. In the opening chapter Susan states: 'I desire one thing only [. . .] I am already set on my pursuit [. . .] Though my mother still knits white socks for me and hems pinafores and I am a child' (*W* 10). The young Susan detests being away at school, preferring home where she can mother and cook for her own father. During school holidays she returns eagerly home to her possessions:

> I shall go upstairs to *my* room, and turn over *my* own things, locked carefully in the wardrobe: *my* shells; *my* eggs; *my* curious grasses. I shall feed *my* doves and *my* squirrel. I shall go to the kennel and comb *my* spaniel. (*W* 39, my emphasis)

Not only does this speech portray Susan's acquisitiveness but, in line with her nurturing nature, it exposes her penchant for owning pets. Woolf clearly felt that mothering was somewhat akin to caring for animals, once writing to Barbara Bagenal: 'Its no good pluming one-self on scraps of learning with you matrons [. . .] who are rearing families and feeding hens' (*L2* 558). Pet maintenance is also emblematic of patriarchal oppression. An example of this can be seen in *The Voyage Out* in a conversation where Terence and Rachel speak about gender power imbalance:

> 'Look at Hirst now. I assure you,' he said, 'not a day's passed since we came here without a discussion as to whether he's to stay on at Cambridge or to go to the Bar. It's his career – his sacred career. And if I've heard it twenty times, I'm sure his mother and sister have heard it five hundred times. Can't you imagine the family conclaves, and the sister told to run out and feed the rabbits because St John must have the school-room to himself – 'St John's working,' 'St John wants his tea brought to him.' [. . .] But St John's sister – ' Hewet puffed in silence. 'No one takes her seriously, poor dear. She feeds the rabbits.'
>   'Yes,' said Rachel. 'I've fed rabbits for twenty-four years; it seems odd now.' (*VO* 197)

Rachel dies before graduating from rabbits to babies, but once learned, the ethos of nurturing animals appears to be difficult to shake. At the beginning of *Jacob's Room* Betty Flanders feeds her hens with her young son in tow and at the end, with 'Morty lost, and Seabrook dead' and 'her sons fighting' – and indeed dying – 'for their country', Betty reverts to wondering: 'But were the chickens safe?' (*JR* 154).

These possessive mothers treat their children and animals like property, but an ability to feed chickens, and in turn children, does not translate into a pacifist attitude. After Percival's death – an untimely end which, like Jacob Flanders's, might befall any child born in a nationalistic society and household – Susan uses her maternal authority to watch over her baby:

> Sleep, sleep, I say, warning off with my voice all who rattle milk-cans, fire at rooks, shoot rabbits, or in any way bring the shock of destruction near this wicker cradle, laden with soft limbs, curled under a pink coverlet [. . .] Sleep, I say, and feel within me uprush some wilder, darker violence, so that I would fell down with one blow any intruder, any snatcher, who should break into this room and wake the sleeper. (*W* 130–31)

The violence of Susan's feelings are in line with Woolf's view of motherhood. They do not suggest that Susan has some maternalist, placatory hidden strength to save mankind or her adult children. If

Motherhood and Food **175**

anything, motherhood makes her even more ferocious, more partial to the type of violent clashes over space that lead to war. Susan is destructive in her patriarchal affiliations. She produces children not only to increase her own possessions, but to strengthen the empire. While her daughters will follow in her (and her mother's) footsteps, carrying on the race in an endless cycle, her sons ensure that she 'shall go mixed with them beyond my body and shall see India' (*W* 131) – the place where Percival dies 'applying the standards of the West' and solving: 'The Oriental problem' (*W* 102). Unlike Mistress Joan or Rachel Vinrace – women who do not want to be part of the domestic foundations underpinning the British Empire – Susan *does* identify with a breastfeeding 'racial other', stating: 'I like best [. . .] the stare of gipsy women beside a cart in a ditch suckling their children as I shall suckle my children' (*W* 73). Susan is contrasted with Jinny, who, offering yet another view of breastfeeding, feels she is 'better than savages in loincloths, and women whose hair is dank, whose long breasts sag, with children tugging at their long breasts' (*W* 149). (Interestingly, Jinny is not anti-imperialist – indeed she rejoices in 'the triumphant procession [. . .] the army of victory with banners and brass eagles and heads crowned with laurel-leaves won in battle' (*W* 149) – she is just anti-motherhood).

As a mother Susan is not only associated with breastfeeding, but with every part of the alimentary process from foraging, growing plants and animal husbandry, to storing and cooking food. This is consistent with Weininger, who writes:

> Another striking aspect of the mother's relation to the preservation of the race reveals itself in the matter of food. She cannot bear to see food wasted [. . .] is stingy and mean [. . .] The mother's object in life is to preserve the race, and her delight is to see her children eat and to encourage their appetites. And so she becomes the good housekeeper. (*SC* 224)

The juxtaposition between the mother's meanness and her joy in encouraging her children to eat can also be seen in *The Waves*, where Susan is an 'unscrupulous [. . .] mother who protects, who collects under her jealous eyes at one long table her own children, always her own' (*W* 174). Vicki Tromanhauser has noted that Susan's 'jealous maternal instinct manifests most forcefully as a means of controlling life processes'. Tromanhauser sees Susan's use of food – 'The kitchen that sustains life – preserving fruit, rising dough, roasting meat, and filling mouths' – as a way of 'fattening and immobilizing her dependents'; raising them as lambs to the slaughter.[56]

Susan's maternal tendencies, as manifested in her cooking, also make her incapable of other achievements. Though Allie Glenny observes that 'Susan's need to possess [. . .] carries undertones of potential tyranny', this maternal way of life arrests Susan's own body and creative spirit as much as, if not more than, her children.[57] While her oppressing love limits them – she nets her infant children over 'like fruit in their cots' (W 147), and as they grow she refuses to allow them to go to London to be schooled – Susan eventually becomes limited herself, rooted to one spot so that, 'fenced in, planted here like one of my own trees [. . .] Life stands round me like a glass round the imprisoned reed' (W 147). Once her children have grown up and gone out into the world, Susan is 'rewarded by security, possession, familiarity. I have had peaceful, productive years. I possess all I see' (W 146). Yet her lot is mixed:

I shall be lifted higher than any of you on the backs of the seasons. I shall possess more than Jinny, more than Rhoda, by the time I die. But on the other hand [. . .] I shall be sullen, storm-tinted and all one purple. I shall be debased and hide-bound by the bestial and beautiful passion of maternity. I shall push the fortunes of my children unscrupulously. I shall hate those who see their faults. I shall lie basely to help them. I shall let them wall me away from you, from you and from you. (W 99)

As an impassioned mother, Susan is 'all one purple' (much like Lily's depiction of Mrs Ramsay in *To the Lighthouse*).[58] Because she is defined by her grand consuming passion/function, Susan's character emerges as one-dimensional throughout the text. Woolf uses food to show how motherhood, like cooking, can be over-exercised: employed, as Tromanhauser writes, to 'sickening excess'.[59] When Susan eventually becomes weary of her 'own craft, industry and cunning' (W 174), Woolf employs the terminology of eating to express this overabundance. Susan dreams of crying: 'No more. I am glutted with natural happiness' (W 131) and wishes 'that the fullness would pass from me and the weight of the sleeping house rise' (W 132).

'The getting of the child': Sexual Intercourse in *The Waves*

Sex & Character offers another way of defining *The Waves*' female archetypes. Weininger conducts his investigation into female archetypes 'by considering the relation of each type to the child and to sexual congress' (*SC* 219). He differentiates between the 'Courtesan' and 'Mother' as follows: 'The essence of motherhood consists [. . .] in that the getting of the child is the chief object of life, whereas in the prostitute sexual relations in themselves are the end' (*SC* 219). This contrast can be seen clearly in Jinny and Susan's attitudes towards sex. While Woolf does not suggest that Jinny is selling sex, her narrative is overwhelmingly about sexual attraction. It describes moments of flirting, physical contact and sensory pleasure. Jinny's relationships, in which she experiences sexual fulfilment with one partner before rapidly moving onto another, are sometimes consummated outdoors:

> on those first spring nights when the tree under the big London houses where respectable citizens were going soberly to bed scarcely sheltered her love; and the squeak of trams mixed with her cry of delight and the rippling of leaves had to shade her languor, her delicious lassitude as she sank down cooled by all the sweetness of nature satisfied. (*W* 212)

The arboreal setting of Jinny's congress is echoed in Susan's sexual experience, but the two scenes are otherwise different. For Susan the sexual act is neither gratifying nor transgressive, instead it is a moment of pastoral begetting:

> in the hot midday when the bees hum round the hollyhocks my lover will come. He will stand under the cedar tree. To his one word I shall answer my one word. What has formed in me I shall give him. I shall have children. (*W* 73)

Unlike Jinny's urban, evening intercourse, Susan meets her lover in a rural setting, while the sun nourishes the land and busy bees fertilise the hollyhocks (a flower that represents fecundity in the Victorian handbook *The Language of Flowers*).[60] Susan's functional attitude towards sex bears the hallmarks of her maternal possessiveness: 'I do not want, as Jinny wants, to be admired. I do not want people, when I come in, to look up with admiration. I want to give, to be given, and solitude in which to unfold my possessions' (*W* 39). In Susan's narrative the language of attainment and ownership is central even in moments of sexual tension. In giving herself, Susan begets children who increase her title both by being her property and by going out into the world to acquire more.

Like Weininger's maternal archetype, who 'accepts any possible man who can make her a mother, and once that has been achieved asks nothing more' (*SC* 220), Susan does not care to be desired, actively seeking solitude. Although Susan bears many children, her narrative offers only one moment of sexual congress. This evokes another of Weininger's concepts – the theory of 'impression'. Weininger states that the 'birth of a human being [. . .] dates from the moment when the mother first saw or heard the voice of the father of her child' (*SC* 217). In *The Waves*, Susan's lover merely offers her 'one word' and this word is enough to cause Susan, who has always been a mother in spirit, to become one in the flesh. Susan and her lover use single words as befits a couple making a baby rather than an author making a text. Indeed, like Woolf's earlier breastfeeding mothers, Susan's fecundity goes hand in hand with a taciturn, monosyllabic nature. Not only is she is 'tied down with single words' (*W* 10) but she sits among her friends 'quenching the silver-grey flickering moth-wing quiver of words with the green spurt of my clear eyes' (*W* 165). Diane Gillespie has suggested that Woolf 'hints at [Susan's] painterly side', with her 'artist's tactile description of [. . .] the hard purity and exquisite colours of a visual life'. However, while parts of Susan's narrative have a visual quality (as a child she notes 'I see the beetle [. . .] It is black, I see; it is green, I see' (*W* 10)) she does not use this potential to access creativity instead using her creative drives to produce children and food.[61] Susan's distance from language and the creation of texts offers further evidence in support of Woolf's argument that motherhood stops women from making art and keeps them – like Susan – limited and 'imprisoned'.

Much like Woolf's own mother, Susan is a muse rather than an artist – 'born to be the adored of poets, since poets require safety; someone who sits sewing, who says, "I hate, I love"' (*W* 190).[62] Susan's status as a mother who protects and nurtures makes her the perfect muse, partly because she allows the poet the time and space to create by taking care of his physical needs. Weininger observes that a 'Mother' will act maternally towards any man, and as a young girl Susan is preoccupied with her father, nurturing and feeding him as she later nurtures her children. The 'Mother' figure is also an ideal muse because she is part of something transcendent. As Weininger explains:

> The enduring security of the race lies in the mystery of [the mother] in the presence of which man feels his own fleeting impermanence. In such minutes there may come to him a sense of freedom and peace, and in the mysterious silence of the idea, he may think that it is through the woman that he is in true relation with the universe. (*SC* 222–23)

As a mother, Susan's relationship to the eternal is expressed through her body when she procreates, but it also extends to other aspects of her mothering, and so can be seen when she 'sits sewing', or prepares and serves food. Woolf had previously explored this relationship with eternity via Mrs Ramsay who, as 'part of her perfect goodness' (*TL* 219) sits and knits while Lily becomes filled with inspiration. This mystical force is also in effect when Mrs Ramsay serves her *boeuf en daube* and the text notes: 'There it was, all round them. It partook, she felt, carefully helping Mr Bankes to a specially tender piece, of eternity' (*TL* 114).

It is important to note the distinction between muses and lovers; the 'Mother' may inspire the artist but she is not a sexual partner. Not only is the attention that a 'Mother' receives from an artist of an order other than sexual, but she marries a man who is creatively limited. This is shown by Mr Ramsay, who will 'never reach R' (*TL* 40) and Susan's husband who is silent and brutal (in the first draft Susan's lover is particularly reminiscent of gamekeeper Oliver Mellors from D. H. Lawrence's *Lady Chatterley's Lover* – a pairing which makes sense, given that Chatterley initially takes her lover in order to have a child).[63] Weininger explains that men who 'are sexually attracted by the mother-type [. . .] have no desire for mental productivity' (*SC* 226). In fact, he echoes Woolf's feelings about the conflict between motherhood and art, arguing that: 'a man only comes to his fulness when he frees himself from the race, when he raises himself above it [. . .] the idea that he is to be lost in the race is repellent to him' (*SC* 223). For Weininger and Woolf the immortality connected with parenthood eradicates or diverts the creative drive, voiding a man or woman's artistic potential. Author Bernard in *The Waves* wrestles with this problem when he marries, and feels:

> a sense that life for me is now mysteriously prolonged. Is it that I may have children, may cast a fling of seed wider, beyond this generation, this doom-encircled population [. . .] ? My daughters shall come here, in other summers; my sons shall turn new fields. Hence we are not raindrops, soon dried up by the wind; we make gardens blow and forests roar; we come up differently, for ever and ever. This, then, serves to explain my confidence [. . .] It is not vanity; for I am emptied of ambition; I do not remember my special gifts, or idiosyncrasy, or the marks I bear on my person [. . .] I am not, at this moment, myself. (*W* 85–86)

For an artist the jeopardy of reproductive immortality is its self-erasing quality. Falling under its spell Bernard becomes 'emptied of ambition [. . .] special gifts [. . .] idiosyncrasy [. . .] myself', he loses the essential self necessary to make art (this is especially interest-

180   *Virginia Woolf and Motherhood*

ing considering the place of self-erasure in modernist writing). It is noteworthy that in this moment Bernard employs Susan-like agricultural imagery – he flings seed, makes gardens grow, his sons turn fields. Unlike Susan, however, Bernard overcomes this creative impediment, 'Yet behold, it returns' begins the next paragraph 'It steals in through some crack in the structure – one's identity' (*W* 86). This is a structural advantage for fathers within a patriarchy but it is not something that Susan can access. Later, when Bernard recalls visiting a heavily pregnant Susan, he remembers the fertile aura of her Lincolnshire estate as 'hateful, like a net folding one's limbs in its meshes, cramping'. 'I thought then how we surrender', he goes on to note, 'how we submit to the stupidity of nature' (*W* 206).

Population Studies, Economics and Gardening in *The Waves*

In addition to engaging with Weininger's theories, Woolf uses food production and motherhood to participate in debates about population science and economics. In the late eighteenth century Thomas Malthus had argued that humanity, like all flora and fauna, reproduce beyond the means of the natural world, noting: 'Through the animal and vegetable kingdoms Nature has scattered the seeds of life abroad with the most profuse and liberal hand; but has been comparatively sparing in the room and the nourishment necessary to rear them'. Malthus explained that checks on humanity such as war, famine and disease were a natural consequence of limited resources. He argued that society could, in theory, prevent large-scale disasters as well as more localised issues of poverty by encouraging abstinence, with those of marriageable age choosing matrimony and childbearing only once they had the means to support a naturally large family. Although he granted that in practice this would prove incredibly difficult, since the 'perpetual tendency [. . .] to increase beyond the means of subsistence, is one of the general laws of animated nature, which we can have no reason to expect will change'.[64]

By focusing on the relationship between gardening, farming, cooking and maternity, *The Waves* engages not only with Malthus's century-old discussion of population and resources but also with contemporary population studies, which were undergoing a revolution at the exact time that Woolf was recording how she 'longed to write the first page of The Moths' (*L3* 424). At the end of August 1927 the first World Population Conference was organised by Margaret

Sanger in Geneva, and was attended by John Maynard Keynes – who was on the advisory council – as well as such British luminaries as H. G. Wells and Havelock Ellis. It was in the conference's opening paper that the influential biostatistician Raymond Pearl introduced the radical idea that population was not unbound as Malthus had claimed, but was, in fact, self-regulating and tied to density. Pearl argued that the birth rate declined when the population grew too fast, even claiming that 'birth rates are markedly affected adversely by small increases in density'.[65] This was controversial and many contemporary academics disputed his models; nonetheless these Neo-Malthusian ideas took root, eventually changing the face of population studies.

Written in an era of fertility decline, *The Waves* participates in these arguments, using Susan's maternity to highlight the links between reproduction and resources. Susan is as laden with food as she is with children. Her kitchen runs over, she handles 'blackberries and mushrooms [. . .] jam-pots [. . .] heavy silver bags of tea', 'damp bags of rich sultanas [. . .] heavy flour [. . .] currants and rices' (*W* 146–47, 74), foodstuffs that signify both the abundance of her own fields, and riches from the empire obtained under less wholesome circumstances and (on occasion) causing hunger elsewhere.[66] As befits Malthusian theory the quantity of food and children are linked; Susan is always sure that, for her family, 'more will come, more children; more cradles, more baskets in the kitchen and hams ripening; and onions glistening; and more beds of lettuce and potatoes' (*W* 132). The text also hints at issues of overcrowding with Rhoda's horror at the dense population of London. Rhoda stands in queues and smells other people's sweat, she is 'hung with other people like a joint of meat among other joints of meat' (*W* 122) and despairs at the proximity of her fellow Londoners – 'oh, human beings, how I have hated you!', she cries: 'How you have nudged, how you have interrupted, how hideous you have looked in Oxford Street, how squalid sitting opposite each other staring in the Tube!' (*W* 156).

The revolution in population studies was not the only event that influenced *The Waves*. Herbert Marder has noted that the novel was written 'in the two-year period between the 1929 Wall Street crash, which began the worldwide Great Depression, and the financial crisis that forced England off the gold standard in September 1931'.[67] Maynard Keynes called the Great Depression 'the greatest economic catastrophe [. . .] of the modern world', yet it was a time of success and security for the Woolfs.[68] Looking at Woolf's book-keeping, Diane Gillespie records how her finances were robust well into

182   *Virginia Woolf and Motherhood*

the 1930s, noting: 'Even in the midst of the depression, earnings remained strong'.[69] With the carnage of war in living memory and hunger marches occurring around the country, *The Waves*' materialist corporeality – Rhoda as 'a joint of meat among other joints of meat' – evoke painful associations. As Tromanhauser notes, the novel has 'returned us to the matter we are made of'.[70] These associations are even more obvious in Woolf's posthumously published 1931 'Cook Sketch', where the cook talks about the cost and quality of the meat for dinner before moving on to gossip about the son of a butcher who is injured.[71] Against these troubling images, Susan's full pantry and her baking – the book's most visceral description of cooking – emerge clearly as emblems of wealth, plenty and new life:

> I knead; I stretch; I pull, plunging my hands in the warm inwards of the dough. I let the cold water stream fanwise through my fingers. The fire roars; the flies buzz in a circle [. . .] The meat is stood in the oven; the bread rises in a soft dome under the clean towel. (*W* 74)

Despite the subtle reminder of decay in the image of the buzzing flies, this is a moment of plenty. 'All the world is breeding' Susan observes as she bakes, her dough rising 'in a soft dome' under a piece of fabric like a mother's swelling belly. Though the term 'bun in the oven' did not become part of the vernacular until 1951, the oven has existed as a metaphor for the womb since Greek antiquity.[72] The materiality of the body is reiterated through the meat in the oven and the dough rising under the towel, both bringing a baby's womb-bound body into focus.

Susan's world of plenty is based on someone of Woolf's class rather than someone affected by the rapidly worsening financial crisis. Similarly the description of baking – the kneading, stretching, pulling and the sensation of the cold water – is based on Woolf's personal experience in the kitchen. Louie Mayer, the Woolf's cook from 1934 until Leonard's death, observed: 'there was one thing Mrs Woolf was very good at doing. She could make beautiful bread'. The same is true of the scenes where Susan carries hives in her car and tallies her jam-pots at Christmas. Woolf was incredibly proud of her honey, and was known in her circle for making jam, as her niece Angelica Garnett wrote: 'well do I remember the pride she took in her cupboard of jade-green gooseberries and sad-purple raspberries on the stairs at Monk's House'.[73] Finally, though Susan's narrative is one of plenty, it directly references Woolf's own experience of foraging for mushrooms and blackberries to supplement her pantry during the rationing of

WW1. In a separate diary that Woolf kept while she was at Asheham, she repeatedly records searching for mushrooms which were sometimes 'so deep in the grass that we probably missed several'; likewise Susan states: 'I feel through the grass for the white-domed mushroom; and break its stalk' (*W* 74). On another occasion Woolf notes 'got enough blackberries to make 4lb jam [. . .] Mushrooms weighed 1½ lb', recalling the moment when Susan and her children 'weigh our blackberries and mushrooms' (*W* 146).[74]

At first it is surprising to see how much of her own life Woolf puts into these metaphors for motherhood. While Woolf's tendency to add autobiographical elements to her fiction are well noted,[75] in the context of her writing on motherhood – something she usually distanced herself from – this is particularly thought-provoking. In her everyday life Woolf had an ambiguous relationship with cooking. After marriage she decided that learning to cook was an important part of modern living. She attended cookery lessons and advised Molly MacCarthy to get her daughter Rachel lessons, noting: 'It is dreadful how we were neglected, and yet its not hard to be practical, up to a point, and such an advantage, I hope' (*L2* 56). However, while Woolf sometimes showed enthusiasm for preparing meals – once writing to Vita Sackville-West 'I have only one passion in life – cooking' (*L4* 93) – her (perhaps ironic) devotion may have been more of a means to an end. Alison Light has associated Woolf's cooking with a desire for independence from live-in staff.[76] In the long-term cooking, and especially baking, was more likely to be a chore that interrupted Woolf's writing. In 1923 she recorded in her diary: 'I have ruined my mornings work by making bread & buns, which require constant voyages to the kitchen' (*D2* 260). Alix Strachey would later recall that Leonard liked Virginia to cook and do other small domestic tasks as a counterbalance to the excitement and over-stimulation of writing. And Louie Mayer was of the opinion that: 'She liked trying to cook [. . .] but I always felt that she did not want to give time to cooking and preferred to be in her room working'.[77] It is possible that Woolf used her own knowledge of baking to access the experience of a more maternal woman – her sister. She associated Bell with growing vegetables and jam- and bread-making, and they were playfully competitive about baking – 'I have made your rolls', wrote Woolf during the war 'not so good yet as yours' (*L2* 108). Later, Woolf records that at Charleston, 'Nessa and Duncan [. . .] seem perfectly happy, painting, making jam, getting all their own vegetables' (*L2* 174). To imagine that Susan has some of Vanessa in her is no great stretch. It has already been noted that Bell was an inspiration for *The Waves*

184 *Virginia Woolf and Motherhood*

and, as Angelica Garnett states, she was also the standard against which Woolf measured her own practical, homemaking abilities.[78]

Gardening is another area of Susan's narrative where Woolf took inspiration not only from her own experience but also from her sister and mother's lives. The description of Susan's garden is sensual: 'Bees boomed down the purple tunnels of flowers; bees embedded themselves on the golden shields of sunflowers. Little twigs were blown across the grass' (*W* 206). The form and language of this description bears a marked similarity to the recollection of Julia's garden at Talland House found in 'A Sketch of the Past': 'The gardens gave off a murmur of bees; the apples were red and gold; there were also pink flowers; and grey and silver leaves. The buzz, the croon, the smell, all seemed to press voluptuously against some membrane' (*MB* 80). The colours and sounds of the fertile garden affected Woolf in a sensory way that she remembered years later. After Julia died, Dr Seton suggested that Virginia take up therapeutic gardening and she noted in her diary: 'the back garden is to be reclaimed' (*PA* 84). Before long, however, Vanessa took over the lion's share of this task and – like their mother – seemed to have a talent for it. In her investigation into Woolf's literary and emotional relationship with gardens, Bonnie Kime Scott notes that 'Woolf learned that gardening was largely a matter of control'; as such it spoke to the maternal gifts of Julia, Vanessa and Susan.[79] While the adult Woolf enjoyed the outdoor spaces of her homes, they were cultivated according to Leonard's passion and vision and she sometimes resented having 'to spend such a measure of our money on gardens' (*D3* 112). Bell, on the other hand, continued to express herself through gardening. As Nuala Hancock notes, 'Charleston garden [. . .] represented a further manifestation of her sister's effortless fertility – "Nessa humming & booming & flourishing over the hill"'.[80]

The Waves is not the only novel where Woolf connects gardening and motherhood. Another example can be found in *Mrs Dalloway*, where Peter thinks of Sally Seton's 'achievements':

> her five sons; and what was the other thing – plants, hydrangeas, syringas, very, very rare hibiscus lilies that never grow north of the Suez Canal, but she, with one gardener in a suburb near Manchester, had beds of them, positively beds! Now all that Clarissa had escaped, unmaternal as she was. (*MD* 209)

Although both are expressions of their maternity, Sally's garden differs to Susan's. Sally's is for display purposes, while Susan's is geared towards the production of food – even her flowers exist for her bees to make honey. The image (and sound) of bees in the description of

Susan's garden – a portrait echoed in Bell's 'humming & booming' – is also tangentially associated with female sexuality and motherhood. At Monk's House the Woolfs kept bees, looking after their hives and extracting honey. Virginia understood the critical role that pollination played in agriculture, and knew about the matriarchal life of the hives with their queen larvae and their workers. She also associated bees with sexuality, writing in her diary when their bees swarmed in 1932:

> Bees shoot whizz, like arrows of desire: fierce, sexual; weave cats cradles in the air; each whizzing from a string; the whole air full of vibration: of beauty, of this burning arrowy desire; & speed: I still think the quivering shifting bee bag the most sexual & sensual symbol. (*D4* 109)

It is possible Woolf made this connection between bees and sexuality because of Jane Harrison's writing on Cybele – the Greek fertility goddess who is associated with bees and sometimes takes the form of one. In *Prolegomena to the Study of Greek Religion* Harrison writes about the 'divine associations' between bees and 'the sacred tradition of the Earth-Mother'. Indeed, Harrison's thinking about Earth-Mother goddesses may have played a part in the formation of Susan's agricultural prowess. Written in the same year as *Sex & Character*, and also using a duality of 'Mother' and 'Maid' to define women (though without the third option of a hysteric), *Prolegomena* describes one of the important tropes of pre-patriarchal civilisation as a 'primitive association of women with agriculture'.[81]

'Lives so opposite [. . .] languages so different': The Impossibility of Class in *The Waves*

Putting aside domestic parallels, one of the most conspicuous connections between Woolf, Bell, Stephen and the character of Susan is their social class. Indeed, all of the central characters in *The Waves* enjoy a similar economic position to Woolf, despite the fact that she originally intended for the novel to be a comprehensive look at a broad cross-section of society. The draft subtitle for the novel was 'The Mind of Anybody' and its earliest pages compare 'Albert whose father was a cowman' to Roger, son of a civil servant, and Florrie, who 'went out [. . .] as kitchenmaid', to Flora and Dorothy, 'going to schools in Switzerland' (*WH* 67). When Woolf chose to forsake working-class characters for a more complete view of her

186   *Virginia Woolf and Motherhood*

final six protagonists she did so with a hint of apology, explaining in the drafts: 'No single person could follow two lives so opposite; could speak two languages so different' (*WH* 68). It is interesting to think of this elimination of working-class figures in light of *Flush*, wherein Woolf chose to comment on Elizabeth Barrett Browning's life through a biography of her dog, despite noting in a footnote that the life of her maid Lily Wilson was 'extremely obscure and thus cries aloud for the services of a biographer' (*F* 94).

Gillian Beer has suggested that Woolf avoided writing the working class into her novels for fear of sounding 'condescending'.[82] Similarly, Finn Fordham argues that:

> Since Woolf's aim is to communicate depth of consciousness and the many layered conflict between a self and the social determinants that crowd round it, she fears caricatures in her sketches. She knows her characterization will fall into this if it attempts working-class 'lives' and 'language'.[83]

Though Fordham claims that: 'The focus on the white-collar (and wing-collar) culture of these characters reflects the minority interest that Woolf feared her mode of writing would excite', Beth Daugherty has emphatically proven (in her transcription of Woolf's correspondence with readers) that the author knew her readership included other classes.[84] However, Woolf made a choice to write about the class she understood because it afforded the best expression of her impressions of the world.[85] While she did not write 'working class "lives" and "language"' into *The Waves*, working-class people still emerge as caricatures. Lacking voices, and observed through the eyes of those in whom they invoke fear, loathing and longing, they are present as distortions of reality. For example, when Susan sees two domestic staff kiss in the garden, she pictures 'a crack in the earth and hot steam hisses up' while 'the urn roars as Ernest roared' (*W* 17); and in the 'sordid eating-house' (*W* 86) Louis frequents he sees the customers as 'prehensile like monkeys, greased [. . .] like guillemots [. . .] slippery with oil' and waitress as full of 'scorn' (*W* 69–72).

Though Woolf chose to eliminate the perspectives of working-class men and women, they still inhabit the text as an impersonal mass or anonymous individuals. In 'Britannia Ruled *The Waves*' Jane Marcus calls class the 'most powerful undertow in *The Waves*', noting: 'The ruling-class characters define themselves as clean, free, and dominant against the dirt and ugly squalor of the masses'.[86] This is true for

Louis and Rhoda, who experience otherness, fear and repulsion when they come into contact with the working class, especially when eating – although this, of course, says more about their own mental state than that of the working-class characters. On the other hand, Bernard likes varied company, claiming: 'Anybody will do. I am not fastidious. The crossing-sweeper will do; the postman; the waiter in this French restaurant' (*W* 88). Bernard evokes his cleaning lady Mrs Moffat as a kind of eternal (and maternal) standard that remains constant when all else wavers. In the first draft of the novel, Roger (who prefigures Bernard) is 'among those who would have nurses; who [. . .] make ~~soft~~ wry & affectionate pictures of old Mrs Constable [. . .] eating her supper ~~dinner~~ & doing her mending over the nursery fire' (*WH* 67). Alongside these amplified responses to class it is particularly striking that Susan, whose house and kitchen runs effortlessly because of an army of maids, does not express any sentiments about the workers she must encounter on a daily basis.

Not only is it strange that Susan never contends with any servants, it is also odd that, as a wealthy woman, she is portrayed as someone who spends so much time cooking and watching over her babies. Upper-middle-class women like Susan and Woolf had little schooling in food preparation or childcare (Woolf took cookery lessons 'at an institution in Victoria St' only *after* marriage – joking of the cross-class experience: 'my views of humanity are changing' (*L2* 55)). As noted, amateur interests such as jam-making and bread-baking aside, Woolf did not spend much time cooking. And when she did cook it was generally only her evening meal and even this would have been something simple like baked potatoes or reheated dishes made by Louie.[87] Having been raised in the country, Susan might have had more practical knowledge than a city-dweller, but she unquestionably would have employed a cook and a nanny. Even bohemian Woolf, who had dreamed for many years about being free from live-in servants, kept Louie as a 'daily', while Bell, with her growing family, had cooks, nannies and governesses.

Susan appears not only responsible for the cooking, but for the childcare too – she describes feeding, soothing and keeping guard over her children in their cots:

> I stoop; I feed my baby. I, who used to walk through beech woods [. . .] who stared at the woman squatted beside a tilted cart in a ditch, go from room to room with a duster. Sleep, I say [. . .] making of my own body a hollow, a warm shelter for my child to sleep in. Sleep, I say, sleep. (*W* 131)

188 *Virginia Woolf and Motherhood*

To today's reader this might seem a natural description of the early years of parenthood but any contemporary of Woolf's would have recognised the pointed choice to not include a nanny or nursery in such a scene. By framing motherhood in this way *The Waves* offers an investigation into the essence of maternity that is very different to the one she conducts in her other works. In contrast, *Jacob's Room* records the uneasiness that creeps into the collaborative caregiving between Betty Flanders and hired help Rebecca:

> 'Did he take his bottle well?' Mrs Flanders whispered, and Rebecca nodded and went to the cot and turned down the quilt, and Mrs Flanders bent over and looked anxiously at the baby, asleep, but frowning. The window shook, and Rebecca stole like a cat and wedged it.
>
> The two women murmured over the spirit-lamp, plotting the eternal conspiracy of hush and clean bottles while the wind raged [. . .]
>
> 'Good-night, Rebecca,' Mrs Flanders murmured, and Rebecca called her ma'm, though they were conspirators plotting the eternal conspiracy of hush and clean bottles. (*JR* 8)

Woolf pinpoints with devastating accuracy the unequal relationship between these women despite their shared responsibility for nursing a child. Later, in *Between the Acts*, Woolf includes a scene where the maternal figure, Isa Oliver, is conspicuously absent from her children's world:

> But what feeling was it that stirred in her now when above the looking-glass, out of doors, she saw coming across the lawn the perambulator; two nurses; and her little boy George, lagging behind?
>
> She tapped on the window with her embossed hairbrush. They were too far off to hear. The drone of the trees was in their ears; the chirp of birds; other incidents of garden life, inaudible, invisible to her in the bedroom, absorbed them. (*BA* 12)

Unlike Susan and even Betty, Isa is so remote from her children that they are living an entirely different experience. Indeed, it is not unreasonable to suggest that the reason Betty is so involved in her children's lives is because she is in a difficult financial situation and thus cannot afford ample childcare.

Though a young Susan predicts 'I shall have maids in aprons; men with pitchforks' (*W* 73) the characters that help her maintain her home and garden are hidden, making it difficult to tell how much of her own cooking she does while circumnavigating the kitchen 'in a blue apron locking up the cupboards' (*W* 73). Having already attempted to investigate motherhood in *To the Lighthouse*, it makes sense that Woolf might try a different, more abstract approach with the character of Susan. By limiting Susan's interactions with the servants and suggesting that she does certain domestic tasks on her own, the text more seamlessly combines motherhood and food production – offering a self-contained view of maternity, and avoiding those moments of heightened tension that raise their heads when Julia Stephen argues for a mistress/maid relationship that might be 'easier [. . .] to bear'.[88] Certainly, when the reader learns that red-haired cook Mildred has been preparing the *boeuf en daube* for three days, questions of class and employment creep in to what can no longer be a pure discussion of modern archetypal motherhood.[89] Though Woolf deliberately avoids this class tension in *The Waves* it is not because she was unaware of it. Indeed, while writing the novel, she would begin – grudgingly – to use her insights into class in 'Memories of a Working Women's Guild'. While these works are vastly different, one thing they have in common is the theme of motherhood. Thus, when conducting her investigations into class, Woolf continued to use maternity as a way to try to write about women who lived very different lives from her own.

'My personal view': 'Memories of a Working Women's Guild' and 'Introductory Letter'

The Waves, with its impression of a pervasive but unknowable working class, is an excellent example of how difficult Woolf found it to write outside her class experience (this is especially stark if the reader considers how easily she entered into Susan's impassioned maternity or the minds of her male characters). Luckily, though she wrote it reluctantly, we have 'Memories of a Working Women's Guild' as a contemporary companion text that marks an important waypoint between representations of the working class in *The Waves* and *The Years*. Woolf was persuaded to write 'Memories' – a preface to the Women's Co-operative Guild's collection of working-class women's memoirs, *Life as We Have Known It* – by Margaret Llewelyn Davies, the Guild's general secretary. Woolf originally met Llewelyn Davies through Janet Case in 1909 and, as a couple, Leonard and Virginia became involved in Guild politics in 1912. The WCG deeply affected Leonard's work, while Virginia – who was an active participant in WCG matters for a decade – had a thorough understanding of the

190   *Virginia Woolf and Motherhood*

movement. In 1913 she attended the Guild annual congress and visited factories, in 1914 she read Co-operative movement manuals and, between 1916 and 1923, she organised speakers while acting as secretary and host for the Richmond branch meetings.[90] While scholars have suggested that Woolf's work in the Guild was socially or politically motivated, there may have been additional reasons why she remained active for so long.[91] Over the years Llewelyn Davies became a good friend (arguably more Leonard's than Virginia's) and she had been a reliable support during Woolf's 1913–15 breakdowns. Indeed in 1915, when Woolf was finally beginning to recover, Llewelyn Davies was one of the few people she consistently wrote to, even dictating letters to Leonard when she could not manage to write herself. These correspondences are among some of the most sensitive in the volumes of Woolf's collected letters. She was incredibly grateful to Llewelyn Davies for her attentions and the way she had helped Leonard, writing on one occasion:

> You saved Leonard I think, for which I shall always bless you, by giving him things to do. It seems odd, for I know you so little, but I felt you had a grasp on me, and I could not utterly sink. I write this because I do not want to say it, and yet I think you will like to know it [. . .] Dear Margaret, I so often think of you, and thank you for what you have done for us both, and one cd. do nothing to show what it meant. (*L2* 60)

and on another:

> No one is really [. . .] quite so inspiriting to see, as you are – and thank God. Those flashing half hours won't destroy us any more. (by which I mean that they were the saving of life to me but not to see you rush out of the room will be so pleasant). (*L2* 70)

It is important to understand this relationship because it had a bearing on Woolf's work for the Guild, and on the writing of 'Memories', both tasks that she may have undertaken, at least in part, because of her feelings about Llewelyn Davies. This is not to undermine the impact that working for the Guild had on Woolf but rather to understand that her motivation to undertake the work may not have been entirely political.

In keeping with her reticence around writing about the lived realities of working-class women, Woolf initially wrote to Llewelyn Davies in 1929 that she felt 'rather doubtful about doing a preface'

(*L4* 65). She claimed that the memoirs did not need an introduction and that she did not know enough about the subject matter. These doubts were never laid to rest, continuing even as the book went to print, and were joined by Woolf's discomfort at the editing process, with the changes she was being asked to make at the insistence of the Guildswomen making her feel 'uneasy and insincere' (*L4* 229). Of course these were simply the concerns that Woolf expressed in writing. There may have been further underlying worries about time (she recorded in her diary that it was written 'with great plodding' (*D3* 304)), the artistic merit of the endeavour, and the reception it might have. The amount of time the letter took – it was a year from when Llewelyn Davies first asked until it was written – might reflect Woolf's disinclination to do it. Clara Jones has noted that Woolf was not alone in her anxiety about the book. Llewelyn Davies was also privately 'dejected about the project', writing in a letter to Dorothea Ponsonby:

> We have been getting through the material for the little book of memories by my coopve women themselves [. . .] I am not very pleased or happy about it. I doubt if it wd. be felt at all interesting & people really dont care about women's lives.[92]

Jones suggests that it was Woolf and Llewelyn Davies's shared concern with the '"obscurity" of women's lives' as well as Woolf's 'literary credentials and specific feminist preoccupations that represented her appeal as a preface writer'.[93] But it was also true that Llewelyn Davies was driven to find an ever-wider platform for the Guild and its campaigns, and might have pushed for Woolf to write the essay because she was well known and popular, and her name could help the book sell.

In an effort not to make the preface a traditional introduction or lay opinion piece, Woolf framed it as a letter to Llewelyn Davies. She sent one copy of the first draft to the *Yale Review* because she had promised them an article, and one copy to Llewelyn Davies. Llewelyn Davies replied with a letter which was generally complimentary but asked for several revisions, and the *Yale Review* replied they wanted to publish it more or less immediately. Woolf then wrote asking if Llewelyn Davies minded her publishing an unedited version in America, if 'I suppressed all real names, did not mention you or Lillian, and made it my personal view of congresses in general?' – thus making the article 'blameless'. She concluded 'I dont suppose any Guildswoman is likely to read the *Yale Review*' (*L4* 191). These

192   *Virginia Woolf and Motherhood*

circumstances led the letter to be published in two different versions – the essay 'Memories of a Working Women's Guild', initially printed in the *Yale Review*, and the modified 'Introductory Letter' in *Life as We Have Known It*. The two renderings have themselves been a focus of some contention over the years. Leonard made a point of including the earlier, unrevised essay when he published a collection of Woolf's essays – *The Captain's Death Bed* – posthumously, but Jane Marcus – who called Leonard's choice 'pronounced editorial bias' – considered the amendment process Woolf shared with the Guild collaborative. Marcus pushed for the primacy of the 'Introductory Letter', arguing that Woolf's 'revisions [. . .] were meant to clarify her opinions about the relation of class to art'.[94] In response to Marcus, Quentin Bell explained that not only was Woolf offended by the changes that Llewelyn Davies wanted, but she was upset at herself for having agreed to contribute an introduction at all. Bell points to a diary entry of 6 July 1930, which labels the letter a 'kind act' and concludes: 'Never – this is the moral – do a kindness in writing. Never agree to use one's art as an act of friendship' (*D3* 307).[95]

In fact, both forms of the essay continue to exhibit Woolf's upper-middle-class anxiety regarding interaction with, and writing about, the working class. Both also use inflammatory language. While neither version is more authentic, most of the quotes in this chapter are taken from 'Memories' as Woolf's discomfort towards working-class bodies and writing are franker in this text, and because it is not complicated by Llewelyn Davies's suggested amendments. In private, Woolf could be vicious about the project, telling Vanessa Bell: 'I have to write about working women all morning – which is as if you had to sew canopies round chamber pots' (*L4* 175), but she also recognised the difference between private snobbery and the opportunity to write something honest that might have a 'chance to get rid of conventionalities' (*L4* 229) and explore an area of life that her texts generally avoided. Indeed as Mary Childers notes: 'Woolf confirms her support for the purposes of the Guild by agreeing to have Hogarth Press publish the collection and by including in her preface several paragraphs that acknowledge the moving content of the volume'.[96] Arguably it was through this process, imperfect as it was, that Woolf finally found a voice that enabled her to represent the daily lives of working-class characters in *The Years*.

Both 'Memories' and 'Introductory Letter' have provoked a range of reactions depending on how much sincerity any given reader affords their narrative tone. Hermione Lee calls 'both versions [. . .] honest' and 'uneasy', and Regenia Gagnier has written that 'Woolf's confrontation with the Co-operative Working Women is one of the most penetrating class confrontations in modern British discourse'.[97] Part of the difficulty with locating Woolf's 'real' feelings about the Guildswomen is her continually shifting narrative voice. As Childers has observed – 'Woolf's writing ranges nervously from pointed, responsible commentary on middle-class women [. . .] to expressions of discomfort amounting to distaste for women whose lives are so restricted by material circumstances that they do not inspire elegant prose'.[98] Though Childers is making a general observation about Woolf's work, this passage could specifically be used to point out the difference between Woolf's views on motherhood in *The Waves* – where the writing is actively limited to the type of upper-middle-class experience she felt capable of representing – and 'Memories' – where Woolf's narrator locates her failure to identify with working-class women's lived experience in her inability to relate to their bodies. There has been a tendency for critics to try to read 'Memories' as a performance, with an unreliable narrator, and to interpret Woolf's intentions as thought-provoking rather than elitist. For example, Alice Wood argues 'that the essay fictionalises Virginia Woolf's relationship with the Guild, concealing her familiarity with Guild activities to better engage an anticipated middle-class readership and promote frank interrogation of class prejudice'.[99] However, this is not the only place where Woolf exhibits discomfort with working women's bodies and writing.[100] Thus it is worth investigating these ideas as representative of her opinions (keeping in mind that she called the essay '*my personal view* of congresses in general' (*L4* 191, my emphasis)), and explaining them in the context of the wider body of her canon.

Motherhood and Shopping: Woolf and the Women of the WCG

Though Clara Jones points out how committed Woolf was to the Guild, and how seriously she took her role organising meetings, it might have been difficult for her to entirely empathise with a society of 'mothers' initially founded on the importance of working-class women's economic influence.[101] Woolf saw the Guildswomen as mothers. She called the Richmond branch 'the Mothers' (*L2* 231) or 'my Mothers' (*L2* 238) in her letters and wrote to one prospective speaker: 'The audience consists of about 12 mothers of families' (*L2* 155). Once, after a disastrous talk on venereal disease, Woolf even wrote to Llewelyn Davies that one member had told the lecturer 'it was a most cruel speech, and only a childless woman could have made it "for we mothers try to forget what our sons have to go

194   *Virginia Woolf and Motherhood*

through"' (*L2* 139). In fact, the Guildswomen overwhelmingly *were* mothers, as Gillian Scott observes: 'Guild branches recruited from the women who shopped at the Co-op stores [. . .] The typical Guildswoman was married [. . .] and in her middle age'. Scott continues that the Guild's 1893 Annual Report showed most of the 6,412 members were wives and mothers, and that 'this pattern became more pronounced as the Guild grew in size'.[102] Indeed in 1920, Llewelyn Davies wrote: 'it is through Cooperation that the married woman living at home finds her work and place in the Labour world'.[103] *Life as We Have Known It* was also not the first book of Guildswomen's writing Woolf had been involved with. In 1915 Llewelyn Davies had approached her with a collection of letters about the strain of repeat motherhood. Woolf urged Llewelyn Davies to publish them, unsuccessfully trying to involve Gerald Duckworth, and, in the end, the Guild self-published the collection under the title *Maternity: Letters from Working-Women*. The 160 letters in this volume show how desperate life was when women bore too many children in reduced circumstances, and they should be taken into consideration when thinking about Woolf's attitude to the Guildswomen.

In addition to finding it difficult to identify with women who were working-class mothers, Woolf found it difficult to empathise with a culture that was built on the power of food shopping. She was reticent about buying her own groceries, writing in her diary: 'I bought my fish & meat in the High Street – a degrading but rather amusing business. I dislike the sight of women shopping. They take it so seriously' (*D1* 8). This sentence in Woolf's diary immediately follows the following passage:

> L. went off to Hampstead to give the first of his lectures to the Women's Guild. He did not seem nervous: he is speaking at this moment. We rather think that old Mr Davies is dying – but I have an idea he'll resist for years to come, although he wants to die, & his life prevents Margaret from much work. (*D1* 7–8)

Given the stream of these thoughts from Guild activism to shopping it seems fair to suggest that the degradation Woolf associated with buying her own dinner was linked, albeit subconsciously, with thoughts of the Guild, and that the 'they' who take shopping so seriously are interchangeable with her working-class Guild associates. After the publication of *Night and Day*, which Llewelyn Davies did not particularly enjoy, Woolf admitted to her: 'You'll never like my books, but then shall I ever understand your Guild? Probably not' (*L2* 399).[104]

The Guildswomen did take shopping seriously. Co-operative stores were the grassroots of the entire Co-operative movement and since – as Scott has noted – 'the stores were dependent upon the trading loyalty of the working-class housewife for their survival and growth', the WCG had a powerful voice within this movement.[105] As many of the Guildswomen also had large families to feed on very little money, shopping was important on a personal level. In a 1913 *New Statesman* article, Leonard Woolf described the average Guild member in the following way:

> no one receives a more terrible or perpetual schooling, than the woman whose husband hands over to her on Saturday a sum which may be as small as 12s or 13s, and leaves it entirely to her to feed him and clothe him, to pay his rent, and to bring up his children.[106]

Maud Pember Reeves's book *Round About a Pound a Week* investigated the food budgets of just such a family. Pember Reeves notes: 'Without doubt, the chief article of diet in a 20s. budget is bread. A long way after bread come potatoes, meat and fish'.[107]

Given the strain on their purses it comes as no surprise when Woolf's diary describes a meeting of the Richmond WCG in which the attendees become particularly animated about food;

> as usual it was only when talk drifted near food that one of the women broke silence. She wanted a bread shop. They all got bread late in the day: for a time they all spoke at once – stories of their own ill treatment & of their neighbours. Oddly phlegmatic these women for the most part; with a passive sort of pleasure in sitting there & watching like so many pale grey sea anemones stuck to their rocks. Still, the children, the housework – excuses enough if one troubled to look. (*D1* 112)

The description of these working-class women is challenging, not only does this diary entry distance Woolf from the Guildswomen but it is particularly unkind about a group on whom she was choosing to exert her energies. This entry was written at the beginning of 1918 when the strain of the household budget was becoming even more difficult due to WW1. With their main foodstuff badly affected by the war it was no wonder the Guildswomen were so animated about bread. In addition, an appeal to open a bread shop fell well within the WCG's policy of using consumption and cooperative economics to actively affect change.[108] The entry is perhaps particularly unsympathetic because it hides some of Woolf's own anxiety. Not only did the war make it difficult to find

196   *Virginia Woolf and Motherhood*

domestic staff but food was scarce for all and, perhaps for the first time in their lives, upper-class women had to do without. Later in the same entry Woolf complains about the paucity of the 'bakers windows' which contained 'almost nothing but little plates of dull biscuits; sections of plain cakes; & little buns without any plums'. The entry continues by noting how quickly things had changed: 'This transformation scene has been stealing on imperceptibly; last year we were still allowed iced cakes? Its unthinkable!' (*D1* 112). Nine months before, in April 1917, a regulation called the Cake and Pastry Order had been brought into effect by the Minister of Food Control, Lord Devonport. The order – which limited the amount of sugar allowed in baked goods made for commercial purposes – was a precursor to rationing, which was officially introduced in London and the South East in February 1918 (exactly a month after Woolf wrote this diary entry).[109] Though bread would not be rationed, King George V issued a proclamation in May 1917, urging the population to 'reduce the consumption of bread [. . .] by at least one-fourth of the quantity consumed in ordinary times'.[110] Although she was actively involved in the Richmond Guild's bread shop discussions, Woolf herself never complained about a lack of bread during the war – possibly because she had the time to bake it herself. Nonetheless everyone was feeling the strain of the shortages and, perhaps more importantly, the war had shrunk the difference between the classes.

'If the dress and body are different': Maternal Physicality in 'Memories of a Working Women's Guild'

The above diary entry is not the only example of Woolf's preoccupation with the working class's interest in food. Written at the same time – Justyna Kostkowska puts the writing between August 1917 and July 1918 – the short story 'Kew Gardens' briefly alights on 'two elderly women of the lower middle-class, one stout and ponderous, the other rosy cheeked and nimble' who are,[111]

> energetically piecing together their very complicated dialogue:
> 'Nell, Bert, Lot, Cess, Phil, Pa, he says, I says, she says, I says, I says, I says –'
> 'My Bert, Sis, Bill, Grandad, the old man, sugar,
>   Sugar, flour, kippers, greens,
>   Sugar, sugar, sugar.' (*CSF* 93)

The women's ironically labelled 'complicated dialogue', descends formally on the page into a catalogue of foodstuffs that is almost a shopping list. It brings to mind the Guildswomen's strength – the economic clout they yielded through their 'basket power' – and their privation. The choice of foods in this list is interesting and once again hints at Woolf's own anxiety. As Pember Reeves notes, sugar, like butter, would be found in small amounts in a working-class home 'according to the length of purse of the mother'.[112] Thus the phrase 'sugar, sugar, sugar' bears a closer association with the Cake and Pastry Order and Woolf's desire for iced cakes than the working-class women's war-related anxiety for bread. When the story was published Woolf was 'pressed [. . .] for copies' by some Guild members but noted with some self-awareness: 'I don't want them to read the scene of the two women. Is that to the discredit of "Kew Gardens"? Perhaps a little' (*D1* 284). This discomfort with the execution and reception of her working-class characters is a precursor of Woolf's reticence to voice working-class characters in *The Waves*.

In 'Kew Gardens' it is not simply the women's conversation that is insensitive. The story also highlights how Woolf distanced herself from working-class women in the way that she wrote about their physicality. The 'stout and ponderous' and the 'rosy cheeked and nimble' women are the only people in the entire story whose physiognomies are described. This corporeal preoccupation can also be seen in 'Memories' where the Guildswomen's bodies are a feature that Woolf chose to highlight, writing such descriptions as: 'they had thickset muscular bodies. They had large hands [. . .] Their faces were firm, with heavy folds and deep lines' (*E5* 180); 'Their arms are undeveloped. Fat has softened the lines of their muscles' (*E5* 182). Unlike *Orlando*, where the nuances of gender are playfully affected by the characters' choice of dress, these women are resolutely tied to their bodies. Not only are working-class bodies (and clothes) irreconcilable with: 'Ladies in evening dress' who 'are lovelier by far' (*E5* 182) but when the narrator declares it would be liberating for both sides to meet as equals 'with the same ends and wishes *even if the dress and body are different*' (*E5* 183, my emphasis), the working-class women are almost reduced to a different species.

There is an element of mind–body dualism in the way Woolf describes the strong physicality of working-class women's bodies versus the weak, but mentally, emotionally and socially developed, 'ladies'. And it is not only the women's bodies that are seen as different for:

> Their eyes looked as if they were always set on something actual – on saucepans that were boiling over, on children who were getting into mischief. Their faces never expressed the lighter and more detached emotions that come into play when the mind is perfectly at ease about the present. (*E5* 180)

Not only are the women physically 'thickset', 'firm', 'heavy' and 'fat' but they have no access to the 'lighter' emotions. A few pages later Woolf notes: 'the range of expression is narrower in working women, their expressions have a force and emphasis, of tragedy or humour' (*E5* 182). As 'Mothers' the Guildswomen are preoccupied with children and food and thus they are unable to contemplate the world or art. With the phrase 'tragedy or humour', 'Memories' depicts these women as assuming the grotesque masks of Greek drama. By describing them in such a way, especially after writing a novel where she uses, yet alters, ancient Greek forms, Woolf is choosing to deny them what she had given her characters in *The Waves*, a modern interiority and psychological perspective.

Although the mothers in 'Memories' are different to *The Waves*' Susan, both are connected with cooking. Indeed, it is through cooking that the narrator fully displays her inability to empathise with her subjects. Though she tries to engage in 'a childish game' of 'Let's pretend', the narrator cannot relate to 'the speaker [. . .] Mrs Giles of Durham City' (*E5* 179) because,

> the imagination is largely the child of the flesh. One could not be Mrs Giles of Durham because one's body had not stood at the wash-tub; one's hands had never wrung and scrubbed and chopped up whatever the meat may be that makes a miner's dinner. (*E5* 179)

Woolf's denial of the sensory understanding of this working-class wife's experience is interesting given her foregrounding of the material aspects of cooking in *The Waves*. Alison Light notes: 'whatever the meat may be' seems 'excessively distancing' and was especially 'odd' given that: 'In her drafts of *The Waves*, she was concurrently imagining the lives of three different men – one homosexual – relying, presumably, on aesthetic sympathy'.[113] This aesthetic sympathy is particularly notable in Woolf's use of her own experience to create Susan's narrative of motherhood and cooking. The 'excessive distance' is also noticeable in the description of the meat. Woolf may have had access to better cuts of meat than the working-class woman she described but she certainly had cooked meat – in 1929 she wrote to Vita Sackville-West 'I cooked veal cutlets and cake today' (*L4* 93), and within the year she would write 'Cook Sketch', putting herself in the place of a working-class protagonist and – as Clara Jones has noted – revealing a 'scrupulous knowledge of various cuts of meat and understanding of wider issues in domestic economy'.[114]

Motherhood and Food **199**

'This book is not a book': Woolf's Guildswomen as Mothers not Artists

Woolf was not writing about the Guildswomen in this way to cause offence, rather she was trying to use honesty to break down barriers, no matter its unpalatability to others. When Llewelyn Davies requested the piece be edited to tone down the physicality of the Guildswomen, Woolf understood why; nonetheless, she resented the revisions. After making any changes that she was willing to concede, she wrote to Llewelyn Davies:

> I'm amused at the importance attached to the size of the Guilders. Vanity seems to be the same in all classes [. . .] What rather appals me [. . .] is the terrific conventionality of the workers. Thats why – if you want explanations – I dont think they will be poets or novelists for another hundred years or so. If they [. . .] cant be told that they weigh on an average 12 stone – which is largely because they scrub so hard and have so many children – and are shocked by the word 'impure' how can you say that they face 'reality'? [. . .] What depresses me is that the workers seem to have taken on all the middle class respectabilities which we – at any rate if we are any good at writing or painting – have faced and thrown out. Or am I quite wrong? And how do you explain away these eccentricities on the part of your swans? It interests me very much. For you see, it is that to my thinking that now makes the chief barrier between us. One has to be 'sympathetic' and polite and therefore one is uneasy and insincere. And why, with such a chance to get rid of conventionalities, do they cling to them? (*L4* 228–29)

Both this letter and 'Memories' portray the Guildswomen as conservative with both upper- and lower-case Cs. Although the writers collected in *Life* are vocal Labour supporters Woolf seems to have felt that those at the head of the WCG 'controlling the masses' (*L2* 19), and those unique women selected to be featured in the collection, were of a different political bent than the everyday Guildswomen she saw at her branch meetings.[115] This letter is particularly inflexible in the way it takes offence at the writers' failure to align their ethics with Woolf's own liberated, artistic morality, while also resolutely denying them any artistic power. For the artist, 'Memories' explains, the most important type of 'reality' was the one found in art, and 'no working man or woman works harder with his hands or is in closer touch with reality than a painter with his brush or a writer with his pen'

(*E5* 182). Yet, though she established the same expectations of them as of any artist – claiming to be alternately 'amused' and depressed by their response to her judgement of their bodies and their rejection of her 'reality' – she had already written that they were not, and in this lifetime would not become, artists. Even where she pictures them as strong, honourable and idealistic, or writes that they bear the 'extraordinary vitality of the human spirit' (*E5* 186), or that they hum with energy and have worked together to build a powerful organisation, Woolf maintains that the women are '12 stone' mothers of children rather than writers. Critiquing the Guildswomen's accounts as if they were fiction rather than memoirs, she writes that, although they 'threw some light upon [. . .] old curiosities and bewilderments' (*E5* 188),

> as literature they have many limitations. The writing lacks detachment and imaginative breadth [. . .]. Here are no reflections; no view of life as a whole; no attempt to enter into the lives of other people. It is not from the ranks of working-class women that the next great poet or novelist will be drawn. Indeed, we are reminded of those obscure writers before Shakespeare who had never been beyond the borders of their own parishes and found expression difficult and words few and awkward to fit together. (*E5* 188)

'[T]his book is not a book' (*E5* 176), notes Woolf; instead, she reads the memoirs as 'fragments' (*E5* 189) such as an archaeologist or historian might uncover, not unlike the 'fragments of yellow parchment' (*CSF* 33) that Rosamond Merridew in 'Mistress Joan' reads. Indeed, Merridew's assessment of these artefacts, that 'only a few people can read & still fewer would care to read if they could' (*CSF* 33), is reminiscent of Llewelyn Davies's fear about whether the collection 'wd. be felt at all interesting & people really dont care about women's lives'.[116]

Typical of Woolf's mothers, these working-class women struggle to express themselves. Though they have 'dauntless energy which no amount of childbirth and washing up can quench entirely' (*E5* 186), their creative ability has been doused by both of these undertakings. They too have verbal impediments, with 'Memories' noting that their 'voices are beginning only now to emerge from silence into half articulate speech' (*E5* 189). Even when Woolf wonders: 'How many words, for example, must lurk in those women's vocabularies that have faded from ours!' (*E5* 183), the rhetorical question puts the women in a position of curiosity rather than culture. As Rachel Bowlby has noted, no matter whether the women are, 'primitive' or 'their language has the naïveté of a childlike freshness [. . .] both place the middle-class listener in a condition of greater linguistic refinement'.[117] Though Woolf had critiqued the way her group of colonial visitors observe the 'native' women in *The Voyage Out*, in 'Memories' she offers the same type of dehumanising gaze with such observations as: 'the women themselves lacked variety and play of feature' (*E5* 188).

Because of their class Woolf could not acknowledge these women as artists. They would never access truth in their kitchens and they needed more than just a room and £500 a year – they needed different minds, different bodies, and two generations to evolve.[118] As Bell notes in a letter to Woolf where she compared her nanny/cook Grace to an eight-year-old Angelica: 'there's something I suppose in having educated grandparents, for already Angelica is capable of understanding things in a way Grace never will'. Although this letter was written by Bell and not Woolf, it is particularly interesting when Bell writes that 'Grace is a very good specimen, not only unusually nice, but much more ready than most to try to understand other things, reading all she can get hold of'.[119] Like Grace, the Guildswomen are voracious readers; there are lists of their favourite books in the back of *Life as We Have Known It*. However, Woolf rebukes them for not following some unwritten syllabus seemingly dictated by upper-middle-class intellectuals. Like Florrie, the maid she tried to write into *The Waves*, who devours 'a great lump of ^greasy white^ heavenly fat' (*WH* 90) until she vomits, these working-class women cannot control their literary cravings; 'they read with the indiscriminate greed of a hungry appetite that crams itself with toffee and beef and tarts and vinegar and champagne all in one gulp' (*E5* 186). This is rather an ironic judgement for a woman who had already written (in the essay 'How Should One Read a Book?'), 'the only advice [. . .] that one person can give another about reading is to take no advice, to follow your own instincts, to use your own reason' (*E5* 573).

Not only does Woolf deem that *Life*'s memoirs are not inspired by great art but she find them, and their authors, uninspiring. She notes how

> questions of sanitation and education and wages, this demand for an extra shilling, or another year at school, for eight hours instead of nine behind a counter or in a mill, leave me, in my own blood and bones, untouched [. . .] my interest is merely altruistic. It is thin spread and moon-coloured. There is no life blood or urgency about it. (*E5* 178)

Woolf understands that the aim of the book – much like the Guild conference – is to stimulate political change, yet this ambition does not rouse her. Initially it seems that Woolf and her contemporaries are unmoved because their social status insulates them from the harsher realities of working-class living. However there is more to this disinterest than Woolf's frank apathy to the Guild's political machinations. The use of 'moon-coloured' and 'life blood' in this passage brings to mind lunar cycles, pregnancy and menstruation. Given the intellectual procreation of *A Room of One's Own*, where 'one takes a sentence of Coleridge into the mind' and 'it explodes and gives birth to all kinds of other ideas' (*AROO* 91), the absence of 'urgency' or 'life blood' suggest that Woolf could not find anything about these women or their work to arouse and fertilise her active writer's mind. For that she looked to those she knew, Vanessa, or Vita, her mother or Thoby, as well as those whose works and theories inspired her – Coleridge, Shakespeare, the Brontës, George Eliot, Marie Carmichael Stopes or Otto Weininger.

Woolf saw a difference between making art and the political and social aspirations of *Life*'s working-class autobiographers. Nonetheless, she does seem – perhaps unknowingly – to have been affected by the Guildswomen's socio-political ambitions, which she called both 'reasonable' and 'forcible' (*E5* 178). She was certainly more inspired by these writings than she initially admitted for, as Clara Jones, Susan Dick, and Heather Levy have shown, she continued to explore working-class voices – especially those of cooks – in a series of unpublished sketches, and these experiments helped her gain confidence to the point where she included a lower-middle-class family meal in *The Years*.[120] Here the mother of the family, Mrs Robson, is approached through the twin motifs of maternity and food, and then compared to an upper-middle-class woman using the same themes.

Form and Maternity in *The Pargiters* and *The Years*

The Years reiterates much of what Woolf had already written about motherhood. The novel includes an image of a pregnant woman holding wasp-ruined fruit and mothers who put the interests of the nation and empire above their own – perhaps unsurprisingly, given the election of right-wing governments in Europe and right-wing economics causing political disruption at home.[121] Like *The Waves*, *The Years* approaches motherhood through food preparation and meals; however, the novels' form and characterisation are remarkably different. This difference offers the reader a glimpse of the evolution of Woolf's thinking about maternity, class and society.

Motherhood and Food **203**

Woolf's earliest inspiration for *The Years* occurred on 20 January 1931, when she 'conceived an entire new book' (*D4* 6) while having her bath. Three days later she recorded that she was having trouble shaking this new fact-heavy project so that she could continue writing *The Waves*, noting: 'The didactive demonstrative style conflicts with the dramatic: I find it hard to get back inside Bernard again' (*D4* 6). With *The Years* evolving out of a polemic, Woolf initially envisaged it as 'Essay-Novel' (*D4* 129). However, in 1933, after writing 60,000 words of alternating essay and fiction, she decided to change the form again 'leaving out the interchapters – compacting them in the text' (*D4* 146). Anna Snaith notes of *The Years*, 'never before had she incorporated so much research into her fiction, and never before had her fiction been so decidedly and openly feminist [. . .] the project was factual, and changing the genre did not remove this foundation'.[122] To prepare for writing her 'Essay-Novel' Woolf kept extensive notebooks of quotes from books, newspaper cuttings, reviews and letters and, though she created two very different works from them, these laid the foundations for both *The Years* and *Three Guineas*.

With an array of disparate interior monologues, *The Years* shows a change from the lyrical poetry of *The Waves* and a return to Woolf's distinctive tonal ambivalence. Snaith notes that *The Years* is one of those works within which Woolf 'seeks structures in her writing which will allow ambiguity'.[123] Similarly, Gill Plain has observed that not only is the novel 'elliptical and fragmented' but it is also 'composed of isolated and alienated characters'.[124] Woolf uses this vocal multiplicity and the resultant unreliable narration to restate and yet also undermine her own earlier archetypal representation of motherhood. This can be seen in the final party scene where North Pargiter watches several people talk about their children. He compares his aunt and uncle, Milly and Hugh Gibbs, to animals in a 'primeval swamp, prolific, profuse, half-conscious [. . .] he looked at his aunt as if she might be breaking into young even there, on that chair – the women broke off into innumerable babies. And those babies had other babies' (*Y* 274–75). North's discomfort continues when another relative, Maggie, comes over to make polite conversation:

> They were talking about *her* children now [. . .] This is the conspiracy, he said to himself; this is the steam roller that smooths, obliterates; rounds into identity; rolls into balls. He listened. Jimmy was in Uganda; Lily was in Leicestershire; *my* boy – *my* girl . . . they were saying. But they're not interested in other people's children, he observed. Only in their own; their own property; their own flesh

204 *Virginia Woolf and Motherhood*

> and blood, which they would protect with the unsheathed claws of the primeval swamp [. . .] How then can we be civilised, he asked himself? (*Y* 277, emphasis in original)

Though these passages reiterate Woolf's earlier ideas about maternity, showing motherhood as a step back in social evolution and highlighting its connections with patriarchal, nationalistic culture, the text also probes these ideas' legitimacy. North is proven to be an unreliable observer during a conversation with another older relative, Kitty Lasswade, in which he makes hasty assumptions about her character which are proved wrong. The reader cannot necessarily trust his opinions and thus they are open to reinterpretation, offering a challenge to Woolf's long-expressed views on maternity. This is not to suggest that motherhood was Woolf's intended target, merely that the narrative style of *The Years* works to undermine all authoritative views.

As noted, *The Years* employs food as a device for comparing and contrasting mothers from different classes. This both provides a fresh perspective on the types of mothers Woolf wrote about in *The Waves* and 'Memories of a Working Women's Guild', and also brings these mothers together within the same text. Pam Morris has argued that as Woolf's writing matured her fictional meals evolved, taking 'her female protagonists out from the patriarchal place into ever wider, more socially heterogeneous spaces'. Morris notes that, unlike *To the Lighthouse*, *Mrs Dalloway* and *The Waves*, meals in *The Years* produce 'no moment of shared communality among the heterogeneous guests. This is perhaps unsurprising since in *The Years*, Woolf explores the challenges as well as the desirability of the common life, underpinned by shared creaturely necessity'.[125] It is important to note that a lack of 'shared communality' is not the only feeling *The Years*' characters experience during these meals. While these events do provoke moments of personal and social discord, they also offer moments of subjective identification felt across a class divide. Never before had Woolf allowed her 'shared creaturely necessity' and 'socially heterogeneous spaces' to include not only people of different ages and genders but also people of different classes.

The Character of Kitty in *The Years*

The most noteworthy connections between motherhood, food and class are found in the 1880 section of *The Years* and centre on the young Kitty Malone, who later becomes Lady Lasswade. Kitty, the daughter of an Oxford Don, is a fascinating character both because she embodies the novel's contradictory form and also because of her connections to other characters within the novel and throughout Woolf's writing. Though she marries a Lord and bears three sons Kitty is an outsider, disrupting expectations, and longing to be free of the patriarchy – to feel like 'nobody's daughter in particular' (*Y* 50). Not driven to join the professions or academia and without the 'culture and intellectual liberty' (*TG* 210) to become an artist, Kitty embodies the ambivalent feminism of *Three Guineas*.[126] By marrying an independently wealthy man (rather than her academic cousin Edward), Kitty – as Sharon Proudfit observes – 'makes the most successful feminine adjustment to life in the novel'. This marriage offers an escape from the stifling life of a college wife while still providing the structure necessary for a woman brought up in a restrictive society. As a woman growing up in the 1880s Proudfit notes that Kitty 'only half knows herself and would not have been able to cope with complete liberation had she been given it'.[127] Although she was still happily married, Woolf knew that matrimony had its risks and costs, recording in her notebook of the 'solemn moment' of marriage: a 'woman has no worldly goods must therefore give her body; must therefore accept her leader' (*RN* 269).[128] *The Years* continues the investigation that Woolf had undertaken in *Night and Day*, examining marriage as an institution that might offer potential freedom but might, equally, mean physical and mental domination. Kitty can be compared with her cousin Eleanor; both are interested in travel and are self-reliant. Like the young Mary Datchet, however, Eleanor is interested in social justice, never marries and eventually manages a contented life as a single woman. Thus, in keeping with its ambiguous form, the book provides no resolutions and neither woman is deemed to have better navigated the social obligations of their age.

In her analysis of 'the complicated figure of Kitty Lasswade', Ann Martin has paid close attention to Woolf's repeated description of Kitty's size. While her incongruous expansiveness is not the same as the weight of the working-class women in 'Memories', Kitty seems to be too big for her surroundings, suggesting a 'poor fit' for the feminine, upper-class role 'she is expected to play'.[129] Martin observes how Kitty is a liminal figure, awkward among society and uncomfortable giving parties. However, Kitty's character is also changeable. While she may be fundamentally unconventional, she does, from time to time, express more conformist opinions: falling, to use Mark Wollaeger's phrase, under the influence of 'the propaganda of everyday life'.[130] When at

206 *Virginia Woolf and Motherhood*

the Royal Opera House watching Wagner's *Siegfried*, for example (an opera which Woolf associated with nationalism and colonialism), Kitty is induced to feel particularly maternal and imperial:[131] 'I've three boys. I've been in Australia, I've been in India [. . .] The music made her think of herself and her own life as she seldom did. It exalted her; it cast a flattering light over herself, her past' (*Y* 134). In this scene the 'flattering light' of patriarchal stimuli colours Kitty's thoughts about her life. Doing the domestic duty of entertaining female guests in her drawing room after dinner also draws out maternal thoughts. Despite these momentary lapses, however, Kitty battles expectations. More than once Woolf makes a point of showing her in the wrong clothes and at odds with her setting. She even eats like a rebel at the final party:

> 'Spoons are coming,' [Delia] said to Lady Lasswade, who was drinking her soup out of a mug.
> 'But I don't want a spoon,' said Kitty. She tilted the mug and drank.
> 'No, you wouldn't,' said Delia, 'but other people do.' (*Y* 291)

Like her body, Kitty's pleasure in food is out of place and her appetite is contextualised by Woolf's *Three Guineas* reading notebooks. These record examples of men disapproving of women eating; for example, C. E. M. Joad – 'Women, I think, ought not to sit down to table with men' – and William Macready – 'How disenchanting in the female character | is a manifestation of relish for | the pleasures of the table!' (*RN* 264).

Although they are different characters, in some ways Kitty offers a somewhat progressive version of *The Waves*' Susan. Kitty's appetite brings Susan to mind – Woolf earlier having written perhaps the most visceral eating scene in her entire canon for Susan:

> There was ~~thin~~ [pheasant in margin] for luncheon [. . .] she ~~thought~~ felt her teeth meet in the rather solid wing of a pheasant; & her tongue roll its fibres; & then the delicious hotness & scent of pheasant, & the grey dry bread crumbs; & the heaping up of soft breadsauce, & the ~~half~~ pungent, curious taste of brussels sprouts – & the [ ], the cold water – ~~she~~ that would be very delicious – Her being would subside into that. (*WH* 190)

Though Woolf does not describe the meal itself, eating alone in her country house Kitty experiences a sense of post-prandial wellbeing similar to Susan's. The text notes: 'She breakfasted; she felt warm, stored, and comfortable as she lay back in her chair' (*Y* 201). A

Motherhood and Food   **207**

shared pleasure in food is not the only aspect of Kitty's narrative that brings Susan to mind. In *The Pargiters* draft Kitty becomes fixated on the idea of becoming a farmer and daydreams of living Susan's life. This aspiration is inspired by a childhood visiting her mother's family in Yorkshire:

> whenever she had had the measles or the whooping cough as a child she had [*been*] <always been> packed [*off to recover to*] [*at*] to Carters, a farmhouse near Settle [. . .] at Carters Kitty had [*gr*] spent far & away the happiest days of her life. She had been allowed to run wild all over the moors [. . .] And she had milked the cows & found the eggs and seen a [*pig killed*] <calf born> & learnt how to make real bread [. . .] & she had eaten huge meals [. . .] in the great kitchen, with the hams swinging from the rafters; [. . .] & once – but this was later, when she was about sixteen, [. . .] the [*boy*] farmer's son, a <splendid young> man of twenty six, had rolled her over in the hay & kissed her & kissed her. [. . .]
>
> Kitty thought of that kiss <again tonight> [. . .] George had a farm of his own now, & was married, & had three squalling babies. And so Kitty [. . .] sank back in her pillows, & thought how one of these days she would buy a farm herself near Carters [. . .] Why should she not become a farmer? That was her dream. She would have to marry she supposed, in order to become a farmer – & her parents wd. never let her marry a farmer.
>
> But no force on earth [she thought] would make her marry [. . .] & settle down, & live in Oxford [. . .] she blew out the candle, & lay, hearing the rain, [*falling*] but in her dreams it became the wind, roaring over the Yorkshire moors. (*P* 104–05)

This reverie offers an approximation of Susan's life; the baking, hams hanging from the ceiling, and a farmer's son (who has had several children in what can only be a few years). However Kitty acknowledges this daydream is not really a potential future. As the 'daughter of an educated man' (*TG* 128) she is expected to marry someone of her own class and have a limited number of well-raised (and, in the case of sons, well-educated) offspring. This longer passage is cut from the *The Years* with Kitty simply telling North at the final party, 'I'd have given anything to be a farmer!' (*Y* 293). Nonetheless it conveys Kitty's departure from Susan and, perhaps, Woolf's departure from archetypal mothers. Kitty might think that she wants to be a farmer, and when the music at the opera reminds her of being kissed by a farmer's son she thinks: 'That's the sort of life I like [. . .] That's the sort of person I am' (*Y* 135), but this is not a complete portrait

208   *Virginia Woolf and Motherhood*

of her character. Unlike Woolf's earlier, more parodic caricatures (like Betty Flanders or Mrs Thornbury), Kitty is ambiguous. She is open to patriarchal, imperial thoughts but they '*seldom*' (*Y* 134, my emphasis) occur to her. She engages with her memories and thoughts of the future with no concern for eternity – she is a gardener, but she is not a farmer and she does not cook. Instead of an apron Kitty feels most comfortable in a travelling dress and 'little tweed travelling-hat' (*Y* 195). Paradoxically, the striking similarity between Kitty's day-dream and Susan's life serve to highlight the differences between both their characters and the novels they are in.

As well as serving as a departure point from Susan, fantasising about being a farmer provides Kitty with a form of rebellion against her own mother; a woman who did grow up on a farm and cannot understand what her daughter dislikes about 'living in Oxford, in the midst of everything' (*Y* 59). Mrs Malone's account of being the mistress of a country home is notably different from Kitty's fantasy.[132] Brought up in the symbolically wintry wasteland of Yorkshire, Mrs Malone spent her youth learning how to keep a house. Thus she is well known in Oxford for the exact thing missing from Susan's narrative – her skill at training and managing servants and cooks. This talent is something Julia Stephen also took pride in, with both Julia and Mrs Malone reflecting the womanly idylls of their time. Woolf's notebooks record a number of artistic, Victorian renderings of such virtuous women. For example, the 'Preface' of Bernard Shaw's *Ellen Terry and Bernard Shaw: A Correspondence* which states: 'A lady is – or in Ellen Terry's generation was – a person trained to the utmost attainable degree in the art and habit of concealing her feelings' (*RN* 272), or Tennyson's *The Princess*, in which a prince describes his ideal wife thus:

> Not learnèd, save in gracious household ways,
> Not perfect, nay, but full of tender wants,
> No Angel, but a dearer being, all dipt
> In Angel instincts, breathing Paradise,
> Interpreter between the Gods and men,
> Who looked all native to her place, and yet
> On tiptoe seemed to touch upon a sphere
> Too gross to tread, and all male minds perforce
> Swayed to her from their orbits as they moved,
> And girdled her with music. Happy he
> With such a mother! faith in womankind
> Beats with his blood, and trust in all things high
> Comes easy to him.[133]

As a rebellion against her mother's stifling domestic and social roles Kitty is reactionary enough to question the point of marriage entirely. However, as a young woman interested in sex, her options are limited. As Woolf observes in *The Pargiters*, 'there was no way in which a woman could earn her living; and [. . .] therefore no way in which she could bear a child without being married' (*P* 129) and Proudfit concludes that in Kitty's case 'marriage was the only profession that would enable her to be her free and true self'.[134] Despite their differences Kitty has a touching and human relationship with Mrs Malone. Like so many mothers and daughters the pair are 'fond of each other; yet they always quarrelled' (*Y* 60). There is an uncomfortable emotional distance between them, typical not only of an inhibited Victorian relationship but also typical of all familial relations. Woolf explores this unease when, after a formal dinner, Kitty is warmly embraced by an unreserved American visitor, Mrs Fripp, and then 'touched [. . .] perfunctorily on the cheek' (*Y* 44) by her mother – 'the only sign they ever gave each other outwardly of their affection' (*Y* 60). Alone in her room Kitty relives Mrs Fripp's kiss which, 'had left a little glow on her cheek' (*Y* 44) and she thinks of leaving Oxford and going to America. Woolf substituted this dream of leaving with Mrs Fripp for *The Pargiters*' passages about Carters farm and both dreams are equally unfeasible.

Thoughts on a Pair of Meals: Motherhood and Class in *The Years*

In *The Years* there are two connected meals placed immediately after one another. Both showcase tea with two different classes of family and two different types of mother. The first meal is a tea that Kitty attends at the house of her friend Nelly Robson and her family. Woolf based Mr Robson, Nelly's father, on Joseph Wright, a professor of comparative philology at Oxford University and a feminist advocate and lecturer for the Association for the Higher Education of Women. Woolf's reading notebooks reference Wright's biography (written by his wife Elizabeth Mary Wright) multiple times. One of these quotes include a letter from Wright to his wife that discusses the false notion of the 'weaker sex' and how he envisions their life together as equals, refuting the suggestions that the life of a married woman is one of 'a detail-tending housekeeper', and promising to uphold their shared 'ideals of the relations between man and wife'.[135]

210 *Virginia Woolf and Motherhood*

Though Woolf does not go so far as to imagine her newly middle-class family as one where the husband and wife share the domestic duties, in the novel Professor Robson is a feminist figure who asserts that his mother, 'a common working woman, [. . .] had a better brain than any professor in the place' (*P* 127). He has a loving, supportive and respectful relationship with his wife and daughter, speaks to women as if he wants to know their opinions and he pushes his daughter to enter the professions.

Though Mr Robson is based on Joseph Wright, Mrs Robson is not based on his wife Elizabeth – a woman educated at Oxford – but is more like his mother Sarah Ann Wright, a working-class Yorkshirewoman who taught herself to read aged forty-five, and worked so hard that 'once [. . .] she fell asleep with her hands in the tub in which she was washing her boys' clothes' (*P* 156). Like the elder Mrs Wright, Mrs Robson is a Guildswoman who daily compares Oxford to 'Mackley (the village where she was born) & [. . .] the Cooperative Stores [. . .] much to the disadvantage of Oxford' (*P* 143).[136] However the resemblance is not exact. Sarah Ann Wright – who 'went out charing' and 'took in washing' – remained within the working class.[137] Her fictional counterpart, having spent many years as the former cook for Mrs Malone's upper-class Yorkshire relatives (a stable and relatively well-paid job), has now moved into the lower-middle class and even employs a couple of servants of her own, albeit reluctantly. Mrs Robson does speak with a Yorkshire accent, an effect Woolf adapted from Wright's biography, where Elizabeth lovingly recreates her mother-in-law's intonation.

Woolf rewrote sections of the Robson's tea several times, trying out several different family names in the process: Gabbit, Hughes and Brook as well as Robson. This aligns with Woolf's anxiety over including working-class voices in her work but it also shows her resolve to get the scene right. As a working-class Guildswoman Mrs Robson's physical description recalls the women in 'Memories'. She is 'short & stout' (*P* 131) in *The Pargiters* and short, 'substantial' (*Y* 68) and likened to the Malone's cook – the aptly named Bigge – in *The Years*. This is in stark contrast with Kitty's mother, whose only defined feature is 'crisp white hair curled stiffly' (*Y* 42). Despite these physical descriptors Mrs Robson is more than a working-class stereotype. In *The Pargiters* (as Mrs Brook), she is fleshed out and given a fierce determination with regard to her daughter's future:

Nell was not to live the life her grandmother had lived before her. [*of*] <About> that Mrs Brook was even more determined than her husband

Motherhood and Food   211

[. . .] Grimly though Mrs Brook regarded the Oxford ladies & their efforts [*organisations*] for the higher education of women, [*sarcastic*] <indifferent> though she might be [*as*] to the architectural beauties of Oxford, & sarcastic though she certainly was as to the amount of food & drink that was consumed by (Dr *An*) Chuffy Andrews & his like at College feasts & Gaudies – but as she cooked her Sam the most succulent Yorkshire pies, cakes, & was famous for her Yorkshire salad her sarcasm [*was*] <in this respect was> to some extent justified, – not withstanding these narrownesses & acerbities, there was no woman in England in 1880 who was more determined that her daughter was to [. . .] be an educated woman & earn her own living than Mrs Brook, [. . .] whose [. . .] mother had been a milk hand & borne seven children to a husband who was a miner. (*P* 147–48)

In this scene, as with 'Memories', Woolf uses food to try to access the lived reality of a working-class mother. This, and Mrs Robson/ Brook's previous life as a cook, further validate the claim that the sketches of cooks that Woolf had been writing were preparation for including a female working-class character in one of her novels. Mrs Robson's biggest success in life, her 'succulent Yorkshire pies, cakes, & [. . .] her Yorkshire salad', give her access to the creative arts. In addition, Woolf uses this depiction of unpretentious Yorkshire cuisine to give Mrs Robson views that align with her own; sanctioning this maternal figure to mock 'College feasts & Gaudies' – something Woolf herself made stinging versions of in *Jacob's Room* and *A Room of One's Own*. In this way Woolf finally provides Mrs Robson some of the empathy (and creative prowess) she felt she could not offer to 'Mrs Giles of Durham City' and her 'miner's' meat (*E5* 179). However, the work Woolf put into the drafts would, in the end, remain yet another practice sketch. In the final novel Mrs Robson's interior monologue is cut, and the impressions of the tea come from Kitty's perspective. Woolf does, however, continue to play with and question her own prejudices. On finding out that Mrs Robson was a cook, Kitty instinctively, and outlandishly (though perhaps not unexpectedly given the limits of her social experience), thinks of 'a great-uncle who rode in a circus' (*Y* 51).

Kitty's impressions of tea with the Robson family are mixed. Upon entering their house she feels 'much too large' and 'too well dressed' (*Y* 49), although this feeling of being out of place is familiar to Kitty and not specifically because she is in a working-class home. Initially she finds the home cheaply and tastelessly decorated and the whole experience of eating with working-class people isolating. Yet as the meal progresses, and especially when the Robson's handsome young

212   *Virginia Woolf and Motherhood*

son Jo – named for Joseph Wright – joins them, she begins to think of this way of life, with its freedoms and gender equality, as vastly superior to her own. Finally she is shown the family treasures, including a photo of the elder Mrs Robson (based on a picture that Woolf saw in the Joseph Wright biography) and, though she continues to find these ornaments distasteful, she becomes carried away with her fantasies about being a part of this world, thinking: 'Did they know how much she admired them [. . .] Would they accept her in spite of her hat and her gloves?' (*Y* 53). Characteristic of *The Years*, Kitty's meeting with the Robsons is ambivalent, full of moments of both truth and self-deception. Her feelings towards them are undermined when, returning to her own home, she immediately dehumanises Hiscock, the butler, thinking: 'Why can't you talk like a human being? [. . .] as he took her umbrella and mumbled his usual remark about the weather' (*Y* 54). Nonetheless, *The Years* does not entirely dismiss domestic, working-class ethics. Woolf certainly admired Joseph Wright, and there was something about his mother's determination that struck a chord. Kitty thinks Mr Robson is 'the nicest man I have ever met' (*Y* 53) and Mrs Robson is a strong character who is resolved to give her daughter intellectual freedom, an intention symbolised by never allowing her to help with the cooking or domestic tasks. In *The Pargiters* Woolf records that although Nelly 'might clear away the tea things <as she was doing now>, she never [*did*] helped in the kitchen <but was driven up to her books>' (*P* 147).

Unfortunately Mrs Robson's resolve is not enough to overturn centuries of patriarchal culture. Edward informs the gathering at the final party that instead of becoming a doctor Nelly died young. This death echoes those of Mistress Joan and Rachel Vinrace, except in this case the death – which allows Nelly to evade becoming a professional rather than a wife and mother – shows how Woolf was beginning to think of the male-dominated professions as almost as menacing as maternity. In addition, the party's actual female doctor, North's sister Peggy, is not only unfulfilled but acutely disenchanted by a profession that teaches her how insidious patriarchal culture is. Peggy is particularly disheartened by her experience of helping women in labour, a view reiterated in Woolf's notebooks, which quote Bertrand Russell on how the 'views of medical men on pregnancy, child-birth, and lactation were until fairly recently impregnated with sadism' (*RN* 363). Nelly's failure to thrive in the professional world can be partly understood using a diary entry Woolf wrote while working on the final pages of *The Years*. After visiting the Labour Party Conference she records how one particular woman delegate stood up and said:

'It is time we gave up washing up. A thin frail protest, but genuine. A little reed piping, but what chance against all this weight of roast beef & beer – which she must cook?' The 'thin voiced & insubstantial' (*D4* 345) woman's rallying call to arms finds little credence in a world where women are systematically suppressed by a society that expects them to be providers and mothers. While there is a class element to this entry it is also true that Woolf felt all women were tied down by domesticity. The sheer weight of this patriarchal culture – alluded to by the use of words of burden and frailness in this passage – explains why Nelly, as a woman, comes to nothing where her father, poor as he is, manages to succeed.

After leaving the Robsons, Kitty returns home to dress for a meal with her own mother. Like Mrs Robson, Mrs Malone has no first name; unlike with Mrs Robson, however, the reader shares Mrs Malone's inner thoughts. During the meal Kitty and her mother eat their 'dull' leftover fish and 'stale bread [. . .] cut in meagre little squares' alone since 'the gentlemen were dining in Hall' (*Y* 55). The absence of these particular men is not troublesome since the majority of Mr Malone's colleagues do not share intellectual conversation with Kitty, instead treating her as a pretty ornament and pawing at her knee. Nevertheless this segregation does serve to show how much more there is to be had from a society which values dialogue between the sexes. Though the food is principally the same 'bread and butter' and 'fried fish' (*Y* 50) as served at the Robsons, Kitty feels the meal and food pale in comparison, and even her mother mentions the 'odd taste in the fish' (*Y* 56). This momentary emotional sympathy does not translate into a feeling of kinship between mother and daughter, instead, Mrs Malone becomes 'increasingly conscious of difficulty with Kitty [. . .] There was always some constraint between them now' (*Y* 58) while Kitty thinks how 'they differed; as they did about so many things' (*Y* 56).

The text weaves food, mistress-hood and the mother/daughter relationship when, after dinner, Kitty reads aloud from a newspaper article about the falling numbers of properly trained cooks:

With the best flesh, fish and fowl in the world [. . .] we shall not be able to turn them to account because we have none to cook them [. . .] Before the rigid and now universal enforcement of school attendance [. . .] the children saw a good deal of cooking which, poor as it was, yet gave them some taste and inkling of knowledge. They now see nothing and they do nothing but read, write, sum, sew or knit. (*Y* 56–57)

214   *Virginia Woolf and Motherhood*

The 1880 Education Act, which made schooling compulsory between the ages of five and ten, meant that, like Nelly, fewer girls were learning the culinary arts at home and fewer were entering domestic service in the kitchen. This dwindling number of trainable girls highlights the change in both Mrs Malone's life as a mistress and Mrs Robson's life as a cook. The lifestyles of Mrs Malone and other characters such as Mrs Ramsay were felt to be becoming less sustainable even before WW1 caused a large number of women to leave domestic service for good. Without prioritising any, *The Years* offers a number of judgements on the education of working-class girls. Kitty thinks the article and its writer 'pompous' (*Y* 57), and Mrs Robson (and, one presumes, her WCG mother-in-law) are invested in female education.[138] Mrs Malone, on the other hand, misses the skills of a good cook and despite her education Nelly neither makes it in the professions nor inherits her mother's culinary skill.

Ultimately the novel provides no settled solutions on either the grander scale workings of society or the more intimate relationships between individuals. There are no answers as to whether the education of girls of any class might benefit society, and Kitty and her mother do not resolve their differences. In addition, Kitty's attitude towards the working class does not offer long-lasting progress. Woolf's depiction of Kitty and her maid Baxter (whose interior thoughts *are* briefly explored) during a night-time encounter in Kitty's bedroom, shows typical old-fashioned tension. Baxter wishes the guests would leave so she can get ready for her own day off and, when Kitty tries an awkward interaction with her working-class co-character, the text notes: 'Baxter gave a queer little bitten-off smile. Maids bothered Kitty with their demure politeness; with their inscrutable, pursed-up faces. But they were very useful' (*Y* 196). This is the type of candid attitude towards domestic help that Mrs Ramsay, Mrs Malone and Julia Stephen, with their maternal authority, avoid. However, as the mother of sons that (like Orlando's children) are missing from the novel, Kitty is not given by Woolf a similar frank encounter with her maternal side. The closest that the novel gets to resolving the tension between middle-class mothers and their working-class domestic staff is when, during WW1, Maggie mostly has to go without domestic help, cooking and caring for her children on her own (to which Eleanor, herself unburdened by maternal domesticity, comments: 'Isn't it much nicer [. . .] not having servants' (*Y* 207)).

Though *The Years* visibly offers many moments of incongruence it is important to note that it also assumes a certain level of human

Motherhood and Food **215**

connection between family members. At the end of their dinner, though Kitty and her mother have no emotional resolution, they do have mutual concerns for one another. Mrs Malone maintains her Victorian, maternal attitude and worries about the loss of her daughter's 'roses' (*Y* 60) – the youth and beauty that will enable her to find a husband. Kitty has a more contemporary concern that her mother should not give in to all her father's desires at the cost of her own health. In light of Kitty's earlier tea at the Robsons' and her identification with Mrs Robson, it would seem plausible to suggest that the detachment between the two Malone women during and after their meal might signify a breakdown in their relationship, but this is not the case. Rather it appears that the instinct for teenage daughters to rebel against their mothers is every bit as innate as the instinct to mother – a revelation that Woolf came to even though she had done neither. Betty Kushen suggests that, through the imagery of a pair of long-lost objects that are found during this scene, Woolf 'demonstrates that the separation of mother and daughter is temporary and less than complete'.[139] Later Kitty looks back on the evening and experiences a moment of grief when she thinks 'I wish I hadn't quarrelled so much with my mother' (*Y* 135). And indeed, in the middle of Kitty and her mother's strained evening a note arrives to inform them that Rose Pargiter has died, denoting another, even more unsatisfying situation, having no mother at all.

From infant-feeding to grand meals, Woolf's pairing of food and motherhood can be found across a wide selection of her texts. It incorporates concerns about wartime pronatalism and rationing, and touches on eugenic anxiety regarding raising healthy children – thus linking back to the previous chapters of this book. However, unlike eugenics or narratives about war, food preparation is a domestic, private affair that is an integral part of women's everyday lived experience. Woolf used images of food to explore prescribed feminine, and particularly maternal, performance and to think about how these roles inhibited the individual creative lives of women. Because inter-class interactions were central to domestic tasks, her representations of the production, preparation and consumption of food, or even of foraging (she associated both blackberry picking and mushrooming with her domestic staff) reveal class anxieties.[140] While these textual moments sometimes show Woolf's bias about working-class (and maternal) artistry, they also demonstrate a desire to broaden her understanding of other classes and her attempts to include working-class voices in her writing: a practice she felt had – as Heather Levy observes – 'radical flaws if attempted by a middle-class pen'.[141] In Woolf's later writing – both published and unpublished – themes of motherhood and food increasingly engage in this struggle to reproduce working-class thoughts and experiences. This not only offers a new perspective to scholarship on her attitude towards class, but proves, once again, how valuable themes of motherhood were in the literary expression of her feminism and politics.

Though Woolf's upbringing shaped her literary associations between gender performance and domesticity, towards the end of her life a woman's place in the home began to take on new significance. The burgeoning discourse of psychoanalysis transformed the sense of gravitas that Victorian culture conferred on the home life of both men and women. It speculated that close domestic relationships – particularly mother–child bonds – were full of emotional disturbance and that they form the basis of the adult character. Given that it is a family saga it is perhaps unsurprising that psychoanalytical impressions of familial relations are seen in a nascent form in *The Years*. Not only are the communication difficulties experienced by the characters especially prominent between family members, but the interactions between Kitty and Mrs Malone reflect the disquiet at the core of mother–daughter relationships. While Mrs Fripp's kiss shows Kitty's yearning for maternal affection, dining with her mother she feels only frustration and sadness that 'they differed; as they did about so many things' (*Y* 56). At the same time Mrs Malone cannot express her love for her daughter but instead, at the same dinner, becomes 'increasingly conscious of difficulty with Kitty [. . .] There was always some constraint between them now' (*Y* 58). It is important to note that mother–child relationships were not the only thing about psychoanalysis that interested Woolf. As critics such as Patricia Cramer have observed, fascism and the threat of violence in Europe was almost certainly the initial prompt that led her to read and borrow from Freud's theories about group psychology and herd instincts.[142] However, given Woolf's abiding interest in motherhood, it is unsurprising that once she began perusing psychoanalytic theory she quickly became affected by its ideas about the formative effects of maternal relationships. Thus, as the following chapter will establish, while *Three Guineas'* investigations of fascism, war-making and patriarchy clearly references Freud, 'A Sketch of the Past', *Roger Fry* and *Between the Acts* all employ both Freudian and Kleinian models of mother–child relationships in their careful rendering of characer.

Notes

1. *Recollections of Virginia Woolf*, pp. 236–37.
2. '"A certain hold on haddock and sausage": Dining Well in Virginia Woolf's Life and Work', in *Virginia Woolf and the Natural World*, eds. Kristin Czarnecki and Carrie Rohman (Liverpool: Liverpool University Press, 2011), p. 162.
3. *Beginning Again*, p. 79. For examples of works that examine Woolf's relationship with food during times of illness see Allie Glenny, *Ravenous Identity* (Basingstoke: Macmillan, 2000) and Shirley Panken, *Virginia Woolf and the Lust of Creation* (New York: State University of New York Press, 1987), pp. 67–69.
4. See Francesca Orestano, 'Virginia Woolf and the Cooking Range', in *Not Just Porridge: English Literati at Table*, eds. Francesca Orestano and Michael Vickers (Oxford: Archaeopress, 2017), pp. 125–34 and Jans Ondaatje Rolls, *The Bloomsbury Cookbook* (London: Thames and Hudson, 2014).
5. Janine Utell, 'Meals and Mourning in Woolf's *The Waves*', *College Literature*, 35.2 (2008), pp. 1–19; Vicki Tromanhauser, 'Eating Animals and Becoming Meat in Virginia Woolf's *The Waves*', *Journal of Modern Literature*, 38.1 *(2014)*, pp. 73–93; See also Andrea Adolph, 'Nostalgic Appetites: Female Desire and Wartime Rationing in Virginia Woolf's *Between the Acts* and Noel Streatfeild's *Saplings*', in *Material Women: Consuming Desires and Consuming Objects 1750–1950*, eds. Maureen Daly Goggin and Beth Fowkes Tobin (Farnham: Ashgate, 2009), pp. 55–72.
6. See Nicola Humble, 'Little Swans with Luxette and Loved Boy Pudding: Changing Fashions in Cookery Books', *Women: A Cultural Review*, 13.3 (2002), pp. 329–30.
7. For more information on the maternalist politics of this time see *Mothers of a New World* eds Seth Koven and Sonya Michaels. For more information about infant and maternal mortality, milk and sanitation see Lewis, *The Politics of Motherhood*, pp. 61–64.
8. In the late 1950s and 1960s Harry Harlow's attachment theory experiments used rhesus monkeys to show that feeding provides more than just nutrients. The effects of different types of infant feeding is a subject still studied widely among the medical academic community. See Harlow, 'The Nature of Love', *American Psychologist*, 13.12 (1958), pp. 673–85 and Manuela Lavelli and Marco Poli, 'Early Mother–Infant Interaction During Breast- and Bottle-Feeding', *Infant Behavior and Development*, 21.4 (1998), pp. 667–83.
9. *Stories for Children, Essays for Adults*, eds. Diane F. Gillespie and Elizabeth Steele (Syracuse: Syracuse University Press, 1987) p. 234. Milk was also central to Silas Weir Mitchell's 'Rest Cure', a treatment that has been explored with relation to Woolf (see, for example, Panken, *the Lust of Creation*, p. 259).

10. 'Perishable and Permanent', p. 14.
11. 'The Milk Problem in *To the Lighthouse*', *Virginia Woolf Miscellany*, 50 (1997), p. 5.
12. Panken, *The Lust of Creation*, p. 26.
13. See Valerie Fildes, 'Infant Feeding and Infant Mortality in England, 1900–1919', *Continuity and Change*, 13.2 (1998), 251–80 and Peter Atkins, 'Mother's Milk and Infant Death in Britain, circa 1900–1940', *Anthropology of Food*, 2 (2003) <http://journals.openedition.org/aof/310> [accessed 11 March 2019].
14. Atkins, 'Mother's Milk and Infant Death', para. 19.
15. For a history of wet-nursing and baby-farming see Valerie Fildes, *Wet Nursing* (Oxford: Basil Blackwell, 1988). For a full description of how milk depots worked, what their milk consisted of and a typical feeding schedule see George F. McCleary, 'The Infants' Milk Depot: Its History and Function', *The Journal of Hygiene*, 4.3 (1904), pp. 329–68.
16. *Mrs Beeton's Book of Household Management* (London: S.O. Beeton, 1861), pp. 1022–23.
17. *Selected Letters of Vanessa Bell*, p. 230, n. 2. Marler doesn't give a reference for her statement, but Merriam-Webster provides a definition, albeit with a difference of spelling <https://www.merriam-webster.com/dictionary/gray_powder> [accessed 27 March 2024].
18. *Stories for Children*, p. 234.
19. *Mrs Woolf and the Servants*, p. 83.
20. *Recollections of Virginia Woolf*, p. 70.
21. *Mrs Woolf and the Servants*, p. 36.
22. *Stories for Children*, pp. 250, 249–50, 252, my emphasis.
23. 'The Politics/Poetics of Motherhood in *To the Lighthouse*', in *Virginia Woolf and Communities*, eds. Jeanette McVickers and Laura Davies (New York: Pace University Press, 1999), pp. 105–06.
24. This is true of the text in general. For an overview of how critics have read 'Mistress Joan' see Anna Snaith, '"A view of one's own": Writing Women's Lives and the Early Short Stories', in *Trespassing Boundaries: Virginia Woolf's Short Fiction*, eds. K.N. Benzel and R. Hoberman (Basingstoke: Palgrave Macmillan, 2004), pp. 130–35.
25. Race, Empire, and Ireland', in *Virginia Woolf in Context*, eds. Bryony Randall and Jane Goldman (Cambridge University Press, 2012), p. 211.
26. 'Woolf, Postcards and the Elision of Race: Colonizing Women in *The Voyage Out*', *Modernism/Modernity*, 8.1 (2001), p. 62.
27. *A History of the Breast* (London: Harper Collins, 1997), p. 126; in rural areas some lower middle-class women also breastfed in certain public places such as at church.
28. 'Woolf, Postcards and the Elision of Race', p. 57.
29. 'From Spaniel Club to Animalous Society: Virginia Woolf's *Flush*', in *Contradictory Woolf*, pp. 159, 164. (Also see Ryan, *the Materiality of Theory*, pp. 144–50). There is a body of work dedicated to Woolf's use

of dogs in her feminist writing: for example, Elizabeth Knauer, 'Of Dogs, Daughters, and the "Back Bedroom" School: Woolf's *Flush* and Women's Education', *CEA Critic*, 73.2 (2011), pp. 1–20. In *A Room* Woolf uses a Blaise Pascal quote to link men's ownership of dogs and women: 'Ce chien est à moi' (*AROO* 46). Interestingly, Leonard Woolf also employs this quote as one of the epigraphs in *Empire and Commerce in Africa*, a work criticising imperialism which Virginia helped research (*D1* 229n).

30. 'Race, Empire, and Ireland', p. 209.

31. Rachel's 'difficult' (*VO* 48) and absorbing Bach can be compared with the villagers' singing which 'slid up a little way and down a little way, and settled again upon the same low and melancholy note' (*VO* 269).

32. In the *Hyde Park Gate News* there is a short story written by Woolf that contrasts autonomy and motherhood. In this comedic story, entitled 'Miss Smith', the titular character ultimately gives up feminism and independence to become a wife and mother. However Smith is an activist and a campaigner rather than an artist (Virginia Woolf, Vanessa Bell and Thoby Stephen, *Hyde Park Gate News: The Stephen Family Newspaper*, ed. with an introduction and notes by Gill Lowe (London: Hesperus, 2005), pp. 164–66).

33. In the introduction to his book *Simple French Cooking for English Homes*, one of the Woolfs' favourite chefs Marcel Boulestin remarks: 'English cooks always tell their mistresses that French cooking is so extravagant because "everything is cooked in pounds of butter"' ((London: Heinemann, 1923), p. v). A glance at any of his books from the 1920s and 30s will show that almost every recipe used butter (see, for example, *A Second Helping* (1925) and *The Finer Cooking* (1937), both used by Vanessa Bell's cook Grace Higgens, and both still found on the shelf at Charleston (Rolls, *The Bloomsbury Cookbook*, pp. 173, 194)). In *To the Lighthouse* Mrs Ramsay takes pride in her French heritage and displays it through food, proudly calling the *Boeuf en Daube* – 'a French recipe of my grandmother's' (*TL* 109).

34. Cited in Richard Davenport-Hines and Judy Slinn, *Glaxo: A History to 1962* (Cambridge: Cambridge University Press, 1992), p. 42.

35. *Glaxo: A History*, p. 42.

36. For more about beliefs on traits being transmitted through breastmilk, see Emily Stevens, 'A History of Infant Feeding', *The Journal of Perinatal Education*, 18.2 (2009), pp. 32–39.

37. 'Woolf, Postcards and the Elision of Race', p. 73.

38. *The Corn King and the Spring Queen* (Edinburgh: Cannongate, 1931), p. 270.

39. Utell, 'Meals and Mourning', p. 2; Glenny, *Ravenous Identity*, pp. 169–71; Tromanhauser, 'Eating Animals and Becoming Meat', pp. 78–79.

40. 'After the Deluge, *The Waves*', in *Virginia Woolf and the World of Books*, eds. Nicola Wilson and Claire Battershill (Liverpool: Liverpool University Press, 2018), p. 78.

41. 'Moments and Metamorphoses: Virginia Woolf's Greece', *Comparative Literature*, 51.3 (1999), p. 230; Also see Patricia Cramer's 'Jane Harrison and the Lesbian Plots: The Absent Lover in Virginia Woolf's *The Waves*', *Studies in the Novel*, 37.4 (2005), pp. 443–63.

42. *After the Deluge*, 2 vols (London: Hogarth Press, 1931–39), I (1931), p. 247. Published the same month as *The Waves*, this text was another influence on Woolf's writing (Macduff, 'After the Deluge, *The Waves*', p. 77).

43. '"The central shadow": Characterization in *The Waves*', *Modern Fiction Studies*, 18.3 (1972), p. 458.

44. *Jane Austen, Virginia Woolf and Worldly Realism* (Edinburgh: Edinburgh University Press, 2017), p. 114.

45. For a time, Woolf called the novel 'The Moths'. In the letter Bell describes her struggle to kill an unusually large moth that had come into her house one night. Knowing how much her children would enjoy having it mounted, she notes: 'My maternal instinct, which you deplore so much, wouldn't let me leave it'. In contrast to Woolf, Bell also uses the letter to posit art and motherhood as equal but different spheres – 'What a lot I could say about the maternal instinct, but then also what a lot about Michael Angelo and Raphael' (*Selected Letters of Vanessa Bell*, p. 315).

46. Ibid., p. 315.

47. Not everyone in the Bloomsbury set who read Weininger liked or agreed with him, Allan Janik notes that G. E. Moore was recommended *Sex & Character* by Ludwig Wittgenstein but saw little of worth in it, something Wittgenstein partly blamed on the 'beastly translation' (*Essays on Wittgenstein and Weininger* (Amsterdam: Rodopi, 1985), p. 66).

48. 'The Sane Woman in the Attic: Sexuality and Self-Authorship in *Mrs Dalloway*', *Modern Fiction Studies*, 51.1 (2005), p. 40. Other scholars who mention Weininger's influence on Woolf's circle include Fassler, 'Theories of Homosexuality', pp. 239–48; and Brenda Helt, 'Passionate Debates on "Odious Subjects": Bisexuality and Woolf's Opposition to Theories of Androgyny and Sexual Identity', *Twentieth Century Literature*, 56.2 (2010), pp. 133–38.

49. *Sex & Character (Authorised Translation from the Sixth German Edition)* (hereafter *SC*) (London: William Heinemann, 1906), p. 222. Further page references will be given within the main text.

50. 'Books in General', p. 704.

51. Elsewhere in the response Woolf does allude to Weininger's suicide but does not name him directly.

52. Vanessa Bell, 'Notes on Virginia's Childhood', in *Virginia Woolf: Interviews and Recollections*, ed. J. Stape (Basingstoke: Macmillan, 1995), p. 6.

53. Fassler, Theories of Homosexuality', p. 250.

54. Ibid., p. 248.

55. Woolf did read *Challenge*, the book Sackville-West wrote as a fictional counterpart to her memoir, in which she cast herself as the dashing Byronic hero Julian.
56. 'Eating Animals and Becoming Meat', p. 78.
57. *Ravenous Identity*, p. 170.
58. Lily paints 'a purple shadow' (*TL* 59).
59. 'Eating Animals and Becoming Meat', p. 78.
60. Kate Greenaway, *Language of Flowers* (London: Routledge, 1884), p. 55. Elisa Kay Sparks notes that alongside roses, the hollyhock was Vanessa's favourite flower ('Everything tended to set itself in a garden', p. 51).
61. 'Virginia Woolf, Vanessa Bell and Painting', in *The Edinburgh Companion to Virginia Woolf and the Arts*, ed. Maggie Humm (Edinburgh: Edinburgh University Press, 2010), p. 135.
62. Woolf's allusion to Catullus's *Odi et Amo*, – 'I hate, I love' – is also a reflection on her intense maternal emotions. Weininger writes that, although a mother's friendly caretaking can be directed towards the community at large – a condition reflected in Julia Stephen, Mrs Ramsay and Susan's visiting of the sick and dying – 'when there is an exclusive choice to be made between her child and others [. . .] she becomes hard and relentless; and so she can be more full of love and more bitter than the prostitute' (*SC* 224).
63. Susan gives herself to 'rather a brutal young man – to a young man in gaiters, slapping his gaiters with a whip, silent. drunk too. That was what she wanted Somebody very dumb too' (*WH* 188). Similarly, *Lady Chatterley's Lover* (published in Italy in 1928) describes 'a man in dark green velveteens and gaiters' who has an air of silent foreboding ((London: Penguin, 2006), p. 46).
64. *An Essay on the Principle of Population*, ed. Joyce E. Chaplin (London: J. Johnson, 1798; repr. London: W. W. Norton, 2018), pp. 38, 137.
65. 'The Biology of Population Growth', in *World Population Conference Proceedings*, ed. Margaret Sanger (London: Edward Arnold, 1927), p. 38.
66. Leonard Woolf wrote about the effect of imperialism on colonial agriculture, see, for example, *Economic Imperialism* (London: Swarthmore, 1920), pp. 69–71.
67. *The Measure of Life: Virginia Woolf's Last Years* (London: Cornell University Press, 2000), p. 43.
68. 'An Economic Analysis of Unemployment', in *Unemployment as a World-Problem*, ed. Quincy Wright (Illinois: University of Chicago Press, 1931), p. 3.
69. 'Adventures in Common: Investing with Woolfs and "Securitas"', in *Virginia Woolf and the Common(Wealth) Reader*, eds. Helen Wussow and Mary Ann Gillies (Liverpool: Liverpool University Press, 2014), p. 208.

70. 'Eating Animals and Becoming Meat', p. 74.
71. Clara Jones, 'Virginia Woolf's 1931 "Cook Sketch"', *Woolf Studies Annual*, 20 (2014), pp. 1–23.
72. Beryl Rowland, 'The Oven in Popular Metaphor from Hosea to the Present Day', *American Speech*, 45.3/4 (1970), pp. 215–22.
73. *Recollections of Virginia Woolf*, pp. 191, 85.
74. *Asheham Diary*, with an introduction by Anne Olivier Bell, *The Charleston Magazine*, 9 (1994), pp. 31–32.
75. See Max Saunders, *Self Impressions: Life-Writing, Autobiografiction and the Forms of Modern Literature* (Oxford: Oxford University Press, 2010), p. 438, and Anna Snaith, '"My poor private voice": Virginia Woolf and Auto/Biography', in *Representing Lives: Women and Auto/Biography*, eds. Alison Donnell and Pauline Polkey (London: Palgrave Macmillan, 2000), pp. 96–104.
76. *Mrs Woolf and the Servants*, pp. 193–95.
77. *Recollections of Virginia Woolf*, pp. 140, 191.
78. Ibid., pp. 83–85.
79. *In the Hollow of the Wave: Virginia Woolf and Modernist Uses of Nature* (Charlottesville: University of Virginia Press, 2012), p. 75.
80. 'Virginia Woolf and Gardens', in *The Edinburgh Companion to Virginia Woolf and the Arts*, ed. Maggie Humm (Edinburgh: Edinburgh University Press, 2010), p. 254.
81. *Prolegomena*, pp. 443, x.
82. *Virginia Woolf: The Common Ground* (Edinburgh: Edinburgh University Press, 1996), p. 89.
83. *I Do, I Undo, I Redo: The Textual Genesis of Modernist Selves in Hopkins, Yeats, Conrad, Forster, Joyce, and Woolf* (Oxford: Oxford University Press, 2010), p. 257.
84. Ibid., p. 255; '"You See You Kind of Belong to Us, and What You Do Matters Enormously": Letters from Readers to Virginia Woolf', *Woolf Studies Annual*, 12 (2006), pp. 1–212.
85. Woolf did experiment with writing working-class voices and eventually worked them into a novel – *The Years*. This will be discussed later in the chapter.
86. 'Britannia Rules *The Waves*', p. 81.
87. *L1* 453, *L4* 407.
88. *Stories for Children*, p. 252.
89. It is important to note that Mrs Ramsay and Susan are very different types of mother. A true maternalist, and philanthropist, Mrs Ramsay's motherhood is outward looking, a way to engage with the world. Mrs Ramsay mothers her guests as much as her own children, approaching mothering in such a professional way that she even, perhaps unconsciously, usurps the mothers of the girls who stay with her. In contrast Susan's motherhood is inward looking, 'netted and covered

over' (*W* 206), Susan is only interested in her own children and she furthers the reach of the empire through private industry.

90. Clara Jones and Alice Wood have recounted Woolf's early involvement with the Co-operative guild. Jones, *Ambivalent Activist*; Wood, 'Facing *Life as We Have Known it*: Virginia Woolf and the Women's Co-operative Guild', *Literature & History*, 23.2 (2014), pp. 18–34.
91. See, for example, Jane Marcus, *Art & Anger: Reading Like A Woman* (Columbus: Ohio State University Press, 1988), p. 148.
92. Quoted in Jones, *Ambivalent Activist*, p. 118.
93. Ibid., p. 118.
94. *Art & Anger*, pp. 117–18.
95. 'A "Radiant" Friendship', *Critical Inquiry*, 10.4 (1984), p. 565.
96. 'Virginia Woolf on the Outside Looking Down: Reflections on the Class of Women', *Modern Fiction Studies*, 38.1 (1992), p. 71.
97. *Virginia Woolf*, p. 361; 'Between Women: A Cross-Class Analysis of Status and Anarchic Humor', *Women's Studies*, 15 (1988), p. 139.
98. 'Virginia Woolf on the Outside Looking Down', p. 62.
99. 'Facing *Life as We Have Known It*', p. 18.
100. Other examples include 'Kew Gardens' (as will be seen) and *A Room of One's Own*, where 'genius [. . .] is not born to-day among the working classes' (*AROO* 44).
101. *Ambivalent Activist*, p. 112.
102. *Feminism and the Politics of Working Women* (London: UCL Press, 1998), p. 16.
103. 'Cooperation at the Fountainhead', quoted in Scott, *Feminism and the Politics of Working Women*, p. 10.
104. This is not to suggest that Woolf did not respect the Guild's work, merely that she could not empathise with it.
105. *Feminism and the Politics of Working Women*, p. 11.
106. 'A Democracy of Working Women', *New Statesman*, 21 June 1913, p. 329.
107. *Round About a Pound a Week*, p. 94.
108. For more on this see Charlotte Taylor-Suppé, '"my comfortable capitalistic head": Virginia Woolf on Consumption, Co-operation and Motherhood', in *Virginia Woolf and Capitalism*, ed. Clara Jones (Edinburgh: Edinburgh University Press, 2024), pp. 70–91.
109. John Hartley, *Bully Beef and Biscuits: Food in the Great War* (Barnsley: Pen & Sword Military, 2015), pp. 276–77, 300.
110. 'A Proclamation', *The Spectator*, 26 May 1917, p. 4.
111. *Ecocriticism and Women Writers* (Basingstoke: Palgrave Macmillan, 2013), p. 14.
112. *Round About a Pound a Week*, p. 97.
113. *Mrs Woolf and the Servants*, p. 204.
114. *Ambivalent Activist*, p. 139.

224 *Virginia Woolf and Motherhood*

115. See Taylor-Suppé, "'my comfortable capitalistic head'", pp. 81–82.
116. Quoted in Jones, *Ambivalent Activist*, p. 118.
117. *Feminist Destinations and Further Essays on Virginia Woolf* (Edinburgh: Edinburgh University Press, 1997), p. 237.
118. A similar eugenic ideal of two generations of evolution is discussed in Chapter 2. However the Guildswomen are two generations from being they type of novelist Marie Carmichael already is.
119. *Selected Letters of Vanessa Bell*, p. 308.
120. Jones, 'Virginia Woolf's 1931 "Cook Sketch"', pp. 1–23; Dick, 'Virginia Woolf's "The Cook"', *Woolf Studies Annual*, 3 (1997), pp. 122–42; and Levy, '"These ghost figures of distorted passion": Becoming Privy to Working-Class Desire in "The Watering Place" and "The Ladies Lavatory"', *Modern Fiction Studies*, 50.1 (2004), pp. 31–57.
121. Both the German Nazi Party and Spanish Radical Republican Party were elected in 1931. In 1932, in a bid to help the worsening depression, the British government decided to pursue a protectionist trade policy and limited free-trade with all but the British Colonies. This led to a mass resignation of Liberal members of parliament.
122. *Virginia Woolf: Public and Private Negotiations* (Basingstoke: Palgrave Macmillan, 2000), pp. 92–93.
123. Ibid., p. 86.
124. *Women's Fiction of the Second World War: Gender, Power and Resistance* (Edinburgh: Edinburgh University Press, 1996), pp. 91–92.
125. *Austen, Woolf and Worldly Realism*, p. 167.
126. Chapter 4 continues the discussion of *Three Guineas* and the professions.
127. 'Virginia Woolf: Reluctant Feminist in *The Years*', *Criticism*, 17.1 (1975), p. 71.
128. *Virginia Woolf's Reading Notebooks* (hereafter *RN*). Further page references will be given within the main text. Here, and in *Night and Day*, Woolf engages with Cicely Hamilton's important feminist book *Marriage as Trade* (1909). For more on this, see Michael Whitworth, *Virginia Woolf (Authors in Context)* (Oxford: Oxford University Press, 2005), pp. 152–55.
129. '"The little bit of power I had myself": Lady Lasswade's Shifting Sense of Place in *The Years*', in *Virginia Woolf and Heritage*, ed. Jane de Gay, Tom Breckin and Anne Reus (Liverpool: Liverpool University Press, 2017), pp. 60–62.
130. 'Woolf, Postcards and the Elision of Race', p. 73.
131. See Emma Sutton, *Virginia Woolf and Classical Music* (Edinburgh: Edinburgh University Press, 2014), p. 81.
132. Given a further entry in her reading notebooks, Woolf may have also considered how different the lived reality of such a woman would have been from all three of her renderings. This entry comes from economist and socialist William H. Beveridge's book *Changes in Family Life* (1932) (Beveridge was most famous for the Beveridge report – officially

titled *Social Insurance and Allied Services*, 1942 – which was influential in the founding of the British welfare state). *Changes* started life as a series of BBC radio monologues and dialogues in which social reformers and academics (including the then General Secretary of the WCG Mrs J. L. Adamson) discussed 'the problems that centre round the fundamental institution of the Family'. The talks were accompanied by a countrywide survey distributed, by selected newspapers and the Co-operative society, to more than 50,000 families across the breadth of society – a project which Beveridge considered an attempt 'to construct a new kind of instrument for social science'. Beveridge wrote a summary of his findings after some 7000 forms had been returned, noting that although not much appears to have changed in family life, 'the changed formal position of the wife and the resultant better companionship of husband and wife come out again and again in every class'. One of the respondents that Beveridge especially acknowledges – and that Woolf makes notes of – is 'a farmer's wife' (*RN* 262) who, though she finds that 'the duties of the farm make it impossible for her and her husband to go out together and thus share pleasures', has such a formidable companionship with him that they even enjoy filling out the form together (*Changes in Family Life* (London: G. Allen & Unwin, 1932), pp. 14, 12, 131–33).

133. Alfred Lord Tennyson, *The Princess*, in *Alfred Tennyson The Major Works,* ed. Adam Roberts, rev. edn. (Oxford: Oxford University Press, 2009) VII. 299–311. It is worth noting that, although this description of an 'Angel' inspiring men with her grasp on eternity brings Susan the muse (and Coventry Patmore) to mind, the poem actually tells the story of Princess Ida, who abandons her betrothed in order to found a women's university. The Princess goes on to reply to this stanza: 'It seems you love to cheat yourself with words:/ This mother is your model. I have heard/ of your strange doubts: they well might be: I seem/ A mockery to my own self. Never, Prince;/ You cannot love me.' (VII. 315–19)

134. 'Virginia Woolf: Reluctant Feminist', p. 72.

135. Elizabeth Mary Wright, *The Life of Joseph Wright*, 2 vols (London: Oxford University Press, 1932), I, pp. 316, 154–55.

136. When she visited Oxford Joseph Wright's mother's commented 'of All Souls that it would make an admirable Co-operative hall' (*P* 127).

137. *The Life of Joseph Wright*, I, p. 28.

138. As Mrs Scott writes in *Life as We Have Known It*: 'I always remember going down a street with great mills on either side and hoping I should never have to bring a child into the world if it was condemned to that life' (Margaret Llewelyn Davies (ed.) (London: Virago, 2012), pp. 84–85).

139. 'Virginia Woolf: Metaphor of the Inverted Birth', *American Imago*, 38.3 (1981), p. 297.

140. See Woolf, *Ashenham Diary*, pp. 27–35.

226   *Virginia Woolf and Motherhood*

141. '"These ghost figures of distorted passion"', p. 49.
142. 'Virginia Woolf's Matriarchal Family of Origins'. See also E. H. Wright, 'Woolf's Pacifism and Contemporary Women Dramatists', in *Virginia Woolf, Europe, and Peace, Vol. 1*, ed. Ariane Mildenberg and Patricia Novillo-Corvalán (Liverpool: Liverpool University Press, 2020), p. 167.

Chapter 4

Motherhood and Psychoanalysis

Introduction

By the time Virginia Woolf started becoming interested in psycho-analytic theory its pioneers had split into two rather distinct factions. Sigmund (and later Anna) Freud advanced theories in which the individual is motivated by two opposing life and death drives known as 'Eros' and 'destruction'. Melanie Klein, on the other hand, was interested in the way infants formed relationships from birth and proposed models which, as Jay Lefer explains, 'saw the mother-child dyad as a building block of psychic structure'. Lefer notes that although these differing philosophies caused quite serious rifts in American psycho-analysis, in Britain there was more tolerance. British psychoanalysts worked together, predominantly focusing on Kleinian object-relations theories in which 'the child's relationship with the mother is internalized and becomes part of his self through time'.[1] This preference for Kleinian psychoanalysis may have been a consequence of the markedly high number of female psychoanalysts working, researching and publishing within Britain. As the preeminent British psychoanalyst Ernest Jones noted in a 1927 letter to Freud, 'for many years there has been a rather special interest taken in the problems of childhood in London, perhaps more than elsewhere. I suppose the reason is that we have a number of women analysts'.[2] Sanja Bahun notes that 'almost half of the practicing members of the British Psycho-Analytical Society in the interwar years were women'. These women and their colleagues focused on a list of gynocentric topics that included 'female sexuality, gender' and 'motherhood' – all topics that are also prominent within Woolf's work.[3]

In the mid-1930s with war once again threatening Europe, Woolf turned to psychoanalysis – a school of thought she had held in disdain

228   *Virginia Woolf and Motherhood*

for most of her adult life – in the hope its theories might offer new ways of understanding and even managing human violence. As Patricia Cramer observes, when 'reading Freud for the first time' Woolf deliberately 'selected his works on social psychology'. Cramer notes that in 'these works Freud [. . .] tries to explain Hitler and the Second World War by analyzing group formations'.[4] While fascism and the threat of violence certainly led Woolf to read and borrow from Freud's theories about herd instincts, this chapter considers how an interest in both Freudian and Kleinian psychoanalysis also led her to explore the lasting psychological effects mothers have on their children and thus changed her writing of motherhood. In her admirable study of Woolf and psychoanalysis Elizabeth Abel argues that Woolf's 1920's interest in early matriarchal societies shows a strong intertextuality with Klein's work, and that the 1930's saw her 'swerve abruptly [. . .] from Klein to Freud as the ideologies of motherhood [. . .] were appropriated and irretrievably contaminated for her by the fascist state'.[5] I would contend, however, that while Woolf's use of psychoanalysis is complex and personalised, broadly speaking the opposite of Abel's hypothesis appears true. As Chapter One demonstrated, Woolf's concerns about the patriarchal ideologies of motherhood were already well-defined by the time of *Jacob's Room* and her interest in matriarchal societies grew not from Klein but from a familiarity with the work of Jane Harrison (who was herself a proponent of Freud rather than Klein). The first concrete appearances of psychoanalytic theory in Woolf's work are predominantly Freudian and can be seen in *The Years* and *Three Guineas*.[6] As Woolf's interest in the subject grew it seems she was exposed to more woman-centric, Kleinian object-relations theories. In 1939, she employed both Klein's maternal-centrality and Freudian self-analysis in 'A Sketch of the Past' as a way to understand the roots of her own character. While she did not finish this memoir the analytic practice she honed in it proved invaluable. At the end of her life psychoanalysis remained central to her writing, not only do its theories form the backbone of *Between the Acts* narrative but Kleinian models of mother-child relationships underpin the novel's characters and their relationships with the world.

'His mother kissed him': Woolf and Psychoanalytic theory

Woolf's familiarity with psychoanalytic language and concepts began in childhood when her father exposed her to the discourse that preceded them – what George Johnson calls 'second wave psychology'.[7]

Leslie Stephen was particularly taken with his friend James Sully's book *Outlines of Psychology* (1884) which influenced Freud with its discussions of the conscious and unconscious.[8] Freud himself began documenting his ideas at the turn of the twentieth-century, though it took almost a decade before his work gained an international following. His theories reached England around the time of the Woolfs' marriage and from 1914 onwards, when Leonard wrote an early review of *The Psychopathology of Everyday Life* (1901), both Leonard and Virginia remained at the forefront of the British (and, indeed, English language) psychoanalytic movement. While preparing his review Leonard also read *The Interpretation of Dreams* and shared his findings with his wife who jokingly recorded a wakeful night when he analysed her according to 'the Freud System' (*L2* 141). Soon after Lytton Strachey became a proponent of Freud (their admiration was mutual) and in 1920 Lytton's brother and sister-in-law James and Alix Strachey went to Vienna to be analysed by and study under Freud, eventually becoming his endorsed English translators. A few years later Woolf's brother Adrian and his wife Karin also began analysis, going on to become the first medically-trained British psychoanalysts. It is important to note these were not merely casual acquaintances but friends and family Woolf spent time with and their diaries and letters are evidence they discussed psychoanalytic theory. The Woolfs also had a business interest in psychoanalysis. In 1924 Hogarth Press became the British publisher of the International Psychoanalytical Library printing the Stracheys' translations of Freud alongside Klein, Ernest Jones, Anna Freud and many others.

Despite this acquaintance with the world of psychoanalysis Woolf was hostile to Freud's theories for most of her adult life, once stating the only thing they proved was the 'gull-like imbecility' (*L3* 135) of the Germans. Part of Woolf's argument with psychoanalysis was its tendency to be used, as Perry Meisel notes, in 'brittle and reductive' ways.[9] In her essay of 1920, 'Freudian Fiction', she described psychoanalysis as 'a patent key that opens every door [. . .] simplifies rather than complicates, detracts rather than enriches' (*E3* 197). Freud's castration theories and his examples of female hysteria were also not as progressive as his pioneering mythos suggested. Indeed, Elaine Showalter observes that the psychoanalytic assertion 'that women were physically deficient and emotionally masochistic beings' was merely a continuation of the 'Victorian psychiatric theory' that 'had evolved to explain mental breakdown in women [. . .] as evidence of innate inferiority'.[10] This was antithetical to Woolf's feminist ethos and is perhaps why, while she disparaged Freud's theories with precise and

230 *Virginia Woolf and Motherhood*

ridiculous parodies, as late as 1932 she still denied having read any of his works (an issue of some critical discussion, with Gabrielle McIntire asserting she may have even set the type for some of them).[11] An example of this satire can also be found in 'Freudian Fiction' where Woolf jokes: 'A patient who has never heard a canary sing without falling down in a fit can now walk through an avenue of cages without a twinge of emotion since he has faced the fact that his mother kissed him in his cradle' (*E3* 196).[12] This lampooning shows that even if she did not agree with his theories, Woolf clearly understood Freud's framing of mother figures as the source of adult neuroses.

Because of Woolf's early antipathy to Freud, and a lack of evidence that she read any of his work until 1939, some critics have felt a burden of proof regarding her understanding of psychoanalytic principles.[13] In fact, a survey of her diary, letters and reading notebooks offer examples of how deep this understanding was. As noted, Leonard shared at least some of his early knowledge of Freudian dream interpretation. Then, in 1918, Woolf's diary mentions a meeting Lytton had attended at the 'British Sex Society', where: 'Incest between parent & child when they are both unconscious of it, was their main theme, derived from Freud' (*D1* 110). By 1923, a year before beginning to publish Freud, Woolf clearly had some thoughts on his theories, reflecting: 'For my part, I doubt if family life has all the power of evil attributed to it, or psycho-analysis of good' (*D2* 242). Her eclectic reading habits also brought her into contact with psychoanalysis. Catriona Livingstone records how in the 1920s and early 1930s, Woolf read several of biologist Julian Huxley's works including *The Science of Life*, a textbook written with G. P. and H. G. Wells.[14] This text would have contributed much to Woolf's understanding of basic psychoanalytic principles. It contains a full chapter on human behaviour that gives a comprehensive account of the work of Freud, Carl Jung and Alfred Adler, and spends several pages outlining the conscious and unconscious, the Oedipus complex and the relationship between repression and neuroses.[15] By 1933, some of what Woolf had heard and read must have begun to register as valuable. She comments in her reading notebook about a line in an Ivan Turgenev novel: 'The [half/long] suspected secret that is strongest in us – Freud' (*RN* 45) (the line is: 'we know that it is what remains a half-suspected secret for ourselves that is strongest in us').[16] This idea of hidden triggers or stimuli would go on to be a central theme of her late writing.

During the 1930s Woolf's interest in psychoanalysis continued to grow. By 1936 she even felt enthusiastic about it, noting of a dinner at Karin and Adrian's home: 'A good deal of p[sycho]. a[nalysis]. talked; & I liked it. A mercy not always to talk politics' (*D5* 32). This dinner coincided with the writing of *Three Guineas*, the first of her works that deliberately employs psychoanalytic theory. This is a somewhat controversial statement with many critics arguing Woolf was influenced by psychoanalysis significantly earlier. Elizabeth Abel starts her study with *Mrs Dalloway* and the influence Freud's *Totem and Taboo* (1919) had on Woolf's contemporaries. Going back even earlier, Dorothy Dodge Robbins writes that while 'there is no tacit evidence to corroborate that in *The Voyage Out* Woolf was rewriting Dora [. . .] There is a suggestion of influence' between the novel and Freud's famous case study of Ida Bauer (since the first draft of *The Voyage Out* was finished by 1912 and Freud was not yet translated or popular among the Bloomsbury group any similarities are likely accidental).[17] Certainly, some psychoanalytic theory was in line with Woolf's earlier writing – though it is impossible to say whether these ideas were absorbed during friendly debate or whether any similarities were the result of common foundations.[18] On the strength of language alone, however, *Three Guineas* marks a significant moment in Woolf's use of psychoanalysis. From the late-1930s, as it became an established part of her writing, she also sought out psychoanalytic discussion. In January 1939 she met both Sigmund and Anna Freud and discussed Hitler and war with this 'old fire now flickering' (*D5* 202). In February she met again with Anna Freud during a sociable day of meetings that were 'frothy' (*D5* 205) with talk. In March, the Woolfs attended the twenty-fifth anniversary dinner of the British Psycho-Analytical Society and Virginia had at least one private meal with Melanie Klein.[19] Both seem to have been intrigued by the mind of a fellow well-known and well-respected intellectual, with Woolf thinking Klein a 'woman of character & force & some submerged [. . .] subtlety: something working underground', even if she did also detect something slightly 'menacing' (*D5* 209). In July, two months after Hogarth Press had published Freud's *Moses and Monotheism*, she wrote to John Lehmann that she was reading 'Moses' because it had 'had a good show' (*L6* 346). By the end of that year, with her interest fully piqued, she recorded in her diary that she was turning to Freud 'to enlarge the circumference, to give my brain a wider scope: to make it objective; to get outside. Thus defeat the shrinkage of age' (*D5* 248).

'The disease of infantile fixation': Psychoanalysis within *Three Guineas*

Alice Wood's excellent genetic analysis exposes *Three Guineas* as a work born of two competing enterprises. Wood notes that while

232   *Virginia Woolf and Motherhood*

Woolf wanted to write a book about 'the oppressive gender roles of her own country', world events kept compelling her to write an anti-fascist diatribe. As a result *Three Guineas* had the most working titles of any of her books. These titles alternated depending on what was foremost in her mind at any given time. For example, Wood finds that Woolf's 1935 reading of Mary Moore's *The Defeat of Women*, 'with its complaint that "women have dropped their sacred task of motherhood"', prompted a 'title change – back from "anti fascist pamphlet" (*D4* 302) to "my Professions book" (*D4* 307)'.[20] Other titles include 'Women Must Weep', the main heading of the two original articles from which the polemic evolved. Given its subject matter and the growing threat of war it is no surprise that *Three Guineas* returns to Woolf's WW1 imagery of weeping mothers as well as themes such as female cooperation in war-making and the state's misuse of women. However, unlike the fictional narratives explored in Chapter 1, the polemic structures these arguments around a body of real-world evidence – or as Woolf famously referred to it, 'enough powder to blow up St Pauls' (*D4* 77). In this search for evidence Woolf looks to psychoanalysis to understand the psychological reasons why patriarchal society encourages men to dominate and women to submit.[21] For example, when discussing why women are compelled to support war despite its 'heavy' cost, 'the price of which [. . .] is mainly paid by women',[22] Woolf explains such collaboration in terms of 'conscious' and 'unconscious' (*TG* 160) motives. While the words conscious and unconscious are not unusual in her writing, they had not previously been used so purposefully as a pair. Repeatedly connecting these two terms, which are ubiquitously linked with psychoanalysis, corroborates her burgeoning interest in the area.

The most significant appearance of psychoanalytic theory is seen in *Three Guineas'* investigation into women's exclusion from the professions. Woolf turns to *The Ministry of Women*, a Church of England report investigating 'the spiritual vocation of women' and the possibility of an expanded, female-inclusive pastorate. The report was commissioned in light of the recent 'general increase' in women's 'freedom and responsibility'. While it concludes that 'the pastoral work of a priest' cannot be 'satisfactorily combined with the responsibilities of a married woman who has [. . .] the care of children', this is only a secondary reflection. Its principal conclusion is two-fold: that the 'continuous tradition [. . .] of a male priesthood [. . .] is based upon the will of God' and that the low number of women who desire entry into the priesthood is insufficient to offset a 'widespread' and 'deep-seated opposition' to such a change.[23] It is not the

Motherhood and Psychoanalysis **233**

designation of the priesthood as historically inflexible, exclusively male and divinely ordained which draws Woolf to the report but its acknowledgement of a widespread hostility to admitting women. Although Woolf (purportedly) had not yet read any exclusively psychoanalytic texts, her burgeoning interest in the area pushed her to explore the 'psychological and not merely historical reasons' (*TG* 253) that women were being excluded from professional life. Or, as *Three Guineas* phrases it, Woolf wishes to understand the: '"Strong feeling [. . .] aroused by any suggestion that women be admitted" – it matters not to which priesthood; the priesthood of medicine or the priesthood of science or the priesthood of the Church' (*TG* 255).

To aid in its psychological inquiry *Three Guineas* contains extensive quotes from one particular part of *The Ministry of Women* report. This is an appendix written by Oxford don, theologian and avid amateur entomologist and psychologist Reverend Professor L. W. Grensted. Grensted's statement uses Freudian concepts to explain society's psychological resistance to emancipating and empowering women. In particular he describes how opposition to a woman-inclusive pastorate arises from 'powerful and widespread subconscious' motives which he labels 'infantile fixation'.[24] While he does not fully outline the mechanisms at play in the formation of this 'fixation', Grensted does reference Freud's Oedipus complex, castration complex and theory of woman as man manqué. These concepts describe the male child's dawning comprehension of physical difference, his dread of castration and incestuous taboos dealing with the desire to replace the father and possess the mother. The mental turmoil that a mother provokes then remains as a lifelong bias which, when perpetuated within a patriarchy, continues to suppress women and enable men.

Woolf understood the basics of these theories and knew that mother figures were at their centre. She had reservations over the gender bias inherent in Freud's models – reservations which can be seen in *Three Guineas*' attempt to exchange the Freudian focus on Oedipus with an examination of his daughter Antigone. Nonetheless, Grensted's psychoanalytic report offered an excellent resource in her attempt to 'analyse' (*TG* 257) society. It describes a tangible obstacle women need to overcome before they can cultivate their own form of public participation and thus prevent fascism. Interestingly, though he concludes that there are no physical reasons for maintaining the exclusivity of the priesthood, Grensted determines that 'infantile fixation' is so deeply felt that allowing women entry might do more harm than good.[25] His evaluation ratifies one of the polemic's early titles: 'On Being Despised' (*D4* 271). This also brings to mind the fact that its final title – *Three Guineas* – reflects, as noted in Chapter 2, an amount quoted in the draft of *The Years* for a Harley Street abortion. Certainly, if Freudian psychoanalysis places society's hatred of women firmly back on the consciences of mothers, this allusion to abortion and the choice to not partake in family life takes on a new dimension.

Regardless of her obvious enthusiasm for Grensted's report Woolf did not believe that 'infantile fixation' was inevitable. *Three Guineas* includes the example of Mr Leigh Smith who was 'completely immune from the disease' (*TG* 264) and his daughter Barbara, a young, empowered woman who became a feminist educationalist and co-founded Girton College. The question of why such a 'strong [. . .] concealed force' (*TG* 265) might be present in most men but not all leads to another subject that psychoanalysis and *Three Guineas* both grapple with – the problem of the instincts and to what extent human emotional responses are inevitable and innate. Woolf had discussed instincts before (in *A Room*, for example) but from *Three Guineas* onwards this exploration would become enmeshed with Freudian psychoanalysis. This inquiry also revisits Woolf's previous theories on maternity, not only aligning it with male violence but also trying to understand if and how such human reflexes might be mutable.

'Eros' and 'Destruction': The 'fighting instinct' and the 'maternal instinct' in *Three Guineas* and Beyond

If *Three Guineas* was trying to show – as E. M. Forster noted in his 1941 Rede Lecture – that the war-oriented European society of the 1930s was a 'tragic male-made mess', then it would certainly have been able to rely on Freud's contemporary writing to prove it.[26] In *Moses and Monotheism*, for example, Freud echoes Jane Harrison's descriptions of early matriarchal civilisations which are characterised by mother-deities and identified through artefacts depicting mother goddesses. However, Freud explains the demise of these matriarchies in a particularly patricentric way, stating:

> This turning from the mother to the father [. . .] signifies above all a victory of spirituality over the senses, that is to say a step forward in culture, since maternity is proved by the senses whereas paternity is a surmise based on a deduction and a premiss.[27]

Freud associates the 'decision that paternity is more important than maternity' with the worship of 'an invisible God', both of which subordinate 'sense perception to an abstract idea'.[28] As a feature of patriarchy and religion, it is this belief in the abstract and unseen mechanisms of nature that, Freud notes, eventually gives birth to science and rationality. As Freud grew older his writing grew more phallocentric and here, in his final work, his theories on the achievements and psychological burdens of civilisation overwhelmingly revolve around the interaction between men in the form of father- and son-figures. This type of thinking may have been antithetical to Woolf but it gave weight not only to the notion that 'uneducated & voteless' middle-class women were 'not responsible for the state of society' (*D4* 346), but that the 'daughters of educated men' (*TG* 118) were especially qualified to work outside of traditional patriarchal social structures in order to affect change.

Both Woolf and Freud suggested the formation of a group of non-conformists to help prevent war. For Woolf this was *Three Guineas*' all-female 'Society of Outsiders' (*TG* 235), a natural successor to the committee she created at the end of WW1 in 'A Society'. In contrast, Freud wrote – in an exchange of open letters with Albert Einstein entitled *Why War?* (1934) – that '*men* should be at greater pains than heretofore to form a superior class of independent thinkers' (my emphasis).[29] Given the previous discussion of when Woolf read Freud's works it is not possible to prove she had read *Why War?* before writing *Three Guineas*; however, there are a number of similarities between the two and there is certainly a possibility that she had. Woolf's last recorded denial of reading Freud is in a letter two years before the publication of *Why War?* – not only did she and Leonard own a copy, but she may have considered the co-authored pamphlet something different to the main body of Freud's writing. Alice Wood notes that Woolf was particularly inspired by the device of letter-writing at the time (two other early titles she considered for *Three Guineas* were 'Answers to Correspondents' (*D5* 3) and 'Letter to an Englishman' (*D5* 18)) and so she might have read such material for inspiration.[30] In addition, *Why War?* was part of a series of open letters published by a committee of the League of Nations. This provenance made it of particular relevance to Leonard's work and Woolf may have associated it with the research she carried out for him on international peace and the formation of the League.[31]

Both *Three Guineas* and *Why War?* directly address the role of the instincts in war-making. In the latter Freud writes to Einstein that it is 'easy to infect men with the war-fever, and [. . .] that man

236 *Virginia Woolf and Motherhood*

has in him an active instinct for hatred and destruction, amenable to such stimulations'.[32] In this passage Freud certainly means *man* and not *mankind*. Aggression was the one instinct he picked out as being unequally shared between the sexes, observing – in a lecture entitled 'The Psychology of Women' – that 'one particularly constant' feature of women's instinctual life is the 'suppression of [. . .] aggressiveness which is prescribed for them constitutionally and imposed on them socially'.[33] This suggestion that there is a 'fighting instinct' (*TG* 311) which is almost exclusively expressed in adult men agrees with Woolf's depiction of WW1 as a destructive, patriarchal activity. *Three Guineas* partially concurs, initially stating:

> though many instincts are held more or less in common by both sexes, to fight has always been the man's habit, not the woman's. Law and practice have developed that difference, whether innate or accidental. Scarcely a human being in the course of history has fallen to a woman's rifle. (*TG* 120)

There are nuanced similarities and differences between Woolf and Freud's formulation of the 'fighting instinct'. Woolf's observation that '[l]aw and practice' have separated the genders' instinctual responses agrees with Freud's finding that women's aggression is suppressed both 'constitutionally' and 'socially'. Both also accept that this 'fighting instinct' can be 'stimulated' or 'developed'. However, while Freud goes on to postulate that the feminine suppression of aggression typically becomes internalised as masochistic behaviour, Woolf looks for an active and outward-looking female counterpart to male hostility – motherhood.

Bearing in mind the destructive view of maternity that Woolf formulated when writing *The Waves*, it comes as little surprise when *Three Guineas* pairs motherhood with aggression by stating that: 'fighting [. . .] is a sex characteristic which she cannot share, the counterpart some claim of the maternal instinct which he cannot share' (*TG* 232). Contradicting her own claim that: 'Scarcely a human being in the course of history has fallen to a woman's rifle', Woolf goes on to cement the connection between fighting and maternity in a footnote. This note recounts the following interview with a Spanish Civil War militiawoman:

> Where were you born? – In Granada – Why have you joined the army? – My two daughters were militiawomen. The younger has been killed in the Alto de Leon. I thought I had to supersede her and

Motherhood and Psychoanalysis   **237**

avenge her. – And how many enemies have you killed to avenge her? – You know it, commandant, five. The sixth is not sure. (*TG* 311)

This woman who has killed at least five people is first and foremost a mother, pushed to violence by the death of her child; however, her ethnicity complicates the association. As a Spaniard and Granadan, the militiawoman is wild and othered like one of *Orlando*'s Gypsies, she is – as Abbi Bardi notes of Woolf's Gypsy trope – 'a ready-made challenge to the nineteenth century project of disciplining gender and sexuality'.[34] Viewed through the colonial, patriarchal gaze of both a group of English parliamentary observers and the author (French war correspondent Louis Delaprée), the woman is described as 'a fauve', a term which can be read as either a wild animal or a wildly vibrant piece of art – although the addition of the words 'of an unknown species' (*TG* 311) favours the former.

While the links between motherhood and fighting are clear in this footnote there remain questions over how universal this violence might be and whether an Englishwoman would be capable of it. Luckily *Three Guineas* was not the last time Woolf examined the maternal and fighting instincts, revisiting this link – with more of a focus on her own social sphere – in the 1940 essay 'Thoughts on Peace in an Air Raid'. A significant passage debates the possibility of restricting these instincts for English men and women:

The young airman up in the sky is driven not only by the voices of loudspeakers; he is driven by voices in himself – ancient instincts, instincts fostered and cherished by education and tradition. Is he to be blamed for those instincts? Could we switch off the maternal instinct at the command of a table full of politicians? Suppose that imperative among the peace terms was: 'Childbearing is to be restricted to a very small class of specially selected women,' would we submit? Should we not say, 'The maternal instinct is a woman's glory. It was for this that my whole life has been dedicated, my education, training, everything . . . ' But if it were necessary for the sake of humanity, for the peace of the world, that childbearing should be restricted, the maternal instinct subdued, women would attempt it. Men would help them. They would honour them for their refusal to bear children. They would give them other openings for their creative power. That too must make part of our fight for freedom. We must help the young Englishmen to root out from themselves the love of medals and decorations. We must create more honourable activities for those who try to conquer in themselves their fighting instinct. (*E6* 244)

238   *Virginia Woolf and Motherhood*

The tone of this passage is unclear. Given Woolf's frequent denigration of maternity and her practised irony it would not be difficult to read sarcasm into these questions around giving up motherhood. Bearing in mind her negative feelings about the Versailles Treaty, suggesting abstinence as a part of 'peace terms' also seems incongruous. However, while there may be some satirical elements the argument is not mere idle sarcasm, nor were these ideas about refashioning the instincts spontaneous. Some months earlier, while corresponding with education reformer Lady Shena Simon, Woolf had speculated: 'Can one change sex characteristics? How far is the women's movement a remarkable experiment in that transformation? Mustn't our next task be the emancipation of man? How can we alter the crest and the spur of the fighting cock?' (*L6* 379). Given that Woolf is talking about gendered behaviours it seems reasonable to conclude that she considered the achievements of 'the women's movement' to include not only financial, political and professional participation, but also the elective freedom from motherhood that enabled such advances. Just as women were becoming free from maternity and able to realise other achievements, so, Woolf reasoned, might men be made free from patriarchally endorsed and instinctually satisfying endeavours such as war-making.

Catriona Livingstone notes that these questions relate back to a segment of *The Science of Life*, which, Woolf recorded in her diary, was about a 'hen that became a cock or vice versa' (*D4* 68–69).[35] However it is also an inquiry into the science of psychoanalysis: the rigour of Freud's theories and to what extent the instincts might prevent strategic social evolution. A month before writing the letter Woolf had noted in her diary: 'Freud is upsetting: reducing one to whirlpool [. . .] If we're all instinct, the unconscious, whats all this about civilisation, the whole man, freedom &c?' (*D5* 250). In recording his ideas Freud was particularly self-assured and left little space for doubting or self-reflection, in addition Woolf's own struggle with motherhood had shown her that defying the 'maternal instinct' was an arduous task. Yet, as she found herself once again suffering through an international war, she felt that questions of how the instincts might be mutable and managed were key not only to the balance of maternity and autonomy but also to helping safeguard the future of humanity.

In an effort to find a remedy for war, 'Thoughts on Peace in an Air Raid' posits art as the antithesis of both motherhood and aggression.[36] Just as Woolf imagines men helping women subdue 'the maternal instinct' by giving 'them other openings for their creative power' so she counsels that to free man from his aggressive instincts, 'we must give him access to the creative feelings' (*E6* 245). This juxtaposition of art and instinct is a continuation of the contrasting themes of creativity and procreativity that this book has found woven throughout Woolf's writing. Here however, the issue is mediated through the psychoanalytic theory that was becoming an integral part of her work. Woolf's two spheres of creativity and procreativity (or fighting) broadly map on to the two competing drives that were a foundational part of Freud's philosophy – Eros (or life) and destruction (or death). In *Civilization and Its Discontents* Freud explains the two drives in the following way:

> beside the instinct preserving the organic substance and binding it into ever larger units, there must exist another in antithesis to this, which would seek to dissolve these units and reinstate their antecedent inorganic state; that is to say, a death instinct as well as Eros; the phenomena of life would then be explicable from the interplay of the two and their counteracting effects on each other.[37]

Woolf's conception of creativity – an activity which promotes all that is promising in oneself and society – and procreativity – a personally and socially damaging pursuit – echo these life and death drives. While it may seem somewhat illogical to associate procreation – the very thing that sustains human life on earth – with a chaotic 'death' drive, Woolf was used to appropriating the parts of ideologies that suited her purpose. It is worth noting that Freud did not see artistic creativity as a quality of Eros since it does not preserve life or cause the proliferation of organic material; instead he saw the making of art as a form of wish-fulfilment (similar to dreaming). Nonetheless both saw, in their distinctive way, a chance to reroute aggression and offer social cohesion. Just as *Three Guineas* offers creativity as an antidote for the destructive instincts, *Why War?* observes that although the 'complete suppression' of aggression is impossible, such tendencies might be diverted by its 'counter-agent, Eros'.[38]

Woolf also comments on Freud's theory of the instincts in a draft of *Between the Acts*, written from 1938 onwards. While the entire novel is highly influenced by psychoanalytic theory one particular passage connects psychoanalysis and neurology. In this scene two central characters, Giles Oliver and Mrs Manresa, pursue each other while watched by Giles's wife Isa. This threesome is observed by a local man named Owen Felkin, who thinks:

> Terms like 'disgusting' were uncalled for. There was nothing obscure in the processes revealed by the slicing of the brain. He had seen through men of action from about the age of seventeen [. . .] why apply heated terms to insects impelled automatically to go through

240 *Virginia Woolf and Motherhood*

> certain gestures? As for the female counterpart of the man of action, he knew them; the Manresas; bubbling cauldrons of impure emotions [. . .] here he jerked round and cast his unimpassioned intellect upon Isa – a woman with a child. Off came her surface, and under it was the lioness with the cub; greed, unscrupulous maternal greed. (*PH* 115–16)

While this passage is deeply ironic and shows a particularly inflexible view of human endeavours, its reference to 'the slicing of the brain' also showcases Woolf's awareness of contemporary neuroscience. The 1930s saw considerable leaps forward in the understanding of the brain. In Germany, Josef Klingler developed a technique for freezing and dissecting brain matter. There were experiments into curing epilepsy by splitting the two sides of the brain and research presented at the 1935 Second International Neurologic Congress in London led to the first lobotomies. *The Science of Life* covered some of these scientific breakthroughs with illustrations such as 'a slice of the cerebrum' and reference to

> the mysteries of that coating of grey matter upon the outside of the cerebrum, which is the seat of Mr. Everyman's dreams and desires, the vehicle of his imagination, the medium of his joys and sorrows, the most important stuff in the universe for every human being.[39]

Mr Felkin's belief that neuroscience reveals 'nothing obscure' is extreme when compared to the scientific textbook's appreciation for the 'mysteries' of the brain. The passage is also a pastiche on the Freudian assuredness that, once under analysis, the human mind could be read like an open book.[40] Felkin is an unusual name and Woolf perhaps knew of Dr Robert Felkin, medical missionary and occultist, whose book title *Hypnotism, or Psycho-Therapeutics* (1890) influenced Freud's development of the term psychoanalysis.[41] Felkin not only parodies Freudian psychoanalysis but also revisits two Weiningerian categories that Woolf had used in earnest in *The Waves*: Manresa as the highly sexualised 'Courtesan' and Isa as the aggressive 'Mother'. Despite Woolf's earnest use of archetypes in the earlier novel, Felkin's estimation that instincts are fixed and cause humans to become character-types contrasts starkly with *Between the Act*'s careful and individual character-building. This passage was written just before Woolf's dinner with Klein and the writing of 'A Sketch of the Past' and, read together, the posthumously published novel and the memoir show an important development in Woolf's thinking about maternity. This seems to have been the moment when Klein's theories became a source of inspiration and both works reflect this. Not only do they engage in a Kleinian exploration of the role that mothers play in the individual's development, they also show Woolf's attempt at fictionally recreating the formation of the human psyche.

'My own case': Kleinian Theory and Self-Analysis in 'A Sketch of the Past'

In April 1939 Woolf was predominantly working on *Roger Fry* but decided to take breaks in the biography to make an attempt at some memoirs. The result, 'A Sketch of the Past', is a work which attempts to 'analyse' 'the invisible presences who [. . .] play so important a part in every life' (*MB* 92). 'A Sketch' begins with Woolf's two earliest memories and a short description of her family history. She is almost flippant about this introduction, declaring that she starts 'without stopping to choose my way' (*MB* 78). However, the decision to begin with these first memories, to – as John Rickman's notes in his introduction to an essay by Klein – trace 'things in the adult back to their origins in infancy', is an active, and psychoanalytically led choice.[42] *Roger Fry* also begins 'before he became conscious' (*RF* 11) and includes, in the first few pages, a description of his family history and his two earliest and most emotive memories. This suggests that Woolf had already been thinking of how to look back into an individual's past and present them as a subject rather than memorialise them as a 'person to whom things happened' (*MB* 79).

Woolf's first two memories relate to her mother and embody Klein's theory of how mother–child relationships impact psychological development. In the first, the infant Virginia is sitting on Julia's lap and looking at 'the flowers she was wearing very close' in their 'purple and red and blue' (*MB* 78). Without attempting to psychoanalyse the memory, Woolf's position suggests that she is staring at her mother's breasts. This is the body part that both Klein and Freud define as a child's primary love object, with Klein stating: 'The child's early attachment to his mother's breast and to her milk is the foundation of all love relations in life' (*LHR* 90).[43] Woolf's second memory is of the nursery at St Ives and identified as 'the most important of all my memories'. It is a joyous recollection of 'feeling the purest ecstasy I can conceive'. Initially the second memory seems unrelated to the first since Woolf is in the nursery alone. However, when the text returns to the scene a page later, Woolf recalls, in a way typical

242   *Virginia Woolf and Motherhood*

of the thought association of psychoanalysis, that the nursery had a balcony which joined that of her parents' room. She notes: 'My mother would come out onto her balcony in a white dressing gown. There were passion flowers growing on the wall [. . .] great starry blossoms, with purple streaks' (*MB* 78–79). Not only are the flowers in both memories connected to Julia (and her breasts) but the second memory evokes her in a very private way – in her dressing gown on her balcony.

By tying her first two memories firmly back to her mother and reiterating the 'ecstasy' of the moments, Woolf engages in a conversation with Klein's 1937 essay 'Love, Guilt and Reparation' – the original of which was in the Woolf's library. Hogarth Press printed 'Love, Guilt and Reparation' alongside Joan Riviera's 'Hate, Greed and Aggression' and together – as a book titled *Love, Hate and Reparation* – they form a pair of Kleinian treatises about the roots of adult love and hate. Klein's essay begins by describing the baby's attachment to the mother. Unlike Freud, who predominantly cast the breastfeeding stage of the baby's development in a negative light (calling it the oral or cannibalistic stage and associating it with frightening images of eating, or being eaten by, a love object), Klein allows for positive associations between the baby and its mother. She describes how an infant who 'is being gratified by the breast' might, when not feeding, still have 'phantasies of a pleasant kind in relation to it' and notes: 'the baby who feels a craving for his mother's breast when it is not there may imagine it to be there, i.e. he may imagine the satisfaction which he derives from it'. Klein associates such 'primitive phantasying' with 'imaginative thinking', explaining it as 'the earliest form of the capacity which later develops into the more elaborate workings of the imagination' (*LHR* 60–61). Woolf's focus on the 'ecstasy' of her early memories may, therefore, have something to do with the importance she attached to her artistic vocation. She describes the sights, sounds and impressions of her second memory as a glorious riot of colour and shape, recording them as if she 'were a painter' (*MB* 79) who uses words as her artistic medium. The pleasure of these memories – a third memory is equally euphoric – and the intensity of Woolf's childhood feelings (both positive and, later, negative) speak to her active imagination and her lifelong passion for creating literary art.

While recording her first, maternal-centric memories Woolf wonders why some reminiscences linger and others fade. She asks: 'Why remember the hum of bees in the garden going down to the beach, and forget completely being thrown naked by father into the sea?' (*MB* 83). Within her earliest memories, the central place of Julia and the relative absence of Leslie corresponds with Klein's insistence

Motherhood and Psychoanalysis **243**

on the primacy of the mother–child relationship. 'Love, Guilt and Reparation' notes:

> Because our mother first satisfied all our self-preservative needs and sensual desires and gave us security, the part she plays in our minds is a lasting one [. . .] The very important part which the father plays in the child's emotional life also influences all later love relations [. . .] But the baby's early relation to him, in so far as he is felt as a gratifying, friendly and protective figure, is partly modelled on the one to the mother. (*LHR 59*)

While Woolf's claim 'we think back through our mothers' (*AROO 69*) may have been a reference to a literary matriarchy, she seemed to welcome Klein's proposal of maternal predominance in early memories. Indeed, Woolf may have been attracted to Klein's work because she saw things from a much more gynocentric position – maintaining Freud's innovation while moving the focus away from the role of penis-envy in female development.

Following on from Woolf's early memories, the next few pages of 'A Sketch' contain a section that is particularly evocative of both psychoanalytic theory and form. Because its practitioners and theorists identified as scientists and because of the dominating influence of Freud, early psychoanalytic writing has a distinct formal style. Case studies in the form of 'Neurotic' episodes or responses are 'analysed' through the use of memories, language-correlations and dreams to uncover their juvenile source.[44] Woolf had long been aware of this writing with its word, theme and image associations. Years earlier she had mockingly written to Molly MacCarthy:

> we are publishing all Dr Freud, and I glance at the proof and read how Mr A. B. threw a bottle of red ink on to the sheets of his marriage bed to excuse his impotence to the housemaid, but threw it in the wrong place, which unhinged his wife's mind, – and to this day she pours claret on the dinner table. (*L3 134–35*)

While this letter shows Woolf's earlier contempt for such Freudian analysis, by the time of writing her memoirs she was clearly interested in its potential. This is verified by her essay 'The Leaning Tower' (1940) which notes of modern authors:

> The leaning-tower writer [. . .] has had the courage to tell the truth, the unpleasant truth, about himself [. . .] By analysing themselves honestly, with help from Dr Freud, these writers have done a great

deal to free us from nineteenth-century suppressions. The writers of the next generation may inherit from them a whole state of mind, a mind no longer crippled, evasive, divided. They may inherit that unconsciousness which [. . .] is necessary if writers are to get beneath the surface, and to write something that people remember when they are alone. (*E6* 274)

Woolf saw psychoanalysis as a step forward in the evolution of writing. She felt that using psychoanalytic techniques to build characters or write autobiography might not only change literature but might also offer readers a way out of society's shared stagnation.

Woolf experiments with this theory in 'A Sketch' by offering an 'analysis' of her 'own case'. Here she explores her anxiety around mirrors – an unease that originated with 'a small looking-glass in the hall at Talland House'. Initially she builds up a picture of herself as a slightly older child. She writes: 'Later we add to feelings much that makes them more complex; and therefore less strong; or if not less strong, less isolated, less complete'. This aligns with psychoanalytic ideas about the development of the ego – as Freud notes, 'primitive impulses undergo a lengthy process of development [. . .] They are inhibited, directed towards other aims and fields, become commingled'.[45] The passage that follows explains Woolf's shameful feelings about the mirror at Talland House and then describes her adult discomfort with mirrors, femininity and dress in general. Next Woolf offers an associated 'memory, also of the hall', which, she notes, 'may help to explain' the 'looking-glass' shame. This memory is of Gerald Duckworth sexually abusing her when she was small – a highly emotional experience which may have caused the mirror to act as a trigger. Finally, the passage recounts a dream in which a 'horrible face' looks over Woolf's shoulder as she stares into a mirror.

The 'looking-glass' passage is in conversation with Freud in several ways. By connecting the experience with some sort of 'ancestral dread' or 'instincts already acquired by thousands of ancestresses in the past' Woolf furthers her investigation of the instincts and their genetic quality. Dream association is also incredibly important here, using dreams was not only one of Freud's earliest methods of analysis but was, as noted, an important introduction for both Leonard and Virginia to his work. In addition, Woolf's mention of her grandfather's liking for cigars – and his subsequent puritanical self-denial – may be a nod to Freud. While only a casual remark, Freud was famous for his cigar addiction and most photographs pictured him holding one (although Hogarth Press chose to use headshots without a cigar in their frontispieces). This addiction caused the mouth cancer which troubled him in his final years and took his life.[46] The passage also has several moments of the type of free association that Freud valued. Not only is the 'looking-glass' shame associated with the hallway, Gerald and the sexual abuse, but there is a moment of word association (although Woolf does not point it out). The hallway mirror had 'a ledge' and Gerald stood her upon a similar item: 'a slab [. . .] for standing dishes upon' (*MB* 81–83). Later, in a letter to Ethel Smyth, Woolf also calls this 'slab' 'a ledge' (*L6* 459–60).

As an emotive moment in the text it is unsurprising that the 'looking-glass' passage has caused a wide range of interpretations.[47] Woolf's motivation for writing it can be found in her letter to Smyth, where she explains:

> as so much of life is sexual – or so they say – it rather limits autobiography if this is blacked out. It must be, I suspect, for many generations, for women [. . .] a painful operation, and I suppose connected with all sorts of subterranean instincts. I still shiver with shame at the memory of my half brother, standing me on a ledge, aged about 6, and so exploring my private parts. (*L6* 459–60)

Here, the 'they' who say 'so much of life is sexual' are, of course, psychoanalysts. Woolf's admission that recounting this memory in autobiographical form is 'painful' shows her willingness to engage in what she describes as 'auto-analysis' (*D5* 226). Such recollections required Woolf to have, like the leaning-tower writer, 'the courage to tell the truth, the unpleasant truth' and she did this to help the next generation. While she did not publish (or even finish) these memoirs in her lifetime, they influenced – and were influenced by – the fiction she was writing at the time. Not only are these Freudian experiments in radical autobiography transformed into *Between the Acts*' atmosphere of candid, physical sexuality, but also a Kleinian focus on mother–child relationships can be seen in the formative (and often hidden) connections that the novel's characters have with their mothers.

'Something hidden': Psychoanalysis and Mothers in *Between the Acts*

Vicki Tromanhauser notes that Woolf wrote *Between the Acts* to 'shed light upon the "scaffolding in the background" against which civilized life defines itself and to illuminate the figures who function

246 *Virginia Woolf and Motherhood*

as its support, those unrecognized parts of ourselves which may in fact be at our very center'.[48] Tromanhauser hits on something incredibly important with her use of the word 'center' here. 'A Sketch' repeatedly refers to Julia as central: she is 'omnipresent [. . .] the creator of that crowded merry world which spun so gaily in the centre of my childhood' (*MB* 95–96). In *Between the Acts* Woolf uses this maternal centrality – one of the founding principles of object-relations psychoanalysis – to fashion her main characters. Developing an understanding of these maternally influenced character profiles offers an opportunity to reassess these characters' relationships to each other and their fictional world.

There are numerous allusions to psychoanalysis throughout *Between the Acts* and even more in its *Pointz Hall* drafts. In the first draft, for example, a pipe-smoking character (reminiscent of Woolf's cigar-loving grandfather), resents 'the suggestion [. . .] that what binds us to life are the bodily pleasures [. . .] smoking; eating; drinking; and other pleasures lodged in us so that the human race may continue' (*PH* 93). In the published version – which is, of course, itself a late draft – an audience member thinks of Miss La Trobe's pageant: 'Did she mean, so to speak, something hidden, the unconscious as they call it? But why always drag in sex' (*BA* 118). This thought could be expanded and applied to the entire novel, since a psychoanalytically inspired focus on sex is an important element of its narrative and influences much of its imagery. In her exploration of nature in *Between the Acts*, for example, Harriet Blodgett notes how Woolf writes animals into the action in order to mirror, and thus call attention to, the 'compulsive sexuality' of its human characters.[49]

Within the novel, Woolf highlights the immediacy and psychic resonance of repressed human sexuality during Lucy Swithin and visitor William Dodge's tour of Pointz Hall:

> She tapped twice very distinctly on a door. With her head on one side, she listened.
> 'One never knows,' she murmured, 'if there's somebody there.'
> Then she flung open the door.
> He half expected to see somebody there, naked, or half dressed, or knelt in prayer. But the room was empty. The room was tidy as a pin, not slept in for months, a spare room. (*BA* 44)

It is interesting that in this scene Woolf associates sexuality and nakedness with prayer. This brings to mind Freud's theories in *Totem and Taboo* and *Moses and Monotheism* linking religious practice

Motherhood and Psychoanalysis 247

with repressed sexuality and, indeed, Lucy is the character in the book who repeatedly engages in spiritual sentiment. This moment was rewritten several times, suggesting that Woolf felt it important to perfect the sense of unnerving expectation and the heavy psychic weight of the room. In the published version Lucy Swithin notes that she was born in the room, while in one draft version she describes it as 'this sort of room. Where, in fact, [my] many things have happened. [My] Wasn't I born here? I rather think so. Born in the flesh' (*PH* 478). In a further draft version of the end of the book William reflects on the intimacy of the house tour and wants to thank Lucy for seeing 'what might have been, if he had been her lover; when she had shown him the house' (*PH* 547).

This scene also brings to mind a description of Woolf's own parents' bedroom found in 'A Sketch':

> the double bedded bedroom on the first floor was the sexual centre; the birth centre, the death centre of the house. It was not a large room; but its walls must be soaked, if walls take pictures and hoard up what is done and said with all that was most intense, of all that makes the most private being, of family life. In that bed four children were begotten; there they were born; there first mother died; then father died, with a picture of mother hanging in front of him. (*MB* 125)

Woolf imagines that the intimate memories of these rooms, which welcome birth, sexual union and finally death, leave as resonating a physical impression as they do a mental one. In the novel, the tour of these private parts of the house continues with the nursery – which Lucy describes as 'the cradle of the race' (*BA* 45). Here the reader glances where an individual begins their journey of character formation or, as Lucy might say, are born in the mind. As the child ages there are also formative moments which occur outside the nursery. Woolf includes an example of this in the novel with Mrs Haines, who recalls how 'she had never feared cows, only horses. But, then, as a small child in a perambulator, a great cart-horse had brushed within an inch of her face' (*BA* 5). There is also a significant formative incident in which Bart Oliver surprises and terrifies his grandson George. This moment is recounted several times and is described as having 'destroyed the little boy's world' (*BA* 120).

Some critics have argued that a sense of hopelessness pervades *Between the Acts*. Alex Zwerdling, for example, not only records 'the increasing grimness' of Woolf's work from *The Years* onwards but also determines that by the time she wrote the novel 'the concept

248   *Virginia Woolf and Motherhood*

of a gradual improvement either in history or in human relationships had been decisively rejected'.[50] As one of the mainstays of the novel, psychoanalysis contributes to its social critique; however, Woolf's enthusiasm for psychoanalytic theory also implies at least some optimism. Not only does it afford her the chance to tell the 'truth about [her] own experiences as a body' (*E6* 483) but *Between the Acts*' Freudian focus on human sexuality and 'Eros' also offers an opportunity to reinvent that artistic creativity which, throughout Woolf's writing, produces moments of (fleeting) unity. As Blodgett observes, while the 'novel recognizes that our deep-seated natural drives may be potent force for evil', the creative energy of its central pageant proves 'that we have our virtues too'. This creativity stands as a positive alternative to the shadowy threat of war in both the book and the real world. Interestingly, Blodgett reflects that this bonding, fruitful energy can be both procreative *and* creative. She notes that the novel is 'both a demonstration of – and a book about – creative power' in which 'our creativity, a primordial force, expresses itself physically in procreation [. . .] and spiritually in the building of civilizations and art, with their ability in turn to effect continuity and some sense of harmony, if only transitorily'.[51] An example of this can be seen when the 'dumb yearning' of a herd of cows rescues the pageant in a moment of paralysis and failure (*BA* 85). In the first draft Woolf writes that the herd's 'primeval voice' – stirred, initially, by a cow that has lost her calf – does what 'no poet could have done; annihilated the gap; bridged the distance; filled the emptiness'. She concludes this passage with an ambivalent phrase – 'Either it was maternal passion [. . .] or Eros had plated his dart' (*PH* 138–39) – and grants a moment of accord between the procreative and creative drives.

It is necessary to note that it is only animals that are afforded this equilibrium of maternity and artistry. In fact, the novel's human creative force, Miss La Trobe, is emphatically not a maternal figure. The first draft reveals that she had a baby at 'the age of eighteen, through no fault of her own' (*PH* 78). Since the child is no longer present, and she has reinvented herself several times, presumably it was adopted, abandoned or died: indeed, the closest that the present-day La Trobe gets to procreation is breeding dogs. As an artist, a lesbian and a woman who has conceived through rape, La Trobe's animal husbandry is not motherly but rather a comment on the value that patriarchal society places on its sexual control of women, domestic animals and other nations (reminiscent of *A Room of One's Own*'s Blaise Pascal quote: 'Ce chien est à moi' (*AROO* 46)). La Trobe's back story is echoed in the newspaper article that Isa Oliver reads

Motherhood and Psychoanalysis **249**

about the horse with a green tail. This is a reference to the 1938 case of a young girl who was raped by soldiers at the Whitehall barracks, became pregnant and was openly given an abortion by a surgeon despite its illegality.[52] Isa reads this article when looking for some reading material which might offer a 'remedy' (*BA* 14) to her situation as a domesticated woman and a citizen of a country on the brink of war. She searches the library shelves for something she might relate to, but when she finally falls to reading the article it offers nothing but a critique of the armed forces and excessive masculine libidinous energy. These direct references to rape are singular in Woolf's fiction and, although La Trobe's youth is expunged from the final draft, they once again reflect the prominence of psychoanalysis and sex.

That art and motherhood are only complementary for animals reconfirms Woolf's assertion that it is civilisation – especially patriarchal civilisation – that distorts and corrupts maternity. This is supported by other negative visions of British, upper-middle-class motherhood, which are as prevalent in this novel as elsewhere in Woolf's writing. Isa, the novel's mother character, is enraged and fettered by motherhood. She insists that her maternity does not define her, and her children are described as a 'strait waistcoat' (*BA* 65), yet she is overcome by the compunction to care for, think about or see them and the desire to create more. Woolf builds maternal imagery into Isa's narrative. In the first scene, for example, she sits on a 'three-cornered chair' (*BA* 6) which brings to mind a birthing stool (this also brings to mind *Three Guineas*' notes on the pervasive 'sadism' (*TG* 268) that pollutes obstetrics). Art and motherhood is firmly juxtaposed when Isa hides her 'abortive' poetry (*BA* 12) from her husband by writing it in a book intended for her domestic accounts. Lucy Swithin, meanwhile, takes up the mantle of Woolf's unmaternal characters. Her brother finds it hard to imagine that she has had children, she is a figure of fun to the domestic staff and she is an ineffective gardener/farmer. Pointz Hall's crop of apricots are ruined by wasps when she decides not to net them because they are 'so beautiful, naked, with one flushed cheek, one green' (*BA* 34).

While broad references to both psychoanalysis and motherhood can be readily found within the novel, the main focus of this study – Woolf's psychoanalytically informed character-building – is much more veiled. Though Zwerdling observes that the 'major characters in *Between the Acts* are substantially less complex than those in Woolf's previous novels [. . .] because they are treated as component parts of a larger organism', in fact, there are developmental histories hidden beneath the surface of each individual.[53] These relationships predominantly revolve around that character's primary love object – their mothers – and are often revealed soon after the individual has been introduced. However, many details of these bonds are only included in the earlier drafts and then expunged. John Whittier-Ferguson notes that the drafts of *Between the Acts* grow 'more elliptical, less discursive, less explanatory with each revision' and that it is 'a novel in which conversations unravel and characters become more opaque as Woolf reworks them'.[54] This is a creative decision that brings to life those questions in 'A Sketch' concerning how remembering or forgetting childhood events might affect our character and relationship with the world. Similar queries are also articulated in the Reverend Streatfield's post-pageant speech, which states: 'Speaking merely as one of the audience, I confess I was puzzled. For what reason, I asked, were we shown these scenes? [. . .] A few were chosen; the many passed in the background'. In fact, under the influence of psychoanalysis, Woolf chose to erase formative facts about her characters and leave in 'scraps, orts and fragments' (*BA* 114) in order to create a novel that was more realistic and ambiguous than she had ever attempted before.

The most thought-provoking characters for this study of motherhood are those within the rural, upper-middle-class Oliver family. This is comprised of patriarch Bartholomew Oliver, his sister Lucy Swithin, Giles (who is Bart's son), and Isa, Giles's wife. As the adult child Giles Oliver is particularly interesting for a psychoanalytic study because, even though he has lost his mother, he has active relationships with his surviving elders, wife and children. Zwerdling notes that Giles spends the novel 'in a state of suppressed rage'. He is angry at the 'old fogies who sat and looked at views over coffee and cream' (*BA* 34), at William Dodge because of his sexuality, he is even 'furiously in love' with his wife.[55] The main object of Giles's ire, however, is his aunt Lucy and the text records that he hangs 'his grievances on her, as one hangs a coat on a hook, instinctively' (*BA* 30). This is not simply a case of the '[s]trong feeling' experienced with Grensted's 'infantile fixation'; rather, Giles is suffering from a much more Kleinian crisis, the loss of his mother when he was a small infant. Although only the first draft reveals this 'great tragedy, Claire's death in India from typhoid when Giles was a baby' (*PH* 118).[56]

Experiencing such a catastrophic event at a formative moment in infancy has had grave effects on Giles's emotional responses. In 'Love, Guilt and Reparation' Klein explains how, during early development, an infant experiences 'destructive phantasies' towards the primary love object in which 'he wishes to bite up and to tear up his mother and her breasts'. These 'phantasies' are followed by fear- and guilt-induced periods in which the child imagines putting the mother back together. Klein argues that children must come to terms with these conflicting feelings of love and hate in order to live happy and emotionally stable lives. However, if this process goes awry 'these basic conflicts profoundly influence the course and the force of the emotional lives of grown-up individuals' (*LHR* 61). In other words, if a mother were to disappear at this stage – as Giles's mother has – it would derail the child's psychic development and thus, the way they, as an adult, relate to others. 'Love, Guilt and Reparation' also discusses the child who has never resolved the feelings of depravation experienced during weaning, who:

> may not have given up his intense desire for his first food, may not have got over the grievances and hatred at having been deprived of it, nor have adapted himself in the real sense to this frustration – and if this be so, he may not be able to adapt himself truly to any other frustrations which follow in life. (*LHR* 90)

Having lost his mother early enough that he would have still been nursing, Giles is filled with 'grievances and hatred'. He has never learned to 'adapt himself' or have appropriate responses in his social interactions. It follows that he reserves the bulk of his anger for Lucy. As a mother-figure without the advantage of a mother–child bond she elicits his most primitive feelings but cannot claim his love.

Another significant part of Giles's narrative is his infidelity. Klein notes that adultery is a form of 'defence' which may be seen in people whose main emotional expression is 'hatred'. An adulterer is described as an adult male 'haunted by the dread of the death of loved people', especially 'his mother, whose death he dreaded because he felt his love for her to be greedy and destructive' (*LHR* 86). Klein explains that when a mother disappears from a baby's life at the stage where he is experiencing 'destructive phantasies', the child believes himself to be culpable and concludes that his love must be harmful. For Klein, infidelity does not mean that a man does not love his wife; in fact, the more he loves her, the more he fears that his love might endanger her and so he distances himself by forming new romantic relationships.

Giles's other important attachment is to his father, whom he loves. The stability of their relationship suggests that Giles has managed to mature through at least the paternal portion of his emotional development. Similarly, Bart loves his son and sees his anger. However, in

252   *Virginia Woolf and Motherhood*

typical Victorian manner Bart makes no attempt to bring Giles's pain out into the open or heal it. When they have company Bart ironically thinks: 'The family was not a family in the presence of strangers' and makes light small talk instead. As a character Bart is entirely different to his son. Notwithstanding the strain of ageing he is largely self-satisfied and confident in his own opinions. His inner world is described using the imagery of a river and others affect this ceaseless, interminable flow so lightly that when Isa enters the room in the first draft: 'Her father-in-law felt as if a flower had been dropped into his stream. No more than that' (*PH* 36). Just as Giles's mother's absence is responsible for his furious interactions with the world, so Bart's mother's affectionate presence is the cause of this self-assurance. The novel offers a short passage on their relationship:

> 'I remember,' the old man interrupted, 'my mother . . . ' Of his mother he remembered that she was very stout; kept her tea-caddy locked; yet had given him in that very room a copy of Byron. It was over sixty years ago, he told them, that his mother had given him the works of Byron in that very room. He paused.
> 'She walks in beauty like the night,' he quoted. (*BA* 6)

The allusion to a gift of Byron and the sentimental quote show that, no matter what her shortfalls might have been – the stoutness and the locked tea caddy suggest a strict and domestic maternal nature – Bart and his mother shared a romantic love.[57] In 'The Psychology of Women' Freud discusses the nature of a mother's love for her son, stating: 'The only thing that brings a mother undiluted satisfaction is her relation to a son; it is quite the most complete relationship between human beings, and the one that is the most free from ambivalence'.[58] This love reaches its zenith when the child, like Bart, is the only son. Freud's account of Goethe's childhood – in which all of his siblings bar one sister died in infancy – attributes the polymath's great success to his mother's uninterrupted love, and notes: 'he who has been the undisputed darling of his mother retains throughout life that victorious feeling, that confidence in ultimate success'.[59]

Further Freudian theories concerning the sexual nature of family relationships can be seen in Bart's bond with Lucy, the unusual character of which has drawn the attention of critics. In the notes to the *Pointz Hall* drafts, for example, Mitchell Leaska observes that a 'Byron legend' (*PH* 39) that Bart recalls 'is almost certainly in part the legend of Byron's incestuous union with his half-sister' (*PH* 194). In addition, during an enthusiastic conversation about the pageant with Miss La

Trobe, the text notes that Lucy 'revealed' an 'unacted part' of herself '... Cleopatra' (*BA* 92). It was customary for Egyptian royals to marry their siblings and Cleopatra was no different, marrying two of her brothers in addition to her famous affairs with Julius Caesar and Mark Antony. Sexual tension can be read in a visceral and emotive early memory that Lucy and Bart share in which she unhooks a fish he has caught. The passage states: 'The blood had shocked her – "Oh!" she had cried – for the gills were full of blood' (*BA* 15). Blood has many sexual connotations and within Woolf's oeuvre fish are often connected to passion or are, as Heather Levy writes, 'a secret password for intimacy'.[60] Leaska notes that Woolf associated fish with 'the early and most intense days' of her ardour for Vita Sackville-West (*PH* 197) and Giles and Isa also meet and begin their love affair while fishing. Woolf's aim here is not to insinuate that Bart and Lucy have an incestuous relationship – Lucy's role as Cleopatra is 'unacted' – but rather to expose the type of incestuous feelings that psychoanalysis sees in all brother–sister bonds. As Klein observes, in a conventional family environment 'sexual desires and phantasies' (*LHR* 89) grow between siblings and close cousins as their development progresses. A draft passage confirms that Woolf was thinking along these lines, with William Dodge contemplating 'how brothers and sisters in the 19th century were different'; directly comparing Bart to Lucy's late husband – whom he calls 'a most suitable match'; and observing of Lucy that she is preoccupied with Bart in such a way that her actions 'always' state '"I follow my brother", as if they were girl & boy in a meadow; & it was her part to [...] <bait the line> – if they fished' (*PH* 547).

Lucy and Bart's sibling status also offers an opportunity to observe how different children react to the same mother. When the reader is first introduced to Lucy, waking up in the bedroom that had previously been her mother's, the text states: 'she remembered her mother – her mother in that very room rebuking her. "Don't stand gaping, Lucy, or the wind'll change ... " How often her mother had rebuked her in that very room' (*BA* 8). This relationship is at odds with Bart's mother–child bond, and the drafts go even further, with Lucy remembering her mother as a critical voice who 'imprinted' 'social morality' (*PH* 43) on her. The word 'imprinted' brings to mind another important scientific discovery of the mid-1930s; animal behaviourist Konrad Lorenz's work on neonatal attachment in geese. By using such language Woolf suggests that Lucy's mother passes on patriarchal social ethics involuntarily, in the same way that animals pass on their social behaviours. Lorenz found that geese follow their mothers because they are the first animal they see and that this bond is irrevers-

254   *Virginia Woolf and Motherhood*

ible for a critical period of their development. This attachment vastly differs from the Freudian model of infant bonding, a contrast which sheds light on the difficult relationship Lucy has with her mother. In 'The Psychology of Women' Freud states that, unlike geese, a fundamental moment of human maturation happens when a girl child transfers her primary attachment from her mother to her father. This necessitates some mother/child discord, with the paper not only arguing that this 'turning away from the mother occurs in an atmosphere of antagonism' but that 'the attachment to the mother ends in hate'.[61] Freud writes that some women retain this hatred into adulthood and some overcompensate with love, nevertheless the majority find their way to an appropriate level of ambivalence. Lucy does not seem overcome with hatred but her recollections of her mother are antipathetic and there is a question of how innate any maternal 'antagonism' is. With her abiding interest in female social education Woolf shapes this relationship to suggest a biological path whereby girls inherit patriarchal self-censorship from their mothers. Whether instinctual or learnt, this socio-biological heritage – the female side of the patriarchal tradition Freud describes in *Moses and Monotheism* – leads to a self-perpetuating anti-matriarchal culture.

Despite coming at the end of Woolf's life, *Between the Acts* sees a return to her earlier realism and, in many ways, comes back full circle to the beginning of her writing career and *The Voyage Out*. While their settings are entirely different both use the juxtaposition of wildness and domesticity to probe questions of motherhood, patriarchal society, relationships, the inheritance of culture and the importance of living a creative life. Over the intervening years Woolf had honed her literary technique and it makes sense that, in the relentless search for ever more effective ways to 'dig out beautiful caves behind' (*D2* 263) her characters, she turned to psychoanalysis. While its practice may not have always been in line with her principles, psychoanalytic models offered a rich point of entry into human affairs. As a study of human emotions, relationships and desires, psychoanalysis offered a new and radical way of looking at individual relationships and group dynamics – both of which constitute important lines of inquiry in Woolf's writing. With her longstanding focus on the place of motherhood in society and its myriad of leitmotifs (women's professional and domestic lives, contraception, family and social inheritance, the juxtaposition of procreativity and creativity, to name but a few) it comes as no surprise that Freud and Klein's notions of how mothers affect psychic development strongly impacted Woolf's writing in her final years. There is undoubtedly more to learn about the nuanced influence that these and other psychoanalytic thinkers had on Woolf's work. Nonetheless it is clear that, once again, Woolf's interest in maternity offers a new way of looking at a complex and much discussed subject of her era

Notes

1. 'Object Relations in Human Sexuality', *International Journal of Mental Health*, 26.1 (1997), p. 16.
2. R. A. Paskauskas, *The Complete Correspondence of Sigmund Freud and Ernest Jones 1908–1939* (Cambridge, MA: Harvard University Press, 1993), p. 628.
3. Sanja Bahun, 'Woolf and Psychoanalytic Theory', in *Virginia Woolf in Context*, ed. Bryony Randall and Jane Goldman (Cambridge: Cambridge University Press, 2012), p. 95. Given Woolf's polemical writing and her feminism, the field's scope for female professionals may also have caught her attention.
4. 'Virginia Woolf's Matriarchal Family of Origins', p. 167.
5. *Virginia Woolf and the Fictions of Psychoanalysis*, p. xvi.
6. This is a controversial statement and will be discussed further below.
7. '"The spirit of the age": Virginia Woolf's Response to Second Wave Psychology', *Twentieth Century Literature*, 40.2 (1994), p. 140.
8. Nicky Platt, 'When Freud Gets Useful', p. 156.
9. 'Woolf and Freud: The Kleinian Turn', in *Virginia Woolf in Context*, ed. Bryony Randall and Jane Goldman (Cambridge: Cambridge University Press, 2012), p. 332.
10. 'Victorian Women and Insanity', *Victorian Studies*, 23.2 (1980), p. 180. For more on psychoanalytic phallocentricity, see the work of Rosemary Balsam, for example, *Women's Bodies in Psychoanalysis* (London: Routledge, 2012).
11. 'An Exchange Regarding Freud and the Hogarth Press', *Virginia Woolf Miscellany*, 77 (2010), p. 16. Elizabeth Abel discusses Woolf's reading of Hogarth Press's psychoanalytical publications (*The Fictions of Psychoanalysis*, pp. 14–19).
12. The book Woolf was reviewing happened to be J. D. Beresford's *An Imperfect Mother*.
13. See, for example, Nicky Platt, 'When Freud Gets Useful' and Murray Roston, *Modernist Patterns in Literature and the Visual Arts* (Basingstoke: Macmillan, 2000) (in particular, the chapter 'Woolf, Joyce, and Artistic Neurosis', pp. 149–83).
14. '"How can we alter the crest and the spur of the fighting cock?": Julian Huxley, Popular Biology, and the Feminist Pacifism of Virginia Woolf', *Women: A Cultural Review*, 31.3 (2020), pp. 315–34.
15. Julian Huxley, H. G. Wells and G. P. Wells, *The Science of Life* (London: Cassell and Co., 1931), pp. 811–21.

256   *Virginia Woolf and Motherhood*

16. *Virgin Soil* (London: Heinemann, 1924), p. 159.
17. 'Virginia Woolf and Sigmund Freud Diverge on What a Woman Wants', *The Centennial Review*, 39.1 (1995), p. 142.
18. When she first read Freud's description of the term 'ambivalence' Woolf was struck by its familiarity – noting of her father in the autobiographical 'A Sketch of the Past': 'It was only the other day when I read Freud for the first time, that I discovered that this violently disturbing conflict of love and hate is a common feeling; and is called ambivalence' (*MB* 108). Around the same time Woolf's diary links the term with her feeling for shopping – 'I dislike this excitement, yet enjoy it. Ambivalence as Freud calls it' (*D5* 249) – and, earlier in her work, these strong conflicting feelings are common (for example *The Waves*' Susan's refrain of 'I hate, I love'). This leads Sanja Bahun to imagine Woolf's early reading of Freud in the following way – 'as she excitedly turns the pages [. . .] she finds, time and again, the confirmation of something she has already put in writing; that human nature is governed by opposing drives interlocked in action' ('Woolf and Psychoanalytic Theory', p. 92).
19. While Woolf only recounts having Klein to dinner once, her pocket diary records a second arrangement less than a fortnight later. See Julie Anne Greer, 'Learning from Linked Lives: Narrativising the Individual and Group Biographies of the Guests at the 25th Jubilee Dinner of the British Psychoanalytical Society at The Savoy, London, on 8th March 1939', EdD thesis, Southampton University, University of Southampton Institutional Repository (2014), p. 9.
20. *Late Cultural Criticism*, p. 71.
21. Amid this evidence there are also numerous non-psychoanalytical entries relating to maternity. Collected over years of research, Woolf's *Three Guineas* notebooks include an entry on John Donne leaving his wife and their 'steadily growing army of babies' so that he could write (*RN* 262) and an account by Julian Huxley disproving the centuries-old theory that a woman's body plays a passive role in conception (*RN* 263). The final published version refers to the lack of positive medical interventions 'in pregnancy, childbirth and lactation' (*TG* 268), the use of chloroform for women during birth (*TG* 295) and articles on what Catherine Stimpson calls 'the Fascist celebration of "The Mother"' (*TG* 175) ('Foreword', in Abel, *Virginia Woolf and the Fictions of Psychoanalysis*, p. x).
22. Woolf credits these words to Ada Lovelace; however, she does very slightly paraphrase the wording that Lovelace used in her essay 'Society and the Seasons' (*The Times' Fifty Years, Memories and Contrasts* (London; T. Butterworth, 1932)], pp. 24–30 (p. 30).
23. *The Ministry of Women*, pp. 6, 9–10.
24. Ibid., p. 81. It is interesting to note that Grensted uses the word 'subconscious' several times in his report – a word that is emphatically not included in Freudian psychoanalysis Freud argued against it

Motherhood and Psychoanalysis **257**

because it was 'topographical' (*Two Short Accounts of Psycho-analysis* (Harmondsworth: Penguin, 1962), p. 108). Except where Woolf copies Grensted's exact words she overwhelmingly uses the correct term 'unconscious'.

25. Ibid., p. 82. Grensted is at some pains to point out that 'infantile fixation' exists not only among men, but across society.
26. *Virginia Woolf: The Rede Lecture* (Cambridge: Cambridge University Press, 1942), p. 23.
27. *Moses and Monotheism* (London: Hogarth Press, 1939), p. 180.
28. Ibid., pp. 186, 178.
29. Albert Einstein and Sigmund Freud, *Why War?* (London: New Commonwealth Pamphlets, 1934), p. 50.
30. *Late Cultural Criticism*, p. 80.
31. For more on the Woolfs and the League of Nations, see Wayne Chapman, 'Synthesizing Civilizations: Leonard Woolf, the League of Nations, and the Inverse of Imperialism, 1928–1933', in *Virginia Woolf and the Common(Wealth) Reader*, ed. Helen Wussow and Mary Ann Gillies (Liverpool: Liverpool University Press, 2014), pp. 18–26.
32. *Why War?*, p. 40.
33. *New Introductory Lectures on Psycho-Analysis* (London: Hogarth Press, 1933), p. 148.
34. '"In company of a gipsy": The "Gypsy" as Trope in Woolf and Brontë', *Critical Survey*, 19.1 (2007), p. 48. Grenada is particularly well known for its Romany community; a fact Woolf may have known, since Vita Sackville-West's book *Pepita* describes much of her grandmother's childhood living close to the city. Elsewhere in Woolf's writing Gypsies represent not only queer desire but have a link with an 'unmaternal' abandon. In the short story 'Gipsy, the Mongrel' a dog both from the Gypsies and called Gipsy gives birth to a stillborn crossbreed puppy and rather than fretting about this loss, 'grins [. . .] in the face of morality' (*CSF* 271). Woolf may have associated Sackville-West's Romany heritage with her tendency to be 'a little cold & offhand with her boys' (*D3* 52).
35. '"How can we alter the crest and the spur of the fighting cock?"', pp. 316–17.
36. *Why War?*, pp. 93–94.
37. *Civilization and Its Discontents* (London: Hogarth Press, 1930), p. 97. The use of the term 'instinct' is a little misleading here. Although the Hogarth Press translation uses the term 'death instinct', in the original German Freud writes 'Todestrieb' which more closely translates to 'death drive'.
38. *Why War?*, p. 93.
39. *The Science of Life*, pp. 86–87.
40. It is interesting to note that Freud started out his medical career with stints in psychology and neurology but later declined to look for

neurological proof of his theories. He stated in *The Interpretation of Dreams*: 'we shall carefully avoid the temptation to determine the psychic locality in any anatomical sense' (London: George Allen & Unwin, 1913, p. 494). For more on Freud and neuroscience, see Steve Ayan, 'Neurotic about Neurons', *Scientific American Mind*, 17.2 (2006), pp. 36–41.

41. Sonu Shamdasani, '"Psychotherapy": The Invention of a Word', *History of the Human Sciences*, 18.1 (2005), p. 4.

42. *Love, Hate and Reparation* (hereafter *LHR*) (London: Hogarth Press, 1937), p. vi. Further page references will be given within the main text.

43. According to Shirley Panken Woolf was only breastfed for ten weeks before being moved onto bottle-feeding while Adrian was nursed 'for more than a year' (*The Lust of Creation*, p. 27). It is difficult to know whether Woolf knew this. However, Klein includes bottle-feeding as a perfectly acceptable, if marginally inferior, form of nursing (*LHR* 59–60).

44. To quote a comprehensive example here would be too lengthy but for some excellent examples of this type of analysis, see Freud's *The Psychopathology of Everyday Life* (London: Benn, 1914) or Klein's *The Psycho-analysis of Children* (London: Hogarth Press, 1932).

45. *Civilization, Society and Religion* (Harmondsworth: Penguin, 1985), p. 68.

46. Interestingly, in 1922, British psychoanalyst Eric Hiller wrote an article on the phallic connotations of various forms of tobacco, a resemblance that was not lost on Woolf, who once described Lord Castlerosse's cigar as 'like a jackass's penis' (*D4* 200). 'Some Remarks on Tobacco', *International Journal of Psycho-Analysis*, 3 (1922), pp. 475–80.

47. Hermione Lee has explored a variety of critical readings of this passage (*Virginia Woolf*, pp. 123–25).

48. 'Animal Life and Human Sacrifice in Virginia Woolf's *Between the Acts*', *Woolf Studies Annual*, 15 (2009), p. 4.

49. 'The Nature of *Between the Acts*', *Modern Language Studies*, 13.3 (1983), p. 30.

50. '*Between the Acts* and the Coming of War', *Novel: A Forum on Fiction*, 10.3 (1977), p. 223.

51. 'The Nature of *Between the Acts*', pp. 34, 27.

52. The resultant case against the surgeon, *R. v. Bourne*, went on to become the standard against which all other abortion cases were measured. For more on this, see Stuart N Clarke, 'The Horse with the Green Tail', *Virginia Woolf Miscellany*, 34 (1990), pp. 3–4.

53. '*Between the Acts* and the Coming of War', pp. 235–36.

54. 'The Burden of Drafts: Woolf's Revisions of *Between the Acts*', *Text*, 10 (1997), pp. 301–02.

55. '*Between the Acts* and the Coming of War', p. 221.

56. Interestingly, in the final text it is Isa's mother who dies in India.

57. Though this mention of Byron is briefer in the final published version, this mother–son relationship exists throughout the drafts and is not expunged by Woolf.
58. *New Introductory Lectures*, p. 171.
59. 'A Childhood Recollection from *Dichtung und Wahrheit*' (1917), in *Sigmond Freud Collected Papers, Vol. 4* (London: Hogarth Press, 1925), p. 367.
60. '"These ghost figures of distorted passion"', p. 41.
61. *New Introductory Lectures*, p. 165.

Conclusion

It feels fitting to begin this conclusion with a section of *Three Guineas* in which Woolf reviews both the demise of Victorian maternity (as explored in the chapters of this book) and also the enduring influence of mothers (as discussed in the previous chapter). Her deliberations begin with the following passage:

> No guinea of earned money should go to rebuilding the college on the old plan; just as certainly none could be spent upon building a college upon a new plan; therefore the guinea should be earmarked 'Rags. Petrol. Matches.' And this note should be attached to it. 'Take this guinea and with it burn the college to the ground. Set fire to the old hypocrisies. Let the light of the burning building scare the nightingales and incarnadine the willows. And let the daughters of educated men dance round the fire and heap armful upon armful of dead leaves upon the flames. And let their mothers lean from the upper windows and cry 'Let it blaze! Let it blaze! For we have done with this "education"!' (*TG* 157)

This scene with its 'Rags. Petrol. Matches.' brings to mind the arson practiced by militant suffragettes, who often used such paraphernalia. Perhaps this is why criticism of this text has focused on what Naomi Black calls 'the bonfire of feminism' – the burning of words and buildings – rather than on the fiery deaths being visited upon the mothers leaning 'from the upper windows' of the burning college (Christine Haskill, for example, writes of the scene, that Woolf draws 'on generational imagery as the daughters and mothers rejoice in the "blaze" of the fire').[1] Because it offers such a strong image of feminist activism it may take a moment of rereading to note that this scene is not simply one depicting mothers cheering on their daughters in demolishing an education system that is not fit for purpose.

Nonetheless, the burning of these mothers revisits an earlier form of 'matricide' – Woolf's desire to kill the 'angel in the house' in 'Professions for Women'.[2] As the introduction to this book notes, Woolf kills the 'Angel' in order to forge her way in the professions, make money and be relevant. Similarly, the mothers in the burning building (and their way of life) must die in order for their daughters to find ways to learn about, enter and influence society. The text goes on to predict that the world can only defeat 'war' and 'tyranny' when the mothers 'laugh from their graves', at which point the 'daughters of uneducated women' (*TG* 208) will finally live free from patriarchal society within an architecture of their own making.

However there is a paradox in *Three Guineas*' handling of motherhood. The words Woolf wants to burn are like a 'corpse', 'dead' and 'without meaning' (*TG* 227), but motherhood, even in its grave, is still alive and laughing. By the mid-1930s Woolf was moving on from simply needing to kill the 'Angel'. Rather than continuing to exist in their current fashion, the mothers of *Three Guineas* willingly die – performing a monumental self-sacrifice – and then live on in a different form after death. In this way Woolf acknowledges that motherhood cannot be entirely eradicated (tainted though it may be) because it is a prerequisite for human existence, a fundamental part of women's lives and because every human – woman or man – has a complex, lifelong emotional relationship with their mother.

This book has observed other moments where Woolf grapples with the task of negotiating this institution which is intrinsic to womanhood, but can also be enlisted to reinforce the patriarchal status quo. In 'A Society' a group of young women experiment with – and reject – celibacy, and one bears a daughter. In *A Room*, the narrator passes on advice that counsels women to go on bearing children 'in twos and threes, not in tens and twelves' (*AROO* 101). Throughout Woolf's works motherhood is a consistently fraught topic that reflects a range of contemporary political and social narratives as well as a set of highly personal associations. Often maternity is seen in a negative light, with bleak depictions of lost mothers, artistic impotence and destructive mothering. Yet far from being a theme that Woolf avoided it is one that her writing constantly questions and reviews. Indeed, where maternal narratives emerge in her work, they offer some of the clearest expressions of her politics, feminism and private life.

It has been this work's aim to demonstrate how every aspect of motherhood interested Woolf – its aesthetics, symbolism, and cultural and political contexts. She used maternity to explore the social connotations of contraception and breastfeeding. She traced the changes in maternal politics from Mrs Ramsay's Victorian maternalism to the working-class mothers campaigning in 'Memories of a Working Women's Guild'. In *Jacob's Room* and *Mrs Dalloway*, she employed mothers as symbols of nationalism. In *Night and Day* and *A Room of One's Own* she used them as a way to think about how art is generated. And throughout her life she used maternity to engage in the major scientific and cultural discourses of her time. While Woolf often represented motherhood irreverently, she always represented it with purpose. She did so in experimental ways, defying traditional conventions and trying to say something true about the material reality before her. From characterisation to the performance of femininity, from eugenics to psychoanalysis, this study of Woolf and motherhood has offered alternative ways of viewing Woolf's engagement with the discourses of her age and added nuance to historicist readings of her social criticism. She lived in a volatile era when not only the role of women but the structure of society itself was drastically changing in response to unprecedented world events, scientific discoveries and economic and political upheaval. Given the political, social and economic turmoil of our own era, the technological changes that have altered human life and the redefinition of gender identity, in many ways Woolf's era was not unlike our own. Now, finally, with women's place in society being reexamined and redefined, perhaps feminist and historicist criticism is ready to recognise motherhood as a fundamental part of women's writing and women's lives – and, as such, a part that must be included in the study of women's literature.

Notes

1. Black, *Virginia Woolf as Feminist* (Ithaca, NY: Cornell University Press, 2004), pp. 29–31. Haskill, 'The Sex War and the Great War: Woolf's Late Victorian Inheritance in *Three Guineas*', in *Virginia Woolf: Writing the World*, ed. Pamela Caughie and Diana Swanson (Liverpool: Liverpool University Press, 2015), p. 46.
2. Anna Snaith uses the term 'matricide' to describe the killing of the 'Angel' in her introduction to *A Room* ('Introduction', in Woolf, *A Room of One's Own and Three Guineas*, ed. Anna Snaith (Oxford: Oxford University Press, 2015), p. xxiv). However, there is an important distinction between these texts; unlike the 'angel' – a spirit that represents any woman who 'excelled in the difficult arts of family life' (*E6* 480) – the women in the burning college are explicitly mothers.

Bibliography

Abel, Elizabeth. *Virginia Woolf and the Fictions of Psychoanalysis* (Chicago: University of Chicago Press, 1989)

Adolph, Andrea. 'Nostalgic Appetites: Female Desire and Wartime Rationing in Virginia Woolf's *Between The Acts* and Noel Streatfeild's *Saplings*', in *Material Women: Consuming Desires and Consuming Objects 1750–1950*, ed. Maureen Daly Goggin and Beth Fowkes Tobin (Farnham: Ashgate, 2009), pp. 55–72

Allen, Ann Taylor. 'Feminism and Eugenics in Germany and Britain, 1900–1940: A Comparative Perspective', *German Studies Review*, 23.3 (2000), 477–505

——. *Feminism and Motherhood in Western Europe, 1890–1970* (Basingstoke: Palgrave Macmillan, 2005)

Allen, Judith. *Virginia Woolf and the Politics of Language* (Edinburgh: Edinburgh University Press, 2010)

Alt, Christina. *Virginia Woolf and the Study of Nature* (Cambridge: Cambridge University Press, 2010)

Andrew, Barbara. 'The Psychology of Tyranny: Wollstonecraft and Woolf on the Gendered Dimension of War', *Hypatia*, 9.2 (1994), 85–101

Angelella, Lisa. 'The Meat of the Movement: Food and Feminism in Woolf', *Woolf Studies Annual*, 17 (2011), 173–95

Atkins, Peter. 'Mother's Milk and Infant Death in Britain, c. 1900–1940', *Anthropology of Food*, 2 (2003) <https://journals.openedition.org/aof/310> [accessed 2 April 2024]

Ayan, Steve. 'Neurotic about Neurons', *Scientific American Mind*, 17.2 (2006), 36–41

Bahun, Sanja. 'Woolf and Psychoanalytic Theory', in *Virginia Woolf in Context*, eds. Bryony Randall and Jane Goldman (Cambridge: Cambridge University Press, 2012), pp. 92–109

Bardi, Abby. '"In company of a gipsy": The "Gypsy" as Trope in Woolf and Brontë', *Critical Survey*, 19.1 (2007), pp. 40–50

Barkway, Stephen. '"Oh Lord what it is to publish a best seller": The Woolfs' Professional Relationship with Vita Sackville-West', in *Leonard and Virginia Woolf, The Hogarth Press and the Networks of Modernism*, ed. Helen Southworth (Edinburgh: Edinburgh University Press, 2010), pp. 234–59

264 *Bibliography*

Barrett, Eileen. 'Matriarchal Myth on a Patriarchal Stage: Virginia Woolf's *Between the Acts*', *Twentieth Century Literature*, 33.1 (1987), 18–37

Beard, George Miller. *American Nervousness: Its Causes and Consequences, a Supplement to Nervous Exhaustion (Neurasthenia)* (New York: G. P. Putnam, 1881)

Bechtold, Brigitte. 'More than *A Room* and *Three Guineas*: Understanding Virginia Woolf's Social Thought', *Journal of International Women's Studies*, 1.2 (2000), 1–11

Beer, Gillian. *Darwin's Plots: Evolutionary Narrative in Darwin, George Eliot and Nineteenth-Century Fiction*, 3rd edn (Cambridge: Cambridge University Press, 2000)

——. *Virginia Woolf: The Common Ground* (Edinburgh: Edinburgh University Press, 1996)

Beeton, Isabella M. *Mrs Beeton's Book of Household Management* (London: S. O. Beeton, 1861)

Bell, Quentin. 'A "Radiant" Friendship', *Critical Inquiry*, 10.4 (1984), 557–66

——. *Virginia Woolf: A Biography*, 2 vols (London: Hogarth Press, 1972)

Bell, Vanessa. 'Notes on Virginia's Childhood', in *Virginia Woolf: Interviews and Recollections*, ed. J. H. Stape (Basingstoke: Macmillan, 1995), pp. 3–8

——. *Selected Letters of Vanessa Bell*, ed. Regina Marler, with an introduction by Quentin Bell (London: Bloomsbury, 1993)

Bennett, Joan. *Virginia Woolf: Her Art as a Novelist*, 2nd edn (Cambridge: Cambridge University Press, 1945; repr. 1964)

Besant, Annie. *The Law of Population, Its Consequences and Its Bearing upon Human Conduct and Morals* (London: Freethought, 1877)

Bettinger, Elfi. '"The journey, not the arrival, matters" – Virginia Woolf and Ageing', *Journal of Aging, Humanities, and the Arts*, 1.3–4 (2007), 177–90

Beveridge, William H. et al. *Changes in Family Life (Seven Wireless Talks)* (London: G. Allen & Unwin, 1932)

Bishop, Edward. *A Virginia Woolf Chronology* (Basingstoke: Macmillan, 1989)

Black, Naomi. *Virginia Woolf as Feminist* (Ithaca, NY: Cornell University Press, 2004)

Blair, Emily. *Virginia Woolf and the Nineteenth-Century Domestic Novel* (Albany: State University of New York Press, 2007)

Bland, Lucy. *Banishing the Beast: English Feminism and Sexual Morality 1885–1914* (London: Penguin Books, 1995)

Blodgett, Harriet. 'The Nature of *Between the Acts*', *Modern Language Studies*, 13.3 (1983), 27–37

Blyth, Ian. 'Do Not Feed the Birds: *Night and Day* and the Defence of the Realm Act', in *Contradictory Woolf*, ed. Derek Ryan and Stella Bolaki (Liverpool: Liverpool University Press, 2012), pp. 278–84

Booth, Allyson. *Postcards from the Trenches: Negotiating the Space between Modernism and the First World War* (Oxford: Oxford University Press, 1996)

Boulestin, Marcel. *Simple French Cooking for English Homes* (London: Heinemann, 1923)

Bourke, Joanna. *Dismembering the Male: Men's Bodies, Britain, and the Great War* (London: Reaktion Books, 1996)

Bowlby, Rachel. *A Child of One's Own* (Oxford: Oxford University Press, 2013)

——. *Feminist Destinations and Further Essays on Virginia Woolf* (Edinburgh: Edinburgh University Press, 1997)

Box, Muriel (ed.). *The Trial of Marie Stopes* (London: A Femina Book, 1967)

Boxwell, D. A. 'The (M)Other Battle of World War One: The Maternal Politics of Pacifism in Rose Macaulay's *Non-Combatants and Others*', *Tulsa Studies in Women's Literature*, 12.1 (1993), 85–101

Boyde, Melissa. 'The Poet and the Ghosts are Walking the Streets: Hope Mirrless – Life and Poetry', *Hecate*, 35.1–2 (2009), 29–41

Bradshaw, David. 'Eugenics: "They should certainly be killed"', in *A Concise Companion to Modernism*, ed. David Bradshaw (Oxford: Blackwell, 2003), pp. 34–55

Briggs, Julia. *Reading Virginia Woolf* (Edinburgh: Edinburgh University Press, 2006)

——. *Virginia Woolf: An Inner Life* (London: Penguin Books, 2006)

Brittain, Vera. 'Our Malthusian Middle-Classes', *The Nation and Athenaeum*, 7 May 1927, pp. 140–41

Bulmer, Michael. 'The Development of Francis Galton's Ideas on the Mechanism of Heredity', *Journal of the History of Biology*, 32.2 (1999), 263–92

Buss, Allen. 'Galton and Sex Differences: An Historical Note', *Journal of the History of the Behavioral Sciences*, 12 (1976), 283–85

Caramagno, Thomas. *The Flight of the Mind: Virginia Woolf's Art and Manic-Depressive Illness* (London: University of California Press, 1992)

Carpentier, Martha C. *Ritual, Myth and the Modernist Text: The Influence of Jane Ellen Harrison on Joyce, Eliot, and Woolf* (London: Routledge, 2013)

Catalogue of Books from the Library of Leonard and Virginia Woolf: Taken from Monks House, Rodmell, Sussex and 24 Victoria Square, London and now in the Possession of Washington State University Pullman, U.S.A. (Brighton: Holleyman & Treacher, 1975)

Chan, Evelyn. 'The Ethics and Aesthetics of Healing: Woolf, Medicine, and Professionalization', *Women's Studies*, 43.1 (2014), 25–51

Chapman, Wayne. 'Synthesizing Civilizations: Leonard Woolf, the League of Nations, and the Inverse of Imperialism, 1928–1933', in *Virginia*

Woolf and the Common(Wealth) Reader, ed. Helen Wussow and Mary Ann Gillies (Liverpool: Liverpool University Press, 2014), pp. 18–26

Childers, Mary M. 'Virginia Woolf on the Outside Looking Down: Reflections on the Class of Women', *Modern Fiction Studies*, 38.1 (1992), 61–79

Childs, Donald J. *Modernism and Eugenics: Woolf, Eliot, Yeats and the Culture of Degeneration* (Cambridge: Cambridge University Press, 2001)

Clarke, Stuart N. 'The Horse with the Green Tail', *Virginia Woolf Miscellany*, 34 (1990), 3–4

Coates, Kimberly Engdahl. 'Virginia Woolf's Queer Time and Place: Wartime London and a World Aslant', in *Queer Bloomsbury*, ed. Brenda Helt and Madelyn Detloff (Edinburgh: Edinburgh University Press, 2016), pp. 276–93

Cohen, Deborah. 'Private Lives in Public Spaces: Marie Stopes, the Mothers' Clinics and the Practice of Contraception', *History Workshop Journal*, 33.1 (1992), 95–116

Cole, Sarah. *At the Violet Hour: Modernism and Violence in England and Ireland* (Oxford: Oxford University Press, 2012)

Committee of Enquiry into 'Shell-Shock'. 'Report of the War Office Committee of Enquiry into "Shell-Shock"' (London: War Office, 1922)

Cooley, Elizabeth. 'Discovering the "enchanted region": A Revisionary Reading of *Night and Day*', *CEA Critic*, 54.3 (1992), 4–17

Cooper, Dana, and Claire Phelan (eds). *Motherhood and War: International Perspectives* (Basingstoke: Palgrave Macmillan, 2014)

Coulter, Myrl. 'Essentialism and Mothering', *Encyclopedia of Motherhood*, 3 vols, ed. Andrea O'Reilly (Los Angeles: Sage, 2010), I, pp. 357–58

Craig, Layne Parish. *When Sex Changed: Birth Control Politics and Literature between the World Wars* (New Brunswick, NJ: Rutgers University Press, 2013)

Cramer, Patricia. 'Jane Harrison and the Lesbian Plots: The Absent Lover in Virginia Woolf's *The Waves*', *Studies in the Novel*, 37.4 (2005), 443–63

——. 'Virginia Woolf's Matriarchal Family of Origins in *Between the Acts*', *Twentieth Century Literature*, 39.2 (1993), 166–84

Cunningham, Valentine. *In the Reading Gaol: Postmodernity, Texts, and History* (Oxford: Blackwell, 1994)

Curl, M. J. "Boston Artists and Sculptors Talk of Their Work and Ideals: IX – Bashka Paeff", *The Sunday Herald*, 6 February 1921, p. 6

Czarnecki, Kristin. '"In my mind I saw my mother": Virginia Woolf, Zitkala-Ša, and Autobiography', in *Virginia Woolf and Her Female Contemporaries*, ed. Julie Vandivere and Megan Hicks (Clemson, SC: Clemson University Press, 2016), pp. 143–50

Daiches, David. *Virginia Woolf* (New York: New Directions, 1963)

Dalgarno, Emily. 'Virginia Woolf: Translation and "Iterability"', *The Yearbook of English Studies*, 36.1 (2006), 145–56

'Dangers of Women's Dress', *Rational Dress Society's Gazette*, April 1888, pp. 2–3

Daugherty, Beth Rigel. 'Feminist Approaches', in *Palgrave Advances in Virginia Woolf Studies*, ed. Anna Snaith (Basingstoke: Palgrave Macmillan, 2007)

——. 'The Whole Contention between Mr Bennett and Mrs Woolf, Revised', in *Virginia Woolf: Centennial Essays*, ed. Elaine K. Ginsberg and Laura Moss Gottlieb (Troy, NY: Whitston, 1983), pp. 269–94

——. '"You see you kind of belong to us, and what you do matters enormously": Letters from Readers to Virginia Woolf', *Woolf Studies Annual*, 12 (2006), 1–212

Davenport, G. C., and C. B. Davenport. 'Heredity of Eye Color in Man', *Science*, 26 (1907), 589–92

Davenport-Hines, Richard. *Universal Man: the Seven Lives of John Maynard Keynes* (London: William Collins, 2015)

——, and Judy Slinn. *Glaxo: A History to 1962* (Cambridge: Cambridge University Press, 1992)

Dekter, Gregory. 'Perishable and Permanent: Industry, Commodity, and Society in *Mrs Dalloway* and *To the Lighthouse*', *Virginia Woolf Miscellany*, 88 (2016), 14–16

Delap, Lucy. '"For ever and ever": Child-raising, Domestic Workers and Emotional Labour in Twentieth Century Britain', *Studies in the Maternal*, 3.2 (2011), 1–10

——. 'The Superwoman: Theories of Gender and Genius in Edwardian Britain', *The Historical Journal*, 47.1 (2004), 101–26

Delegates of Second International Conference of Women. 'Resolutions of the Zürich Congress 1919' (Geneva: Women's International League for Peace and Freedom, 1919) <http://www.ja1325.org/PDFs/Resolutions%20of%20the%20WILPF%20Zurich%20Congress%201919.pdf> [accessed 12 January 2013]

Dell, Marion. *Virginia Woolf's Influential Forebears: Julia Margaret Cameron, Anny Thackeray Ritchie and Julia Prinsep Stephen* (Basingstoke: Palgrave Macmillan, 2015)

DeSalvo, Louise A. 'Lighting the Cave: The Relationship between Vita Sackville-West and Virginia Woolf', *Signs*, 8.2 (1982), 195–214

——. *Virginia Woolf: The Impact of Childhood Sexual Abuse on Her Life and Work* (New York: Ballantine Books, 1989)

Dick, Susan. 'Virginia Woolf's "The Cook"', *Woolf Studies Annual*, 3 (1997), 122–42

——. '"What fools we were!": Virginia Woolf's "A Society"', *Twentieth Century Literature*, 33.1 (1987), 51–66

Dodge Robbins, Dorothy. 'Virginia Woolf and Sigmund Freud Diverge on What a Woman Wants', *The Centennial Review*, 39.1 (1995), 129–45

Dreher, Nan H. 'Redundancy and Emigration: The "Woman Question" in Mid-Victorian Britain', *Victorian Periodicals Review*, 26.1 (1993), 3–7

Drewery, Sarah. 'Recruitment and Fundraising Posters, World War One', *Liddell Hart Centre for Military Archives*, King's College London (2008) <http://www.kcl.ac.uk/lhcma/summary/xr30-001.shtml> [accessed 8 May 2013]

268 Bibliography

Dubino, Jeanne et al. 'Introduction', in *Virginia Woolf: Twenty-First-Century Approaches*, ed. Jeanne Dubino et al. (Edinburgh: Edinburgh University Press, 2015), pp. 1–14

Duckworth Stephen, Julia. *Stories for Children, Essays for Adults*, ed. Diane F. Gillespie and Elizabeth Steele (Syracuse, NY: Syracuse University Press, 1987)

Einstein, Albert, and Sigmund Freud. *Why War?* (London: New Commonwealth Pamphlets, 1934)

Elkins, Amy E. 'Old Pages and New Readings in Virginia Woolf's *Orlando*', *Tulsa Studies in Women's Literature*, 29.1 (2010), 131–36

Evans, Suzanne. *Mothers of Heroes, Mothers of Martyrs: World War I and the Politics of Grief* (Montreal: McGill-Queen's University Press, 2007)

Fassler, Barbara. 'Theories of Homosexuality as Sources of Bloomsbury's Androgyny', *Signs*, 5.2 (1979), 237–51

Fielding-Hall, H. 'Eugenics and Common Sense', *The Atlantic*, September 1914, pp. 348–54

Fildes, Valerie. 'Infant Feeding and Infant Mortality in England, 1900–1919', *Continuity and Change*, 13.2 (1998), 251–80

——. *Wet Nursing* (Oxford: Basil Blackwell, 1988)

Fordham, Finn. *I Do, I Undo, I Redo: The Textual Genesis of Modernist Selves in Hopkins, Yeats, Conrad, Forster, Joyce, and Woolf* (Oxford: Oxford University Press, 2010)

Forster, E. M. *Virginia Woolf: The Rede Lecture* (Cambridge: Cambridge University Press, 1942)

Fowler, Rowena. 'Moments and Metamorphoses: Virginia Woolf's Greece', *Comparative Literature*, 51.3 (1999), 217–42

Freeden, Michael. 'Eugenics and Progressive Thought: A Study in Ideological Affinity', *The Historical Journal*, 22. 3 (1979), 645–71

Freud, Sigmund. 'A Childhood Recollection from *Dichtung und Wahrheit*' (1917), in *Sigmond Freud Collected Papers, Vol. 4* (London: Hogarth Press, 1925) pp. 357–67

——. *Civilization and Its Discontents* (London: Hogarth Press, 1930)

——. *Civilization, Society and Religion* (Harmondsworth: Penguin, 1985)

——. *The Interpretation of Dreams* (London: George Allen & Unwin, 1913)

——. *Moses and Monotheism* (London: Hogarth Press, 1939)

——. *New Introductory Lectures on Psycho-Analysis* (London: Hogarth Press, 1933)

——. *The Psychopathology of Everyday Life* (London: Benn, 1914)

——. *Two Short Accounts of Psycho-analysis* (Harmondsworth: Penguin, 1962)

Friedman, Susan Stanford. 'Creativity and the Childbirth Metaphor: Gender Difference in Literary Discourse', *Feminist Studies*, 13.1 (1987), 49–82

Fromm, Harold. 'Leonard Woolf and His Virgins', *The Hudson Review*, 38.4 (1986), 551–69

Froula, Christine. '*Mrs Dalloway*'s Postwar Elegy: Women, War, and the Art of Mourning', *Modernism/modernity*, 9.1 (2002), 125–63

——. *Virginia Woolf and the Bloomsbury Avant-Garde* (New York: Columbia University Press, 2005)

Gagnier, Regenia. 'Between Women: A Cross-Class Analysis of Status and Anarchic Humor', *Women's Studies*, 15 (1988), 135–48

Galton, Francis. 'Eugenics: Its Definition, Scope, and Aims', *The American Journal of Sociology*, 10.1 (1904), 1–25

——. 'Family Likeness in Eye-Colour', *Nature*, 34 (1886), 137

——. *Hereditary Genius: An Inquiry into Its Laws and Consequences* (London: Macmillan, 1869)

Garner, Les. *Stepping Stones to Women's Liberty: Feminist Ideas in the Women's Suffrage Movement 1900–1918* (London: Heinemann Educational, 1984)

Garrity, Jane. *Step-Daughters of England: British Women Modernists and the National Imaginary* (Manchester: Manchester University Press, 2003)

Garstang, Walter. Review of Robert Heath Lock, *Recent Progress in the Study of Variation, Heredity, and Evolution*. Second Edition (1909), *The Eugenics Review*, 1.3 (1909), pp. 210–12

Gerard, Andre. 'Blog #55: A Tendentious Lighthouse: Virginia Woolf and Marie Carmichael Stopes' <http://patremoirpress.com/blog/?p=629> [accessed 12 March 2018]

Gilbert, Sandra M., and Susan Gubar. *No Man's Land: The War of the Words* (New Haven, CT: Yale University Press, 1988)

Gillespie, Diane F (ed.). 'Adventures in Common: Investing with Woolfs and "Securitas"', in *Virginia Woolf and the Common(Wealth) Reader*, ed. Helen Wussow and Mary Ann Gillies (Liverpool: Liverpool University Press, 2014), pp. 205–11

——. *The Multiple Muses of Virginia Woolf* (Columbia: University of Missouri Press, 1993)

——. 'Virginia Woolf, Vanessa Bell and Painting', in *The Edinburgh Companion to Virginia Woolf and the Arts*, ed. Maggie Humm (Edinburgh: Edinburgh University Press, 2010), pp. 121–39

Ginsberg, Elaine K., and Laura Moss Gottlieb (eds). *Virginia Woolf: Centennial Essays* (Troy, NY: Whitston, 1983)

Glaxo. 'Builds Bonnie Babies' poster (1918) 'Medical Advertisement from Days Past', Waiuku Museum, Waiuku <https://waiukumuseum.wordpress.com/2014/10/27/medical-advertisement-from-days-past-3/> [accessed 26 March 2019]

——. 'Remembrance', *Illustrated London News*, 25 January 1919, p. 19, The British Newspaper Archive <https://www.britishnewspaperarchive.co.uk/viewer/BL/0001578/19190125/061/0019?browse=true> [accessed 26 March 2019]

270 Bibliography

Glendinning, Victoria. *Leonard Woolf: A Biography*. (London: Simon & Schuster, 2006)

——. *Vita: The Life of Vita Sackville-West* (New York: Knopf, 1983)

Glenny, Allie. *Ravenous Identity: Eating and Eating Distress in the Life and Work of Virginia Woolf* (Basingstoke: Macmillan, 2000)

Gorsky, Susan. '"The central shadow": Characterization in *The Waves*', *Modern Fiction Studies*, 18.3 (1972), 449–66

Gottlieb, Freema. 'Leonard Woolf's Attitudes to His Jewish Background and to Judaism', *Transactions & Miscellanies*, 25 (1973–75), 25–37

Greer, Julie Anne. 'Learning from Linked Lives: Narrativising the Individual and Group Biographies of the Guests at the 25th Jubilee Dinner of the British Psychoanalytical Society at The Savoy, London, on 8th March 1939' EdD thesis, Southampton University, University of Southampton Institutional Repository (2014)

Graves, Robert. *Goodbye to All That* (London: Penguin, 2000)

Grayzel, Susan R. *Women's Identities at War: Gender, Motherhood, and Politics in Britain and France during the First World War* (Chapel Hill: University of North Carolina Press, 1999)

Green, Stephanie. *The Public Lives of Charlotte and Marie Stopes* (Abingdon: Routledge, 2016)

Greenaway, Kate. *Language of Flowers* (London: Routledge, 1884)

Gurney, Peter. *The Making of Consumer Culture in Modern Britain* (London: Bloomsbury, 2017)

Hall, Ruth. *Marie Stopes* (London: Virago, 1978)

Hancock, Nuala. 'Virginia Woolf and Gardens', in *The Edinburgh Companion to Virginia Woolf and the Arts*, ed. Maggie Humm (Edinburgh: Edinburgh University Press, 2010), pp. 245–60

Hankey, Maurice P A. 'Recommendations of the Committee (3rd Revise)', Cabinet Memorial Services (November 11th) Committee, *The National Archives*, Public Works Record, Public Records Office, CAB 24/114/65 (5 November 1920)

Hankins, Leslie. '"To kindle and illuminate": Woolf's Hot Flashes against Ageism – Challenges for Cinema', in *Virginia Woolf and Her Influences* ed. Jeanette McVickers and Laura Davies (New York: Pace University Press, 1998), pp. 26–35.

Hanson, Clare. *Eugenics, Literature, and Culture in Post-War Britain* (Abingdon: Routledge, 2013)

Harlow, H. 'The Nature of Love', *American Psychologist*, 13.12 (1958), 673–85

Harrison, Austin. 'For the Unborn', *The English Review*, May 1915, pp. 231–36

Harrison, Jane Ellen. *Ancient Ritual and Art* (Oxford: Oxford University Press, 1913; repr. Bradford-on-Avon: Moonraker, 1978)

——. *Peace with Patriotism* (Cambridge: Deighton Bell, 1915)

——. *Prolegomena to the Study of Greek Religion*, 2nd edn (Cambridge: Cambridge University Press, 1903; repr. 1908)

Hartley, John. *Bully Beef and Biscuits: Food in the Great War* (Barnsley: Pen & Sword Military, 2015)

Haskill, Christine. 'The Sex War and the Great War: Woolf's Late Victorian Inheritance in *Three Guineas*', in *Virginia Woolf: Writing the World*, ed. Pamela Caughie and Diana Swanson (Liverpool: Liverpool University Press, 2015), pp. 43–48

Hauck, Christina. '"To escape the horror of family life": Virginia Woolf and the British Birth Control Debate', in *New Essays on Virginia Woolf*, ed. Helen Wussow (Dallas, TX: Contemporary Research, 1995), pp. 15–37

Haule, James. '*To the Lighthouse* and The Great War: The Evidence of Virginia Woolf's Revisions of "Time Passes"', in *Virginia Woolf and War: Fiction, Reality and Myth*, ed. Mark Hussey (New York: Syracuse University Press, 1991), pp. 164–79

Hawke, Ellen. 'Woolf's "Magical Garden of Women"', in *New Feminist Essays on Virginia Woolf*, ed. Jane Marcus (Lincoln, NE: University of Nebraska Press, 1981), pp. 31–60

Helt, Brenda. 'Passionate Debates on "Odious Subjects": Bisexuality and Woolf's Opposition to Theories of Androgyny and Sexual Identity', *Twentieth Century Literature*, 56.2 (2010), 131–67

Hill, Katherine C. 'Virginia Woolf and Leslie Stephen: History and Literary Revolution', *PMLA*, 96.3 (1981), 351–62

Higonnet, Margaret. 'Suicide: Representations of the Feminine in the Nineteenth Century', *Poetics Today*, 6.1/2 (1985), 103–18

Hiller, Eric. 'Some Remarks on Tobacco', *International Journal of Psycho-Analysis*, 3 (1922), 475–80.

Hilton, Matthew. 'The Female Consumer and the Politics of Consumption in Twentieth-Century Britain', *The Historical Journal*, 45.1 (2002), 103–28

Himmelfarb, Gertrude. 'In Defense of the Victorians', *Wilson Quarterly*, 12.3 (1976), 90–99

Hirsh, Elizabeth. 'Mrs Dalloway's Menopause: Encrypting the Female Life Course', in *Woolf in the Real World*, ed. Karen V. Kukil (Clemson, SC: Clemson University Press, 2005), pp. 76–81

Hite, Molly. 'Tonal Cues and Uncertain Values: Affect and Ethics in *Mrs Dalloway*', *Narrative*, 18.3 (2010), 249–75

Holland, Kathryn. 'Late Victorian and Modern Feminist Intertexts: The Strachey Women in *A Room of One's Own* and *Three Guineas*', *Tulsa Studies in Women's Literature*, 32.1 (2013), 75–98

Holtby, Winifred. *Virginia Woolf: A Critical Memoir* (London: Continuum International, 2007)

Holtzman, Ellen M. 'The Pursuit of Married Love: Women's Attitudes toward Sexuality and Marriage in Great Britain, 1918–1939', *Journal of Social History*, 16.2 (1982), 39–51

Homberger, Eric. 'The Story of the Cenotaph', *Times Literary Supplement*, 12 November 1976, pp. 1429–30

Bibliography

Humble, Nicola. 'Little Swans with Luxette and Loved Boy Pudding: Changing Fashions in Cookery Books', *Women: A Cultural Review*, 13.3 (2002), 322–38

Humm, Maggie. *Feminisms: A Reader* (London: Harvester Wheatsheaf, 1992)

Hussey, Mark. 'Refractions of Desire: The Early Fiction of Virginia and Leonard Woolf', *Modern Fiction Studies*, 38.1 (1992), 127–46

——. *Virginia Woolf A–Z* (New York: Facts on File, 1995)

—— (ed.). *Virginia Woolf and War: Fiction, Reality, and Myth* (New York: Syracuse University Press, 1991)

Huston, Nancy. 'The Matrix of War: Mothers and Heroes', in *The Female Body in Western Culture: Contemporary Perspectives*, ed. Susan Rubin Suleiman (Cambridge: Harvard University Press, 1985), pp. 120–36

Huxley, Julian. *What Dare I Think?* (London: Chatto & Windus, 1933)

——, H. G. Wells and G. P. Wells. *The Science of Life* (London: Cassell and Co., 1931)

Hyslop, T. B. 'A Discussion on Occupation and Environment as Causative Factors of Insanity', *British Medical Journal*, 2.2337 (1905), 941–44

Jameson, Anna. *Sisters of Charity; and, the Communion of Labour: Two Lectures on the Social Employments of Women* (London: Longman, Brown, Green, Longmans, and Roberts, 1859)

Janik, Allan. *Essays on Wittgenstein and Weininger* (Amsterdam: Rodopi, 1985)

Jensen, Tracey. 'Why Study the Maternal Now?', *Studies in the Maternal*, 1.1 (2009) <http://doi.org/10.16995/sim.166> [accessed 22 October 2019], 1–3

Johnson, George. '"The Spirit of the Age": Virginia Woolf's Response to Second Wave Psychology', *Twentieth Century Literature*, 40.2 (1994), pp. 139–64

Jones, Clara. *Virginia Woolf: Ambivalent Activist* (Edinburgh: Edinburgh University Press, 2016)

——. 'Virginia Woolf's 1931 "Cook Sketch"', *Woolf Studies Annual*, 20 (2014), 1–23

Kato, Megumi. 'The Milk Problem in *To the Lighthouse*', *Virginia Woolf Miscellany*, 50 (1997), 5

——. 'The Politics/Poetics of Motherhood in *To the Lighthouse*', in *Virginia Woolf and Communities*, ed. Jeanette McVickers and Laura Davies (New York: Pace University Press, 1999), pp. 102–09

Kaula, David. 'The Time Sense of Antony and Cleopatra', *Shakespeare Quarterly*, 15.3 (1964), 211–23

Kawash, Samira. 'New Directions in Motherhood Studies', *Signs*, 36.4 (2011), 969–1003

Kealey, E. J. 'Women of Britain Say "Go!"', poster (Parliamentary Recruiting Committee, 1915), Imperial War Museum, London <https://www.iwm.org.uk/learning/resources/first-world-war-recruitment-posters> [accessed 9 September 2013]

Keynes, John Maynard. 'An Economic Analysis of Unemployment', in *Unemployment as a World-Problem*, ed. Quincy Wright (Chicago: University of Chicago Press, 1931), pp. 1–42

——. 'Opening Remarks: The Galton Lecture', *The Eugenics Review*, 38 (1946), 39–40

Kime Scott, Bonnie. *In the Hollow of the Wave: Virginia Woolf and Modernist Uses of Nature* (Charlottesville: University of Virginia Press, 2012)

——. 'The Word Split Its Husk: Woolf's Double Vision of Modernist Language', *Modern Fiction Studies*, 34.3 (1988), 371–85

King, Julia, and Laila Miletic-Vejzovic (eds). *The Library of Leonard and Virginia Woolf: A Short-Title Catalogue* (Pullman: Washington State University Press, 2003)

Kingsley Kent, Susan. *Making Peace: The Reconstruction of Gender in Interwar Britain* (Princeton, NJ: Princeton University Press, 1993)

——. *Sex and Suffrage in Britain 1860–1914* (Princeton, NJ: Princeton University Press, 1987)

Klein, Melanie. *The Psycho-analysis of Children* (London: Hogarth Press, 1932)

——, and Joan Riviera. *Love, Hate and Reparation* (London: Hogarth Press, 1937)

Knauer, Elizabeth. 'Of Dogs, Daughters, and the "Back Bedroom" School: Woolf's *Flush* and Women's Education', *CEA Critic*, 73.2 (2011), 1–20

Kore Schröder, Leena. 'Tales of Abjection and Miscegenation: Virginia Woolf's and Leonard Woolf's "Jewish" Stories', *Twentieth Century Literature*, 49.3 (2003), 298–327

Kostkowska, Justyna. *Ecocriticism and Women Writers* (Basingstoke: Palgrave Macmillan, 2013)

Koven, Seth, and Sonia Michel. *Mothers of a New World* (London: Routledge, 1993)

——. 'Womanly Duties: Maternalist Politics and the Origins of Welfare States in France, Germany, Great Britain, and the United States, 1880–1920', *The American Historical Review*, 95.4 (1990), 1076–108

Kushen, Betty. 'Virginia Woolf: Metaphor of the Inverted Birth', *American Imago*, 38.3 (1981), 279–304

Ladd-Taylor, Molly. *Fixing the Poor: Eugenic Sterilization and Child Welfare in the Twentieth Century* (Baltimore, MD: Johns Hopkins University Press, 2017)

Laurence, Patricia. *The Reading of Silence: Virginia Woolf in the English Tradition* (Stanford, CA: Stanford University Press, 1991)

Lavelli, Manuela, and Marco Poli, 'Early Mother–Infant Interaction During Breast- and Bottle-Feeding', *Infant Behavior and Development*, 21.4 (1998), 667–83

Lawrence, D. H. *Lady Chatterley's Lover*, ed. Michael Squires, with an introduction by Doris Lessing (London: Penguin, 2006)

Lee, Hermione. *Virginia Woolf* (London: Vintage, 1997)

274 Bibliography

Lefer, Jay. 'Object Relations in Human Sexuality', *International Journal of Mental Health*, 26. 1 (1997), 15–22

Letherby, Gayle, and Catherine Williams. 'Non-Motherhood: Ambivalent Autobiographies', *Feminist Studies*, 25.3 (1999), 719–28

Levenback, Karen. *Virginia Woolf and the Great War* (New York: Syracuse University Press, 1999)

——. 'Virginia Woolf's "War in the Village" and "War from the Street"', in *Virginia Woolf and War: Fiction, Reality and Myth*, ed. Mark Hussey (New York: Syracuse University Press, 1991), pp. 40–57

Levitan, Kathrin. 'Redundancy, the "Surplus Woman" Problem, and the British Census, 1851–1861', *Women's History Review*, 17.3 (2008), 359–76

Levy, Heather. *Servants of Desire* (New York: Peter Lang, 2010)

——. '"These ghost figures of distorted passion": Becoming Privy to Working-Class Desire in "The Watering Place" and "The Ladies Lavatory"', *Modern Fiction Studies*, 50.1 (2004), 31–57

Lewis, Jane. *The Politics of Motherhood: Child and Maternal Welfare in England 1900–1939* (London: Croom Helm, 1980)

Lewis, Paul. 'Life by Water: Characterization and Salvation in *The Waste Land*', *Mosaic*, 11.4 (1978), 81–90

Light, Alison. *Mrs Woolf and the Servants* (London: Penguin Books, 2008)

Little, Judy. '*Jacob's Room* as Comedy: Woolf's Parodic Bildungsroman', in *New Feminist Essays on Virginia Woolf*, ed. Jane Marcus (Lincoln, NE: University of Nebraska Press, 1981), pp. 105–24

Livingstone, Catriona. '"How can we alter the crest and the spur of the fighting cock?": Julian Huxley, Popular Biology, and the Feminist Pacifism of Virginia Woolf', *Women: A Cultural Review*, 31.3 (2020), 315–334.

Llewelyn Davies, Margaret. 'Cooperation at the Fountainhead', *Life and Labour*, 7 (1920), 199–202

—— (ed.). *Life as We Have Known It: The Voices of Working-Class Women* (London: Virago, 2012)

—— (ed.). *Maternity: Letters from Working Women* (1915) (retitled *No One but a Woman Knows* (London: Virago, 2012))

Longenbach, James. 'The Women and Men of 1914', in *Arms and the Woman: War, Gender and Literary Representation*, ed. Helen Cooper, Adrienne Munich and Susan Squier (Chapel Hill: University of North Carolina Press, 1989), pp. 97–123

Lovelace, Ada. 'Society and the Seasons', in *The Times' Fifty Years, Memories and Contrasts* (London; T. Butterworth, 1932), pp. 24–30

Lowe, Alice. '"A certain hold on haddock and sausage": Dining Well in Virginia Woolf's Life and Work', in *Virginia Woolf and the Natural World*, ed. Kristin Czarnecki and Carrie Rohman (Liverpool: Liverpool University Press, 2011), pp. 157–62

MacCarthy, Desmond [Affable Hawk, pseud.]. 'Current Literature: Books in General', *New Statesman*, 2 October 1920, p. 704

McCleary, George F. 'The Infants' Milk Depot: Its History and Function', *The Journal of Hygiene*, 4.3 (1904), pp. 329–68

MacDuff, Sangam. 'After the Deluge, *The Waves*', in *Virginia Woolf and the World of Books*, ed. Nicola Wilson and Claire Battershill (Liverpool: Liverpool University Press, 2018), pp. 76–82

McIntire, Gabrielle. 'An Exchange Regarding Freud and the Hogarth Press', *Virginia Woolf Miscellany*, 77 (2010), 16

MacKay, Marina. 'The Lunacy of Men, the Idiocy of Women: Woolf, West, and War', *NWSA Journal*, 15.3 (2003), 124–44

MacKenzie, Donald. 'Eugenics in Britain', *Social Studies of Science*, 6.3/4 (1976), 499–532

Maggio, Paula. 'Taking Up Her Pen for World Peace: Virginia Woolf, Feminist Pacifist. Or Not?', in *Virginia Woolf: Writing the World*, ed. Pamela Caughie and Diana Swanson (Liverpool: Liverpool University Press, 2015), pp. 37–42

Maitland, Frederic William. *The Life and Letters of Leslie Stephen* (London: Duckworth, 1906)

Malamud, Randy. 'Splitting the Husks: Woolf's Modernist Language in *Night and Day*', *South Central Review*, 6.1 (1989), 32–45

Malthus, Thomas Robert. *An Essay on the Principle of Population*, ed. Joyce E. Chaplin (London: J. Johnson, 1798; repr. London: W. W. Norton, 2018)

Marcus, Jane (ed.). 'Alibis and Legends: The Ethics of Elsewhereness, Gender and Estrangement', in *Women's Writing in Exile*, ed. Angela Ingram and Mary Lynn Broe (Chapel Hill: University of North Carolina Press, 1989), pp. 269–94

——. *Art & Anger: Reading Like a Woman* (Columbus: Ohio State University Press, 1988)

——. 'Liberty, Sorority, Misogyny', in *The Representation of Women in Fiction*, ed. C. Heilbrun and M. Higonnet (Baltimore, MD: Johns Hopkins University Press, 1983), pp. 60–97

——. *New Feminist Essays on Virginia Woolf* (Lincoln, NE: University of Nebraska Press, 1981)

——. *Virginia Woolf and the Languages of Patriarchy* (Bloomington: Indiana University Press, 1987)

——. 'Wrapped in the Stars and Stripes: Virginia Woolf in the U.S.A.', *The South Carolina Review*, 29.1 (1996), 17–23

Marder, Herbert. *The Measure of Life: Virginia Woolf's Last Years* (London: Cornell University Press, 2000)

Marshik, Celia. 'Thinking Back through Copyright', in *Modernism & Copyright*, ed. Paul K. Saint-Amour (Oxford: Oxford University Press, 2011), pp. 65–86

Martin, Ann. '"The little bit of power I had myself": Lady Lasswade's Shifting Sense of Place in *The Years*', in *Virginia Woolf and Heritage*, ed. Jane De Gay, Tom Breckin and Anne Reus (Liverpool: Liverpool University Press, 2017), pp. 60–66

Mayhall, Laura E. Nym. 'Defining Militancy: Radical Protest, the Constitutional Idiom, and Women's Suffrage in Britain, 1908–1909', *The Journal of British Studies*, 39.3 (2000), 340–71

276 Bibliography

Meisel, Perry. 'Woolf and Freud: The Kleinian Turn', in *Virginia Woolf in Context*, eds. Bryony Randall and Jane Goldman (Cambridge: Cambridge University Press, 2012), pp. 332–41

'Memoranda', *British Journal of Inebriety*, 10 (1912), pp. 105–14

Meyer, Jessica. '"Not Septimus now": Wives of Disabled Veterans and Cultural Memory of the First World War in Britain', *Women's History Review*, 13.1 (2004), 117–37

Mills, Jean. *Virginia Woolf, Jane Ellen Harrison, and the Spirit of Modern Classicism* (Columbus: Ohio State University Press, 2014)

The Ministry Of Women: Report Of the Archbishop's Commission (London: Press and Publication Board of the Church Assembly, 1935)

Minow-Pinkney, Makiko. '*Virginia Woolf and the Problem of the Subject* (Brighton: Harvester, 1987)

Mitchison, Naomi. *The Corn King and the Spring Queen* (Edinburgh: Cannongate, 1931)

Moore, Madeline. '*Orlando*: An Edition of the Manuscript', *Twentieth Century Literature*, 25.3/4 (1979), 303–55

——. *The Short Season Between Two Silences* (London: George Allen & Unwin, 1984)

Moran, Patricia. 'Virginia Woolf and the Scene of Writing', *Modern Fiction Studies*, 38.1 (1992), 81–100

Morganroth Gullette, Margaret. *Declining to Decline: Cultural Combat and the Politics of the Midlife* (Charlottesville: University Press of Virginia, 1997)

——. 'Inventing the "Postmaternal" Woman, 1898–1927: Idle, Unwanted, and Out of a Job', *Feminist Studies*, 21.2 (1995), 221–53

Morris, Pam. *Jane Austen, Virginia Woolf and Worldly Realism* (Edinburgh: Edinburgh University Press, 2017)

Mosse, George L. 'Shell-Shock as a Social Disease', *Journal of Contemporary History*, 35.1 (2000), 101–08

Mothers' Union. *To British Mothers: How They Can Help Enlistment* (London: Mothers' Union, 1914)

Mott, Frederick. 'The Neuroses and Psychoses in Relation to Conscription and Eugenics', *The Eugenics Review*, 14.1 (1922), 13–22

National Birth-Rate Commission. *Problems of Population and Parenthood: Being the Second Report of and the Chief Evidence Taken by the National Birth-Rate Commission, 1918–20* (London: Chapman and Hall, 1920)

Neushul, Peter. 'Marie C. Stopes and the Popularization of Birth Control Technology', *Technology and Culture*, 39.2 (1998), 245–72

Neville-Rolfe, Sybil. *Social Biology and Welfare* (London: George Allen & Unwin, 1949)

Nicolson, Nigel. *Portrait of a Marriage* (London: Weidenfeld and Nicolson, 1973)

Nuhn, Ferner. *The Wind Blew from the East: A Study in the Orientation of American Culture* (New York: Harper & Brothers, 1942)

Office of the Registrar-General. *The Census of Great Britain in 1851*, ed. Thomas Milner (London: Longman, Brown, Green, and Longmans, 1854)

Ondaatje Rolls, Jans. *The Bloomsbury Cookbook* (London: Thames and Hudson, 2014)

Orestano, Francesca. 'Virginia Woolf and the Cooking Range', in *Not Just Porridge: English Literati at Table*, ed. Francesca Orestano and Michael Vickers (Oxford: Archaeopress, 2017), pp. 125–33

Overy, Richard. *The Morbid Age: Britain and the Crisis of Civilisation, 1919–1939* (London: Allen Lane, 2009)

Panken, Shirley. *Virginia Woolf and the Lust of Creation* (New York: State University of New York Press, 1987)

Pankhurst, Dame Christabel. 'Women and the War', in *Women's Writing of the First World War: An Anthology*, ed. Angela K. Smith (Manchester: Manchester University Press, 2000), pp. 71–85

Park, Sowon. 'Suffrage and Virginia Woolf: "The mass behind the single voice"', *The Review of English Studies*, 56.223 (2005), 119–34

Paskauskas, R. A. *The Complete Correspondence of Sigmund Freud and Ernest Jones 1908–1939* (Cambridge, MA: Harvard University Press, 1993)

Patmore, Coventry. *The Angel in the House*, 4th edn (London: Macmillan, 1866)

Pawlowski, Merry M. *Virginia Woolf and Fascism* (Basingstoke: Palgrave Macmillan, 2001)

Payne, Michael. 'Erotic Irony and Polarity in *Antony and Cleopatra*', *Shakespeare Quarterly*, 24.3 (1973), 265–79

Peach, Linden. 'Historical Approaches', in *Palgrave Advances in Virginia Woolf Studies*, ed. Anna Snaith (Basingstoke: Palgrave Macmillan, 2007), p. 169

——. 'Woolf and Eugenics', in *Virginia Woolf in Context*, ed. Bryony Randall and Jane Goldman (Cambridge: Cambridge University Press, 2012), pp. 439–48

Pearl, Raymond. 'The Biology of Population Growth', in *World Population Conference Proceedings*, ed. Margaret Sanger (London: Edward Arnold, 1927)

Pedersen, Susan. *Family, Dependence, and the Origins of the Welfare State: Britain and France 1914–1945* (Cambridge: Cambridge University Press, 1993)

Pember Reeves, Maud. *Round about a Pound a Week* (London: G. Bell, 1914)

Periyan, Natasha. *The Politics of 1930s British Literature: Education, Class, Gender* (London: Bloomsbury Academic, 2018)

Pethick-Lawrence, Emmeline. 'Motherhood and War', *Harper's Weekly*, 5 December 1914, p. 542

Plain, Gill. *Women's Fiction of the Second World War: Gender, Power and Resistance* (Edinburgh: Edinburgh University Press, 1996)

Plant, Rebecca Jo. *Mom: The Transformation of Motherhood in Modern America* (Chicago: University of Chicago Press, 2010)

278 Bibliography

Platt, Nicky. 'When Freud Gets Useful: Retaining the Commonplace in Virginia Woolf's *Pointz Hall*', *Woolf Studies Annual*, 16 (2010), pp. 155–74

Plomin, R. *Genetics and Experience: The Interplay between Nature and Nurture* (Thousand Oaks, CA: Sage, 1994)

Poole, Roger. *The Unknown Virginia Woolf* (Brighton: Harvester, 1982)

Port, Cynthia. '"Ages are the stuff!"': The Traffic in Ages in Interwar Britain', *NWSA Journal*, 18.1 (2006), pp. 138–61

Potter, Jane. *Boys in Khaki, Girls in Print* (Oxford: Oxford University Press, 2005)

Priest, Ann-Marie. 'Between Being and Nothingness: The "Astonishing Precipice" of Virginia Woolf's *Night and Day*', *Journal of Modern Literature*, 26.2 (2003), pp. 66–80

——. *Great Writers, Great Loves: The Reinvention of Love in the Twentieth Century* (Melbourne: Black Inc. Books, 2006)

Prins, Yopie. '"OTOTOTOI"': Virginia Woolf and "The Naked Cry" of Cassandra', in *Agamemnon in Performance 458 BC to AD 2004*, ed. Fiona Macintosh et al. (Oxford: Oxford University Press, 2005), pp. 163–85

'A Proclamation', *The Spectator*, 26 May 1917, p. 4

'Proposals that Leonard Woolf take over work of Non Conscription Fellowship and the National Council for Civil Liberties', University of Sussex Special Collection, SxMs-13/1/G/2/A (1916)

Proudfit, Sharon L. 'Virginia Woolf: Reluctant Feminist in *The Years*', *Criticism*, 17.1 (1975), 59–73

Provine, William B. *The Origins of Theoretical Population Genetics* (Chicago: University of Chicago Press, 1971)

Radeva, Milena. 'Re-visioning Philanthropy and Women's Roles: Virginia Woolf, Professionalization, and the Philanthropy Debates', in *Woolf Editing/Editing Woolf*, ed. Eleanor McNees and Sara Veglahn (Liverpool: Liverpool University Press, 2009), pp. 206–15

Raitt, Suzanne. 'Virginia Woolf's Early Novels: Finding a Voice', in *The Cambridge Companion to Virginia Woolf*, ed. Sue Roe and Susan Sellers (Cambridge: Cambridge University Press, 2000), pp. 29–49

——. *Vita & Virginia: The Work and Friendship of V. Sackville-West and Virginia Woolf* (Oxford: Oxford University Press, 1993)

Randall, Bryony. *Modernism, Daily Time and Everyday Life* (Cambridge: Cambridge University Press, 2007; repr. 2011)

——. 'Virginia Woolf's Idea of a Party', in *The Modernist Party*, ed. Kate McLoughlin (Edinburgh: Edinburgh University Press, 2013), pp. 95-111

——. 'Woolf and Modernist Studies', in *Virginia Woolf in Context*, ed. Bryony Randall and Jane Goldman (Cambridge: Cambridge University Press, 2012), pp. 28–39

Rathbone, Eleanor. 'The Remuneration of Women's Services', *The Economic Journal*, 27.105 (1917), 55–68

——. 'Separation Allowances: An Experiment in the State Endowment of Maternity II', *Common Cause*, 7.362 (1916), 648–49

——. 'Separation Allowances: I', *Common Cause*, 7.359 (1915), 611–12

Rational Dress Society's Gazette, April 1888, p. 1

Report of Proceedings of the First International Eugenics Congress, Held at the University of London, July 24th to 30th, 1912 (*Problems in Eugenics*, vol. II) (London: The Eugenics Education Society, 1912)

Review of Virginia Woolf, *Night and Day* (1919), *Times Literary Supplement*, 30 October 1919, p. 607

Ricoeur, Paul. *Time and Narrative*, 3 vols, trans. Kathleen McLaughlin and David Pellauer (Chicago: University of Chicago Press, 1984–1988)

Robb, George. 'Race Motherhood: Moral Eugenics vs Progressive Eugenics, 1880–1920', in *Maternal Instincts: Visions of Motherhood and Sexuality in Britain, 1875–1925*, ed. Ann Sumner Holmes and Claudia Nelson (New York: St Martin's, 1997), pp. 58–74

——. 'The Way of All Flesh: Degeneration, Eugenics, and the Gospel of Free Love', *Journal of the History of* Sexuality, 6.4 (1996), 589–603

——. *Consumerism and the Co-operative Movement in Modern British History* (Manchester: Manchester University Press, 2009)

Rosenman, Ellen Bayuk. *The Invisible Presence: Virginia Woolf and the Mother–Daughter Relationship* (Baton Rouge: Louisiana State University Press, 1986)

Rosenthal, Michael. *Virginia Woolf* (London: Routledge & Kegan Paul, 1979)

Roston, Murray. *Modernist Patterns in Literature and the Visual Arts* (Basingstoke: Macmillan, 2000)

Rowland, Beryl. 'The Oven in Popular Metaphor from Hosea to the Present Day', *American Speech*, 45.3/4 (1970), 215–22

Rubio-Marín, Ruth. 'The Achievement of Female Suffrage in Europe: On Women's Citizenship', *International Journal of Constitutional Law*, 12.1 (2014), 4–34

Ruddick, Sara. 'Private Brother, Public World', in *New Feminist Essays on Virginia Woolf*, ed. Jane Marcus (Lincoln, NE: University of Nebraska Press, 1981), pp. 185–215

Rupp, Leila J. 'Constructing Internationalism: The Case of Transnational Women's Organisations, 1888–1945', *The American Historical Review*, 99.5 (1994), 1571–600

Russell Noble, Joan (ed.). *Recollections of Virginia Woolf by Her Contemporaries* (London: Cardinal, 1989)

Ryan, Derek. 'From Spaniel Club to Animalous Society: Virginia Woolf's *Flush*', in *Contradictory Woolf*, ed. Derek Ryan and Stella Bolaki (Liverpool: Liverpool University Press, 2012), pp. 158–65

——. *Virginia Woolf and the Materiality of Theory* (Edinburgh: Edinburgh University Press, 2013)

——, and Stella Bolaki. 'Introduction', in *Contradictory Woolf*, ed. Derek Ryan and Stella Bolaki (Liverpool: Liverpool University Press, 2012)

Sackville-West, Vita. *The Dragon in Shallow Waters* (London: G. P. Putnam's, 1921)

——. *Family History* (London: Virago, 1996)

280 Bibliography

——. *Heritage* (London: William Collins, 1919)

——. *The Letters of Vita Sackville-West to Virginia Woolf*, ed. Louise DeSalvo (San Francisco: Cleis, 2004)

——, and Harold Nicolson. 'Marriage', *Listener*, 26 June 1929, 1.24, pp. 899–900

Saguaro, Shelley. '"Something that would stand for the conception": The Inseminating World in the Last Writings of Virginia Woolf', *Green Letters: Studies in Ecocriticism*, 17.2 (2013), 109–20

Sarsfield, Rachel. 'Cassandra's Worms: Unravelling the Threads of Virginia Woolf's Lepidoptera Imagery', *Hungarian Journal of English and American Studies*, 9.1 (2003), 101–17

Saunders, Max. *Self Impressions: Life-Writing, Autobiografiction and the Forms of Modern Literature* (Oxford: Oxford University Press, 2010)

Savage, George. 'Discussion on Insanity and Marriage', *British Medical Journal*, 2.2599 (1910), 1242–44

——. 'A Lecture on Neurasthenia and Mental Disorders', *The Medical Magazine*, 20 (1911), 520–30

Schwartz Cowan, Ruth. 'Francis Galton's Statistical Ideas: The Influence of Eugenics', *Isis*, 63.4 (1972), 509–28

Scott, Gillian. *Feminism and the Politics of Working Women* (London: UCL Press, 1998)

Shamdasani, Sonu. '"Psychotherapy": The invention of a word', *History of the Human Sciences*, 18.1 (2005), 1–22

Shattuck, Sandra. 'The Stage of Scholarship: Crossing the Bridge from Harrison to Woolf', in *Virginia Woolf and Bloomsbury: A Centenary Celebration*, ed. Jane Marcus (Basingstoke: Macmillan, 1987), pp. 278–98

Shields, E. F. 'The American Edition of *Mrs Dalloway*', *Studies in Bibliography*, 27 (1974), 157–75

Showalter, Elaine. *A Literature of Their Own: British Women Novelists from Brontë to Lessing* (Princeton, NJ: Princeton University Press, 1977)

——. 'Victorian Women and Insanity', *Victorian Studies*, 23.2 (1980), pp. 157–81

Simpson, Kathryn. *Gifts, Markets and Economies of Desire in Virginia Woolf* (London: Palgrave Macmillan, 2009)

Snaith, Anna. 'A Room of One's Own', in *The Literary Encyclopedia* (March 2001) <https://www.litencyc.com/php/sworks.php?rec=true& UID=7038> [accessed 2 October 2019]

——. 'Introduction', in Woolf, *A Room of One's Own and Three Guineas*, ed. Anna Snaith (Oxford: Oxford University Press, 2015)

——. 'Leonard and Virginia Woolf: Writing Against Empire', *The Journal of Commonwealth Literature*, 50 (2015), 19–32

——. '"My poor private voice": Virginia Woolf and Auto/Biography', in *Representing Lives: Women and Auto/Biography*, ed. Alison Donnell and Pauline Polkey (London: Palgrave Macmillan, 2000), pp. 96–104

——. 'Race, Empire, and Ireland', in *Virginia Woolf in Context*, ed. Bryony Randall and Jane Goldman (Cambridge University Press, 2012), pp. 206–18

——. '"A view of one's own": Writing Women's Lives and the Early Short Stories', in *Trespassing Boundaries: Virginia Woolf's Short Fiction*, ed. K. N. Benzel and R. Hoberman (Basingstoke: Palgrave Macmillan, 2004), pp. 125–38

——. *Virginia Woolf: Public and Private Negotiations* (Basingstoke: Palgrave Macmillan, 2000)

Soloway, Richard. 'Marie Stopes, Eugenics and the Birth Control Movement', in *Marie Stopes, Eugenics and the Birth Control Movement: Proceedings of a Conference Organized by The Galton Institute, London, 1996*, ed. Robert A Peel (London: The Galton Institute, 1997), pp. 49–76

——. 'Neo–Malthusians, Eugenists, and the Declining Birth-Rate in England, 1900–1918', *Albion: A Quarterly Journal Concerned with British Studies*, 10.3 (1978), 264–86

Sparks, Elisa Kay. '"Everything tended to set itself in a garden": Virginia Woolf's Literary and Quotidian Flowers A Bar-Graphical Approach', in *Virginia Woolf and the Natural World*, ed. Kristin Czarnecki and Carrie Rohman (Liverpool: Liverpool University Press, 2011), pp. 42–60

Spurgeon, Dickie. 'The Athenaeum', in *British Literary Magazines: The Romantic Age, 1789–1836*, ed. Alvin Sullivan (Westport, CT: Greenwood, 1989), pp. 21–24

Squier, Susan M., Louise A. DeSalvo and Virginia Woolf. 'Virginia Woolf's "The Journal of Mistress Joan Martyn"', *Twentieth Century Literature*, 25.3/4 (1979), 237–69

Stanley, Adam. 'Hearth, Home, and Steering Wheel: Gender and Modernity in France after the Great War', *The Historian*, 66.2 (2004), 233–53

Stape, John Henry (ed.). *Virginia Woolf: Interviews and Recollections* (Basingstoke: Macmillan, 1995)

Staveley, Alice. 'Marketing Virginia Woolf: Women, War, and Public Relations in *Three Guineas*', *Book History*, 12 (2009), 295–339

Stephen, Leslie. *The Science of Ethics* (London: Smith, Elder, 1882)

——. *Social Rights and Duties: Addresses to Ethical Societies* (London: Swan Sonnenschein, 1896)

——. *Studies of a Biographer*, 4 vols (London: Duckworth, 1898–1902)

Stephens, Julie. *Confronting Postmaternal Thinking: Feminism, Memory, and Care* (New York: Columbia University Press, 2012)

Stevens, Emily. 'A History of Infant Feeding', *The Journal of Perinatal Education*, 18.2 (2009), 32–39

Stimpson, Catherine. 'Foreword', in Elizabeth Abel, *Virginia Woolf and the Fictions of Psychoanalysis* (Chicago: University of Chicago Press, 1989), pp. ix–xi

Stopes, Charlotte Carmichael. *British Freewomen* (London: Swan Sonnenschein, 1894)

Stopes, Marie Carmichael. *Contraception* (London: John Bale, 1923)

——. *Contraception its Theory, History and Practice: A Manual for the Medical and Legal Professions* (London: Putnam, 1952)

282   *Bibliography*

——. *Love's Creation: A Novel* (London: John Bale, 1928; repr. Eastbourne: Sussex Academic, 2012)

——. *Married Love: A New Contribution to the Solution of Sex Difficulties*, 6th edn (London: A. C. Fifield, 1919)

——. *Mother England: A Contemporary History* (London: John Bale, 1929)

——. *Radiant Motherhood: A Book for Those Who are Creating the Future* (London: G. P. Putnam, 1920)

——. *Wise Parenthood: The Treatise on Birth Control for Married People: A Practical Sequel to Married Love*, 4th edn (London: A. C. Fifield, 1919)

—— et al. *Queen's Hall Meeting on Constructive Birth Control: Speeches and Impressions* (London: G. P. Putnam, 1921)

Storr, L. 'Letter from L. Storr (Secretary of Memorial Services Committee) to J. T. Davies', *David Lloyd George Papers*, House of Lords Record Office, F/23/3/20, 28 October 1920, quoted in Susan Grayzel, *Women's Identities at War* (Chapel Hill: University of North Carolina Press, 1999), p. 230

Strange, Julie-Marie. *Death, Grief and Poverty in Britain, 1870–1914* (Cambridge: Cambridge University Press, 2005)

Sutton, Emma. *Virginia Woolf and Classical Music* (Edinburgh: Edinburgh University Press, 2014)

Taylor Suppé, Charlotte. '"My comfortable capitalistic head": Virginia Woolf on Consumption, Co-operation and Motherhood', in *Virginia Woolf and Capitalism*, ed. Clara Jones (Edinburgh: Edinburgh University Press, 2024), pp. 70–91

Tennyson, Alfred Lord. 'The Princess', in *Alfred Tennyson The Major Works,* ed. Adam Roberts, rev. edn (Oxford: Oxford University Press, 2009), VII. 299–311

Toner, Anne. *Ellipsis in English Literature: Signs of Omission* (Cambridge: Cambridge University Press, 2015)

Topping Bazin, Nancy, and Jane Hamovit Lauter. 'Woolf's Keen Sensitivity to War', in *Virginia Woolf and War: Fiction, Reality and Myth*, ed. Mark Hussey (New York: Syracuse University Press, 1991), pp. 14–39

Toye, John. *Keynes on Population* (Oxford: Oxford University Press, 2000)

Trautmann, Joanne. *The Jessamy Brides: The Friendship of Virginia Woolf and V. Sackville-West*, Penn State Studies, No. 36 (University Park: Pennsylvania State University Press, 1973)

Tromanhauser, Vicki. 'Animal Life and Human Sacrifice in Virginia Woolf's *Between the Acts*', *Woolf Studies Annual*, 15 (2009), 67–90

——. 'Eating Animals and Becoming Meat in Virginia Woolf's *The Waves*', *Journal of Modern Literature*, 38.1 (2014), 73–93

Turgenev, Ivan. *Virgin Soil* (London: Heinemann, 1924)

Usui, Masami. 'The Female Victims of the War in *Mrs Dalloway*', in *Virginia Woolf and War: Fiction, Reality and Myth*, ed. Mark Hussey (New York: Syracuse University Press, 1991), pp. 151–63

Utell, Janine. 'Meals and Mourning in Woolf's *The Waves*', *College Literature*, 35.2 (2008), 1–19

Warwick, Frances Evelyn Maynard Greville (The Countess of Warwick). *A Woman and the War* (London: Chapman & Hall, 1916)

Webb, Sydney. *The Decline in the Birth-Rate*. (London: Fabian Society, 1907)

Webster, Charles (ed.). *Biology, Medicine and Society 1840–1940* (Cambridge: Cambridge University Press, 2009)

Weininger, Otto. *Sex & Character (Authorised Translation from the Sixth German Edition)* (London: William Heinemann, 1906)

Whittier-Ferguson, John. 'The Burden of Drafts: Woolf's Revisions of *Between the Acts*', *Text*, 10 (1997), 297–319

Whitworth, Michael. 'Historicising Woolf: Context Studies', in *Virginia Woolf in Context*, ed. Bryony Randall and Jane Goldman (Cambridge: Cambridge University Press, 2012), pp. 3–12

——. 'Introduction', in Virginia Woolf, *Night and Day*, ed. Michael Whitworth (Cambridge: Cambridge University Press, 2018)

——. *Virginia Woolf (Authors in Context)* (Oxford: Oxford University Press, 2005)

Wilson, Peter. *The International Theory of Leonard Woolf: A Study in Twentieth-Century Idealism* (Basingstoke: Palgrave Macmillan, 2003)

Wolfe, Jesse. 'The Sane Woman in the Attic: Sexuality and Self-Authorship in *Mrs Dalloway*', *Modern Fiction Studies*, 51.1 (2005), 34–59

Wollaeger, Mark. 'Woolf, Postcards and the Elision of Race: Colonizing Women in *The Voyage Out*', *Modernism/Modernity*, 8.1 (2001), 43–75

Wood, Alice. 'Facing *Life as We Have Known It*: Virginia Woolf and the Women's Co-operative Guild', *Literature & History*, 23 (2014), 18–34

——. *Virginia Woolf's Late Cultural Criticism* (London: Bloomsbury, 2013)

Woolf, Cecil. 'Cecil Woolf Remembers Leonard Woolf', *Virginia Woolf Miscellany*, 72 (2007), 9–12

Woolf, Leonard. *After the Deluge*, 2 vols (London: Hogarth Press, 1931–39)

——. *Beginning Again* (New York: Harcourt Brace Jovanovich, 1975)

——. 'A Democracy of Working Women', *New Statesman*, 21 June 1913, pp. 328–29

——. *Downhill All the Way* (New York: Harcourt Brace Jovanovich, 1975)

——. *Economic Imperialism* (London: Swarthmore, 1920)

——. *Letters of Leonard Woolf*, ed. Frederic Spotts (New York: Harcourt Brace Jovanovich, 1989)

——. *The Wise Virgins* (New Haven, CT: Yale University Press, 2007)

Woolf, Virginia. *Asheham Diary*, with an introduction by Anne Olivier Bell, *The Charleston Magazine*, 9 (1994), 27–35

——. *Between the Acts*, ed. Stella McNichol, with an introduction and notes by Gillian Beer (London: Penguin, 1992)

——. *The Complete Shorter Fiction of Virginia Woolf*, ed. Susan Dick (San Diego: Harcourt, 1989)

284 *Bibliography*

———. *The Diary of Virginia Woolf*, 5 vols, ed. Anne Olivier Bell with Andrew McNeillie (Harmondsworth: Penguin, 1979–85)

———. *The Essays of Virginia Woolf*, 6 vols, ed. Andrew McNeillie and Stuart N. Clarke (London: Hogarth Press, 1986–2012)

———. *Flush: A Biography*, edited and with an introduction and notes by Alison Light (London: Penguin, 2000)

———. 'Introductory Letter', in *Life as We Have Known It*, ed. Margaret Llewelyn Davies, with an introduction by Anna Davin (London: Virago, 1977)

———. *Jacob's Room*, edited and with an introduction and notes by Sue Roe (London: Penguin, 1992)

———. *The Letters of Virginia Woolf*, 6 vols, ed. Nigel Nicolson and Joanne Trautmann Banks (London: Harcourt, Brace, Jovanovich, 1975–82)

———. *Melymbrosia*, edited and with an introduction by Louise DeSalvo (San Francisco: Cleis, 2002)

———. *Moments of Being*, ed. Jeanne Schulkind, revised and with an introduction by Hermione Lee (London: Pimlico, 2002)

———. *Mrs Dalloway*, ed. Stella McNichol, with an introduction and notes by Elaine Showalter (London: Penguin, 2000)

———. *Mrs Dalloway*, with a foreword by Maureen Howard (New York: Harcourt, 2002)

———. *Night and Day*, ed. Stella McNichol, with an introduction and notes by Julia Briggs (London: Penguin, 1992)

———. *Orlando: A Biography*, ed. Brenda Lyons, with an introduction and notes by Sandra M. Gilbert (London: Penguin, 2019)

———. *The Pargiters: The Novel-Essay Portion of 'The Years*, edited and with an introduction and notes by Mitchell A. Leaska (London: Hogarth Press, 1978)

———. *A Passionate Apprentice: The Early Journals, 1897–1909*, ed. Mitchell A. Leaska, with an introduction by David Bradshaw (London: Pimlico, 2004)

———. *Pointz Hall: The Earlier and Later Typescripts of Between the Acts*, edited with an introduction, annotations and afterword by Mitchell A. Leaska (New York: University Publications, 1983)

———. *Roger Fry: A Biography*, with an introduction by Frances Spalding. (London: Hogarth Press, 1991)

———. *A Room of One's Own and Three Guineas*, ed. Stella McNichol, with an introduction and notes by Michèle Barrett (London: Penguin, 2000)

———. *To the Lighthouse*, ed. Stella McNichol, with an introduction and notes by Hermione Lee (London: Penguin, 2000)

———. *Virginia Woolf's 'Jacob's Room': The Holograph Draft*, transcribed and edited by Edward L. Bishop (Oxford: Pace University Press, 1998)

———. *Virginia Woolf's Reading Notebooks*, edited and with an introduction and notes by Brenda Silver (Princeton, NJ: Princeton University Press, 1983)

———. *Virginia Woolf 'The Hours': The British Museum Manuscript of Mrs Dalloway*, transcribed and edited by Helen Wussow (New York: Pace University Press, 1996)

———. *The Voyage Out*, edited and with an introduction and notes by Jane Wheare (London: Penguin, 1992)

———. *The Waves*, edited and with an introduction and notes by Kate Flint (London: Penguin, 2000)

———. *The Waves: The Two Holograph Drafts*, transcribed and edited by J. W. Graham (London: Hogarth Press, 1976)

———. *Women & Fiction: The Manuscript Versions of 'A Room of One's Own'*, transcribed and edited by S. P. Rosenbaum (Oxford: Blackwell, 1992)

———. *The Years*, ed. Stella McNichol, with an introduction and notes by Jeri Johnson (London: Penguin, 1998)

———, Vanessa Bell and Thoby Stephen, *Hyde Park Gate News: The Stephen Family Newspaper*, edited with an introduction and notes by Gill Lowe (London: Hesperus, 2005)

Wright, E. H. 'Woolf's Pacifism and Contemporary Women Dramatists', in *Virginia Woolf, Europe, and Peace, Vol. 1*, ed. Ariane Mildenberg and Patricia Novillo-Corvalán (Liverpool: Liverpool University Press, 2020), pp. 134–35

Wright, Elizabeth Mary. *The Life of Joseph Wright*, 2 vols (London: Oxford University Press, 1932)

'Wright's Coal Tar Soap Advertisement', *The English Review*, 20 May 1915, p. xi

Yalom, Marilyn. *A History of the Breast* (London: Harper Collins, 1997)

Yeo, Eileen Janes. 'The Creation of "Motherhood" and Women's Responses in Britain and France, 1750–1914', *Women's History Review*, 8.2 (1999), 201–18.

Zwerdling, Alex. '*Between the Acts* and the Coming of War', *Novel: A Forum on Fiction*, 10.3 (1977), 220–36

———. '*Jacob's Room*: Woolf's Satiric Elegy', *ELH*, 48.4 (1981), 894–913

———. 'Mastering the Memoir: Woolf and the Family Legacy', *Modernism/modernity*, 10.1 (2003), 165–88

———. '*Mrs Dalloway* and the Social System', *PMLA*, 92.1 (1977), 69–82

———. *Virginia Woolf and the Real World* (Berkeley: University of California Press, 1986)

Index

A Room of One's Own, 6, 15–16, 38, 58, 87, 108, 123, 130–9, 171

Asheham Diary, 183

'A Sketch of the Past', 7–8, 17, 48–9, 241–5, 247

'A Society', 8, 15, 49–59, 235

Abel, Elizabeth, 228, 231, 255n

abortion, 129–30, 137, 248–9

Alt, Christina, 105, 132

the 'androgynous mind', 134–6

'Angel in the House', 9–10, 225n, 261, 262n

artistic procreation, 5–6, 67, 108–9, 123, 133–6, 202

ageing, 62–5, 69

babyfarming, 154–5

Bahun, Sanja, 227, 256n

Bardi, Abby, 237

Beer, Gillian, 186

Bell, Vanessa, 6–7, 67, 97–8, 113, 118, 123, 154–7, 168–9, 183–4

Bennett, Arnold, 51, 56

Bettinger, Elfi, 70

Between the Acts, 17, 239–40, 245–54

birth control, 4, 22n, 87, 116, 122–30

and sexual pleasure, 134

birth rate, 44

decline, 4, 8, 29, 76, 124, 181

Black, Naomi, 12, 260

Blair, Emily, 13

Blodgett, Harriet, 246, 248

Blyth, Ian, 101

Bowlby, Rachel, 6, 200–1

Bradshaw, David, 87

Briggs, Julia, 83n, 107, 112

Brittain, Vera, 11, 116, 145n

'The Censorship of Books', 131

Childers, Mary M., 192–3

Childs, Donald, 77, 68, 115, 131–2, 134, 148n

class, 3–4, 16, 154–5

VW's class bias, 53, 156, 192–202

and eugenics, 76, 95–6, 108, 115–16, 125–9, 139–40

working-class in VW's novels, 157, 162–6, 187–8, 201–2, 204, 209–16

clothing, 69, 126–7, 172, 197

Cole, Sarah, 46–7

Coleridge, Samuel Taylor, 133, 135, 202

contraception *see* birth control

cooking, 150–2, 163, 175, 182–4, 187, 198, 211–14, 219n

Cooley, Elizabeth, 107, 145n

Craig, Layne Parish, 98, 123, 134

Craig, Maurice, 85n, 93–5

Cramer, Patricia, 80n, 216, 228

Index   287

Darwin, Charles, 85, 89–90, 102–2, 138, 162
Daugherty, Beth Rigel, 82n, 186
Davies, Margaret Llewellyn, 128, 152, 189–94, 199
Dekter, Gregory, 153, 155
DeSalvo, Louise, 118, 146n
Dick, Susan, 51–2, 57, 202
Duckworth Stephen, Julia, 7–8, 89, 153–7, 184, 241–2, 246

Einstein, Albert, 235
Ellis, Havelock, 134–5, 169, 181
eugenics
  The Eugenics Society, 86–8, 105, 115, 124, 141
  feminist eugenics, 15, 87, 116, 120, 128, 141n
  multiplicity of, 87
  VW's eugenic doctors, 77, 86, 92–8
  VW's eugenic friends, 115–17, 119–20
  VW's personal eugenics, 113–15, 121

farming, 168, 175, 179–80, 207–8
Fassler, Barbara, 135, 172
First World War, 2, 11, 108, 214
  memorials, 24, 42, 41–5, 232
  peace negotiations, 52–6
  propaganda, 15, 24–9, 32–4, 165–6
  food shortages and rationing, 182–3, 195–6
  'shell-shock', 60, 70–1, 76–7
Flush, 143n, 160, 186
Fordham, Finn, 186
formal experimentation, 8–9, 36–7, 167, 203–4, 243–5
Forster, E. M., 150–1, 234
Friedman, Susan Stanford, 5–6
Freud, Sigmund, 17, 216, 227–54, 256n, 257n
'Freudian Fiction', 229–30
Froula, Christine, 6, 13, 85n

Galton, Frances, 76, 88–92, 96, 99–106
gardening, 168, 175, 184–5
gender performance, 5–6, 11–12, 14, 39–40, 152
  and war, 25, 34–5, 44, 70–1, 235–9
  and eugenics, 99, 105, 143n
  shifting gender identity, 169–72
Gillespie, Diane, 178, 181–2
Glaxo baby formula, 163–6
Glenny, Allie, 167, 176
Graves, Robert, 33–4
Grayzel, Susan, 15, 25, 27, 31, 43, 71
Great Depression, 181–2

Hancock, Nuala, 184
Hanson, Clare, 140
Harrison, Jane, 37–41, 48, 80n, 167, 185, 228, 234
Haskill, Christine, 260
Hill, Katherine, 90
Hite, Molly, 72, 75
Holtby, Winifred, 11, 107
homosexuality
  and artistry, 135, 171–2
  and Septimus Smith, 70
'How should One Read a Book', 201
Hussey, Mark, 13, 46n
Huxley, Julian, 230, 256n
Hyslop, T. B., 93–5

imperialism, 4, 71–2, 158–9, 163, 165, 175, 181, 205–6
infant feeding
  breastfeeding, 154–66, 175, 241–2
  bottle feeding, the rise of, 154–5, 163–4
  wet nursing, 154–5
'The Intellectual Status of Women', 56, 170–1
'Introductory Letter' *see* 'Memories of a Working Women's Guild'

288 Index

Jacob's Room, 2, 15, 34–49
Jones, Clara, 10, 110, 198, 202
'The Journal of Mistress Joan
    Martyn', 8, 29–30, 157–62,
    200

Kato, Megumi, 153, 155, 157
Kawash, Samira, 14
'Kew Gardens', 196–7
Keynes, Maynard, 54, 86, 115,
    145n
Kingsley Kent, Susan, 31
Klein, Melanie, 17, 227–31, 241–5,
    250–4
Koven, Seth and Sonya Michel, 10,
    20n
Kushen, Betty, 215

Lady Chatterley's Lover, 131, 179,
    221n
'The Leaning Tower', 423–45
Lee, Hermione, 13, 89, 98, 114, 192
Levenback, Karen, 26, 79n
Levy, Heather, 202, 216, 253
Light, Alison, 156, 183, 198
Little, Judy, 48
Livingstone, Catriona, 238
Longenbach, James, 32
Lowe, Alice, 151

MacCarthy, Desmond, 5, 56,
    170–1
MacDuff, Sangam, 167
McIntire, Gabrielle, 230
MacKay, Marina, 35
MacKenzie, Donald, 105, 139, 149n
Malthus, Thomas, 180–1
Marcus, Jane, 1, 12, 81n, 131, 186,
    192
Marder, Herbert, 181
marriage, in VW's works, 41, 58,
    103–13, 122, 161–2, 205,
    209, 224n
Martin, Ann, 205
matriarchal civilisations, 38–9,
    185, 234–5

maternalism, 10–11, 20n, 29–31
  maternal philanthropy, 10–11,
    152, 155–6
  maternal metaphors, 1–3, 5–6,
    133–6
  maternal/motherhood studies, 2,
    13–14
Melymbrosia, 3–4, 9, 19n, 155,
    159–62
'Memories of a Working Women's
    Guild', 16, 153, 189–202
menopause, 62–70
miscarriage, 4–5, 125–6, 137
Mitchison, Naomi, 166
Morganroth Gullette, Margaret,
    62, 69
Morris, Pam, 167, 204
Mosse, George L, 70
motherhood
  and ambivalence, 2, 6, 8–9,
    17–18, 112, 203–4, 254
  Archetypal motherhood, 167–8,
    173, 240
  essentialist and anti-essentialist
    views of, 11–12, 78n, 169
  mother muses, 178–9
  mourning mothers, 41–5
  as possessive/aggressive, 168–70,
    173–4, 178, 236–7
  of sons/daughters, 39–40, 45–6,
    57–8, 111
  vs art, 4–5, 67, 161–2, 178–9,
    200, 238–9, 248
  VW's relationship with, 6–8,
    18–19, 29, 92–8, 168–9
*Mrs Beeton's Book of Household
    Management*, 155
Mrs Dalloway, 2, 15, 24, 59–77,
    98, 114–15, 122, 162–6, 18
  and Kitty Lushington Maxse,
    65–6
  and the motif of time, 64–5, 69
  'Mrs Dalloway in Bond Street',
    62, 64
  Septimus Smith, 60–1, 64–5,
    68–77, 98, 114–15

Nicolson, Nigel, 113, 118–19
Night and Day, 8, 15–16, 87–9, 92, 98–114, 139, 205, 224n
nursing *see* infant feeding

Ondaatje Rolls, Jans, 151
Orlando, 5, 64, 117–19, 127, 172
Overy, Richard, 87

pacifism
   maternalist pacifists, 25, 29–33, 78n
   VW's pacifism, 24–5, 53–4
Pankhurst, Dame Christabel, 31–2, 78n
Park, Sowon, 112
patriarchy values, 87, 103–5, 128, 136–7, 159–61, 175, 205–6, 234–5
   and women, 30, 37–41, 58, 62, 162, 179–80, 205, 232–3, 213, 248
   and Victorian culture, 42, 44, 89
   and war-making, 35–6, 46–52, 71–4, 236–7
patriotism, 25–35
The Pargiters, 18–19, 203, 207, 209–13
Pawlowski, Merry M., 71
Peach, Linden, 12, 87
Pearl, Raymond, 181
Pember Reeves, Maud, 140–1, 195, 197
Pethick-Lawrence, Emmeline, 30–2, 54–5
Plant, Rebecca Jo, 11
Pointz Hall, 246–53
Poole, Roger, 93–4
Port, Cynthia, 63
Priest, Ann-Marie, 104, 107, 145n
Proudfit, Sharon L., 205, 209

Raitt, Suzanne, 43, 121
Randall, Bryony, 68
Rathbone, Eleanor, 11, 20n
Rational Dress Society, 127

'Reminiscences', 7
Ricoeur, Paul, 64
Roger Fry, 216, 241
Rubio-Marín, Ruth, 31–2
Ruddick, Sara, 14, 37, 43
Ryan, Derek, 12, 160

Sackville-West, Vita, 116–21, 171–2, 253, 257n
Saguaro, Shelley, 133–4
Sarsfield, Rachel, 105
Savage, George, 93, 95–7, 115
Scott, Gillian, 194–5
Shakespeare, William, 132, 135, 145n, 149n, 202
   Cymbeline, 68
   Anthony and Cleopatra, 72–3
Shakespeare, Judith, 17–18, 133
Shaw, George Bernard, 85n, 101, 115–16
shopping, 63, 152, 193–6
Showalter, Elaine, 9, 12
Snaith, Anna, 159, 160–1, 203, 262n
Soloway, Richard, 124
Spanish Civil War, 236–7
Sparks, Elisa Kay, 74–5, 81n, 221n
Stephen, Leslie, 15, 89–92, 97, 121, 143n, 146n, 228–9, 242
Stephens, Julie, 11
Stopes, Charlotte Carmichael, 126–7, 132, 149n
Stopes, Marie
   in *A Room of One's Own*, 131–6
   and eugenics, 87, 124–6, 134, 137–8, 145n
   Love's Creation, 128, 130–9
   Married Love, 120, 122–4, 126, 134
   Radiant Motherhood, 126, 128, 136–7
   Wise Parenthood, 124, 126
suffrage, 11, 29–32, 109–10, 144n, 260–1

Tennyson, Alfred Lord, 208, 225n
To the Lighthouse, 130, 150, 152, 157, 219n
'Thoughts on Peace in an Air Raid', 56, 237–9
Three Guineas, 11, 32, 81n, 129–30, 249, 260–1
  alternative titles, 232, 234, 235
  and class, 139–40
  notebooks, 17, 203, 206, 256n
  and psychoanalysis, 230–7
  and war, 43–4, 48, 82n
Tromanhauser, Vicki, 151, 167, 175–6, 182, 245–6

unmaternal women, 61, 67–9, 76, 118–19, 184, 257n
Usui, Masami, 71
Utell, Janine, 151, 167

The Voyage Out, 8, 155, 157–62, 174, 231, 254

'The War from the Street', 34
The Waves, 16, 34–5, 166–89, 203, 206
Webb, Sidney and Beatrice, 94, 115–16, 142n
Weininger, Otto, 169–80, 220n, 221n, 240
Whitworth, Michael, 12, 144n
Wollaeger, Mark, 159, 165
Women's Co-operative Guild, 16, 128–9, 140, 192–3, 195
  and motherhood, 193–4
  VW's involvement in, 152, 156, 189–90

women's writing, 6, 8, 10, 57, 116, 119, 123, 133, 138, 200–1, 249
Wood, Alice, 193, 231–2, 235
Woolf, Leonard, 54, 66, 74, 108, 113–19, 146n, 151, 166–8, 183–4, 192
  and the decision not to have children, 7, 18, 93–8
  and psychoanalysis, 229–30, 235, 244
  and the WCG, 189–90, 195
Woolf studies overview, 1–2, 12–13
Woolf, Virginia
  and feminism, 1–2, 9, 12, 15, 66, 87, 103, 120, 133, 159, 203, 229–30, 260–2
  marriage to Leonard, 18, 94, 113, 146n
  and mental illness, 7, 60, 77, 93–8, 113–15, 190, 229–30
  on having a baby, 6–7, 18–19, 94, 98, 130, 168–9
  sexual abuse, 244–5
  see also individual works by title
working women, 9–10, 126, 129–31, 156, 210–13, 231–4, 260–1
Wright, Joseph, 209–12

The Years, 16–17, 47, 75, 129, 153, 192, 202–16, 228

Zwerdling, Alex, 7, 12, 36–7, 70, 247–50